# JAMAICA

# JAMAICA
## A HISTORICAL PORTRAIT

Samuel J. Hurwitz

and

Edith F. Hurwitz

**PRAEGER PUBLISHERS**
*New York • Washington • London*

63453

PRAEGER PUBLISHERS
111 Fourth Avenue, New York, N.Y. 10003, U.S.A.
5, Cromwell Place, London SW7 2JL, England

Published in the United States of America in 1971
by Praeger Publishers, Inc.

Library of Congress Catalog Card Number: 70–153835

Printed in the United States of America

*To*
Arthur Charles
and
Shelah Joyce

# Contents

ILLUSTRATIONS FOLLOW PAGE 84

# Preface

This is an account of Jamaica from its historical origins to the present day. An attempt has been made throughout to stress the factors that have contributed to the making of contemporary Jamaica. Although the broad framework is chronological, emphasis has been placed on the major themes of Jamaica's development.

A small island, isolated in the Caribbean Sea, Jamaica has nevertheless experienced many of the social and political developments that have engulfed Western civilization. Discovered during the age of exploration which ushered in the capitalist era, Jamaica was shaped and forged by the same forces that created the new economic and political order. As was true of other territories flung far and wide over the earth, the mercantilist era that followed the age of exploration brought colonial rule. The English wrested control of Jamaica from the Spanish and then ruled it uninterruptedly for more than 300 years. As a colony, Jamaica was profoundly influenced by England. In the economic sphere, Britain created the export-oriented, commercial-crop agriculture that was the mainstay of the island's livelihood. In the political sphere, the British brought the rule of law, which gave stability to the local governments of successive generations.

Economic, political, and social development was very much dependent on the relationship between colony and colonizer. The economic ambitions of the British in Jamaica were responsible for the dislocation of a people from their homeland. The forced migration of Africans to the Western Hemisphere had few precedents in world history. The slave trade, an important source of commercial wealth in the seventeenth and eighteenth centuries, brought large numbers of Africans to the island to create the plantation economy. They were forced to suffer the degradation of slavery, which left emotional scars on subsequent generations. Deprived of their culture and society, these people salvaged some of the old customs and traditions, adding on to them much that was new from their adopted land.

The British also created economic, social, and political institutions that remained long after their usefulness disappeared. Jamaica did not find a place in the industrial era that followed mercantilism, and became a casualty. With the abolition of preferential duties in 1849, the last vestige of the mercantile support that had sustained the Jamaican economy was pulled away. Great Britain had forced the emancipation of the slaves in 1833, creating a free labor force that had no market in which to sell its labor. Assets in one era, the black masses were liabilities in the next. The swarm of humanity that had been transported to the island was cast adrift.

Throughout the nineteenth century, the political control held first by the white elites and later shared with the colored elite steadily diminished, especially when, in a moment of panic, the colonists voluntarily yielded their right to self-government in 1865. Still, the position they had once maintained seemed only to congeal the narrowness of their vision with respect to the black masses. The paternalistic governors of the Crown-colony era depended on the elites for advice if not consent. The best of the governors had a broader vision, however, and, by improving and expanding the educational system, streamlining and modernizing the governmental apparatus, and encouraging the development of a native peasantry, they laid the foundation for a modern Jamaica.

In the very broadest sense, the history of Jamaica until 1938 revolved around groups that did not form a society. The formation of Jamaican society began in 1938 with the development of a politically oriented labor movement. The political parties emerging from that movement have become the integrating mechanisms for the creation of a unified society.

It is a major goal of the nationalist movement to change the image of the colonial past by creating a new cultural identity. Here the new leaders are trying to forge a synthesis between the past and the present. Mindful of the historical traditions that have shaped the new nation, they are giving them a positive focus and contemporary relevance that their mass following can understand and, it is hoped, identify with. Through economic, social, political, and educational programs, the new leaders have begun to cope effectively and on a broad scale with the needs of the citizens of Jamaica.

Jamaica is facing and will continue to face major problems that do not lend themselves to easy solutions. But Jamaicans are accustomed to doing things gradually, for, unlike many other newly emerging nations, Jamaica achieved independence through gradual reforms. A polyethnic society, it has one of the most stable governments of the new nations that have been created from former colonial societies. Already the present is an improvement over the past, and, more important, Jamaica's leaders and the nation as a whole look forward to a better future.

In a work of this scope, the authors are inevitably indebted to numerous persons and institutions. A Fulbright Award enabled us to live and work among the people of Jamaica, and we are grateful to friends and our colleagues at the University of the West Indies who helped us in our early research in Jamaican history. Important sources have been manuscript material in the Public Record Office in London, the Public Record Office in Spanish Town, Jamaica, and the Jamaica Government Archives. To the library and staff of the University of the West Indies and the Institute of Jamaica we give thanks for help given at the inception of this study. Brooklyn College and the University of Hawaii aided in securing sources not in their own collections. The British Museum, the John Carter Brown Library, the Columbia University Library, the Cornell University Library, the Library of the New York Historical Society, and the New York Public Library are among the institutions to which we had recourse for unusual and rare material. We owe special thanks to the Henry E. Huntington Library in San Marino, California, for providing a research grant that enabled us to explore the library's valuable collection of papers from the Hope Estate of Jamaica. The library of the Research Institute for the Study of Man helped in providing information on contemporary Jamaica.

# JAMAICA

# 1. Jamaica in the Age of Exploration

In the sweep of historical time, no age saw more rapid exploration and exploitation of unknown continents and territories
than the age in which the recorded history of Jamaica began.
Like the rest of the Western Hemisphere, Jamaica was discovered in the great age of discovery, the fifteenth and sixteenth centuries, when explorers set out on expeditions that led
them to the geographical limits of the earth. Not content with
sketching the rough outlines of the inhabited world through
their daring exploits, these men also established national outposts almost everywhere they landed—small and scattered, but
permanent.

Settlements were necessary because the great explorers of
the period were primarily interested in discovery not for its
own sake but rather to attach to their particular countries
areas that were known or believed to be of economic importance. Precious metals and lands were the principal sources of
wealth in those times, and the seizure and exploitation of new
land, either unoccupied or occupied by "useless" or intract-
able peoples, offered fortunes for those who would find it. The
economic success of the colonies of Spain and Portugal in
Madeira and parts of the Canary Islands in the fifteenth century encouraged the search for territories still farther removed
from the known continents. Trade, especially of the long-distance kind, was somewhat less sure, and hence a less attractive
way to new wealth, but it was highly lucrative when successful.
Precious commodities from the East exchanged for staples

3

from the West brought great wealth to those who would chance the investment. Two large-scale oceanic trades, the westward trade of Spain and the eastward trade of Portugal, arose in the sixteenth century; national in character, they were established by governmental decree and guarded by naval force. Most of the explorations by other nations during the century were inspired by the hope of breaking or circumventing one or another of these monopolies. Of the two, Spain's was the greater in both bulk and value. It was within its empire, the first colonial empire in the New World, that the fortunes of Jamaica were originally cast.

Jamaica's historical pattern was established at the very beginning of its historical life. Originally a tool of the Spanish Empire and eventually of the British, it became an exploited land, useful only for the wealth that was culled from its soil. This wealth went into the making of foreign fortunes; little was returned for the benefit of Jamaica. But, to return to the beginning, Jamaica's was inauspicious; its discovery, accidental.

The recorded history of Jamaica begins with the voyages of Christopher Columbus. Looking for gold and a shorter route to the East, Columbus found instead the New World. He saw a group of islands that he described as "far surpassing all the rest of the world in beauty and conveniency." Impressed with the beauties of Tortuga and Hispaniola, which he discovered on his first voyage, Columbus went back to Spain impatient to return to the newly found territories. Though it had taken him seven years to persuade the King and Queen of Spain to finance his first voyage, in less than seven months Columbus was again on his way to the New World for his second.

Success had bred confidence, and King Ferdinand and Queen Isabella—anxious to claim as many new territories as possible before the King of Portugal, Spain's bitter competitor in the search for empire, laid similar claims—gladly furnished Columbus with the necessary provisions for his second voyage. This expedition left Spain on September 25, 1493. Twelve islands were sighted and named by Columbus as he sailed westward from the Canary Islands and then northwestward toward Hispaniola. He established a viable settlement there and set out to sea again. Jamaica was the last landfall to be discovered. After visiting the south coast of Cuba, Columbus sighted Jamaica on May 4, 1494. He had been told about Jamaica by the Indians of Cuba, who had called it the source of the "blessed gold." Although he never found gold, he did find natural beauty; when he landed on the north coast of Jamaica, he named the area Santa Gloria because of its extreme beauty. A member of the crew described his reactions and impressions: "It is the fairest island that eyes have beheld; mountainous and the land seems to touch the sky; very large, bigger than Sicily, and all full of valleys and fields and plains."

Stopping on the north shore, Columbus came into contact with Indians who were of the same type as those of Cuba and Hispaniola but who seemed much more warlike and hostile. Columbus described their villages as "very big" and "very close together," located "on the edge of the seas as well as inland." These original inhabitants of Jamaica, 60,000 to 75,000 in number, lived on a level of development anthropologists call the Polished Stone Age. They were called Tainos and were a branch of the Arawaks, the general name given to the Indian inhabitants of the Caribbean isles. Fragmentary evidence indicates that their small-scale society was defined largely in terms of age and sex differences, kinship connections, and village communities. They cultivated a variety of plants. They supplemented their meager yields from the soil with some hunting, fishing, and gathering. At the head of their political organizations were hereditary town chiefs, or *caciques*, who played religious and economic roles as well.

Though the Tainos, or Arawaks, had no written language or history, it is believed that they had migrated from the Latin American mainland less than five centuries before Columbus discovered them. They first went to Trinidad; then some of their number moved gradually north to the other islands until some reached Jamaica.

It was not until his fourth voyage, in 1503, that Columbus really explored Indian life in Jamaica. At that time, because storms had damaged his ships as the fleet made its way back to Hispaniola from the South American mainland, he was forced to land in approximately the same area where he had landed in 1494. Here, at Santa Gloria, known today as St. Ann's Bay, Columbus and his crew remained for twelve months. His men mutinied and deserted the settlement to pillage the Indians, but Columbus eventually brought them under control and was able to return to Hispaniola on new ships sent over by his loyal lieutenants Ovando and Mendez. Soon thereafter, Columbus left for Spain and never returned to the West Indies. The legacy he left behind, a group of island territories, would soon become the prizes of European empires.

In 1510, the Spaniards began in earnest to make their first permanent settlement in Jamaica (the third Spanish settlement in the West Indies), eighteen years after Columbus had made a permanent settlement in Hispaniola and just one year after Juan Ponce de Leon had settled Puerto Rico. The Viceroy of the New World, Diego Columbus, Christopher's son, had appointed as governor Juan de Esquibel, who had already proved to be a valiant soldier in Hispaniola. Esquibel founded the town of Seville on the spot where Christopher Columbus had landed. But it was under the administration of Francisco de Garay in 1515 that the colony began to export foodstuffs and hemp. Thus Jamaica experienced its first period of prosperity and very early in its recorded history began the export economy that would become the lifeline of its existence in future centuries.

The center of the Spanish settlement was moved to the southern part of the island in 1534, when Villa de la Vega, today's Spanish Town, was founded. Most of the Spanish settlers in the West Indies at that time were wanderers and adventurers who did not intend to settle permanently on the island. As a result, some cattle herds roamed wild and such tropical products as sugar could not be cultivated in quantities sufficient for export.

Much more important were colonies on the mainland of South America, which completely overshadowed the Caribbean islands in wealth and population and had replaced them in the affections of Europe. Francisco de Garay, just a few years after becoming governor, deserted Jamaica to investigate a gold strike on the mainland. It was apparent that Jamaica and its neighbors had become way stations on the route to the real fortunes to be made in South America. Jamaica was also out of favor because in 1536 it had been given as a personal estate to Don Luis, the grandson of Columbus. Though Don Luis and his successors never came to Jamaica, the fact that he held it as a fief made the titles of other settlers suspect, as Columbus's descendants could legally claim the land.

Jamaica was not an attractive area for Spaniards to settle in from an economic point of view, either. Mining of precious metals was the important business of Spain in the New World. The lure of the mainland, with its gold and silver, made it difficult to keep men for long in small, tropical island outposts.

Spain rendered the rest of Europe the immense service of making the first great experiments in colonization in the Western Hemisphere. In the seventeenth century, the varied assemblage of lands under the Spanish crown made up a vast colonial empire. Spanish colonization had attained its greatest extension. Other European nations would soon challenge Spain by attempting to wrest from it various territorial possessions, but up until the end of the sixteenth century Spain's right to the territories in the West Indies remained unchallenged.

That is not to say that non-Spanish nationals were not attracted to the West Indies. Adventurers, pirates, and privateers came to the islands, but they confined their activities to smuggling and raiding rather than settling. Quick and lucrative returns were to be had from raids on Spanish colonies or ships. Booty and treasure could be seized by the quick and the strong. They—and those who did not possess these qualities fell by the wayside—were attracted to the "business" of plunder. More than ever, it became an axiom that one of the great hazards of foreign trade was the risk of being plundered.

It was an age of pirates and robbers, press gangs and mutineers. Armed aggression was the heart of commerce. Piracy and trade were practically synonymous. There was no code of chivalry at sea. The strength of a maritime nation was linked with the durability and toughness of its seafaring men. Even treachery was a virtue—if profitable and successful.

Nations were not above using rogues and pirates for their own advantage. Besides being the age of the pirate, the sixteenth and seventeenth centuries were the age of the privateer —the private individual who, after arming his own ship, on which he was also chief officer, received commissions from governments to capture merchant ships of competing powers. For the privateer, the advantage lay in receiving a cloak—however thin and ragged—of legitimacy; for the country commissioning him, there was the possibility of profit without risk.

Jamaica's initial contacts with the European power that would some day guide its destinies were through the English privateers. Sir Francis Drake sailed for the West Indies in 1585 to begiñ eighteen years of private expeditions of organized plunder. His exploits became known throughout England, and Queen Elizabeth and the English Government profited immensely and closed their ears to charges of piracy. Drake and others were encouraged rather than restrained. Success encouraged enlargement of the enterprise.

Leading privateers like Drake and Sir John Hawkins thought it a good idea to hold a base within the Spanish Indies from which to conduct their operations. To this end, Puerto Rico was captured in 1598, but it was immediately abandoned. The unopposed occupation of Jamaica's single settlement, Villa de la Vega, in 1597 by Anthony Shirley might have been used advantageously for the same purpose. Shirley, driven by a domineering wife and family bankruptcy to seek a quick fortune in privateering, came to Jamaica after suffering heavy losses in an expedition to the Cape Verde Islands. Sickness during the Atlantic crossing further reduced the numbers of his fighting men, and only because Shirley met no opposition in Jamaica could his expedition there be called a "success." Having had no earlier "victories," the members of the crew looted every scrap of available property of any value. Even mattresses were torn open in the search for valuables that might be hidden there. A large quantity of meat and bread was also taken during the forty days spent on the island. Shirley then tried to take Honduras, but Jamaica remained his only victory, and he returned to England at the end of 1597, "alive but poor."

In 1603, a large joint force of English and French corsairs began operating in the Caribbean. Five hundred of them landed in Jamaica on January 24 of that year. Though the Spaniards claimed to have driven them off, it is more likely that this Anglo-French force was not interested in conquering anything more than its hunger and, after obtaining the meat that was Jamaica's livelihood, pressed on toward greater objectives. An earlier attempt to capture Jamaica had been made by Captain Christopher Newport ("of the one hand"), a privateer in the service of English merchants. By 1595, he had established a position in the front rank of privateering captains, "specializing" in West Indian ports. The ships he commanded were the *Golden Dragon* and, after 1595, the *Neptune*; it was on the latter that he came to Jamaica in 1601. For all his formidable reputation, Newport could not storm the city of Villa de la Vega. This time, having experienced the ravages of Shirley's expedition, the Spanish settlers were prepared. According to contemporary accounts, though Newport used 1,500 men, he went only halfway to Villa de la Vega and then retreated, the only consolation for his failure being the tales he heard of the poverty of the country.

Though the seventeenth century continued to be an age of pirates and privateers, Jamaica was free from their scourge from 1603 until its capture in 1655 by the English, except for the expedition of Captain William Jackson in 1643. Unlike Newport, Jackson was successful in storming the city of Villa de la Vega, and he lost only forty of the five hundred that had disembarked for the expedition. Though his commission bore the Great Seal of the realm, the purpose of Jackson's voyage was privateering rather than military occupation. Jackson added to his personal profits by setting a price upon the city: 7,000 pieces of eight, 10,000 loaves of cassava bread, and 200 head of cattle. Ravaged by the attack, Villa de la Vega was a shambles, and the beaten and distressed Spanish settlers paid the ransom only with great difficulty.

The daring and adventurous privateers virtually pioneered in exploring the Caribbean Sea for England. The appearance of English seamen in those waters, rare in 1580, was common by 1600, and with it came a great improvement in the means of shipping and seamanship. Knowledge of the ocean and its shores and mastery of the organization and conduct of large, long-distance expeditions were skills of vital importance for the period of settlement and colonization that were to create a British empire in the West Indies in the seventeenth century.

It was in England rather than Spain that the economic arguments in favor of permanent settlements in the colonies were strongly heard. The Spanish pattern in the West Indies of conquest, trading post, and stockade was for a purpose different from that of the patterns developed by the English to secure the greatest wealth for their nation. England's leaders perceived that colonies would enrich the crown and also the English merchants and manufacturers by serving as a market for English products. Also, as a source of commodities that were needed at home or could be re-exported to the continent at higher prices, the colonies would provide a lucrative trading asset. The key to what later would be known as Mercantilism was the enrichment of the nation; the state had become the economic unit, the object of the greatest economic gains. International trade, with exports greater than imports, was considered the most lucrative kind of commercial activity. The profit would be in the form of gold and silver, the media of exchange and the foundation, it was held, of power. Mercantilism became the program of government. The advantage lay with England, because England possessed banks, joint stock companies, and settlement companies—the mechanisms of international trade. Spain had hardly any.

There were several avenues that Britain could use in quest of colonies for the settlement of its people. One was to send them to unclaimed territories, establishing a kind of protectorate over the area in the name of the English crown. In North America, this was done at Jamestown, Plymouth, and Massachusetts Bay. Scots, Irish, Welsh, and English settlers had also moved into the outer islands of the West Indian chain. In 1624, St. Kitts was settled, and in 1632, Antigua and Montserrat. Those who did not have the means to stake their own claims came as indentured servants, hoping to acquire land for themselves at the expiration of their indentures. The West

Indian islands were much more popular as places for settlement than the mainland territories to the north. In 1640, the population of Barbados was equal to that of Virginia and Massachusetts combined: More than 30,000 people, or 200 to the square mile, lived on that small island. In the same year, the much smaller island of St. Kitts had a population of 20,000. This, indeed, was overcrowding. The first great leap across the barrier of the Atlantic had been made, and Englishmen, initiating an era of rapid movement of men, plants, animals, and technology, would become the leaders in establishing colonial settlements in the New World.

Another course that was pursued in the quest for colonies was to seize by force the weaker links of the Spanish Empire. Not setting their sights for the great land settlements of Mexico and Peru, which seemed impregnable, first the Dutch and then the English concentrated on the West Indian islands that already had Spanish outposts. Jamaica, it would seem, was a likely target for English conquest, but the island nation initially set itself a more ambitious goal, Hispaniola. It was Jamaica, however, that was to be captured. The British occupation of Jamaica was an afterthought, a face-saving action to redeem the failure to capture Hispaniola.

Oliver Cromwell, who became Lord Protector of England in 1653, cherished a scheme, known as the "Western Design," for capturing all of the Spanish possessions in the Caribbean. Advised by the powerful Lord Willoughby, Colonel Thomas Modyford, and others that the Spanish hold on the West Indian islands was weak, he assumed these prizes of empire could easily be won. The instructions given to Admiral William Penn, who was put in charge of the fleet, and General Robert Venables, who led a 2,500-man army, were to concentrate their forces on taking Hispaniola and St. John's Island (Puerto Rico). Cuba was a valuable target as well, but nothing was said about Jamaica when the forces departed in December, 1654. The fleet arrived in Barbados in January, 1655, where, with the aid of the governor, the force was augmented by 3,000 recruits, who were, according to Venables, "so loose as not to be kept under discipline, and so cowardly as not to be made to fight."

Mutual antipathies between the commanders and the mutinous mood of the army, due to an order issued by the commanders against looting, militated against the success of the expedition even against a weak foe. Indeed, after the failure to capture Santo Domingo, at the end of April, 1655, General Venables wrote, "We are ashamed of the cowardice of our men, and were not the enemy as cowardly as themselves, they might with a few destroy our Army." Whatever remained of the British forces left the coast of Hispaniola on May 4, 1655, ending probably the most humiliating defeat to be suffered by the British in the West Indies for more than a century to come. To save their reputation, the commanders had to return to England with some success. After Hispaniola, they dared not try Havana or any other large and well-defended place. They recognized that Jamaica was hardly a prize but felt it to be the best target, as it was known to be thinly populated and weakly garrisoned. Of utmost importance was the necessity of raising the spirit of the army by some "smaller success" so that perhaps at a future date a major prize could be taken.

Upon the arrival of the English army on May 10, 1655, the Spaniards in Jamaica did not put up effective opposition. Within a week after the landing of the British, articles of capitulation were signed. Villa de la Vega surrendered without a shot fired; many of its inhabitants fled into the countryside. Women and children from among those who managed to reach the north side of the island were sent to Cuba. The Spaniards surrendered the capital, but last-ditch resistance to the invaders was to be made through guerrilla warfare; trusted Negroes were armed. It was five years before the Spanish capitulation could be turned into a complete English conquest.

The undisciplined army of Penn and Venables that occupied the south side of the island was obsessed with the hope of getting from Jamaica the fruits of victory that had been too long in coming. Like many other treasure-hunters, they soon found that there was no treasure to be had. In desperation, they destroyed herds of cattle and hogs and dug up the crops the Spaniards had planted, hoping to be sent home once the food supply was destroyed.

The English beginnings in Jamaica were thus hardly auspicious. Harassed from the north by guerrilla bands of Spaniards and Negroes, rendered feeble by the deficiencies of its conquering army, England did not fare much better than Spain in making Jamaica a successful settlement. Bitterly disappointed at the failure of his "Western Design," Cromwell was nonetheless determined to change a booby prize into a grand prize. Jamaica had to be colonized: An adequate population, established for "planting," would be of fundamental importance in repulsing future aggressors. Instead of relying only on private enterprise, as in Barbados and St. Kitts, in Jamaica the resources of the state were also marshaled. More troops were sent out to reinforce the garrison, and those men already there, particularly army officers, were encouraged to settle. Grants of land were generously given out, chiefly in the fertile, well-watered bottom lands of the Rio Minho Valley. Of the first group of English settlers, few succeeded, for they lacked the discipline, self-control, and will needed to pioneer in a strange climate and territory. Colonel Modyford, a leader of the successful settlement in Barbados, remarked in 1665 that the population of Jamaica was generally intemperate, while the "old army officers" had turned from "strict saints" into the "most debauched devils."

Other methods to augment the population were tried. Prisoners taken in Royalist risings were sent out as servants of the state. In October, 1655, it was ordered that 1,000 Irish girls and 1,000 Irish boys fourteen years of age or under be sent, and the following year 1,200 men from Ireland and Scotland were provided with transportation and sent out. Cromwell also hoped to recruit settlers from North America, and 300 did arrive at the end of 1655. Settlers came from Bermuda and Barbados—some in the hope of improving their condition, and others to evade payment of their debts or punishment for their crimes. From that time on in the West Indies, the movement of English settlers from island to island was an established pattern. Those who came to the English Caribbean were not immune from the restlessness that characterized frontiersmen all over the hemisphere.

Despite government propaganda and the promises of low taxation and virgin land, there was no wave of migration toward Jamaica as there had been to Barbados and the Leeward Islands in the 1630's and 1640's. The second half of the seventeenth century did not bring a flourishing tropical agricultural economy to the island. There did emerge a flourishing commercial center, situated on a narrow strip of land that juts off like an arm from the south coast of Kingston. Called Port Royal, it became the center for the trading of the loot of the buccaneers, those daredevils who raided the Spanish and Dutch. Here they heaped the plunder of Spanish cities or galleons taken at sea. Church plate, gold- and silver-embroidered heavy cloths, silks, and laces were some of the booty. It was easy to bargain for low prices with the buccaneers, who were not skillful business-men, and as a result merchants rushed to the island to take advantage of the "bargains." By 1668, Port Royal was said to have eight hundred houses, which, according to a traveler, were "as dear-rented as if they stood in well-traded streets in London." The same writer, Richard Blome, reports that there was a "Jews street" with a synagogue. It is little wonder that the first Jews to settle in Jamaica came to Port Royal. Trading and traveling had been the lot of the Jews for many centuries, and Jamaica offered them abundant opportunities to do both.

Most legendary and famous of the buccaneers who stormed Port Royal and made it their own was Henry Morgan. He received commissions from the governor of Jamaica, Colonel Modyford, for it was the Spanish enemy that Morgan was forever weakening by his raids. Cuba was one of Morgan's tar-gets, and, after marching forty miles inland there in 1668, he almost succeeded in storming Havana and seizing the city of Puerto Principe. Although the boldness of the assault spread terror throughout Cuba, only 50,000 pieces of eight were col-lected in plunder. But the attempt had been on a scale that suited Morgan, and he returned to Port Royal claiming victory over the Spaniard. He soon achieved it in a more material sense when a few months later he successfully looted Porto Bello on the Isthmus of Panama, the town from which the treasures of Peru were shipped to Spain. Morgan's success in a venture no buccaneer before him had dared brought Jamaica international renown. Morgan and his men always returned to their home base of Port Royal. In 1670 Morgan settled in Jamaica for a time to supervise the cultivation of the large estates that had been granted to him by Governor Modyford.

Panama was Morgan's last victory. There he amassed a treasure of 750,000 pieces of eight. The Anglo-Spanish peace brought Morgan's activity to an end, and as part of the terms of peace the Spaniards demanded Morgan's neck. But King Charles II, after delaying two years, pardoned Morgan and knighted him for his exploits. Appointed lieutenant governor of Jamaica, Morgan returned to the island, where he was to be long remembered by the sobriquet "the hammer against the Spaniards."

Privateering, conquest, and settlement had been the English imprints on Jamaica as the seventeenth century drew to a close. Economic returns had been plentiful, but they had come spasmodically. The mercantile design—that the colonies would provide ready markets for a high volume of exports at high prices and return to the mother country needed imports at low prices—had not yet been realized. Two things were needed for this scheme to work in the West Indies: a crop that was cheap and easy to produce and a large labor force that could work effectively in a tropical climate. Sugar became the crop, and Negroes from Africa provided the labor. Negro slavery and the plantation economy closed the century of conquest and ushered in the era of settlement for Jamaica.

# 2. Political Life in the Era of Slavery

The institutions that made up the structure of Jamaica's political life during the first two centuries of its existence were created soon after the English conquest. Military government, in force since the conquest of the island, officially came to an end on February 13, 1661, when Charles II, restored King of England, commissioned the military governor, Colonel D'Oyley, to set up a council from among the inhabitants. To encourage intensive settlement and to establish a viable and stable society by the settlers, Lord Windsor, who replaced D'Oyley the following year, was empowered by the King to grant greater privileges and concessions to the inhabitants. In a proclamation issued by Windsor on December 14, 1661, the King declared,

> . . . that all the children of our natural borne subjects of England to be born in Jamaica, shall from their respective births, be reputed to be, and shall be, free denizens of England, and shall have the same privileges, to all intents and purposes, as our free born subjects of England.

To induce prospective settlers to quit their country and settle in a remote area of the world, and to ensure the allegiance of those already living on the island, the King thought it expedient to make clear to all those interested in Jamaica that there would be a reciprocal relationship between himself and his subjects, regardless of whether they lived in England or emigrated to a distant corner of "His Majesty's Plantations" in the New World. With this principle in mind, the King could offer nothing less to his resettled subjects than the forms of civil government already established in England. The Windsor Proclamation made it clear that so long as they remained loyal to their King and country, relocation in a different part of the world would not change the method by which they were governed. Many generations of settlers would jealously guard and defend this principle.

Already a great principle of English law at the time that civil government was established in Jamaica was the right of some of the governed to have a voice in the making of all laws by which they were to be bound. In keeping with this principle of the proclamation, Windsor was also instructed by the King and his councilors to appoint a twelve-member council and to work together with them to call

> . . . Assemblys together, according to the custome of our Planta-
> cons, to make lawes and uppon eminent necessityes to leavy moneys,
> as shall be most conduceable to the honor and advantage of our
> Crown and the good and welfare of our subjects provided they be
> not repugnant to any of our Lawes of England.

With the ending of martial law in Jamaica and the arrival of Lord Windsor, the English Government had immediately outlined the framework of civil government that would be with the island for almost two centuries. An elaborate analysis of the form and functions of the Assembly was given by the King and his councilors to another early governor, the Earl of Carlisle. Representatives would be "duly elected by the major part of the freeholders of the respective parishes and places and so returned shall be called and held the general assembly of the island of Jamaica." The Assembly would then proceed "with the advice and consent" of the governor and the Council "to make constitute and ordain laws, statutes, and ordinances for the public peace, welfare, and good government of the said island."

Using the British governmental structure as a model, there was established in Jamaica at the end of the seventeenth century a representative Assembly that was an "exact resemblance" of the House of Commons, a governor who represented the wishes of the crown, and a Council to substitute for the House of Lords as the upper house of the legislature. Jamaica was the only colony besides the Bahamas to make adequate provision for the regular printing of its statutes. A local governmental structure was also established on the English model; officers such as coroners, constables, and justices of the peace performed the same jobs in Jamaica as in England. Despite its structural likeness to the British Government, the Jamaican counterpart worked quite differently.

The judicial system of Jamaica was streamlined and functional. At the apex was the Supreme Court, which handled both civil and criminal cases. The two Courts of Assizes located in parishes away from the government were presided over by the Chief Justice of the Supreme Court, so that in effect, as has been said, the Supreme Court went "on circuit." Minor judicial disputes concerning payments were settled in the local courts of common pleas, while minor criminal offenses were dealt with at the quarter sessions. Both the Court of Chancery and the Court of Ordinary were presided over by the governor alone, while the Vice Admiralty Court was under his jurisdiction as well. The governor, the chief justice, and the members of the Legislative Council, sitting together, formed the Court of Appeals.

Financial support of the judiciary was wanting. The local government was responsible for the salaries of justices, and in Jamaica only enough money for one salary was voted by the Assembly. As a result, the chief justice was the only qualified law officer. If the legislature had been willing to pay enough, English lawyers could have been recruited for the jobs. But, because it was not, the entire judicial system, except for the Supreme Court, was left in the hands of local citizens.

There were more than thirty judgeships open at various levels, but, except for the Supreme Court, all those appointed served without pay. As in other areas of Jamaican life, the judicial system suffered from a "want of public spirit." In 1792 and again in 1809, committees of the Assembly warned that the courts were "in general very negligently attended" by the justices and that the whole judicial system was in a shocking state. If something was not done to alter the situation, a committee of 1809 concluded, justice would most likely "fail altogether." To assemble sufficient numbers of white Protestants for jury duty was always a problem on the island. To help the situation, the coroner was allowed to fill out an affidavit when he was unable to get twelve men to sit, and then a smaller number was permitted. Though modeled on the English structure in its operations, the government of Jamaica would be modified and regulated both in England and by local conditions and problems.

Rather than being an executive in his own right, the governor had to be guided in his actions by instructions from the king and his councilors. In the administrative and judicial areas, he had the right to establish courts and commission justices to issue writs and grant reprieves and pardons and to summon, prorogue, and dissolve the Assembly. The governor had a voice in making the laws, because all legislation needed his approval. Some of his most important executive duties included making appointments to colonial offices, dispensing money from the public treasury by warrant, granting land, calling up the militia, proclaiming martial law, and suspending councilors and others from office in case of misconduct.

There was little danger that these powers would be abused. The governor's actions were severely circumscribed on two sides: by the local legislature and by the King's instructions, usually issued through the secretary of state. All laws made on the island needed the approval of the King and his Privy Council. The governor was also required by the terms of his commission to consult the Council before any major decisions were made. Although this was not necessarily a handicap, as councilors were usually either his appointees or drawn from the groups friendly to his administration, the governors of Jamaica and the other West Indian islands found that they could not always profit from the advice of the body, because most of the members were landowners who spent very little time on the island. The Assembly presented by far the larger obstacle. As the articulate voice of local residents, it had a most important role in government and often challenged the gov-

ernor's power. Local legislatures had the last word in many
disputes between themselves and the governor. Laws that were
at variance with the wishes of both the governor and the
Privy Council in England were frequently passed by the Assembly. Though the governor had the power of veto or could
add a suspension clause so that the law could not take effect in
Jamaica until it was approved in England, these powers were
in fact rarely invoked. Colonial governors resident in Jamaica
for a limited time preferred to remain at peace with people.
As a result, the Assembly and its subcommittees wielded
powers that were usually delegated to independent national
assemblies. This had the effect of taking away from the governor many of the powers that according to British imperial
theory were officially his. Many a Jamaican governor wrote
dispatches complaining of the arrogance of the popular Assembly and how it encroached on his power. Governor Robert
Hunter commented, "In the infancy of the Colonies the Crown
was lavish of privileges as necessary for their nursing but a full
grown boy makes commonly but indifferent use of that indulgence requisite toward a child."

Of all his administrative powers, the governor's authority
might have been most effectively utilized in his power to suspend colonial officials under him who were insubordinate or
disloyal. Lord George Germain wrote to Lieutenant Governor
Campbell of Jamaica in 1781 that he, Campbell, had "authority
over all officers of the Crown within the island in every Department; and they are all so far amenable to you that you
may suspend them for flagrant misbehavior." Despite this clear
directive, the governor's authority was also circumvented by
officials in England, who often terminated suspensions after
a short period of time. The governor's dignity and status most
certainly suffered in the eyes of those he governed if an individual who had the reputation for being disloyal to him was
returned to a powerful position in government. In the long
run it was safer for the governor merely to complain about an
official rather than to remove him. With his suspension powers
severely weakened, the governor could not effectively supervise

the colonial civil service, and as a result laxity, inefficiency, and blatant corruption were widespread.

The office of the governor was further weakened by the failure of the King to delegate any real or meaningful patronage power to him. Though the governor had the power to appoint the judges of the different courts of the island and name the members of the Council and many of the officers of local government, most of these positions offered no monetary rewards. The positions on the island that did offer rich emoluments were within the King's prerogative. Those who received lucrative appointments of this nature were called patentees because they held patents or commissions from the crown. Such offices as secretary of the island, provost-marshal-general, clerk of the court, collector of customs, and receiver general and treasurer of the island yielded their incumbents incomes of over 6,000 pounds per annum. Adding to the attractions of these appointments was the further provision that those who took them need not be residents of the island and were entitled to the income of the office regardless of whether they ever set foot there. They appointed deputies, who, in the words of a contemporary, "notoriously and avowedly" obtained their situations by purchase directly from the patentee. The practice was curbed by a law passed at the end of the eighteenth century that required patentees to be residents, but this did not improve the governor's weak position, because the patronage power remained with the crown.

In only one major area of state operation did the governor have meaningful power. If not as strong as he might be as an executive, as commander-in-chief of the militia the governor had at his disposal all of the officers' commissions in that body, independent of any legislative or royal interference. Thus the governor held the safety and internal security of the island in tight rein. Having no other way to gain friends and influence, every governor who came to the island would make new appointments to the officer corps of the local fighting force, sometimes completely changing its make-up. Those who lost their commissions were not compelled to serve in an inferior rank. More often than not an experienced man was replaced, in the words of the historian Edward Long, by an inexperienced opportunist, "to regale the passions and humors" of various governors, who had little "interest in the fate of the country nor did they care about it, after their present turn was served."

Because the governor was commander-in-chief, executive head of the government, director of the court system, and representative of the King, "it is not to be expected," wrote Bryan Edwards, an eighteenth-century historian of the West Indies, "that every Governor should on every occasion bear his faculties meekly." Those who received the office were, in the words of Edwards, "men whose education and past pursuits have not given them opportunities of acquiring much acquaintance with the principles of our liberal government." For, like the other lucrative positions in the Jamaican Government, these were simply products of royal patronage. "Party merit and connections" were the "most forcible recommendations" of a candidate. Often the appointment was given to a military officer who had virtually no experience with governmental problems, let alone the knotty points of law connected with a complicated judicial system. Some who received such appointments had already lost their fortunes in dissipated living. Hoping to retrieve the irretrievable, they ventured to the hardship posts of empire in search of self-enrichment. Edward Long, the great historian of eighteenth-century Jamaica and a resident of the island, furnishes this description of the chief executives and their advisers:

> A faithful description of provincial Governors and men in power, would be little better than a portrait of artifice, duplicity, haughtiness, violence, rapine, avarice, meanness, rancour and dishonesty, ranged in succession; with a very small portion of honour, justice and magnanimity, here and there intermixed to lessen the disgust, which otherwise, the eye must feel for so horrid a group.

The most talented and experienced of men would find the job difficult, while the mediocre would find it all but impossible. In 1762 Governor W. H. Lyttleton complained to the Board of Trade that it was "extremely difficult for the King's Governor to support His Majesty's authority in this island with a Council assuming the powers of the House of Lords and an Assembly those of the House of Commons in Great Britain."

The Council, as a constituent part of the legislature, approved all legislation before it became law. The Council was generally considered to be closely allied with the governor. Given their appointment by the governor, its members were expected to support his measures. Because the Council was also constituted as the highest court of appeal on the island, there was a fusion of judicial functions at the very highest levels. Its judicial powers, in concert with the governor, were significant. The Council had less legislative power. It usually served as the governor's voice when hammering out compromises on legislative matters with the lower house.

It was the forty-three-member House of Assembly that was the voice of legislative authority in the land. Drawn from every corner of the island—each "parish" or county was entitled to two representatives ( Kingston and Spanish Town had three each)—the members of the Assembly were the political voice of the permanent settlers. Assembly representatives had to be white Christians and were chosen from either of two groups— merchants and planters—because to qualify for a seat the law required that a man have an income of 300 pounds per annum. No artisan, small freeholder, or laborer could meet this qualification. Resident planters who owned their own estates did not make up a large segment of the population in Jamaica, but they were usually favored by the local parishioners as their representatives. The records of the House of Assembly of the island from the earliest days until the abolition of representative government are blazoned with the heat of angry debate between the governor and the legislature, which more often than not chose to ignore the wishes of the King. In the end, some sort of compromise was usually worked out between their opposing points of view, but before that agreement was reached the governor often lost the respect and good will of the legislature and the people he governed.

From earliest times, the Assembly challenged the prerogatives of the crown. In 1677 it refused to pass a permanent revenue bill and declared that all money appropriated was to be used on the island. The Lords of Trade, who were the King's overseers for the colony, thought they would put down the upstarts by imposing on the colony Poyning's law, the instrument by which Ireland was ruled. But the Jamaican settlers would have no part of this arbitrary form of government, whereby no Assembly could be called without the King's consent and money bills could be promulgated by decree. The Assembly, reported the Earl of Carlisle, "rejected the new constitution with indignation." Through the efforts of one settler, Samuel Long, who went to England to plead Jamaica's cause, the ruling was rescinded after the Assembly agreed to a seven-year revenue bill and legislation to guarantee the perpetual payment of the governor's salary. The major objective of the Lords of Trade eluded them, as they failed to get a permanent revenue bill from the Assembly.

Determined to have absolute control over its own purse strings, the Assembly had refused to allot a sum from the general revenues collected by the state for the use of the crown. Neither the power of the governor nor the loyalty of His Majesty's subjects resident in the island could induce the Assembly to yield to the demands of the King. The struggle between England and the Jamaican Assembly would continue on this issue until 1728, when a perpetual revenue bill was enacted. Money already granted in the form of quitrents, fines, and import duties on wine was the major source of this revenue, so the 8,000 pounds to be granted annually did not represent any new tax burden on the colony. The Assembly agreed to pay an annual revenue of 8,000 pounds to England, and the King in return granted his retroactive approval to all laws enacted during the disputed period.

Problems of monetary control were a constant source of contention. In 1757, for example, the House of Commons passed three resolutions condemning the 1753 assertion by the Jamaican Assembly that

> . . . it *is* the inherent and undoubted right of the Representatives of the people to raise and apply monies for the Service and Exigencies of Government and to appoint such person or persons for the receiving and issueing thereof as they shall think proper.

The Assembly was never cowed, and serious conflicts arose when governors sought to follow specific instructions sent to them from England. Though the governor was charged by his commission to represent the King's wishes, the colonists and their representatives usually thought of the governor's interference as an infringement upon their rights as British subjects residing in Jamaica, rights guaranteed to them by the Windsor Proclamation in 1661. Edward Long, in his *History of Jamaica,* written in 1776, noted that "the Assembly consider their privileges as derived to them from their constituents; and that they are not concessions from the Crown, but the right and inheritance of the people." In the view of the colonists, the instructions from the crown to the governor were recommendations rather than obligations. The colonists regarded the relationship between themselves and the English sovereign as reciprocal. In exchange for their allegiance and loyalty to the crown, they felt that they were entitled to assent to all laws they were to be obligated to obey.

Though all legislation passed by the government of Jamaica required final approval by the King and his Privy Council, it remained, unless otherwise specifically stated, the law of the land until the King's pleasure was known. Approval or disapproval from England was sometimes two or three years in coming, and, by the time it came, because the law had been accepted locally, there was little real concern over what the King's pleasure would be. Edward Long wrote that men who were "entrusted with public offices so far from the mother state, require a chain instead of a thread to hold them in place." The residents of Jamaica preferred the thread.

The Assembly's behavior was a most accurate and sensitive barometer of the tensions and conflicts inherent in the social and economic structure of Jamaican society. The Assembly was composed of various factions usually representing the major economic interests of the island. That is not to say that all planters were in one faction and all merchants in another. Factions of planters opposed other planters, merchants opposed other merchants, and planters and merchants opposed each other.

Laws were created to deal with a wide range of problems covering every area of island life—public works projects, repairing of roads, voting of appropriations to maintain the government, and legislation for ordering community affairs. The Assembly was intent on dealing independently with the problems of Jamaican society. In a dispatch to the Board of Trade in 1762, Governor W. H. Lyttelton offered his analysis of the Assembly's frame of mind. There was, he said,

> . . . such an eager desire to be freed from those restraints which the wisdom of His Majesty's councils have put them under and such an aspiring endeavor to acquire in their Assemblies and within the sphere of their activity the same power and privileges as are enjoyed by the British House of Commons.

The Assembly was the voice of the white Christians, a varied and diversified lot represented in several social strata. Its leaders were often the large property-owners who were permanent residents of the island. They were small in number, as most of the Englishmen who owned estates in Jamaica did not reside there, preferring to live in England, where they could enjoy the profits from their investment without suffering any of the hardships connected with living in a tropical wilderness. Ownership of a plantation on the island of Jamaica was considered but another business enterprise by those who were wealthy enough to invest in it.

The absentee landlord, even though much of the safety and security of his property and consequently its ultimate success as an investment depended upon an efficient government on the island, had, generally, no interest in the local affairs of Jamaica. The negation by the absentee Jamaican landowners of the first principle of organized society—that every member is equally bound to contribute to its common safety, defense, and support—was never questioned.

Those who remained on the island were, however, aware of the consequences of absenteeism as early as 1746. At that time, the local government tried to subject the absentees to additional taxation on the principle that they should compensate for their lack of personal service to the island by supplying greater financial aid. There were some among the assembly-men who also thought that it might compel the absentees to live on the island if they had to pay a price for remaining away. Despite ardent pleading for the tax by the King's own representative on the island, Governor Trelawny, it was dis-allowed by the Privy Council and the King in England. A very strong and powerful "lobby" of nonresident proprietors with good royal connections—many of them ranked high in the aristocracy—had thwarted the attempt to change conditions. The complaint of Governor Trelawny fell on deaf ears: "I truly think that there is hardly any evil we labor under, but what is owing ultimately to the small number of inhabitants: it makes the duties of magistracies and all Commissions, civil and military, very hard on the residents and there is no choice."

Those "elite" inhabitants with whom the governor worked or whom he appointed to civic responsibilities were often men whose occupations gave them very little understanding of administrative functions. Such were the men who were sup-posed to fill the offices of public trust and be responsible for parish government and the running of the local courts. Some, who had no qualification other than the ability to read and write, filled crucial administrative positions. It was common practice for one man to hold several offices at the same time, doing none of the jobs well.

Local jealousies were also quite common, particularly with respect to Jamaica's major urban centers, Spanish Town and Kingston. The former, an inland city, opposed all measures benefiting the latter, a coastal mercantile town. In 1755, King-ston replaced Spanish Town as the capital city, only to have the honor taken away in 1758 and restored to Spanish Town. (More than a century later, in 1872, Kingston was made the capi-tal permanently.) There were many factional conflicts between city and city and between rural and urban areas. The legis-lature failed to provide funds for the building of a reservoir in Kingston as a safety precaution against fire. There was also the failure to build a customs house in Kingston for want of rural support. The lack of a decent jail in Spanish Town was attributed to the fact that some "indulged a principle of wantonly opposing every scheme and project offered."

Failure of public spirit and a weak sense of community responsibility affected the security of the island. Every man was bound by law to serve in the militia, but, drawing from a white population composed chiefly of hired servants and indentured laborers, this military force was never a strong, well-disciplined or effective instrument. Governor Hunter, commenting on the state of the island in the 1730's, described the militia as composed of "servants and these sort whose hearts are not with us," with the consequence that "their hands are of little use to us." They could not be depended upon, he continued, because they felt obligation neither of honor or interest "for the defense of their master's properties."

All males above the age of sixteen who had been residents of the island for one month were enlisted. Civic duty required that all except commissioned officers serve without pay. Though there were permanent stations at various trouble spots on the island, manned on a rotating basis, most militia members were on inactive duty. Like the reservists of today, they could be called to action without prior notice. Here, as in every other area of Jamaican life, public spirit and concern for the common good were lacking. Although there was monthly training as well as maneuvers, local militia units were very poorly prepared for effective fighting. Mobilizations were occasions for merry-making rather than serious effort. Commissions were vehicles for prestige, and favoritism was common. To aid local defenses, companies of the British army were intermittently stationed in Jamaica from 1730 on. The Assembly and the British Government were constantly haggling over their support, while relations between the standing army officers and the proprietors were far from cordial. As holders of militia commissions, the proprietors were jealous of the professionals and contemptuous of the motherland's rank-and-file. In 1792 the militia numbered 8,172 men, divided into a small cavalry division and a large infantry section.

The Assembly's controversy with England over Jamaica's share in helping to support the army companies stationed there was characteristic. The Assembly held that the primary purpose of government was to protect Jamaica and to guard against the servile population, but it was unwilling to pay the price and looked to Britain for protection. It accepted colonial status only insofar as it was useful, and this outlook was held until the old representative system was abolished.

# 3. The Plantation Economy and International Trade

Jamaica was founded as a state enterprise. Unlike most of the British colonies, neither a single proprietor, a settlement company, nor a joint stock company was initially instrumental in creating Jamaica's first settlements. In Cromwell's "Grand Design," Jamaica was considered valuable to the state as a base for operations against the Spanish Empire. Before the conquest there had been no advanced plans to exploit the colony agriculturally. After the conquest, and with the restoration of Charles II, the King and his councillors played a major role in recruiting investors and planters, who turned Jamaica's lands into agricultural ventures.

Sugar became the major crop of the West Indies and of Jamaica by a process of trial and error. Tobacco was the original choice of those early settlers in the West Indies who came to the Leeward Islands and Barbados in the 1630's and 1640's. However, tobacco from Virginia fetched a much higher price on the London market because of its superior quality, and the islanders soon found they needed a crop that was better suited to a tropical environment. Climate and geography demanded a product that would bring a high price on the European market and would have a high yield per acre. Sugar became the obvious choice. There was an ever increasing, almost insatiable, demand for it in Europe, and it could be cultivated intensively and for long periods on the same land without exhausting the soil. In Jamaica the initial capital investment in any agriculture was high because the area of

30

usable land was limited and often had to be cleared for plant-ing at great cost; hence, only the crop that would give the greatest return could justify the expenditure. Sugar had a high yield per acre.

It was the Dutch who taught the English the methods of sugar cultivation and refining, which they had learned in Brazil. Expelled by the Portuguese from Pernambuco, many Dutch settlers sought refuge in the West Indies. With them they brought agricultural gold—sugar planting. By the time the English had consolidated their position and opened the islands wide for settlement, sugar and economic success had become linked together by an unbreakable bond.

Sugar cultivation, to yield a maximum profit, required in those times a large, highly organized, and regimented labor force. In the early stages of the industry, white laborers, most of whom had come to the West Indies as indentured servants, were used. Every method of recruitment, including force, was employed to bring workers to the islands. Transportation to the islands became a regular punishment for vagrants, political prisoners, and many convicted felons. This class of desperate and despised men "such as, had there been no English Foreign Plantation in the World, could probably never have lived at home to do service to their country," as Edward Long writes, could hardly be successful at working long hours in the sugar fields under the heat of the tropical sun. Besides, their term of servitude was limited; they lived in the hope of escape from the hardships of plantation labor. Although they were some-times derided by the Negroes as "white slaves" and received worse treatment, the status of "servants" and not "slaves" gave them an independence of mind that was almost impossible to curb. Thus they did not fit in with the highly organized labor situation necessary on the sugar plantation.

As the sugar-planting "fever" spread in the islands, the de-mand for labor increased. Large numbers of laborers were needed and were to be supplied from Africa through a large-scale commercial enterprise. The slave trade had existed since the sixteenth century, when the Portuguese pioneered the west coast of Africa in search of human cargo. Slaves, or "black ivory," as they came to be called because they were such a precious commodity to the New World, were utilized by the Spaniards in the Caribbean as early as 1502. At first the majority were brought to Hispaniola, under the *asiento* given by the King of Spain to German traders in 1537.

A century later it was the Dutch who first supplied the British islands with slave labor. This practice soon attracted adverse criticism in England. It was in complete contradiction of the mercantilist ideology to buy so valuable and expensive a commodity from foreigners. The Navigation Acts forbade Dutch ships to trade in English colonies. Seeking to add to what a contemporary economist, Thomas Munn, called "England's Treasure by Foreign Trade," Charles II granted a charter to a group of investors known later as the Royal African Company. The crown itself did not have the resources to undertake the building of forts and the provision of armed ships. Therefore, just as the crown had chartered settlement companies such as the Massachusetts Bay Company in the earlier part of the century, so in 1663 it lent its strength and prestige to back a slave-trading company. Several members of the royal family were shareholders in this enterprise, which was organized to supply the English sugar colonies with three thousand slaves a year. Its beginnings were inauspicious, and many investors feared the Royal African Company would never reach its goal.

The demand for slaves in the second half of the seventeenth century was great, but it was particularly pressing in Jamaica. In area, Jamaica is two or three times larger than any other British territory in the West Indies, and this vast virgin land, opened to all comers, was ready for sugar cultivation, provided sufficient labor could be had. The Royal African Company did not prove to be a good supplier to Jamaica. After 1690 Jamaica received most of its slaves from private traders. While the Royal African Company supplied 34,480 slaves in all, private merchants from 1690 to 1713 supplied 42,000.

The conditions under which the slaves were transported to the new world and the sufferings in the middle passage were horrendous. A slave who made it to the island was immediately sold. Prices varied with quality—that is, tribal stock and the age and health of the individual slaves. The full acclimation or "seasoning" period lasted three years. Mortality rates were high during this period. It has been estimated that one-fourth of the slaves who reached Jamaica died during their first three years in the new land, mostly by suicide, from dysentery, or from other illnesses.

Despite the setbacks of the middle passage and the seasoning period, Jamaica's Negro population grew bigger and bigger. In 1658 there were 1,400 Negroes, in 1722 there were 80,000, and in 1800 there were 300,939. Slaves were an indispensable part of economic life in Jamaica.

A minimum of 250 slaves were needed to perform the tasks related to cultivation, refining, and maintenance for a sugar plantation to be profitable. After evaluating all costs for establishing a plantation, the largest portion of the investment was that reserved for the purchase of slaves.

The absentee owner living in England often made his investment as part of a larger consortium composed of like-minded businessmen. The independent investor's prospects for success were much slimmer: He had less money for the initial outlay and hence depended more on creditors, who would foreclose at the first indication of failure. Bryan Edwards wrote that "the business of sugar planting is a sort of adventure in which the man that engages must engage deeply. There is no medium. It requires a capital of no less than 30,000 pounds sterling to embark in this employment with a fair prospect of adventure." Investors tended to buy up small holdings and consolidate them into larger ones. The number of small farmers rapidly decreased.

Complaining of this development, an island resident told the Board of Trade, "The decrease of small freeholders was by reason of the greater eating up or buying out all the lesser planters and keeping vast tracts of land unoccupied." The island resident was justified in complaining. Just before the American Revolution, in the parish (county) of St. James, 132 proprietors held 106,352 acres of land. Of these only 10 held less than 50 acres each, and by the end of the century each proprietor held, on the average, 900 acres. Primogeniture tended to perpetuate and even aggravate the situation.

The estates of the absentee landlords were left in the hands of attorneys or agents who were paid a salary or, more commonly, a commission, generally 6 per cent of the annual yield. The position was lucrative. The agent lived in the great house on the estate, was served by the master's blacks, used his horses and carriages, and, without risking any of his own money, received his compensation as the first charge against the season's crops.

Attorneys were hired also to audit and supervise the accounts of the estate plantations. Most had charge of several plantations. This factor tended to weaken responsible supervision, and extravagance in the operation of an absentee's holdings was widespread. Supplies were frequently wasted, and very little effort was made to promote economies in buying them. Because improvements temporarily reduced net earnings (and the agent's commission), these were held to a minimum.

Personnel were needed to organize and discipline the labor force. In Jamaica the man who directly supervised the slaves was called an overseer, but at times he was also a bookkeeper. On very large estates these jobs were often split: The overseer had charge of over-all maintenance of the property, and the bookkeeper was responsible for directly supervising and disciplining the agricultural labor gangs in the field. The bookkeeper's job was more specialized; the overseer's was to see that the operation was efficient and well organized. Because his job was so intimately related to the work and life of the slave, contemporary opinion thought of the bookkeeper as "doomed to a kind of banishment and bondage."

Attorneys and overseers were interested primarily in greater production, because the immediate return on investment was the test by which most of them were judged. The incentive, therefore, was to force output. Many of the abuses and sufferings of the slave laborers resulted from the desire on the part of those directing tropical agricultural production to increase production or at least to maintain it in the face of increasing soil exhaustion. By driving their slaves hard they hoped to bring in the largest crops possible, which would yield a lucrative commission. The picture of the cruel overseer is derived largely from this group of "hired hands." It was not so much the resident and creole plantation owners living permanently in Jamaica who were the cruel masters; cruel acts were, according to Long, the "execrable misdeeds of British refugees." Permanently warped, said Long, by "unprincipled hearts and abominable tempers," the hired supervisors of the estates were to be blamed for the wanton torture inflicted on the slaves in their charge. Often incapable of doing a competent job, they cared little for the problems of the estates and even less for the Negroes working on them. They had come to the island not because of their interest in tropical farming but rather to make a fortune for future use in England. Most of them had no experience with agricultural pursuits. A property in Jamaica, said Bryan Edwards, was like a "lottery ticket," for it awakened "extravagant hopes and expectations."

Contemporaries had harsh comments for attorneys and overseers. One wrote in 1785 of the advantages of being an attorney, "Fat managers and lean employers; to be an attorney of an estate of a non-resident is better than to be its owner, the first receiving benefits without the least risk, while the latter was subject to every loss without receiving the advantages which ought, consistent with justice, to be his and not his steward's." An heir, inspecting his legacy at almost the same time, called the attorneys "the locusts of the West Indies."

In general, on a plantation 600 to 900 acres in size, one-third of the estate land was allocated to the growing of cane; another third was given over to pasture for the grazing of work animals such as horses and oxen, as well as to provision grounds; and the rest was woodland, used as a source of both timber for construction and fuel for refining the cane.

A routine of sugar cultivation was adopted that kept the slaves fully employed throughout the year. The creole cane, grown in Jamaica, matured for harvest fifteen months after planting. As it was usual to let half the land lie fallow for six months, the harvest of one crop coincided with the planting of the other. Maintained the year round on the plantation, the slaves worked all the time, deprived by this system of the seasonal rest that would normally occur after the planting season.

After the brush was cleared away with cutlasses and then burned, a field was prepared for planting. This was done by digging, with hoes, parallel lines of holes about 2 feet wide and 6 inches deep. The slaves worked in pairs—the weaker person doing the easier part of the process, the stronger the more difficult. "Holing," as the process was called, was the hardest work and was performed by a large number of slaves, some specially hired for the job. In a few cases where fertilizers were used, female slaves carried baskets of dung or ashes on their heads and dumped them into the trenches. Cane cuttings were inserted, and planting was complete. It remained only to fight weeds by pulling or hoeing and to harvest the ripe sugar cane stalks with machetes. Ratoons developed from the roots of the original canes after they had been cut and carted off, and they yielded decreasing quantities of liquid. When the soil was exhausted, the field was abandoned and the exploitation of another area begun.

Though relatively inefficient, this was the process of planting that continued to be used, with but slight modifications and improvements, into the nineteenth century. During refining in the sugar mills, boiling was done in open copper pots. Three products resulted: molasses, rum, and "muscovado," or raw sugar. The syrupy mass granulated, and, after draining had removed much of the molasses, the muscovado sugar was packed in barrels for shipment to overseas refineries. Rum was distilled from the scum arising during the boiling and from molasses collected into casks for transportation to market.

Although scientific agriculture in England was making progress in the latter half of the eighteenth century, Jamaica, along with the other West Indian islands, did little in the way of improving its agricultural production. Edward Long declared in 1774 that the sugar industry in Jamaica was less than one-third efficient, and William Beckford, a resident from 1773 to

1788, held that one-seventh of each crop was regularly wasted. In the nineteenth century a visitor complained, "The people of Jamaica make no novel experiment" to improve their antiquated methods.

In time, the custom of the past hardened. A Jamaican proprietor who arrived to take possession of his estates in the first decade of the nineteenth century found that it was most difficult to introduce innovations. He found:

> The greatest obstacle to improvement, was the *bigotry* and the *refractory* disposition of the professional planters, by whom I mean the regular hired overseers, who are employed to conduct the ordinary business of plantations and in the old *habits* of professional agents who have reached the highest situations of confidence and responsibility by becoming the superintendents of a multiplicity of plantations, and the representatives of absentees.

As late as 1840, a Baptist missionary, a twenty-year resident in Jamaica, wrote, "The old methods are the rule—the improvements the exception."

The center of life and authority on the estate was the "great house." It usually stood in a commanding position on the estate, often facing the sea. Despite its name, the great house was not always imposing. Built of wood, with stone supports, it ranged from a miserable thatched hovel to a porticoed, colonnaded mansion. Interiors were plain. All culinary operations were performed in separate buildings. Servants lived in adjacent quarters, while the settlement that housed the estate's Negroes was situated a short distance away, to the rear of the great house.

By the end of the eighteenth century practically all plantations had provision grounds—plots allotted to slaves to grow the yams, potatoes, and corn that were the staples of their diet. And on many plantations the slaves could not only provide for themselves but produce a surplus to sell at the market on Sunday. They used the cash proceeds to buy the provisions they could not grow—salt beef, salt fish, and other items. By the middle of the eighteenth century—the "golden age" of prosperity in Jamaica—the provision ground system had become an integral part of the economy. Edward Long expressed the belief that during this period most of the small silver coins circulating in Jamaica were in the hands of the slaves. The slaves became the major producers of vegetables and other cash crops on the island.

The amount of provision ground per slave varied with many circumstances, but the average was about half an acre. In addition, the slaves were permitted to cultivate the grounds behind their huts. They tended to grow staple foods, such as yams and plantains, and also pumpkins, bananas, and ackee. Slaves were also permitted to keep cows and chickens, which were often owned in common.

Just as the amount of provision land varied, so too did the number of hours the slaves were permitted to be away from their regular work. The Consolidated Slave Laws set a minimum standard of one day a week, but whether the law was adhered to on every plantation is uncertain.

The slave-dominated Sunday markets that became a distinctive feature of the internal economy of Jamaica were at first opposed by law. One of the reasons was that goods stolen from the masters were sold by the slaves at the market. By the end of the eighteenth century it was an accepted feature of life in the islands, as economic necessities forced planters to rely on the provision ground as a major source of sustenance for the slaves. The market was a natural outgrowth of the slaves' independent endeavors.

Such was the plantation, the major unit of agricultural production in Jamaica. Its major product, sugar, would have been of little value without an external market to absorb it. Jamaica was a link in the economic system of empire that Great Britain had fashioned through mercantilism. As a specialized economic entity serving an export market, Jamaica would for a time flourish.

The British West Indian colonies were intended for exploitation. Put into law with the Navigation Acts, which took effect in 1651, the British Government's policy was aimed at the enrichment of the mother country. Trade was synonymous with wealth and was the best vehicle for acquiring riches.

The "triangular" trade with Africa, the American colonies,

and Great Britain filled the prescription of the mercantile ideology. It involved the procuring of slaves in Africa, their transportation to the British colonies, and, in the case of the West Indies, the sending of sugar (semirefined and its byproducts) to Great Britain. It generally took a full year to complete the cycle, and there was an inseparable link between the slave trade and the sugar trade. Ships sailed from British ports for the African coast, where they bartered commodities such as manufactures, firearms, and liquor for slaves, whom they took to the West Indian colonies. There they were sold to the planters, mostly in exchange for sugar, which was then carried back to England. It was a hazardous but largely profitable trade. During the infamous "middle passage" from Africa to the West Indies, many slaves were lost because of disease and other hardships. Adam Smith called the slave traders "the refuse of the jails of Europe." The slave traders and the sugar barons (the absentee owners of West Indian plantations) formed a powerful lobby in England, influencing public opinion and Parliament.

The triangular trade among Britain, North America, and the West Indies brought the greatest fortunes. Intra-empire commercial relations provided guaranteed markets for colonial products. Unable to cultivate sugar, England and North America brought their supplies from the West Indies, while the islands, because they specialized in certain tropical crops, needed foodstuffs and manufactured goods.

Not the local merchants but the commercial agents in England handled the accounts for the absentee owner. After a crop on a given estate was ready for export, it was hauled to the nearest port of clearance, loaded aboard a merchantman, and shipped across the Atlantic, usually in April, June, or August. Upon arrival in England, the hogsheads, casks, puncheons, and parcels, which had already been marked to designate their ownership, were claimed by the merchant designated by the estate owner. The crop was disposed of by this agent, usually to several buyers, one part here and another there, over a period of time. Price varied according to quality and the trend of the market. The produce sold early in the season, when supplies were ample, brought less than did that held over until stocks had been largely cleared. When an entire shipment had been sold, a commission, usually 2½ per cent, was charged against sales, the remainder of the gross receipts going to the credit of the owner. The West Indian merchants, usually centered in London, performed other business operations for the proprietor besides the marketing of his tropical products. Absentee proprietors, as a rule, had no interest in their business except to know the amount of money it made, so they gladly assigned to the commerical houses the job of being their personal representatives for all dealings. It was the merchant who purchased supplies for the plantation—cloth, hardware, crockery, furniture, plate, salt-cured meat, and even the last word in feminine fashions. If a crop failed to bring a good price, it was the merchant who extended the planter credit for the next year. Because of this system, little money actually passed through the planter's hands. There was considerable waste and extravagance, and, because the merchant was paid a percentage commission, it was not necessarily in his interest to pay low rather than high prices for purchases made for the planters.

By the mid-eighteenth century, there were comparatively few large English merchants who did not trade with Jamaica. The value of this trade was said to be four times greater than the value of trade with the rest of the world. Unlike the East Indies trade, which required export of bullion to pay for spices and other exotic items, the trade with Jamaica and the West Indies consisted in the simple exchange of cheap manufactured goods for African slaves, of slaves or manufactured goods for West Indian foodstuffs, and of these products for a high return in cash either in the home market or on the continent of Europe. Opulent living, in the past the sole preserve of the gentry, was now also the way of life of a new "millionaire class" of merchants who, like the overseer, estate manager, and absentee landlord, were well served by the soil of Jamaica.

A group of local merchants in Jamaica carried on business first at Port Royal and then, after the earthquake of 1692 and the hurricane of 1703 had destroyed that town, moved either to Spanish Town, the island's capital, or to Kingston, the chief port. Port Royal Street, situated close to the harbor, was the chief merchants' thoroughfare in Kingston. Favored by nature with a wide, basin-like shore surrounded by flat terrain that gradually rose in elevation, Kingston was, from the eighteenth century on, Jamaica's equivalent to Boston or New York. And it has remained ever since.

Acting as representatives of English mercantile houses was one way in which local businessmen earned their living. They saw to it that the crop was safely loaded onto the eastward-bound merchantmen. When a vessel arrived with stores and manufactured goods for the estate, it was the representative's job to unload it, pay all the duties and port fees, and arrange for the inland transportation.

Without its commercial agent and its local representative, the plantation would not have flour to bake the daily bread, meat for dinner, or dried herrings, which were the protein staple of the slave's diet. Unlike the small farmers in North America, who were often self-sufficient, the estate owner was largely dependent on imports from North America and England for his very subsistence. Usually both the independent merchants and those who represented English mercantile houses did not have to wait for customers. They did a kind of mail-order business with the country estates, constantly sending them supplies ordered in advance. Sale in bulk was usually the rule, for transportation costs from town to country were high while poor roads prevented many shipments from arriving intact. As a result, retail shops were almost unknown; merchants and commercial representatives operated out of large warehouses, where they stored the goods from abroad. Here they filled their orders, and from here they shipped the goods. Local independent operators who were not representatives of English firms supplemented their incomes by supplying various goods to peddlers who roamed the countryside and frequented the town markets, selling to slaves, free Negroes, white servants, and small farmers.

Trinkets, colorful cloth for bandanas, or shiny pots for the ladies—these were the kinds of wares given on consignment

by the town merchant to the peddler. If he was a good sales-
man, the peddler might in the course of time become a merchant himself by saving enough money to establish himself.
But this was unusual. Many of them died on the road or, as
soon as they saved enough money to pay their passage, sailed
for North America, where they hoped to find a more lucrative
calling.

There was an absence of banking facilities in Jamaica, as on
the other West Indian islands, and bills of exchange drawn in
Great Britain were used to meet the planters' obligations. The
exchange was rarely at par and fluctuated with the demand
for bills. Although pounds, shillings, and pence were used to
set prices, these were not on a British sterling basis and varied
in value.

Many of the local merchants obtained credit from the
London merchantile houses to purchase their own wares to
sell and increase their earnings. Edward Long said that "most
of the merchants and petty storekeepers of Jamaica would be
in a little better state than beggary" were it not for the
"fountainhead of credit" supplied by the "merchants of the
mother country."

There was, however, one group of businessmen who gained
good profits by trading with the Spanish Main and with Hispaniola and Cuba. Jamaica's geographical position was closer
to these islands and the Spanish mainland than was any other
English colony at the time. One writer called Jamaica the
"key to the Indies" because it lay "in the very belly of all
commerce." The wealth accumulated by the Jamaican merchants trading with the Spaniards was an affirmation of this
belief.

Jews in particular were quite active in the Spanish trade.
According to Edward Long, their "knowledge of foreign languages and intercourse with their brethren, dispersed over the
Spanish and West Indian colonies have contributed greatly to
extend trade and increase the wealth of the island." As a result,
the Jewish community in Kingston was very large, and its
synagogue was a "handsome, spacious building" with a gallery
"for the reception of women, who do not mingle with the
other sex in their public devotion." As independent dealers,

Jews were often money-changers and provided credit services as well. They were, states Long, always chief importers of bullion and carried on a "profitable business by purchasing dollars with ryals of old plate." They also accepted the dollars of "soldiers and indentured tradesmen," allowing them to purchase "small necessaries" and "made considerable sums on exchange." And, if a planter could not get a loan from a representative of an English mercantile house, a Jew would oblige him with a loan, charging 6 per cent above the regular interest rate. Successful in their livelihood, Jews had, Long concluded, "solid attachment to the interests and security of Jamaica; which they consider their home."

The years 1713 to 1739 witnessed a great expansion of the trade carried on between Jamaica and the Spanish Main. When England, under the Treaty of Utrecht (1713), was granted the *asiento*, the exclusive right to supply Spanish America with slaves, Jamaica was the greatest beneficiary among all the British possessions. Slave ships going to Spanish America would stop at Jamaica for the "refreshment" of slaves before continuing to the mainland. Local merchants would sell the slavers goods, which could be smuggled onto, or sold openly on, the mainland at high prices. Before crossing the Atlantic or setting out for British North America, the slave ships from the coast would once again stop at Jamaica, where they would spend some of their proceeds while reloading their holds for the return journey with Jamaican products. While the *asiento* trade enriched merchants, it was a constant thorn in the side of the planters, who found themselves competing with the Spanish settlements for a sufficient supply of high-quality bondsmen. Despite the huge imports of slaves to Jamaica, demand always exceeded supply. The *asiento* trade was from 1713 to 1739 a major source of the discrepancy.

During the eighteenth century some diversification in the cultivation of tropical products had taken place. Coffee was introduced in the 1720's as a crop for small farmers; exports rose from 65,700 pounds in 1763 to 402,800 pounds in 1775. Also in operation were 110 cotton properties, 100 pimento farms, 8 indigo estates, and 30 estates growing ginger.

Successful as Jamaica and the other British colonies were in their plantation economies, they could not meet the competition of the French sugar islands, which, because of lower production costs and prices, were fast moving in on the established markets in North America and Europe. In 1717, 300 acres in the French islands could be worked profitably by 30 to 40 Negroes and a few horses and cattle, while the same amount of land in the English colonies would require 150 Negroes, 50 or 60 head of cattle, and 12 horses. Despite the Navigation Acts of 1660, 1663, 1673, and 1696, which made the English islands the sole legal supplier of sugar to North America, illegal trade between British North America and the French sugar islands was on a steady rise from 1713 on. Rum and molasses from the French islands were particularly abundant and cheap because France's mercantile laws discouraged importation, in the interest of French wines and brandies. As the trade grew to great proportions in the eighteenth century, the West Indian interests in England, whose political influence and economic power were substantial, persuaded the government in 1733 to enact a law known as the Molasses Act, designed to prevent loss of the North American market to the French West Indies.

In general, Jamaica had been less seriously affected by French competition than the other English islands. It still had considerable tracts of uncultivated land, and its natural resources were far from exhausted. Nevertheless, it strongly, though belatedly, supported the other islands in their demand for the suppression of the French trade with North America. It hoped in this way to increase its sales of molasses, which went at double the French price. Greater outlets in North America would allow Jamaica to fulfill its great agricultural potential.

Whether the Molasses Act would have helped Jamaica to fulfill its potential—a goal that was never reached—will never be known. The weakness of the imperial machinery for enforcing the trade laws in British America prevented the Molasses Act from having a meaningful, long-lasting effect. Evasions became, almost immediately after its passage, a matter of common knowledge among officials. The powerful West

Indian lobby pressed the British Government to find still another solution to the economic depression of the West Indian islands. Too many influential persons had investments in Jamaica and the other islands for the situation to be tolerated indefinitely. High production costs in the British islands prevented them from besting the French islands in open competition, so some saw the only alternative in crippling French sugar production by burning cane and carrying off slaves to work on the British islands. In times of intense rivalry, war could be an effective instrument for doing away with the major competitor. The British had made destructive forays into the Spanish colonies since 1739. They turned on the French in 1744, when the European War of Austrian Succession entered its last phase. The British efforts were frustrated. When the war ended, in 1748, no question had been resolved with France and no territory had changed hands; nor had any commercial disputes been settled.

That the sugar trade was generally less profitable for the British colonies than it had been earlier was already apparent at the end of the Seven Years' War, in 1763. Heavy fighting in the Caribbean between British and French squadrons gave Britain an occasion to order its commanders not only to pillage but also to capture enemy islands. Guadeloupe was seized from the French in 1759, and the flooding of the London market with sugar from that island evoked bitter complaints from the West Indian interests. This experience was to have a great impact on the outcome of the war.

As a result of the war, Great Britain had the opportunity to acquire Guadeloupe and Martinique, both very productive sugar islands. But if it did, the economies of the British Caribbean islands would be destroyed. Faced with the opposition of the sugar barons and the West Indian merchants, Great Britain did not annex Guadeloupe and Martinique—which would have given strong competition to the existing British West Indian sugar interests—but acquired Canada instead. Canada posed no such threats and was a source of supplies needed by the British West Indies.

What can only be termed an "unnatural" settlement is explainable by the importance and influence of the West India interests both in the West Indies and, particularly, in Great Britain. The acquisition of the French sugar colonies would have been, because of competition, a blow to the existing monopoly of the British West Indian islands and those who benefited from it.

Nevertheless, conditions in the British West Indies, especially in Jamaica, did not return to "normal." The war had interrupted the century-old highly profitable trade between Jamaica and the Spanish islands of Cuba and Puerto Rico. This trade was illegal under Spanish law but was approved of by the British authorities. Cuba and Puerto Rico exchanged mules and cattle for Negroes and supplies. Most important, because the trade balance was in its favor, Jamaica received large quantities of sorely needed bullion and money.

The confiscation of all Spanish vessels in Jamaican harbors at the beginning of hostilities and some illegal extractions of fees from the Spaniards by officers in Jamaica seemed largely responsible for the failure of the old trade to be renewed. The eighteenth-century historian Long stated that the commercial decline of Kingston was apparent and there was distress and poverty.

Still another struggle, that between the North American colonies and Great Britain, created fear and alarm in the British Caribbean. The decision of the first Continental Congress to close the ports of the thirteen colonies to British produce and then to close them to exports from the British Caribbean worried and aroused the West Indian interests both in Britain and in the colonies.

The Jamaican Assembly took strong action. In December, 1774, in a petition, the Assembly expressed loyalty to the King and asserted that it had no intention of opposing the British Government but that it was an established principle of the empire that no law could bind its subjects unless it had been approved by their representatives. The Assembly deplored past attempts to override that principle, declared that depriving colonials of equal rights with Englishmen dissolved the relationship between Jamaica and England and appealed to the King to mediate the differences between his British and American subjects.

The West Indian interests in London called a general meeting to decide on what action to take in the crisis. A petition to Parliament was signed, and funds were collected. It was of little avail against the opening of actual hostilities between the British Government and the thirteen colonies. Although in no danger before France joined the war on the side of the colonies, the West Indies, including Jamaica, suffered economically from the cutting off of their sources of supply and the loss of markets. The American Revolution brought serious hardships and deprivations to Jamaica and its sister colonies in the West Indies. Essential foodstuffs long supplied by the mainland colonies were no longer available to the West Indies after September 10, 1775, when the Continental Congress forbade American ships to call at British ports in the West Indies. Abundance turned to scarcity, and prices for such essential products as rice, Indian corn, and flour doubled and tripled during the war years. Added to these troubles was a scarcity of freighters to carry the crops to the English markets and the high wartime duties levied on the shipments. A severe hurricane in 1781 ravaged the island and destroyed great stretches of crop land. The golden prosperity of the preceding decades collapsed in a long night of revolution and war.

It was at this time that what became two major staples of the Jamaican diet—ackee and mango—were introduced on the island. Indigenous to West Africa, cuttings of these plants were first sent to the island by Admiral Rodney, who discovered them on a French slave ship he had seized. Still a third food, thought of today as Jamaican but really native to Tahiti—the breadfruit—was brought at this time to the island by Captain Bligh of the H.M.S. *Bounty*. While the slaves readily ate the mangoes and ackee, they spurned the breadfruit. For more than forty years breadfruit was fed to pigs, and not until after emancipation did it become an important source of food for the peasant communities. Cultivation of staples was encouraged by the Jamaican Assembly in an effort to make the island less dependent on the American colonies for food. Besides mangoes, ackee, and breadfruit, yams, cocoa, corn, and plantains were grown in greater abundance than ever before. But such gestures toward self-sufficiency on the part of the planters could not offset the troubles caused by the American Revolution.

Having somehow survived the war, the Caribbean colonies encountered problems posed by the recognition of the United States as a sovereign state: Would there be a restoration of the old trading relations, or would there be a breaking off, by action of the British Government, of the former trade? Would imperial commercial policy prevent the normal flow of trade between the British Caribbean colonies and the now independent United States of America?

In Jamaica there was no doubt as to what should be done. Nor was there any in the minds of influential Americans. John Adams wrote in 1783:

> The commerce of the West India Islands is part of the American system of commerce. They can neither do without us, nor we without them. The Creator has placed us upon the globe in such a situation that we have occasion for each other. We have the means of assisting each other, and politicians and artful contrivances cannot separate us. Wise statesmen, likeable artists of every kind, study nature and their works are perfect in proportion as they conform to her laws.

Adams was, of course, thinking of the economic interests of the United States; Jamaica supported the same sentiments because they favored its interests. But, in the eyes of the British, still held by the gospel of mercantilism, the United States was a foreign state and had to be treated as such. British interests and British shipping had to be protected. Adam Smith's opinions could not be supported. Instead, Caribbean sugar would be protected by the continuation of extra duties on sugar produced by foreigners. The old colonial system had to be strengthened and protected. In the light of the then prevailing opinion, to allow free trade between the West Indian islands and the Amercian colonies would mean to surrender the advantages of empire while continuing to offer the colonies protection under the mercantile system.

Because the British Government stood firm on its position,

large-scale smuggling became a practice. At the same time, the fishing and lumber industries of Canada were greatly stimulated. Nevertheless, prices of the goods imported by the West Indians, either legally or illegally, remained considerably above those of the prewar period. The cost of living was very high in the islands. Sugar prices, meanwhile, fell.

The Jamaican Assembly petitioned Parliament to allow the free importation of supplies from the United States. In the petition it painted a sad picture of estates facing ruin. Some temporary relief was granted, but the growing of sugar was becoming less profitable, and the increase of coffee production was not sufficient to overcome the generally bad economic situation. In 1790 the Jamaican Assembly, in a petition to the King, warned that Jamaica was becoming bankrupt. Recovery from wartime depression never came, and great dissatisfaction and apprehension were felt on the island. Owners of estates faced ruin; famine swept the island in the 1780's along with severe hurricanes, killing over 15,000 slaves. Of the 767 sugar estates in operation in 1791, only 451 were in the hands of their prewar proprietors, while 177 had been sold for debt and 92 were held by mortgagees. The decade 1783–93 witnessed the worst economic depression Jamaica experienced in the eighteenth century. Already tottering because of structural weakness and inefficient production methods, the Jamaican plantation system had been shaken to its foundation. Only extraordinary good fortune could save it from total collapse.

The withdrawal from the world sugar market of Jamaica's greatest competitor—Santo Domingo—was just the stroke of luck the island needed. Santo Domingo, a French colony since the sixteenth century, was able to produce at lower prices almost as much sugar as all the British tropical American colonies combined. Boasting the proud label "Queen of the Antilles," it had already raced ahead of Jamaica and captured a great portion of the North American and European markets.

Santo Domingo was severely tarnished by the French Revolution—never really to shine again. Inspired by the doctrines of liberty, equality, and fraternity, first the free Negroes and then the slaves rose up in revolt against the large resident white plantocracy. The slave revolt could not be checked, and before long an island-wide war between the races was in progress. "Clothed with spoils and covered with the blood of Europeans," the slaves, a contemporary writer said, "spread over the fairest portions of the new world the barbarism that still covers their native deserts." The cultivation of sugar and other crops was brought to an abrupt standstill. Santo Domingo's misery was Jamaica's opportunity. Never before had there been such a great demand for Jamaican sugar, coffee, and other tropical products. Planters could scarcely begin to meet it. The general demand for tropical products stimulated the Jamaican planters to try to improve their output. Primary attention was paid to the introduction of new species of sugar cane—bourbon and tahitian —which yielded greater quantities of juice. Despite these innovations, past failure to exploit Jamaica's virgin lands would be paid for with a lower volume of profits. If its agricultural potential had been fully exploited, the members of the Jamaican Assembly declared in an address to the King, this "accidental and temporary increase in the value of our staples could have saved this Island from absolute bankruptcy." Nevertheless, because demand was greater than supply, it was a time of great prosperity for the entire island.

This brief period of prosperity notwithstanding, the plantation system in Jamaica was on the decline. Sugar was at the base of the economy, and Great Britain alone could not absorb all the sugar produced. Prosperity, therefore, rested on both a lack of effective competition and the fact that after being imported and refined in Great Britain some of the sugar was also exported to foreign countries. Jamaican prosperity depended on its having a market both in Great Britain and in Europe. During the Napoleonic Wars, Jamaica was deprived of the European market by Napoleon's "Continental System," aimed at barring Great Britain from markets in Europe. An even greater long-term result of the Continental System was the development and growth of the beet sugar industry in Europe.

With Europe's becoming self-sufficient in sugar, the London market was once again glutted with supplies of tropical products. By 1807 the position of the proprietary class had become critical. Prices of sugar, cotton, and coffee fell drastically during the first decade of the new century, while the government raised import duties to new highs to meet the costs of the war. Prices of sugar on the London market were so low that Jamaican growers were not even meeting their production costs. A committee of the Jamaican Assembly reported that the average planter was losing approximately 236 pounds on a season's crop. One of the most prosperous and well-situated plantations in Jamaica, Hyde Hall, which had made at least a 12 per cent profit during the last decade of the eighteenth century, was making 3 per cent in 1805, and in 1807 was barely meeting operating costs.

Many suggestions, schemes, and plans were offered by the West Indian interests in London to relieve the distress of the planters. To this end, the British Parliament in the acts of 1808, 1810, and 1813 forbade the distillation of grain. It was expected that rum would then have an increased importance as a beverage and that the demand for it would substantially rise. Thus more sugar would be needed and bought. To further encourage the consumption of rum, its market price was lowered when the government cut the import duties on it. These regulations, however, failed to raise prices substantially on the London market. Plantation values suffered a sharp decline.

Once again a painful outcry came from Jamaica. Addressing the Prince Regent, the Assembly declared that sugar properties were being cultivated at a loss, resulting in foreclosures and confiscations to pay the debts owed mercantile houses in England. So numerous were these seizures of property for debt that, according to the Assembly in 1811, there were "large tracts, whole parishes, in which there is not a single proprietor of a sugar plantation resident."

Prices reached new highs for food and other provisions needed for subsistence, further aggravating Jamaica's already depressed domestic situation. The practice of allowing slaves to grow their own fruits and vegetables on provision grounds was still further encouraged, as the plantation owner could no longer afford to feed them. Feeble attempts were made to encourage domestic production of needed foodstuffs. The assembly offered prizes of 200 pounds for curing and salting at least ten barrels of beef or for cultivating a 20-acre patch of yams, but to no avail. By the last years of the Napoleonic Wars, the Jamaican sugar planters had already fallen under their burden of accumulated distress and discouragement. Conditions would be further aggravated if they failed to regain their continental markets at the end of the Napoleonic Wars or faced new competition at home, and the prosperity they craved might never come.

Before the Napoleonic Wars, Jamaica and its sister colonies in the Caribbean had been faced with serious competition from Santo Domingo. After the wars, their monopoly of the British and continental markets was challenged by serious competition from within their own colonial empire—a challenge they could not effectively meet. Great Britain added, among other territories, the island of Mauritius to its colonial possessions—the fruit of victory in the Napoleonic Wars. Though Mauritius lies off the southeast coast of Africa in the Indian Ocean rather than the Caribbean Sea, this former French island was the center of an extensive, efficient, and cheap sugar industry that could easily win in any price competition with the West Indies. That island's exports to Great Britain rose substantially between 1814 and 1823. Besides Mauritius, a still greater threat to the West Indian monopoly was East Indian sugar, which was produced more cheaply and efficiently than all others. Although West Indian sugar had lower duties levied on it than the East Indian product, giving it a preferential position on the British market, there was a growing lobby of the East India interests in Parliament that demanded equalization. Reasoning that they would give the domestic market a quality product at a cheaper price if the West Indies lost its preferred position, the East India merchants and their parliamentary supporters gradually gained allies.

At the same time, not only were continental consumers turning to beet sugar, but, more important, the intensive sugar production of Cuba and Brazil had the advantages of a renewable labor supply (slaves), a deep rich soil that had been relatively little exploited, and an open market in which to sell its products. Large tracts well suited for sugar were intensively and extensively developed for the first time in the two colonies after the Napoleonic Wars. Not barred, as the British islands were after 1808, from importing slaves, Cuba alone received 320,000 slaves between 1791 and 1825. The plantations were on virgin territories whose soil had not been depleted by a hundred or more years of cultivation and whose producers were not dependent on a single group of merchants or on a government that raised the price of their commodity by placing varying duties on it. Hopes of regaining the continental market for the West Indies were dashed forever, as Brazilian and Cuban merchants were regularly in a position to undersell English dealers throughout continental Europe. Cuban cultivators made rich profits and grew opulent at a price of 30 shillings per hundredweight, about half the price required by the British for a profitable transaction on the continental market.

Property values declined drastically as profits dwindled. A Jamaican plantation producing 200 hogsheads of sugar per annum was worth on the average only 43,000 pounds in local currency; in 1820, several sold for as low as 30,000 pounds. With the falling off of real estate values came a tightening of credit, without which the plantations could neither purchase the next year's supplies nor plant a new crop. "The calamities impending over the colonies must be aggravated by the inability of the Mercantile body to supply those funds which will be necessary for their relief," the West India Society of Merchants and Planters declared in 1823. The Jamaican Assembly petitioned the crown regularly from 1821 to 1823, complaining of the competition from India and Mauritius and asking for an increase in the duty rate of East India sugar. It also demanded lower import duties for products coming from the Caribbean and direct trade with the United States.

In 1822, influenced by the Caribbean distress and by the policy of *laissez-faire*, then beginning to take hold in Great Britain, the planters were allowed direct access to foreign markets and the sugar trade was opened to American businessmen. The struggle for the right to trade directly with the United States, a natural and major source of supplies, was finally marked by success. But the triumph was short-lived. Having depended on British merchants since the beginning of the sugar trade, the planters found that they could not now engage in trade on their own. Most of them were already greatly indebted to their British agents, and their estates were heavily mortgaged. Nor did the United States reciprocate; instead, interested in promoting trade in American ships, it taxed the British ships coming into American ports. The British Government retaliated.

Instead of giving the West Indies the great push it needed, the lifting of mercantile restrictions became a boomerang. Preferential tariffs favoring West Indian staples over those from East India and Mauritius became increasingly difficult to justify. The chief argument for this special treatment had been that it was a form of compensation for subjecting the West Indies to mercantile restrictions under the Navigation Laws. With the restrictions dropped, East Indian interests lost no time after 1822 in attacking the preferential tariffs: If tariff charges were equalized, they declared, the Orient could easily undersell the Occident. Back into the pockets of the consumer would go the several million pounds per annum that now went to the West Indian planters because of their higher prices. "The people of England," the Liverpool East India Association announced, "are compelled to submit to . . . a clear, undisputed and acknowledged tax, to force up the price of an article 6½d., . . . which the people could get for 2½d."

Other arguments favoring equalization of duties between East and West Indian sugar were that it would increase rather than decrease the government's revenues, because low prices would bring higher consumption, and that it would enlarge the exports of British manufactures to the Orient, a market that would constantly expand while the West Indian market was contracting. Properties were worth so little in the West Indies that not to adopt equalization, it was charged, would be to prop up a decrepit enterprise—"to bribe a parcel of slave-holders to continue a losing business." The controversy raged throughout the 1820's; the West Indians on the whole rested their case on sentiment and tradition, and their rivals on practicality, expediency, common sense, and reason.

Great Britain, on the threshold of the Victorian era, was an extremely practical society, and its political leaders, seeing no logical reason to grant the West Indies preferential tariffs, equalized the rate between the West Indies and their new competitor, Mauritius, as of 1826. This was the beginning of the end of the West Indian monopoly. Those who had economic interests in Jamaica saw it as a foreshadowing of things to come. Real estate values, already low, plummeted. A plantation in St. Elizabeth parish, Jamaica, for which 5,000 pounds in currency had been refused in 1824 was sold for one-third of that figure in 1829. Another, valued at 64,000 pounds in 1817, could not be disposed of locally or by auction in London in 1830. A private home bought for 2,000 pounds in 1821 was resold in 1831 for 400 pounds. Widespread discussions of the problem throughout the 1820's and early 1830's stimulated both the Board of Trade and Parliament to make extensive investigations of the situation. But instead of being used as a basis for action, their reports remained on the shelf.

The privilege and power that in the eighteenth century had been the reward for those who took economic risks in Jamaica had been transferred to economic interests in the Orient, South America, and Cuba. Like its soil, much of which was worn out by continuous use, Jamaica itself had been used and thrown away when it could no longer compete with societies that held many economic advantages over it.

In terms of economic stability and security, the promise of Jamaica was never fulfilled. It was clear, long before the emancipation of slaves, that crude methods of cultivation coupled with an insufficient and costly labor supply had knocked Jamaica out of the front rank in the world market for tropical products. When Great Britain in the 1820's scrapped its long-standing policy of maintaining a preferential tariff for West Indian products, the competitive weakness of Jamaica and its sister colonies was nakedly and brutally exposed. What had been apparent to interested observers since the end of the eighteenth century, what had been predicted by friend and foe alike, became reality.

The omens of economic doom in the eighteenth century became a self-fulfilling prophecy. Stagnation and decay set in, and observers would forever wonder at the natural riches that remained unexploited or unexplored. Colonial officials and public-spirited citizens tried at various times to retrieve the economy from the state of desuetude into which it had fallen. The path to success was so slippery that most fell by the wayside in their efforts. Dependent on outside markets in tropical products for its livelihood, Jamaica was forever at a disadvantage with its high-priced exports and still higher-priced imports. After 1833, the loss of servile labor on the plantations complicated matters and further affected Jamaica's competitive position.

Jamaica was allowed to wither on the economic vine in the nineteenth century. The situation was summed up by one resident in a gloomy exclamation: "The trunk is at length bent to the ground, and although the hurricane has passed away, it can use no more—its vegetation and its life had fled."

# 4. The Social Order in the Slave Society

Jamaica's many ethnic groups have provided a strong stimulus to the island's life. After the original Arawaks came the heterogeneous elements that make up the white population. Coming as indentured servants, overseers, planters, estate managers, or merchants, these Spaniards, English, Irish, Welsh, Scots, French, and Jews braved the island's frontier hardships to look for fortune in its plains and valleys. Less than a hundred years after the English conquest of the island, an English official reported to the Duke of Newcastle: "'Tis well known that this island is inhabited by four different nations, by the English, Scots, Irish and Jews." He did not include the black slaves, who were the overwhelming bulk of the population, because they were thought of as property rather than people.

The first of the "nations" to settle permanently on the island was not the English but probably the Jews. As Marranos (Jews who professed conversion to Catholicism), some came to trade with the Spanish colonies in South America while Jamaica was still a Spanish territory. The first will of a Jew was recorded soon after the British conquest. As early as 1673, David Gomez, a merchant living in Port Royal, left money and land to relatives in Amsterdam. There was a continuous Jewish immigration throughout the slavery era. Out of a white population of 7,148 in 1730, there were 900 Jews. In the early nineteenth century this figure reached nearly 2,000. Though most Jews were merchants and therefore were concentrated in Kingston and Spanish Town, the Jewish landowner and planter was not unknown in

Jamaica. Many Jewish cemeteries exist in every nook and corner of Jamaica.

From earliest times until the nineteenth century, Jews labored under various disabilities. From 1698 to 1739 they paid a special tax to the Jamaican Government called the "Jew's tribute." In 1711 Jews were prohibited from holding public office, being employed by the government, sitting on juries, and exercising the franchise. Content to avoid open conflict, happy with their religious privileges and with the absence of governmental economic discrimination, most Jews turned their backs on the legal manifestations of anti-Semitism. Edward Long, secretary to Governor Henry Moore, comments in his *History of Jamaica* that the Jews worked hard and were fertile, healthy, and "remarkably long lived." This he attributes to their sparing use of strong liquors. He observes that the Jews were most diligent in the performance of those duties Voltaire had called indispensable above all others to their people, "namely the getting of money and children."

Success as merchants and as planters came quickly. Although the Jews won the respect of important elements of Jamaican society, that respect was mixed with envy. Thus, despite the efforts of individual Jews in 1750 and 1820 to exercise the franchise, it was not until 1831 that they were freed of all restrictions. Throughout the period they remained a strong, close-knit group supporting their religious life from within while holding an influential position in the economy of the island.

Early action taken by the King in the form of proclamations and commands brought a trickle instead of a flood of white inhabitants. His promise of religious toleration for residents of the island and the gift of 30 acres of land to every adult settler made in the Windsor Proclamation of 1661 brought no crowds to Jamaica's doorstep. Settlers from other areas of the Caribbean, including Barbados and what later would be called Guiana, failed to change the picture drastically.

Local efforts began in 1703, when the first "deficiency law" was passed. The island legislature tried to place responsibility for securing white settlers on the individual plantation owners by requiring them to maintain a certain proportion of whites on their plantations. A ratio of one white to every ten or twenty Negroes was the usual requirement. The planter was subject to a fine based on the number of whites short of the requirement on his plantation. This law was renewed annually by the legislature, but it was wholly uneconomical and impractical. The cost of transporting indentured servants from Europe was high enough, but the biggest expense was to maintain them on the plantations, where they were likely at any moment to fall prey to a tropical disease or prove worthless as workers. From the point of view of the manager and the estate owner or his business attorney, it was far more practical, expedient, and inexpensive to pay the fines than to fill the deficiencies. Eager for the revenues the law brought in, the legislature continued to renew it until emancipation. Jamaica prized the ideal behind the deficiency law, but plantation owners did little to translate the ideal into reality.

Various land settlement programs were also devised on the island to encourage white settlers. Much of the most fertile land was taken up by large sugar estates, but Governor Hunter in the 1730's devised a plan whereby the local government could use the uncultivated portions of these estates for families who wished to settle. Grants the newcomers received were never more than 100 acres, and, to help them through the first and most difficult year, a year's provisions were supplied. As an added inducement, transportation was free. Costly to implement, this immigration plan failed to attract significant numbers. In a typical five-year period, a mere 347 immigrants arrived. They could not have sent very encouraging letters home.

Poor planning, bad administration, and uninspired leadership marred other settlement plans. Small farmers did not feel welcomed in a land where sugar was king. Large estates functioned as isolated units, and there was no sense of community life or welcome in the countryside. Forced to do it alone on his small farm, the new settler soon became discouraged and unwilling to undergo the hardships of climate and strange physical surroundings. Variable weather conditions brought poor crops, which fetched low prices. New settlers who were tradesmen or artisans often found it difficult to find customers, because slaves had been trained to do their jobs. After 1762, immigration schemes were permanently discontinued, not to be renewed until the mid-nineteenth century, and then only on a sporadic basis.

Jamaica, then, was not a place for the "little man." This was the basic reason why deficiency laws, settlement schemes, and the like were doomed to failure. A member of the Jamaican Assembly described the situation succinctly in 1737 when he said, "The only way to bring additional settlers to the island was to make Jamaica a good poor man's Country." Unfortunately, his practical suggestions for accomplishing this were never followed. Four years before, in 1733, another public-spirited citizen complained that Jamaica was "too valuable a jewel in the crown of England to be lost" by "the exorbitant avarice of a few leading men, who have eaten up all their poor neighbors and expelled [them] from the island."

Factions within the legislature sought to fill the ranks of the white population with more "responsible" individuals. Fully aware of the dangers inherent in the Jamaican situation—an unbalanced population ratio between Negroes and whites—they sought to recruit new people so as to stabilize the situation. Various programs were put forward to deal with absenteeism and the high turnover in the white population. Efforts were often intense, but the results they brought never came anywhere near fulfilling the desired goals.

For the rest of the white population, rank and title had little significance. All white Christians felt the bond that comes from belonging to a powerful minority among the subservient majority. "The poorest white person," Bryan Edwards wrote, "seems to consider himself nearly on a level with the richest." Excessive individualism was characteristic of the whites. Most of them were adventurers and upstarts seeking fortunes through sweat and cunning. Their work on the plantations demanded a maximum of self-reliance and detachment. Isolated on large estates and surrounded by seas of blacks, they tended to think in terms of the here and now, of individual gain rather than the collective good.

Native whites were commonly called "creoles." As described by Edward Long, they were physically tall and well built, though "some of them rather inclined to corpulence."

Of all the groups within the white population, the creoles, according to eighteenth-century observers, seemed to have the most pleasing personalities. Besides being "tender fathers," they were "humane and indulgent masters," not a common characteristic of the English members of Jamaican society. Other positive qualities attributed to them included generosity, sensibility, bravery, and hospitality: "Their tables were covered with plenty of good cheer and they regaled" their guests with a "profusion of viands."

This is not to say that the creoles had no negative side. Being independent in spirit, "they are liable to sudden transports of anger; but these fits, like hurricanes, though violent while they last, are soon over and subside into calm." But it would appear that the outstanding fault of the entire group was their impractical and erratic nature. They were forever haunted by "creditors and deputy marshals." As a group, the creole families were close knit, most of them allied by intermarriage, as their ancestors came from among the early white settlers of the island.

Many of the early Scottish and Irish settlers of humble origin were indentured servants. In 1730 there were 3,009 white male servants and 948 white female servants in a total white population of 7,148. It was from this group, approximately half of the white population, that many of the permanent white settlers came. By the 1760's they held many positions of political importance in the island. The more ambitious among them had become planters, working their way up from supervisor to owner of land and slaves. Many of them raised cacao, coffee, timber, and livestock. Throughout the slavery period the descendants of indentured servants were the most enduring element within the white population.

Still another stratum of white society was the class of very large and wealthy sugar planters, a few of whom resided on the island. They usually held the highest appointed posts in the government, though some were Assembly representatives. These men were from wealthy families in England and owned huge tracts of land or had bought up several estates at one time when economic misfortune had set in. It was not a common practice for them to cultivate all their holdings at any one time. Often they sent their families back to England, and after a while many of them returned there themselves. What could be said of the large landowners would apply to other segments of the white population—the turnover in the number of residents was high. A survey of 307 wills probated in Jamaica between 1625 and 1792 reveals that more than half of the testators were living in England at the time their wills were made.

Another important but often transient element within the white population was made up of the professional groups. Of the professional skills, law and medicine were most in demand. Lawyers in particular did a flourishing business because almost all transactions between town and country were done on credit. Prompt payment of debts was not characteristic, and incessant litigation for their recovery was common. Still another source of business for the lawyer was the legal disputes arising from defective land titles. But the majority of lawyers were employed by absentee landlords to audit and check their estates' accounts. Because a large number of the plantations in Jamaica were owned by absentees, many lawyers were needed on the island. Young men, usually possessing a minimum of legal training and a maximum of ambition, were sent from England to Jamaica as "plantation attorneys." Inexperienced as lawyers in general and plantation attorneys in particular, they were usually burdened with numerous properties to superintend. Records show that some of them had in their charge as many as forty properties. With inexperience and inefficient management techniques the rule, neither agricultural production nor account auditing was carried on with great success in Jamaica.

Medical men were more in demand in the towns because only a free population could support them. Those doctors who resided in the country were hired by estates to care for the slaves and were engaged for a year at a time. Each served several proprietors and visited the various properties weekly. Compensation was computed in terms of the number of Negroes cared for. In 1790, the Jamaican estate doctor earned 6 shillings a head, plus other payments for additional services such as inoculation or setting of a cast. Despite attempts by the legislature to set up a licensing system, many quacks not qualified to practice medicine came to the island. Shortages of trained personnel made Jamaica a fertile ground for incompetents—not only in medicine and in law but in estate management as well.

Careful not to establish any permanent roots in the island, professional men and estate personnel made sure not to commit themselves to any enduring relationships with women. Even if they wanted to, there were so few white women on the island that marriage was difficult if not impossible. Female slaves and free Negro women became excellent substitutes, offering the comforts without the responsibilities or inconveniences of married life. "He who should presume to show any displeasure against such a thing as simple fornication," Long writes, "for his pains would be accounted a simple blockhead; since not one in twenty can be persuaded that there is either sin or shame in cohabiting with a slave." In the eighteenth century, concubinage was, like slavery, an established institution of Jamaican society. With no one to check their behavior on the estates, the white managers indulged in all kinds of excesses. Inevitably, Long reports, "in a place where, by custom, so little restraint is laid on the passions," men are "too easily led aside" to indulge in "every kind of sensual delight." As the slave was merely a thing to be used, marriage was never considered, but children were inevitable. Bequeathed to Jamaica was a large population of mulattoes, who, unlike their natural fathers, remained a permanent part of the society into which they were born. Some of them were given freedom and to others were left the fortunes their fathers had acquired. A few were looked after by their fathers and even sent to Westminister, Eton, or some other school in England. Mixing freely and equally with white society in England, they were shocked to learn when they returned to Jamaica that their mother was a slave and that their skin color barred them from equal access to the social and political institutions of the island. A few returned to England, where they were accepted because they were wealthy and foreign. Most remained in Jamaica, where they formed an in-between class, higher in status than the slaves but much lower in the estimation of Jamaican society than the poorest white man.

Freedom in Jamaica conferred on Negroes no privileges other than the right to own property. The courts of law interpreted manumission as nothing more than the abandonment or release of property authority, and no civil or political rights went with it. Although there is no evidence that Negroes were exercising these rights earlier, laws were passed in 1711 barring Negroes from holding public office or sitting in the Assembly. They were also excluded from the franchise and, until 1795, from testifying in the regular courts of the island.

There was a small group of property-owners within the free Negro class who individually sought privileges denied to them as a group. They resorted to a procedure long established in England—the device of a petition—to secure the enactment of private bills in their behalf by the Jamaican legislature. That there was great reluctance on the part of the government to approve these bills is demonstrated by the small number passed—a total of 128 in the eighteenth century. Of these, only 4 granted all the civil rights of white men.

Despite rejection by white society, free Negroes remained loyal to Jamaica. They gave their full and conscientious support to the island when its security was threatened. There were 1,889 free Negroes in the island militia in 1792 though none was offered a commission. One way of proving their undivided allegiance was to fight in battle. Companies of free Negroes were raised in both the First Maroon War of 1733 and the Second Maroon War of 1795. Only after the second war did they receive a special commendation from the Jamaican legislature. This was because a successful slave revolt in the neighboring island of St. Domingo caused the governor of Jamaica, the Earl of Balcarres, to believe that the Trelawny Town Maroons were plotting revolution with the help of French agents. The island militia was called out to capture the Maroon Camp. The war between the Government of Jamaica and the

Trelawny Maroons lasted from July to December, 1795. Over 1500 British troops plus twice that number of local militia failed to subdue the three hundred Trelawny Maroons. The use of bloodhounds, imported from Cuba, finally forced them to surrender. Fearful of a slave revolt in their own island inspired both by the events in St. Domingo and the successful fighting of the Trelawny Maroons, the island residents depended on the help of the two militia companies of free Negroes. Yet, their only reward was a legislative act which granted all free Negroes the right to testify in self-defense in criminal actions in the courts of the island. Nevertheless the free Negroes never waivered in their support of the government. It was not until 1830 that free Negroes of Jamaica were given the rights of white Protestants.

Although the free mulatto may have been the child of a white man, his inheritance did not include the rights and privileges of his father. Suspended as he was between the heaven of the white man's superior position and the hell of degradation of the slave, the free Negro found himself in an eternal purgatory from which there was no purgation. The majority of free Negroes were commonly called "people of color" because they were the progeny of white fathers and black mothers. This group attempted to cling to its white ancestry, reflected in a lighter shade of skin color. The difference in appearance between the mulatto and the slave was important to the mulatto, even though society did not grant him the rights and privileges of a free man. What was called in the laws "the unfortunate circumstances of birth"—his Negro or slave ancestry—was a stigma he could not erase, but his lighter skin gave him a subjective affinity with the white race.

Freedom was meaningful only when the free man's position in society was contrasted with that of the slave. From this vantage point, the free Negroes could indeed consider themselves far superior to the majority of their race. Far better off than the masses, they learned to hate all slaves, who reminded them of an ancestry they considered degrading. Edward Long, in his *History of Jamaica*, reported that a distinguished eighteenth-century Jamaican free Negro, Francis Williams, "looked down with sovereign contempt on his fellow blacks." Williams expected and received great deference from the slaves about him while behaving toward them "with severity bordering on cruelty." The slaves, for their part, feared and hated the free Negroes. William Burge, a former attorney general of Jamaica, remarked that there was "much greater hostility" and "decidedly more hatred" between free Negroes and slaves than between the slaves and the whites because of the slave's "inveteracy" toward the free Negroes. Cruelty toward the slaves was the stereotyped behavior of the free Negroes.

It is clear that the free Negroes derived whatever sense of well-being they may have had in the community not from what they were but from what they were not. They were not slaves and did not work at "slave work" such as agricultural or other menial labor. To live in the cities and away from the plantations, with their overwhelming slave population, was their chief object. Being insecure about their origins and their group membership, the free Negroes were always troubled by an inferiority complex.

As the rejection of ancestry was the only way to derive status, the free Negroes sought to identify completely with the white men. Anxious to clothe themselves in the culture of the agents of power and control, they adopted, with an almost religious fervor, the customs and habits of the white population. Sloughing off the external shackles of servitude, they retained, internally, an unquestioning slavish devotion to the clothes, language, manners, and religion of white society. One traveler, Rev. Richard Bickel, noted "a great number of free blacks" in Kingston "who are mechanics" and "are more respectably clad than white men of the same class in Europe." James Stewart, another visitor, writes the "independent people of color, shut out from general white society form a separate society of their own, fully as gay and expensive as that of the whites." They were in "constant attendance at churches," and most of them were "attached to the Church of England."

Custom and law encouraged these proclivities. To be a concubine of a white man was considered a proper role for the mulatto woman by her own mother. Rather than marry one of the Negro race, it was considered more desirable for a mulatto woman of any age to be the concubine of a white man. "Excluded as they are from all hope of ever arriving to the honor and happiness of wedlock, insensible to its beauty and sagacity; ignorant of all Christian and moral obligations; threatened by poverty, urged on by their passions, and encouraged by example, upon what other principles," Bryan Edwards asks, "can we ask these ill-fated women to act otherwise than they do?"

Social pressures and precedents were strengthened and enforced by the laws of the land, which clearly reflected the mores and attitudes of the various occupational and social strata of white Jamaican society. Appearing regularly in the election laws of 1733, 1756, and 1780 was a clause to the effect that all mulattoes who were three generations removed from their Negro ancestors "shall have all privileges and immunities of His Majesty's white subjects provided they are brought up in the Christian religion."

The English abolitionist James Stephen once cynically but appropriately remarked that in Jamaica "enfranchisement of the progeny is a premium for concubinage." With this ultimate reward ever in view, both free mulattoes and the white men, whose world they desired to enter, were very much aware of complexion differences between dark- and light-skinned Negroes. A classification system labeled the first generation removed from 100 per cent black ancestry (one parent being white) as a *mulatto*, the second generation removed from Negro ancestry (the offspring of a mulatto and a white person) as a *quadroon*, and the third generation removed from Negro ancestry as a *mustee* (the offspring of a quadroon and a white person). These terms were regularly used both in the common speech of the island and as descriptive words in the laws of the land. Free Negroes who petitioned the legislature for the civil rights withheld from them because they were not born with a white skin were usually, but not always, described in the preamble of the bill as free mulattoes, quadroons, or mustees. In the 1790's the legislature, in an attempt to ascertain the number of free Negroes on the island, required each parish to keep a register of those residing in its locality. Each registry book had a column for complexion, usually following immediately after the individual's name. The lawmakers in Jamaica were not color-blind but, rather, very color-conscious. Like the individuals they represented, they valued, in the vast sea of black faces around them, skin colors that were nearer to their own. Miscegenation, whether the result of sexual union between a white man and Negro woman or between a Negro man and a white woman (which was far rarer), was thus encouraged. If marriage was possible with a member of the Negro race, it was less desirable, as it did not bring the advantages to future generations of being equal to the white man.

Like its private life, the cultural, educational, and religious life of the free white Jamaican society was hardly of the highest caliber. The Christian church, which in other parts of the New World played a leading role in bringing culture and learning to colonial outposts, totally failed to provide such leadership in Jamaica. The island's official church, like that of England, was Anglican. Although the Bishop of London appointed twenty-nine churchmen to the island between 1745 and 1784, they failed to establish a really authoritative and lasting influence over the population.

The Anglican clergymen who were sent to the islands were given no supervision, help, or preparation for the tasks ahead. Those recruited for the job were often men who had been failures at home and were sent to the colonies because the church did not know what else to do with them. Ministers were also drawn from the ranks of unsuccessful overseers. John Riland, the son of a Jamaican planter, sadly remarks in his *Memoirs*, published in 1827, that the clerical office in Jamaica was a last resort for men who had not succeeded in other professions. Many of them were addicted to "lewdness," drinking, gambling, and "iniquity." Charles Leslie, author of *A New History of Jamaica* (1749), considered the Anglican clergymen to be "the most finished of our debauchers!"

It was the governor's duty to supervise the clergy; by a grant of royal authority he was the supreme head of the church. He had the right to suspend any clergyman if the parishioners so requested. Rarely did the governor do so, for if a clergyman tended to neglect his duties few of his parishioners were disappointed. The whites of the island were hardly known for their piety. Except on the occasion of weddings and funerals, churches were empty, the planters having little or no interest in regular religious worship. In Kingston and Spanish Town there were large cathedrals with their own organs, but churches in other parishes of the island were crude affairs, simple one-room bungalows made of wood. A combination of inferior representatives and the indifference of the general population toward religious matters made the established church in this period a force of no significance in religious, educational, or cultural matters.

If nothing was done by the establishment to promote religion among those who knew of it, something was done by non-Anglicans to bring religion to those who knew nothing of it. Totally neglected by the Anglican church, the slaves became the special charge of religious groups that in England were called "dissenters" because they dissented from the Anglican church. First of these groups to come to Jamaica and preach to the slaves was the Moravians in 1754. Using simple language and preaching elementary religion and morality that could be understood by the slaves, the Moravians tried to convince the slaves that the moral life was the only life. Baptism and confirmation into the church were the rewards offered to those who showed evidence of changed ways. North American Baptists fleeing the Revolution were the next group of missionaries to work with the slaves. In 1784, George Liele, a Virginia Negro born in slavery and freed by his master, came to Jamaica with several Southern loyalists. A native preacher in America, he took up his calling in Kingston and organized the first Baptist church in Jamaica with four other Americans. According to one observer, Liele was particularly effective when preaching to slaves. After amassing a considerable following, estimated by him at 15,000 people, in 1790 he asked that this Jamaican branch of the Baptist sect be taken under the wing of the English Baptists. In 1813, John Rowe was sent out as the first English Baptist missionary. The Baptists were a mighty force among the slaves because it was their practice to train lay leaders who could communicate with the masses. This system, combined with fiery preaching, gave the Baptists the largest following among the Jamaican Negroes.

On the heels of the Baptists came the Wesleyan Methodists under Thomas Coke in 1789. Because the Methodists, unlike the Anglicans, did not regard Negroes with contempt and were deeply aware of their need to be respected as free human beings, they gained a large following among the free Negroes. In 1803 the Methodist church in Kingston had 530 members.

Supported by parent organizations in England and acting under their official instructions, the missionaries were a completely independent cultural and social force working with the slaves. Their doctrine of brotherly love and their belief in the equality of all men before the eyes of God were considered dangerous beliefs for the slaves to hold. Planters and overseers quickly came to distrust the missionaries, fearing their doctrines would incite the slaves to rebellion. Missionaries were barred from preaching to the slaves on a great many estates, while planters forbade their slaves to attend services in the dissenting chapels in the towns. Zealous and undaunted in their cause, the missionaries operated secretly among the slaves. Despite obstacles, they managed to create a loyal following.

Free white society took no interest in the education of the masses and little in the education of its own sons and daughters. Because many of those who came to Jamaica thought of their life on the island as a temporary interlude, there was little lasting interest on the part of the legislature in the eighteenth century to organize an educational system for the island. This was not unusual, for state-supported public education was also unknown in England. More unusual was the fact that little public support was given to the private academies that were started at various times during the century with bequests: John Woolmer, a Kingston goldsmith, left a devise to start a school in that city in 1734, and Martin Rusea, a resident of Hanover, left a sum of money in 1710 to start a free school in that parish. After the money had been used up, it would have been up to the Assembly or the inhabitants of the area where the school was located to perpetuate its existence by giving it additional support. Sometimes this was forthcoming, but more often there was a lack of public interest. Even if subscriptions were raised to continue a school, after a while the original supporters lost interest in the project and a rapid decline of the institution set in. This is not to say that there were no funds available to establish schools: Between 1667 and 1736, 218 bequests were made to churches, to the poor, and for educational purposes. But lack of public concern prevented these bequests from being put to proper educational use. The sums were either mismanaged or poorly applied. James Stewart, a twenty-year resident in the island, threw up his hands in horror at the thousands that were thrown away on trifles by the West Indian legislatures while they were doing so little about providing money for the general good. Charles Leslie commented in the 1720's that "learning is here at the lowest ebb."

Deep public interest and intense vigilance to secure good schools for the coming generation were attitudes all but unknown in eighteenth-century Jamaica. To the residents of the island, their tropical wilderness was a frontier—a rude environment and not a center of culture, manners, and refinement. Therefore, it was not the best place for educating children. Rather than try to create their own native cultural environment, the Jamaican creoles looked to England as the center of civilization and depended on the mother country to give their children the background and learning that could not be found in Jamaica.

Everything that was English was ideal. Clothing, food, furnishings, entertainments, and the education of children—all had to be properly English if they were to have any value and meaning to them. Jamaica provided the most lucrative livelihood the creoles could acquire. Deprived by economic exigencies of residences in the center of civilization, they brought British culture with them and sought to nurture it and keep it ever blooming, like some rare plant. Planters who had their families with them and creoles knew in their hearts, however, that there was no substitute for living in England, so they prepared their sons (few girls were sent) to go to Eton or some other famous secondary school. They did so by hiring someone to teach the rudiments of reading, writing, and arithmetic to their children. Hardly learned themselves, those who tutored the sons of planters were half-educated adventurers, commanding neither the respect of the parents nor the obedience of their pupils. In 1720 Charles Leslie commented that the occupation of tutor was "looked upon as contemptible." Usually the tutor was but one step ahead of his pupils.

Often the resident of Jamaica had no relatives or friends to take on the responsibility of caring for his children in England. Consequently children were given over upon their arrival in England to their father's business agent, consigned as one contemporary put it, "like a bale of dry goods." After this they were left on their own, supported by an allowance. With no parental or other authority to guide them, Jamaican youth, who were only thirteen or fourteen when they landed in England, easily and quickly succumbed to the vices of their new country. Studies and other serious pursuits were set aside in favor of drinking, gambling, and other tavern sports. With no one about to offer them discipline or lead them from the crooked to the straight path, many never learned to be responsible individuals. The island of their birth seemed but a primitive, out-of-the-way place, unsuited to a life of pleasure. Many of them remained in England to become absentee landlords, depriving Jamaica of a new generation of native leaders. Those who did return resented their birthplace because all notions of the gracious and gentlemanly life were related to England, to which they longed to return. Lack of local pride and little or no interest in the island's problems, characteristics so marked among the white population, can be traced in large measure to the educational procedures of the island. By failing to establish an educational system, the creoles still further depleted the already weak reserve of island leaders. They inculcated in their sons a contempt for the homeland. All the good in the world seemed to be in England, and all the bad in Jamaica. Except that its lands were a source of income, the island had no value; its society meant nothing, when compared to the splendor of "glorious" England. Little wonder that by 1770 three-fourths of all the proprietors' male children from the island were educated in England. Up to 300 youths left the island each year, many never to return.

The creoles' sons who did return to Jamaica had learned nothing about the management and improvement of the estates on which their livelihood depended. The young men of the island showed little interest in their properties and even less in running them. Instead, they would hire overseers to supervise their properties and would move to Kingston or Spanish Town, if not away from Jamaica, and live on the income from the land. The education to which the planters wished to subject their children was, paradoxically, in direct contradiction to the needs and problems of Jamaican life.

There was a group of 500 to 600 Negroes in Jamaica who were not slaves and did not live within the bounds of the culture of the society. Called the "Maroons," from the Spanish word *marrano*, meaning wild boar, these were the descendants of the Negro slaves of the Spaniards who, when the English invaded Jamaica, had fled into the interior parts of the island. Never making peace with the new settlers, they constantly harassed them from their almost impenetrable positions in the bush. Offering a ready refuge for runaway slaves most of whom were recent arrivals from Africa, they were like a magnet, drawing them away from the plantations in the northeastern and northwestern parts of the island where their band was situated. Until the 1730's, the Jamaican legislature had tried various methods to suppress them, incorporated in at least forty-four laws. More than 240,000 pounds was spent from the resources of the local treasury to stamp out the menace.

From 1734 to 1738, the island was in the throes of the final phase of the First Maroon War. The British Government failed to supply the troops needed to meet the danger, so the free Negroes were organized into regular militia companies for the first time. Mosquito Indians from Honduras were also brought to the island to bolster the ranks of the regular militia. After four years of intensive warfare, a treaty of peace was signed between the leader of the Maroons, General Cudjoe, and the Jamaican Government. Under the terms of the treaty the rebels were given their freedom and 15,000 acres of land, which set the Maroons apart from the rest of the Negro population on their own reservations. Still more important in terms of law and order for Jamaica was the provision of the treaty that enlisted the aid of Cudjoe and his men to fight against the Windward rebels and to return for cash rewards all runaways that came to the Maroon camp. The Maroons were thus set apart from the mainstream of civilization, and they remained at a primitive level of development.

Except for their leaders, the Maroons were ignorant of the English language, speaking among themselves a dialect of African origin. They hunted wild boar and sold them at the local markets, where they bought liquor, tobacco, salted beef, and firearms. Contemporaries describe them as wearing "little or no clothing of any kind" and speaking a language that sounded like a "barbarous dissonance of the African dialects, with a mixture of Spanish and broken English" thrown in. Like the great majority of the slaves, they adhered to a mystical religion that placed authority in certain old men of their group— called the "obeah-men"—who were thought to possess the supernatural spirit of the obi. While the men hunted, the women made some effort to grow such vegetables as corn and yams. Polygamy was universally practiced among the Maroons, some of their leaders having from two to six wives. Women had no status in the eyes of the community and were regarded as "beasts of burden." Paternal authority was harshly asserted, particularly toward daughters who were offered as prostitutes to any and all who frequented the villages. If they felt the guests were worthy of it, the Maroons entertained them with a mock battle, using shrill war whoops and fierce shouts, following this up with a meal of wild boar, land crabs, and fish. In 1760, they loyally allied themselves with the government in putting down a revolt of slaves in the northeast section of the island. It is said that after capturing the leader, Tacky, they preserved his head "as a trophy of victory" and "roasted and actually devoured the heart and entrails of the wretched victim."

Except for a flare-up between the government and the Maroons living in the northwest portion of the island, which resulted in the deportation of almost the entire group to Nova Scotia in June of 1796, the Maroons remained peacefully settled on their reservations, where they can be found today. Though not primitive or warlike as they were in the eighteenth century, they are proud of their separate identity. Their leader displays to visitors the sword said to have been worn by General Cudjoe in the 1730's. Living in an area known as "cockpit" country because of its many valleys and plateaus, they scratch out a living from some of the poorest soil on the island.

Revolts were not an exclusive prerogative of the Maroons. White Jamaica forever lived under the threat of collective slave violence. As early as 1673, three hundred African slaves murdered their master and thirteen other whites.

There were three major disturbances that shook the whole island—the First Maroon war (1725–1740), the Coromantee rebellion of 1760, and the slave revolt of 1832—each of which involved more than a thousand slaves. The major reasons for the large number of revolts were the high ratio of slaves to white men and the nature of the slave population itself. As slave breeding was not encouraged, there was a constant flow of new arrivals from Africa onto the Jamaican plantations. In the mid-eighteenth century, Africans accounted for about half of the slave population. Unable to adjust to their servile status, the Coromantee slaves revolted in 1760. Rather than be re-enslaved, the survivors of the revolt committed mass suicide—an indication of their inability to cope with enslavement. Five years later, Gold Coast slaves revolted on seventeen estates, and in 1766 the Coromantees struck once again. The Coromantee and Gold Coast Negroes came from highly developed militaristic regimes in Africa and were skilled in jungle warfare. A bill came before the House of Assembly in 1765 to bar the entry of African slaves from these regions but failed to pass. The smug selfish, individualistic white population of Jamaica could not think in terms of collective good, as their attitude toward slave revolts oscillated between extreme hysteria and unbelievable optimism. One resident commented: "No people are more thoughtless of danger at a distance, so I must own they are apprehensive of it enough when it is at hand."

Among the slave population, it was but a minority that would risk their lives as rebel slaves. The majority lived and died in the dull, hard-driving workaday life of the servile laborer.

Contemporary opinion considered the Negro slaves to be not part of society but simply tools, in human form, to be used to exploit the land for the profitable gain of others. The Negro was thought naturally suited for the ends he served, a *thing* rather than a *being*, and as such incapable of playing an independent role in society. Therefore, the masses of Negro slaves were placed far below the lowest rung of the social ladder.

The majority lived in their own communities with other slaves on the plantation grounds. Cottages were made of wood and built by the slaves themselves. They were usually fifteen to twenty feet in length and barely high enough for the occupant to stand up straight. Thatched roofs made of palm or coconut leaves were common, while the floors were of natural earth. Furnishings were simple and bare. A bed was some boards built as a platform with a mat and blanket on top. Perhaps there was a small table or one or two stools in the hut as well. Cooking was done outdoors on an open fire with an iron pot, while gourds known as "calabashes" were used as serving dishes and bowls. Plantains, yams, and sweet potatoes were the common diet, sometimes mixed into a pudding or served with pork, fish, or salted beef. A fresh broth called "pots," highly seasoned with peppers and okra, was a regular feature of the slaves' diet. Individual houses were usually situated near fruit trees—avocado, orange, and banana were the most common. Each slave received a small piece of land next to his hut as "provision ground." All the greens, vegetables, cauliflower, and tomatoes that the slave might eat would come from this plot. If there was a scarcity of imported food because of delayed shipments to the plantation, the slave would have to rely on wild fruits and his provision grounds as the sole means of subsistence. Clothing was given out on an annual basis, a year's allowance consisting of linen, woolen, and checked cloth, which would be fashioned into various kinds of coverings by their owners. Hats, handkerchiefs, needles, and thread were sometimes supplied by the plantations. Usually, a clothing provision would be made to last two or three years. Plantation directors and owners might neglect to give out a new allowance if there had been a poor harvest or sugar prices had declined on the European market. A scant supply of clothing was no great hardship to those who lived under Jamaica's tropical sun.

Supplied with the bare essentials of life, the slaves labored long hours for their owners and their supervisors. The skills they acquired and the jobs they were responsible for covered a wide range of occupations, from highly skilled to menial. Except for the main gang, which employed the vast majority of male field hands, women in general outnumbered men in field gangs. Men had other areas of the plantation economy to work in. A small but important minority of men were skilled artisans, while others were involved with livestock and sugar-processing. Domestic servants were of both sexes and usually received better housing and clothing supplies. While the field hand lived in a hut made of poles driven into the ground, the skilled servant lived in a wooden house with board floors and a permanent roof. The domestics had to look presentable to those they served. There was a high number of servants employed in the great houses of the estates. Twenty to forty of them were commonly used at one time. On the farm as well as in the home, poor organization and wasteful practices were common.

Laborers forced to work long hours would slacken their pace as a resut of overwork. Eventually, if still driven on, they might become sick or permanently disabled. Death from over-work and exhaustion was not unknown. When a slave was re-placed, the planter paid a price that ate up the profits he had gained from overworking the slave. The absentee owner in England had no idea about what took place on the plantation. He might deplore the high costs of production, but he usually did not understand what caused them. Being ignorant, he placed the blame on the oppressed, not the oppressor, with the result that the long-term value of the estate was forever in jeopardy. Edward Long deplored this situation: "Humanity operates here like virtue; it is its own sure reward."

Like their "superiors" on the plantations and in the towns, the male slaves had several female relationships, not always on the same estate. Children who were born from these unions were usually raised by grandparents too old to labor in the fields. The elderly were looked upon with veneration and respect by the rest of the slave population. They were addressed as "Ma" for mother and "Ta" for father, designations meant to convey not only the idea of filial reverence, but also of esteem and fondness. Parents were not addressed in this manner, nor were other relatives. Feeling that it was an accomplishment to reach old age in the harsh conditions of life on the plantation, Jamaican slaves gave special respect and support to the elderly.

To their children, the Negroes displayed a severely critical attitude. They chastised them at the least provocation but were, at the same time, capable of expressions of great love, sympathy, and intense attachment. They held filial obedience in much higher estimation than conjugal fidelity. Children were named for the day of the week on which they were born, but males and females had different names. For example, a boy born on Monday was named "Cudjoe," and a girl, "Juba"; on Wednesday, "Quaco" and "Cuba"; and on Sunday, "Quashee" and "Quasheba." Among the Negroes native to the island, ages were determined from holiday to holiday on a yearly basis. Thus, a child was said to be born on a Christmas ago, even if its birthdate was in July or September.

As soon as they were physically capable, those children who had survived the first years of life (the infant mortality rate was very high) joined their parents and elders in the fields, working a full day soon after starting. Initiation into the life of toil without rewards came early. On Rose Hall Plantation in the Parish of St. James it was common practice to start the children working at the age of four. Boys and girls were put on the weeding gang at that age, but by the age of six boys were put to more difficult tasks. Some were cattle boys, while others worked in the overseer's house and still others in the fields. Girls worked in the meat smokehouse until the age of nine, when they too were deployed in various sections of the plantation economy—tending stock, domestic work, and personal service. Children were also thought of in economic terms by their natural parents. Whether it was to provide them with some additional subsistence when they were too old to work or as an additional helper in maintaining the provision ground, the child had a useful function to the slave community. There was very little change from one generation to the next in the life of the plantation Negro.

It was not common practice to encourage child-rearing on the large sugar plantations, as it was generally considered better economics to purchase new Negroes than to rear their children. As a result, more males than females were brought to the island as slaves, and there were 30,000 more males than females in 1789. With no understanding of what a monogamous marriage was, population inequities dictated excessive promiscuity and little interest in the possibility of offspring. Abortions were widely practiced, a fact noted by many observers of Jamaican life. If children were not killed by abortions, neglect, unhygienic conditions, and poor treatment of pregnant women led to miscarriages and an excessive death rate among children in the early years of life.

In an environment that so thoroughly discouraged child-bearing for the slaves, family life was almost nonexistent in slave communities. Estate owners cared not at all how offspring were brought into the world, and certainly did not want the slaves to develop any family attachments. With both fathers and mothers free to pursue a variety of mates, there was nothing to bind the natural parents of slave children. The average slave was not expected to be responsible for the raising of his children, though there were instances when fathers showed great pride in their children and strove to attend to their needs. Generally such fathers were prominent slaves in leading positions of authority and trust. Children of these unions felt little kinship with their brothers and sisters. Every child had a great many half-brothers and half-sisters; it was not possible to develop a strong, intimate family relationship in the slave culture.

In his relations with the white world, the Negro displayed, according to observers, a talent for flattering those in superior positions. He was a loquacious and artful talker when trying to gain something from his superiors. Never complaining of any injury or wrongdoing, he suppressed his hurt and waited for the opportunity to retaliate or take revenge even if it came years later. The Negroes could be easily shamed, and words of rebuke from those in authority had a stinging and lasting effect. Holding them up to the ridicule of their fellow blacks was the worst form of degradation; the sneers of fellow Negroes directed their anger away from the authority figure and against themselves. Ridicule was a most deadly weapon for those who knew how to use it.

Among the slaves, there were strong distinctions drawn between creole or Jamaican-born Negroes and Africans. The creoles felt contempt for the Africans; they felt their own Jamaican birth gave them a heritage, manner, and decorum that the "foreigners" lacked. Imported Negroes were called "salt water Negroes" and "Gurney Birds" and were thought to be prone to drunkenness and thievery. New arrivals usually lived separately from the others. Easily provoked and often quarrelsome, their bad tempers made them stand out like sore thumbs among the majority of creoles in the population. Like the society of free men in Jamaica, estate communities of slaves exhibited a stratified ranking system among its members. African-born Negroes were at the bottom of the scale, not only because of their personalities and bad manners, but also because the majority of them worked in field gangs, the lowest job on the occupational ladder. Creole slaves born into the culture of the plantation had moved up to skilled agricultural jobs connected with sugar-refining, building, and other trades or had become domestic servants. Subject from birth to a continual process of acculturation, the native-born were far better adjusted to their milieu and were able to derive greater benefits from it than their African-born counterparts.

During the eighteenth century, the generations of Negro slaves who came to know Jamaica as their home created a cultural life apart from the society of their overlords. As among the American Negro slaves, music was a favorite form of diversion from life's drudgery. They sang songs using soloists and chorus, making up the verses as they went along.

One observer distinguished three different types of folk songs among the slaves—digging songs, dancing songs, and ring songs. Digging songs were work chants sung with great spontaneity by a soloist and chorus. In tone and spirit, the songs were laments about their cruel and oppressive life or direct complaints about harsh treatment by an overseer. American Negro slaves rarely directed their laments to the cruelty of a particular person, but Jamaican slaves commonly did. The lack of stable, paternalistic leadership on island plantations accounts, perhaps, for the differences of expression.

Dancing and ring tunes had similar content but were far more melodious. All three types followed a format similar to that of African songs: short musical phrases sung first by the leader and repeated by the group, then a short refrain taken from one group to another. Like the African counterpart, the Jamaican song was topical, extending to a wide range of subjects. Primitive instruments were fashioned to accompany the singers. One, called the "merry-wang," was a gourd with skin stretched over its largest section and four strings, which were plucked. An ornate handle was attached to the end of the gourd, giving the instrument the appearance of a primitive banjo. Another favorite was the "goombah," a large drum fashioned from a hollow log covered with sheepskin. It was beaten with a stick about six inches in length by one man, while another rolled a stick over a notched piece of wood fixed across one end of the instrument. The dances were strongly accented by heavy rhythms, for which the merry-wang and goombah were well-suited. Melodies were either brisk or slow. The men dancers were all action, fire, and gesture; the women, slow and languid, wiggling their hips as they confronted their partners. Dancing was an art learned early in life, and most of the slaves seemed to have a natural talent for rhythmic improvisation. By the 1820's, observers reported the introduction of fiddles and other European instruments among the slaves. Also, Scottish and English dances at this time replaced some of the African ones.

At Christmas time in the towns the Negroes paraded in masquerade through the streets, led by several "tall robust fellows dressed in grotesque habits, and a pair of oxhorns on their heads" and "a mask, on their faces . . . about the mouth . . . rendered very terrific with large boar-tusks." This kind of Christmas festival would in later decades be known as John Connu, the name given to the men who led the parades. Each group of Negroes had its own "Connu" to lead its parade, but the original John Connu was a John Conny, revered by the Negroes along the Guinea coast.

Besides singing, dancing, and the annual Connu festival, the only other outlet the slave had from a life of drudgery was religion. Various contemporary observers reported seeing funerals followed by feasts and dances with sacrifices made to ancestral graves. Magico-religious conceptions and mystical ideas were the stuff of the slaves' religion. Place-spirits ("jubies") and dead spirits ("duppies") were feared and propitiated. Magical spirits varied, but they were usually not worshiped by the group together.

Group rituals were more common among the newly arrived African slaves than among the creoles. As Negroes were often imported as a group from the same tribe and sold that way in Jamaica, each plantation had slaves who together practiced their own African religions. The Coromantee Negroes believed in a god called Accompong, the creator of all things and a diety of infinite goodness, while the Dahomeans had two gods, Naskew and Timnew, which were vaguely associated with good and evil. Other gods were designated for earth and sea, while each family had its own special deity who was supposed to be the original ancestor. Praises and supplications were offered to all the gods, but there was no community sacrifice of a material nature. Eboes and the Whidah tribe had no spiritual communications, as they worshiped reptiles, particularly a species of lizard known as the iguana. Circumcision was a common practice in both tribes.

Regardless of native origin, cultism and mysticism were common. Under the name "Obi," they were propagated by obeah men or women, who had the combined powers of witches and medicine men. They were able not only to cure a disease, but to cause the outbreak of one as well. Strange powers also enabled them to raise a man from the dead or make him invulnerable. Slaves who wanted to revolt or commit crimes sought out the obeah man to receive protective spells. Objects such as blood, fowls' feet, feathers, teeth, and earth from burial grounds were utilized by the witch doctors. They could cast spells on innocents that would force them to perform evil deeds or help those who sought revenge on others to work up their emotions to sufficient heat. Slaves feared the obeah man, for he was supposed to have the power to strike without warning. Planters and overseers were always on guard for the obeah cult, for it paralyzed all those who became victims of it and, in extreme moments, brought self-inflicted death to some. Slave revolts were said to be caused or inspired by obeah men.

This was the world of those below the social ladder. Though the slave worked long, hard hours—from sunrise to sunset—he managed to fashion some cultural life of his own, contradicting through his behavior those who tried so hard to deride his status as a man.

The legal structure that supported the institution of slavery defined the slave's relationship to the world in terms of the following basic categories: in relation to his master, in relation to the rest of society, in relation to the government, and in relation to his own freedom. As could be expected, in the first category the master's power was absolute (with the exception that it was a crime for a master to kill a slave). This was explicit in all slave laws from 1674 on. It meant the slave could be sold to settle debts or for cash. In Jamaica it was once reported that some planters consulted with their slaves before selling them. Richard Hakewell stated: "The only transfers which take place are of domestic or tradesmen Negroes, and no man would buy a slave who did not previously agree to live with him." More common, however, was the practice criticized by Edward Long, a member of the plantocracy and an ideological defender of slavery. Negroes, he declared are "liable to be seized for bond and simple contract debts and hurried from one part of the island to another," and "their servitude is more bitter and intolerable; and produces a very great annual loss to the public, by the mortality which it produces." Despite these criticisms, selling individual Negroes went on, according to Bryan Edwards, "every day and under the present system will continue to occur." Edwards, in June, 1797, was successful in having the House of Commons repeal the section of the slave code that allowed slaves to be sold for debts. Because the practice was so common, however, the Jamaica Assembly in 1809 reinstated the clause retroactively. The directive from the House of Commons had never been heeded.

Concerning the slave's relation to freemen, the slaves could neither sue nor be sued. Until 1831 slaves could not testify in the regular courts of the island. Instead, specially created tribunals comprising (with minor variations) two justices of the peace and three freeholders tried slaves for various petty crimes and misdeameanors. It was not unusual for the owner of the defendant to sit on the court. In 1772, the Jamaica legislature passed a law prohibiting the "improper" selection of justices and freeholders to sit in trials of slaves. The law was not enforced. These tribunals were thus incapable of administering impartial justice.

The slave could either buy his freedom or be manumitted by his master for loyal service or for being his offspring. The slave could also be freed by an act of the Assembly in exchange for some service to the state. This usually meant loyal fighting against a rebellion, betrayal of a conspiracy, or testifying against rebellious slaves.

At the end of the eighteenth century, the Jamaica legislature attempted to lay down guidelines for the slave-owner to ensure the humane treatment of slaves. The Consolidated Slave Act of 1781, revised in 1787 and 1788 and still further revised and re-enacted in 1792, was considered the model statute of its day. The provisions of the code were an attempt to protect the slave from those who set no limits on the economic exploitation of the Negro. An eleven-hour day was declared the maximum working day for the slave, and the code further stipulated that every other week the slave should be given a free day to work on his provision ground. For the first time in the history of Jamaican slave laws, instruments of enforcement were provided; these were strengthened by subsequent revisions of the law. The 1781 act stipulated that the justices and vestry of each

The national coat of arms

Paul Hogel, leader of the rebellion
at Morant Bay in 1865

*Jamaica Information Service Photos*

George William Gordon, member
of the Jamaican Assembly who
supported the Morant Bay
rebellion

Malachi Reynolds, called Kapr, leading a pocomania
ceremony in Kingston

Devon House, a restored mansion of old Jamaica

Cricket, the national game of Jamaica, played at Sabine Park in Kingston

*Jamaica Tourist Board*

Folk dancing in a rural district

Louise Bennett, author of *Jamaica Labrish,*
in traditional costume

Square in Spanish Town, with old government buildings

Members of the National Dance Theatre Company

A member of the
religious cult called
Rasta Fari

*Jamaica
Tourist Board*

Sir Alexander Bustamante,
leader of the Independence
Movement and first
Prime Minister of
the new nation

*Jamaica Tourist Board*

Kingston Industrial Estate in 1958, when seventeen manufacturing plants were in operation

*Jamaica Industrial Development Corporation*

Kingston Industrial Estate
in 1969, with more than
seventy manufacturing
plants

*Jamaica
Industrial Development
Corporation*

Hugh Shearer,
Prime Minister
of Jamaica
since 1968

*Jamaica
Information Service*

parish were constituted as a council of protection over the slave, and the 1787 revision required that the master or overseer swear on oath once a year that his slaves were maintained and clothed properly; that the doctor of every plantation give an annual account of the increase or decrease of slaves with reasons for deaths; and that if a local justice had any information on the mutilation of slaves, he was required to issue a warrant for examining the slave. Limitations on slave punishments were incorporated into the code as well. Though they were not rigid (thirty-nine lashes was the limit for flogging), they did demonstrate the legislature's recognition that the master's power over a slave was not absolute. The Consolidated Slave Law of 1792 required all owners of slaves in town and country to provide for the disabled; to instruct slaves in the Christian religion; and to allow them three holidays a year at Easter, Whitsuntide and Christmas, plus one day every two weeks, exclusive of Sunday, to cultivate their provision grounds. Work hours for field hands were set from 5 A.M. to 7 P.M. with a half hour for breakfast and two hours for dinner; overseers and planters were subject to fines of 50 pounds for driving the slaves a longer period of time. The penalty for the mutilation of a slave was set at a 100-pound fine or twelve months in prison, while the "wanton, blood-minded" killing of a slave was punishable by death. Arbitrary floggings and other punishments defined as excessively cruel by the law were also subject to penalties. Special courts were to meet in every parish of the island to hear grievances and disputes between masters and slaves.

In theory, it would appear that the local leaders of Jamaican society were very much concerned with the welfare of their slaves, and as individuals some of them were. But when it came to enforcing the provisions of the Consolidated Slave Law, as a group they were lax. On the plantations there was no police force for the slave to call when his rights were infringed, and he most likely would not be aware of his rights under the law in any event, because most slaves could not read. Consequently, it was left to the planters to see that they themselves or their employees observed the law, an almost impossible responsibility for men who had, for so many years, thought of the slave as below the level of human respect. So the Slave Law remained largely a dead letter, reflecting the ideal rather than the real.

Slave laws, codes, and rules notwithstanding, the bound Negro was not the beneficiary of justice. Courts served the master's interest, not the slave's and nowhere in the statute books were there laws that defined the slave's rights. Instead, the slave code defined what he could not do, the limits of his behavior in the world outside the plantation. Inside the plantation, it was the owner's place to set those limits. The state as an agent of enforcement was weak. Into the hands of the owner went the power to determine the proper behavior pattern of the slave.

It can be seen from this account that the Jamaican society of the eighteenth century consisted of a complex set of interrelationships among its various groups. Legally, there were three main categories of social differentiation: the free with full civil rights, the free with limited civil rights, and the great bulk of unfree with no civil rights. Whites were all free by the beginning of the nineteenth century. Catholics, free Negroes, and Jews enjoyed only limited civil rights, and black slaves were unfree and had no claim to legal privileges in society. Culturally, there was a wide gap between the free and unfree sections of society. Religious observances and concepts of kinship and mating patterns, family organization, language, community organization and associations, recreation, and folklore had their own patterns of development in each group in society.

# 5. Jamaica and the Antislavery Crusade, 1787–1833

The dawn of the nineteenth century saw no appreciable change in the social and political life of the island. Time had little effect on the social forces operating in Jamaican society. The old was far more important than the new. The present and past were joined, and few thought of the future. Change was feared; left to itself, Jamaica would have remained a static society.

Jamaica, however, was not left alone, for it was not an independent society. The physical mass which was the island was owned mostly by people living abroad, not by local citizens. The economy was dependent upon England both for imports and as a ready market for its tropical produce. As a polity, Jamaica's government was subordinate to the King and Parliament. In the eighteenth century the disputes between local officials and the English Government had usually turned on points of law: violations of English mercantile policy, local interference with the rights of individuals, or the general inexpediency of proposed laws. England had intervened in Jamaica's internal affairs for the most part in peripheral areas.

In the nineteenth century, however, all this changed. Jamaica and England became embroiled in a controversy of a magnitude far greater than any dispute of the past. For the first time in history, the imperial government openly questioned and criticized what was considered the very foundation of Jamaican society and economy—the institution of slavery.

Ironically, Jamaica itself had questioned the importance of the slave trade, the first target of the English attack on slavery. In 1760, the Assembly of Jamaica, in an act that reflected the fears of the white minority, had imposed a duty on slaves imported into the island with the view to diminishing their numbers. The great disparity in population between Europeans and Africans was a matter of great concern on an island that was subject to slave revolts and had just experienced one that year by the Coromantee slaves. The British Government had refused to sanction the 1760 measure. Statutes passed by the Jamaica legislature in 1765 and 1774, which restricted the number of slaves imported into the island, had been similarly disallowed. Jamaica's protests had been rejected with arguments such as the one offered by the Secretary of State for the Colonies: "We cannot allow the colonies to check or discourage in any degree a traffic so beneficial to the nation." Another Secretary of State for the Colonies, the Duke of Portland, would some twenty years later commend the Jamaica Act of 1797, which put a 10-pound duty upon the the importation of all slaves over twenty-five years of age. The preamble to the act stated that it was difficult to civilize and train older Africans, they were an economic liability, and they usually turned out to be the instigators of revolt. Jamaica had sought to curb the slave trade, only to be rebuffed. When the notion was subsequently embraced by England, Jamaica was no longer interested.

Vital to the prosperity of England was the wealth of Jamaica and its sister islands. Maintenance of slavery and the slave trade was necessary, regardless of its great inequities, as prosperity and wealth were its fruits. The importation of Africans had to be supported and protected, for as a commercial, seafaring nation, Britain benefited from the trade not only because of its ties to the West Indies but also because it provided profits for its shipping industry.

A nation in which diverse opinions and varieties of thought flowered, if not always freely, England toward the end of the eighteenth century saw the development of a movement whose major concerns were moral rather than economic. Greater to them than any material achievement was the satisfaction derived from striving to drive evil from the world. They considered slavery and the slave trade such an evil, a national sin, and looked to the British Government to correct the wrong.

Aware of the difficulties involved in doing away with slavery completely, the Abolitionists first concentrated their fire on the slave trade. If, they reasoned, the evils connected with the commerce in human beings could be abolished, then ultimately slavery would correct itself. To do away with the abominable traffic would destroy a major bulwark of the slave system—its source of supply. Slave-owners would be forced to take good care of their slaves when fresh supplies from Africa were no longer forthcoming. Negroes would be better fed, better housed, and not driven beyond their physical capacity. Marriage would be encouraged, thus providing a more stable upbringing for future generations. Self-interest would require planters to concern themselves with the emotional as well as the physical growth of their slaves. Religious instruction among the slaves would have their support and encouragement.

Without immediately infringing on the institution of slavery, they hoped to reform it—to change somehow the attitude of the planter toward the slave without changing the basic relationship. Slavery was a disease that killed the moral feelings of both the owner and the owned, and finding a cure for it would make all the difference. Free of the illness, the slave-owner would change his ways and so would the slave. Abolition of the slave trade by England, the United States, and the European powers would be the cure, as the planters would at first take better care of their slaves and ultimately discover that free labor was more profitable. Secure in the righteousness of their cause, the Abolitionists confidently predicted a successful outcome.

When the first cure failed to wipe out the disease, a new one was tried—the general registration of slaves. This would provide a mechanism for protecting the Negro. When this failed to bring the desired results, the Abolitionists sought still another form of relief—parliamentary intervention to promote the amelioration of the conditions of slave life. When this, the last of the cures, failed to work, they came up with the strongest prescription of all—a proposal for the abolition of slavery itself, not through gradual measures, but immediately!

To be successful, it was necessary for the Abolitionists to

capture public interest and support, which in turn would influence Parliament and ultimately the government to steer a course toward abolition. They used a variety of devices to influence public opinion. First, they conducted a campaign to educate the public regarding the evils of slavery by circulating pamphlets and books. Second, they established local Abolitionist societies in cities, towns, and shires to distribute their literature and to draw up petitions to be sent to Parliament. Finally, they secured the backing and commitment of several leading political figures to carry on the fight in Parliament. With these tools of reform, the Society for the Abolition of the Slave Trade was ultimately successful in securing from the British Parliament a law that abolished the slave trade in the British Empire.

Twenty years elapsed between the founding of the Society for the Abolition of the Slave Trade in 1787 and the abolition of the slave trade by Parliament in 1807. Earlier, in 1783, the English Quakers had formed a committee and issued their first pamphlet, which stated their purpose to be the "discouragement of the slave trade on the coast of Africa." This original group began to attract non-Quakers to its ranks. Among them was Thomas Clarkson, who would become a leading figure in the English antislavery movement and one of its lifelong workers. He had graduated from St. John's College of Cambridge in 1785, where he had won the University's Latin Prize for an essay entitled "Is It Right to Make Men Slaves Against Their Will?" Clarkson would later write a history of the abolition of the slave trade, as well as numerous other pamphlets, books, and articles. Besides being a propagandist, Clarkson was the organizer for the antislavery forces in the country, riding on horseback to the various towns, cities, and counties to recruit members for the antislavery committees being formed throughout England and Scotland. As a result, the objectives of the society gained national support. It was now important to gain a voice in Parliament. Slave-trading was not illegal by British common law, and the only way to abolish it was by an act of Parliament.

The cause of the slave found its Parliamentary champion:

William Wilberforce of Hull, scion of a wealthy Yorkshire family, whose personal magnetism and utter lack of malice brought him many friends and admirers. Wilberforce, an Anglican by birth, had joined a dissenting movement within the Church of England known as the Evangelicals, or the Clapham Sect. Evangelicalism was a reaction to the easy and cold certitudes of the eighteenth-century church and sought practical ways for men to do service to God. In addition to working for the betterment of slaves, Wilberforce supported legislation for the "improvement of manners" and the suppression of vice.

He and his fellow Evangelicals were by no means social revolutionaries. They embraced rather than rejected the social patterns of their day. Their call was for greater self-discipline through intensive good works that would find favor in God's eyes. The betterment of the Negro slave was the outstanding cause promoted by the Claphamites. But they were as opposed to slave revolts as they were to the formation of unions by working men. For the slave as for the working man, it was not collective self-help that was needed but benevolent acts by understanding authority figures. Thus they were sure that if masters and factory owners were duly exhorted to act morally, they would change their ways for the better.

As the Parliamentary orator for the antislavery cause, Wilberforce moved Parliament to action. His strategy was, as he said, "to excite the flame as much as possible in a secret way, but not to allow it to smoulder until after I have given notice of my intention to bring it forward. This must be a signal for the fire's bursting forth." As the movement's political leader, he intended to clear the path for popular support to express itself in a way that would bring the most pressure to bear on the government.

Wilberforce met with some success. The King instructed his Privy Councilors to investigate the complaints against the slave trade. A standing committee was formed on February 11, 1788, to collect information on the problem. Investigations, however, do not necessarily lead to action.

It was popularly known that the King and his Court were opposed to abolition. The Duke of Clarence was the foremost protagonist for the slave trade in the House of Lords, and King George III himself had been turned against Abolitionism by distaste for the methods of popular agitation used in its cause. Though Wilberforce was able to gain the support of Prime Minister Pitt, he failed to win over the rest of the Cabinet, with the exception of Lord Grenville. Other prominent political leaders, such as James Fox, Lord John Russell, Sir William Yonge, and Edmund Burke, became advocates of abolition, but there was no substantial political movement in its favor.

The slave trade was backed by tradition and property, two great mainstays of British society. Slaves were property, and the antislavery forces were, in effect, questioning the right of Englishmen to private ownership. Once let it be established, ran the argument, that the British legislature could confiscate property, and no property would be safe. Little wonder, then, that in 1791 a motion in the House of Commons to abolish the trade was handily defeated. Horace Walpole remarked, "Commerce clinked its purse and the sound is generally prevalent with the majority."

The Abolitionist forces, though defeated, refused to surrender. The following year they secured 312 petitions from England and 180 from Scotland in support of their cause. Forced, by this pressure, to reconsider the issue, many Members of Parliament discarded their old policy of direct and complete opposition to abolition and devised new tactics. Henry Dundas, for example, proposed in Parliament that slavery be regulated and the conditions of the slaves be improved. This, he argued, would be far more effective and helpful to the slave than abolition of the trade. Wilberforce countered that abolition of the slave trade would compel the planters to make immediate improvements in the conditions of their slaves. The public interest would also be safeguarded, as, with no further importation of slaves, the dangers of slave insurrections would be minimized. Pitt argued that, as a commercial endeavor, the slave trade should be regulated as were other "branches of trade." Every new commerical regulation, tax, or prohibitory duty affected "some man's property and some man's expectations" but nonetheless was not forbidden to Parliament.

Persuaded by argument and pressure, the House of Commons, in a compromise typical of the British, voted to "gradually abolish" the slave trade in 1792. The House of Lords failed to support this proposal. Reform might bring revolution as it had done in France. Besides, Wilberforce had been given a place in the National Convention in France. This was a dubious honor, since to most lords the line between sedition and reform was razor thin.

The turn the French Revolution took after 1792 and the slave revolt in the French Caribbean island of Santo Domingo, where thousands were massacred and plantations destroyed, pointed up, it seemed to many, the dangers of tampering with the established order, whether at home or in the West Indies. Wilberforce himself was painfully aware that circumstances were working against abolition. He observed in a letter: "People here are panic-struck with the transactions in St. Domingo and the apprehension or pretended apprehension of the like in Jamaica and other of our islands. I am pressed on all hands to defer my motion till next year." Reform now became equated with dreaded revolution; the fact that the slave trade had been abolished by France during the Revolution was a good reason to retain it in Great Britain. The arguments of Pitt, Fox, and Wilberforce that abolition was a good English doctrine even if it was a radical French one was lost amid the gains that were accruing to the British. It seemed the height of folly to cut off vast commercial profits for the sake of principle.

As for the Jamaica legislature, the "excesses" of the French Revolution were not needed to convince it that abolition of the slave trade would be disaster. On December 3, 1789, fearful of action by Parliament, the legislature set forth its opposition and sought to portray the advantages of not only slavery as a commercial system but the advantage to the slaves themselves. It asserted that the island's "slaves in general are not only treated with kindness and humanity but . . . are also protected by law from immoderate chastisement, or cruel treatment, and enjoy more easy, comfortable and happy lives than the multitudes of the labourers in Great Britain." Parliament apparently took no official notice of the communication from

Jamaica, and on November 5, 1790, the Assembly sent a petition directly to the King protesting that "a representation of matters of the highest importance to our present and future welfare was withheld or suppressed." In 1797 the Assembly claimed, in an address to the British Government, that "we are actuated by motives of humanity only and not with any view of termination of the slave trade."

Unfortunately for Jamaica, its idea of humanitarian action was not the same as that of the friends of the slave in England. To them the slave could not be thought of as property, for no human could be made the property of another. Ideally the slave, like every other human, should be a self-sustaining member of society having certain legal rights to protect him from the unlimited powers of others. The realities of life on the Jamaican plantation made such notions irrelevant. The slave was an instrument of production, to be exploited to the extremes of human capacity; human characteristics were only of accidental interest. Certainly they would never be utilized to develop an independent self.

Philip Francis, who in 1796 introduced a motion in Parliament for regulating slavery, did not concur. The object of his proposal was to raise the slave to a level of civilization where he could live a moral life. Too many colonial laws were punitive in regard to the slave and failed to recognize and develop his moral capacities. Give the slave a definite nonservile status in society, equivalent to an English laborer, Francis said, or allow him to buy his freedom at a just price fixed by law, and he will be well prepared to accept religious teachings and live the moral life. The representatives of West Indian interests in Parliament, many of whom had never seen a plantation or worked with slaves, supported the Francis motion for reasons of expediency. They hoped it would put off the Abolitionists' crusade against the slave trade. If the West Indian legislatures would pass laws bettering the conditions of the slaves, the birth rate would go up, indicating the slaves were better protected. Meanwhile, abolition of the slave trade could be put off indefinitely until it was proved whether or not the natural population growth fostered by better treatment would lessen the demand for native Africans, rendering slave-trading unprofitable and making an act to abolish it unnecessary.

Pitt's government welcomed the West Indian support of amelioration and took steps to translate Francis's resolutions into practical terms that the West Indian legislators would understand. In two circular dispatches sent by the Duke of Portland on May 6, 1797, and April 23, 1798, recommendations were made for legislation. The largest number of them dealt with ways to increase the slave population. It was suggested that some sort of tax be devised that would make it advantageous for the planter to work women and children less hard. Another suggestion was that a pregnant woman be exempted from field labor for the last six weeks or two months before delivery and that she be exempt from all labor except child care after the baby is delivered. Mothers of large families should be exempted from all labor as "a reward for high productivity." Though population increase was the object of the dispatch, moral education was not forgotten. Planters were told to allow missionaries to work among slaves on their estates, and legislatures were told to reward such masters by decreasing their property taxes. Finally, it was suggested that slaves be given permanent status on the land, that they be legally attached to it as villeins.

So far were these suggestions from the realities of slave life in Jamaica and its sister islands that little was done to implement them. Thus the West India Association's hope that amelioration would thwart the Abolitionists were quickly dashed.

The cause of the Abolitionists was, however, helped by the capture by the British of many Caribbean "sugar islands" from the Dutch and French (not including Santo Domingo). These became an additional source of trouble for the West India interests. As lesser islands they had not been extensively cultivated; if they were now, they might offer serious competition to Britain's older sugar colonies. The traditional West India interests in Parliament had made their fortunes in the older islands and were fearful of new competition from fresh sources. If African labor were supplied to the new colonies at a rapid rate, the possibility of their outstripping the older ones in sugar production was very real.

Since 1799, sixty-five estates had been given up in Jamaica and thirty-two had been sold for debts. By 1807, suits were pending against one hundred fifteen others. It was said that "debt, disease and death" were the major topics of conversation on the island. On November 13, 1807, a committee of the Jamaican Assembly reported on the economic conditions in the island. One of the major reasons for the difficulties, it said, was that "the total output of sugar from the British and conquered islands greatly exceeds the consumption in Britain and Ireland." Jamaica's explanation for its economic problems was supported by Parliamentary investigating groups.

Before the Jamaican Assembly issued its report, the British Government took steps to curtail the economic development of the ceded colonies—Grenada, the Grenadines, Dominica, St. Vincent, and Tobago—by first limiting and eventually completely cutting off their slave labor supply. Two Orders of Council and an act of Parliament were involved. An Order of Council of August 15, 1805, limited slave imports in the newly acquired colonies to 3 per cent of the existing number of slaves, and an Order of September 13, 1806, barred slave imports in Guiana. Superseding these acts of the Privy Council was the act of May 23, 1806, which prevented British ships from carrying slaves to, or engaging in the slave trade with parties in, any conquered, ceded, or foreign colonies. Without fresh supplies of new laborers, the virgin lands of these possessions could not be intensively developed.

With abolition now established and supported by the government, the antislavery forces intensified their efforts to have the slave trade abolished not only in the ceded colonies but throughout the empire. Between 1804 and 1807, the Abolitionists had secured new support from Irish members of Parliament who had been brought to Westminister by the Act of Union. Once again a bill to abolish the slave trade passed in Commons. The House of Lords postponed action on the bill, to which Wilberforce could only remark: "It was truly humiliating to see four of the Royal Family come down to vote against the poor, helpless, friendless slave."

The West Indian groups solidly opposed abolition of the slave trade, particularly after the labor supply to the ceded colonies had been drastically curtailed. General meetings of the Society of West Indian Planters and Merchants vigorously opposed abolition in 1805 and, in December, 1806, reaffirmed its desire to "employ the most vigorous and incessant exertions in opposing so baneful a project." Petitions were sent to both houses of Parliament.

The sudden death of Pitt in January, 1806, was probably the most decisive event in favor of the Abolitionists. The new Cabinet, known in history "as the ministry of all talents" was dominated by men who were prepared to support abolition at all costs. Whereas Pitt's second Cabinet contained a group of avowed anti-Abolitionists—eight in number—the new government headed by Charles James Fox, an unflagging, advocate of Abolitionism, had ten pro-Abolitionists. The possibility of obstruction from the House of Lords was considerably lessened, as the Prime Minister was in the upper house. With the coming to power of the "talents," the King's influence on Parliament was weakened, clearing still another obstacle from abolition's path. The fact that the danger of French invasion had been removed and the fear of Jacobinism had died down also favored abolition. The general public had done its share by exerting political pressure on its Parliamentary representatives, with the result that abolition of the slave trade had passed in Commons in 1804 and 1806, only to be blocked from becoming the law of the land by the House of Lords. Gestures of public support, coupled with the successful passage of the law of 1806, which prohibited British ships and merchants from supplying slaves to foreign territories, allowed Fox to put all his political strength behind a resolution for suppression of the slave trade in the British Empire. This too was passed by both houses of Parliament in 1806. Though this measure expressed Parliament's sentiment that the slave trade should be abolished with "practicable expedition," it was not until 1807 that statutory abolition was achieved. On March 25, 1807, the abolition of the slave trade became law. According to the statute, the slave trade was "utterly abolished, prohibited and declared to be unlawful." Under the terms of the act, no slavers were to clear from ports in the United Kingdom after May 1, 1807, and no slaves were to be landed in the colonies after March 1, 1808. Lord Grenville could justly be proud of his government for its success in efforts to bring about what he described as "one of the most glorious acts that had ever been done by any Assembly of any nation of the world."

Those most directly involved with slaves and slave-trading in the West Indian colonies did not feel "glorious" at all. The Society of West Indian Planters and Merchants petitioned the King "to avert the approaching destruction of [their] fellow subjects who are inhabitants of these colonies." Harsher measures were advocated in Jamaica. In retaliation, a committee of the Assembly recommended that the subsistence of 3,000 troops stationed in the islands be discontinued. A heated debate followed between those for the recommendation and those against it. When the opponents prevailed, the principals on each side, a Mr. P. Stewart and a Mr. J. Shand, fought a pistol duel in which both were wounded. Blood-and-thunder resolutions in the Assembly denounced Parliament's authority to enact legislation regulating local affairs. Abolition left deep-seated resentment in the hearts of the colonials.

Reactionary forces took the lead. Some of Jamaica's most progressive slave statutes were repealed. A law that gave a 3-pound bounty annually to every overseer on whose plantation births exceeded deaths expired in 1807 and was not renewed. In 1809, clauses were dropped from the Consolidated Slave Act requiring owners, overseers, and managers to return annual accounts, under oath, of all births and deaths of slaves within the year under penalty of a 50-pound fine for every default. With much exasperation, the Abolitionist James Stephen commented that, just when the abolition act of 1807 was passed as a check on the slave system so as to make the "native population take an interest far deeper than ever and even vital to the colony, the Assembly displayed increased indifference about it; and instead of adopting new means for

ascertaining its progress or decline, put an end to such provisions for that purpose as already existed." This, Stephen
said, was "very suspicious and very contumacious conduct on
the part of the Jamaica legislature."

The abolition of the slave trade was intended to do away
with an inhuman practice, but it was also conceived of as part
of a larger scheme to better the lot of the slaves already in the
colonies. Concern for the slave's material improvement was
coupled with concern for his spiritual welfare. Missionary
societies were sending representatives to the West Indian islands
to convert the heathen, and their efforts were warmly endorsed
by the Abolitionist movement. By far the most missionaries
were members of the Baptist, Methodist, and other dissenting
sects. Living in the villages and towns, they came into close
contact with the daily life of the people. Reports of their
activities were sent regularly to England, and it was from
these that vigilant Abolitionists evaluated the living conditions
of the slaves.

The laws of the colonies were a source of concern, as legislation more often than not failed to serve the slaves' best
interests. The Abolitionists often succeeded in having the laws
they objected to "disallowed" or declared null and void by the
Privy Council. The laws of Jamaica were the object of particular scrutiny. As the largest island in the British West Indies,
Jamaica's slave population was greater than all other British
possessions in the Caribbean.

Over the course of the first quarter of the nineteenth century,
the internal affairs of the island were the object of intense
scrutiny by the Colonial Office. The Abolitionists were often
successful in bringing pressure to bear on the Colonial Office
to have legislation disallowed that they felt was detrimental
to the slaves' best interests. As a result, disagreements between
local politicians and British officials were common. Though these
encounters were usually skirmishes, serious flareups occurred
from time to time. A law of 1802, which had the effect of
prohibiting dissenting missionaries from preaching or teaching,
was objected to, but the legislature would not change it. Even
when the Privy Council disallowed the act, the legislature in-

cluded the restrictions in a different form in the Consolidated
Slave Act of 1807.

The intransigence of the Jamaica legislature stemmed from
a combination of arrogance and fear. Baptists, Methodists, and
other dissenters, it was felt, were allies of the Abolitionists
and were in effect aiding enemy forces. Besides, the slave-
owners could not comprehend why the teachings of the missionaries were applicable to the slaves. Brotherly love seemed
nonsense to them when applied to black and white, slave and
free. Then, too, the notion smelled of equality, an idea of
great repugnance to all slave-owners. Planters prohibited the
building of chapels and the instruction of slaves on their
properties.

The fear and hatred of religious dissenters would manifest
itself often in the coming decades. As one assemblyman phrased
it, the dissenters represented "dark and dangerous fanaticism,"
which, "grafted on to African superstitions and working on the
uninstructed minds and ardent temperament of the Negroes,
has produced the most pernicious consequences to individuals
and is pregnant with imminent danger to the community." The
governor of Jamaica—the Duke of Manchester—described the
mood of the Assembly when he said it assumed "to itself an
independent and paramount jurisdiction rendering ineffectual
every other authority."

The reaction of the "slave interests" to the Abolition Act
only convinced the Abolitionists that the struggle must be
waged with ever more vigor. The Abolitionists did not take
lightly the intransigent attitude of Jamaica and sought new
means to force compliance from the colonists. In 1815, Wilberforce proposed that legislation be enacted to compel Jamaica
and its sister colonies to keep a registered list of all slaves.
The registers would be sent to Great Britain and inspected
regularly. Their purpose was to keep a check on the slave-
owners to determine whether they were improving the conditions in which their slaves lived. Harsh treatment would be
reflected in higher death rates, and because the measure would
also provide for the recording of other pertinent data, such as
causes of death and the physical condition of each slave, what-

ever a planter was doing wrong could easily be determined and corrected. Illegal imports of slaves would also be detected. Free Negroes would be protected, for if they were not listed in the registers, they could more easily overcome the legal presumption of slavery for all nonwhites.

The protest of the Jamaica legislature at this attempt to "violate" what it saw as its "constitutional right" was immediate. It expressed its "surprise, grief, and concern"—and refused to obey. The *Jamaica Gazette*, in more than one issue, called the registration proposal a cloak for emancipation. In England, British merchants and absentee landlords declared slave registration an "unnecessary impolitic and unconstitutional measure." The West India Association and the Society of West Indian Planters and Merchants directed the legislatures of each island to send official protests to London. These protests were published in the English press as part of a skillful plan to win support. They were, in part, responsible for a compromise proposal agreed to by the British Government, under which each colony was to enact its own registry bill.

The Jamaica legislature passed its slave registry bill in 1816. (Lord Bathurst had warned the legislative colonies that Parliament would enact a registration bill if the individual colonies did not.) The looseness of the law was matched by the laxity of its enforcement. No machinery was created to enforce the law, and it remained, in its effect, a dead letter. Jamaica's slave registry law was but a token gesture designed to placate critics and also to gain continued preference in England for its sugar exports. As competition from sugar producers in the East Indies increased, token compliance with the British Government's policies would be judicious if it meant Jamaica and its sister islands would continue to receive favored treatment. The slave registry law was but one attempt made by the Jamaica legislature to return to the good graces of the British Government. Other reforms, some more meaningful, were also to be enacted. For the first time, positive steps were taken to provide for the religious education of the slaves.

The Curate's Act of 1816 appropriated funds for the maintenance of an Anglican minister in each parish. By the terms of his appointment, he was to devote every Sunday afternoon plus two other days a week to instructing the slaves. Planters were required to give time off on Sunday afternoon and two other days for these religious instructions. This was done in good part to offset what many felt was the revolutionary influence of the Moravians, Baptists, and other missionaries and not to increase religious instruction among the slaves.

If the Assembly's zeal for reform was not notable, its actions reflected the pressures it was facing. The legislators privately agreed with the apprehensions voiced by one of their number that "concessions" to free Negroes were "highly prejudicial to the white population of the island" and a "great danger, in general, and productive of greater mischief," but the driving force was the realization that, unless Jamaica granted increased rights to its Negroes, the British Government would withdraw its special privileges to the West Indian "sugar interests." Just three years before, in 1813, free Negroes had been given the right to testify in all judicial disputes, both civil and criminal, and in all courts of the island. Now, in 1816, a "legacy law" of 1761, which limited the amount of property free Negroes could inherit, was repealed. To present a better image to the British Government, the Assembly's Committee on Correspondence instructed its colonial agent in England to let it be known that the free Negroes were put on the same legal footing "with a very respectable class of inhabitants, the Hebrews."

The Assembly's efforts to offset criticism were token gestures, which critics in England quickly discounted. Missionary and Colonial Office reports of events in the colonies failed to show significant changes in attitudes and actions. The Abolitionists were further dismayed by the failure of Great Britain to secure the international abolition of the slave trade. A new approach was devised. The root of all evil—the institution of slavery itself—would be abolished.

Immediate emancipation was not their goal. Their aim, as described by Sir Thomas Fowell Buxton, was "not the sudden emancipation of the Negro; but such preparatory steps, such measures of precaution, as, by slow degrees, and in a course of years, first fitting and qualifying the slaves for freedom, shall gently conduct us to the annihilation of slavery."

In 1822, under Zachary Macaulay's leadership, Thomas Clarkson, William Allen, James Cropper, and several other prominent Quakers joined forces with Henry Brougham and other
public figures for a new campaign. After several preliminary
meetings, in January, 1823, they formed the Society for the
Mitigation and Abolition of Slavery Throughout the British
Dominions. Branches were organized in provincial centers and
larger cities. Pamphlets, such as Wilberforce's *An Appeal to
the Justice, Religion and Humanity of the Inhabitants of the
British Empire on Behalf of the Negro Slaves in the British
West Indies* and Clarkson's *Thoughts On the Necessity of Improving The Slave's of the British Empire With The View of
Their Ultimate Emancipation*, were distributed, and petitions
were circulated throughout the kingdom. The entire organiza-
tional structure that had existed during the earlier campaign
to abolish the slave trade was reactivated with the personal
guidance of Thomas Clarkson, who rode circuit throughout
the country enlisting members of the first organization to be
charter members of the new society. Once again, corresponding
moves were made in Parliament. Sir Thomas Fowell Buxton
and his associate, Stephen Lushington, replaced the aging and
ill Wilberforce as Parliamentary spokesmen. Buxton opened
the Parliamentary battle in May, 1823, by moving "that the
state of slavery is repugnant to the principles of the British
constitution and of the Christian religion, and that it ought to
be gradually abolished throughout the British colonies."

The British Government under Canning, pressed by the
Abolitionists, who demanded reforms, and by the colonists,
who insisted that private property and the principle of local
self-government could not be interfered with, sought to meet
the demands of both sides by attempting to persuade the West
Indian colonies to institute "voluntary" reforms on a local level
and thus avoid intervention by the imperial government. The
West India interests in Parliament, recognizing that the attacks
on slavery could best be resisted by ameliorating the conditions
of the slaves, endorsed Canning's proposals. The survival of
the institution of slavery might be insured by a recognition—
and reform—of its worst features and an imaginative defense
addressed to both emotion and reason. The Society of West

Indian Planters and Merchants therefore advised the colonies that "it is not less the part of prudence" to cooperate with the government's efforts on amelioration. It warned that, if cooperation was not forthcoming, the British Government "will inevitably be driven by public opinion" to "decided acts of interference."

Having the support of the West Indian interests in Parliament, the Tory government was quite justified in believing that the colonial legislatures would carry forward the program of amelioration. A dispatch was sent to the colonial governors on May 28, 1823, instructing them to advise the colonial legislatures to enact measures to improve conditions for the slaves. And less than a year later, on March 16, 1824, Canning issued as an Order in Council for Trinidad, a model slave code to be used by the legislatures of other colonies as well to revise their slave laws. The principal notion guiding the framing of these codes and all other reform suggestions was the idea that the slave must be treated in a Christian manner—as a human with human needs. Its major provision was that a protector and guardian for slaves be appointed to act for them in legal proceedings. The code stipulated that the whip must not be used at work, that females must not be punished by whipping, that families must not be separated, that marriage and manumission must be facilitated, and that the slave's evidence must be admitted in the regular courts of the island. The code required that the slaves be allowed to spend more time in cultivating their own provision grounds in order to accumulate savings, which might then be used to buy their own freedom. It was also proposed that children born after a fixed date be free. Provisions for more religious instruction, deemed so essential to "building character," were considered extremely important. Religion would spur the Negro on to greater industry and trust.

Reform proposals from official government sources fell on deaf ears in the colonies. Not even the Society of West Indian Planters and Merchants, which represented the interests of the West Indies, could persuade the colonial legislatures of the wisdom of enacting reforms, because the constellation of forces that held power in the legislatures included other groups besides the Society's members. William Wilberforce wrote, in a pamphlet published in 1823, that a class had developed in the colonies whose members had no status but that derived from being white. They looked upon any extension of "privileges" to Negroes as a threat to their own position and were extremely hostile to any attempt at amelioration. They were, as Wilberforce phrased it, bound by a "peculiarly strong *esprit de corps.*"

The unwillingness of the West Indian governments, as Thomas Clarkson complained, to "elevate the condition of the Negro or to do anything for him as a human being" was largely substantiated by the actions of the Jamaica legislature throughout the 1820's. Its response tells much about why emancipation became a reality in 1833.

In Jamaica the reaction of the colonists to the amelioration program was extreme; they took it to be not a compromise but a declaration of war. The Jamaica legislature and the groups it represented rejected the whole idea and refused to cooperate with the new colonial policy. Meetings were held in every parish, and resolutions were sent to London newspapers protesting Parliament's attempt to infringe the colonists' "right" to regulate their own particular social order. Jamaica, according to an Assembly declaration, was being offered as a "propitiatory sacrifice at the altar of fanaticism." On June 28, 1823, it sent a violent statement to the British Parliament: "We will pray the Imperial Parliament to amend their origin, which is bribery; to cleanse their consciences, which are corrupt; to throw off their disguise, which is hypocrisy; to break with their false allies, who are the Saints; and finally to banish from them all the purchased rogues, who are three-fourths of their number."

Much of this anger stemmed from a fear of slave revolts. With the British Parliament now on the side of the Negro, all violent actions would seem to the slaves to be justifiable. Fixed in the memory of white Jamaicans was what happened in Santo Domingo thirty years before, when slaves were given "rights."

Several slave "conspiracies" were unearthed in the half-year following the Jamaican Assembly session of 1823. They confirmed the fears of those who believed that the slaves no longer respected local authority and were preparing for open revolt against it. Though whatever skirmishes occurred were minor incidents, the white residents, ever fearful of the black masses, gave them a significance far beyond their actual proportions. They strongly supported, therefore, the adamant stand taken by the Assembly.

The Assembly's final resolution on the amelioration proposals was to take "the most firm, strong and constitutional measures to resist such an attempt, and to preserve to the inhabitants of this Colony those rights which have been transmitted to them by their ancestors."

With this principle in mind, the Assembly declined to pass any of the suggested melioration measures save one protecting females from violence against their persons. The creation of an Anglican Diocese in Jamaica through Royal Letters Patent in 1824 did little to facilitate religious instruction among the slaves. The new Anglican Bishop was viewed as still another representative of the enemy out to spy on the condition of the slaves. As the church of the establishment, the Anglican body in Jamaica, even as an independent diocese, could have little effect on the life of the slave.

The recommendations of the imperial government could be thought of as revolutionary only by those who were responsible for, and lived in the midst of, the slave labor system. The suggestion that slaves' evidence be admitted in the courts of the island was considered particularly dangerous. As one member of the Jamaica Legislature put it in 1825:

Can any measure be adopted which would have the effect of depressing the character of the higher classes and elevating the lower it would be admitting slave evidence. What could our enemies devise which would more effectually destroy the high feeling of superiority with which the white population are regarded than to place their lives and liberties at the mercy of slave evidence.

Jamaica's example was not lost on the other West Indian islands. An exasperated Colonial Secretary, the Earl of Bathurst, complained that they made the example of Jamaica "their apology for doing so little," yet the British Government was not eager to take up the challenge and could only counsel patience to those who demanded stronger steps against the recalcitrant wayward colonies.

The Abolitionists were not as patient as the Colonial Office. The Parliamentary team that carried on their work—Thomas Fowell Buxton, Henry Brougham, Stephen Lushington, and William Smith—became "Ajaxes in battle" who were "vigilant on the watch to bring before Parliament flagrant cases of abuse." The persecution of missionaries of the various dissenting sects became common practice in some of the islands. This was particularly true whenever a change of policy was instituted in Britain. As symbols of reform, of abolition and humanitarianism, and of a different view of the Negro, the missionaries were easy targets for the rage of the planters. Thus, when the amelioration program was embarked upon in 1823, individual missionaries became the objects of abuse. In Jamaica, the Reverend George Bridges, an Anglican clergyman obviously on the side of the establishment, led the attack. A Wesleyan Chapel was damaged, and slaves were forbidden to attend meetings led by dissenters. Those who did found their services broken up by gangs of rowdies while their ability to congregate was soon curtailed by laws designed to check nonconformist activities.

The Reverend John Smith of the London Missionary Society was the martyr of the age. His death in prison after being sentenced to death for inciting rebellion became a *cause celebre* of the Abolitionists. In June, 1824, Brougham called for a full investigation by Parliament; though ably supported by Wilberforce, who made his last speech before that chamber on the issue, the motion was defeated. If the Abolitionists lost in Parliament, they were compensated for the loss by the huge gains they made in public opinion. Outraged by this attack on an agent of God, pious citizens once apathetic to the antislavery cause now became its champion.

Another case that contributed greatly to the fortunes of the Abolitionists was that of two Jamaican free Negroes, Lewis Lescene and John Escoffery, who became the subjects of debate in Parliament when the Abolitionists championed their cause. They had been secretly tried in Jamaica in 1823 for allegedly plotting an insurrection. Though there was little real proof to back up the charges, the governor of Jamaica, the Duke of Manchester, secretly deported them. In 1824, before they were expelled, Brougham moved in Parliament that the case be debated, but the motion was rejected. Ultimately, on June 16, 1825, the case came before Parliament. Thanks to the hasty action of the Duke of Manchester, the free Negroes of Jamaica found a forum outside of Jamaica in which their grievances would be heard, for the debate was used not only to discuss the specifics of the case but also to publicize the general condition of the free Negroes.

Stephen Lushington stated that, though the Assembly had rejected the demands of the free Negroes for civil rights, their loyalty and devotion remained unquestioned. They were, however, "smarting under the rejection of their prayers." The white population, he added, could not be "speedily brought to view the importance of the people of mixed blood" as "the prejudices which had for so many generations led them to consider the blacks as an inferior race, naturally extended to all who had a mixture of African blood in their veins." They thus had a "natural jealousy of any approach by the colored to equal rights."

Under the forceful leadership of Lushington (whose family had large holdings in the West Indies) and others, the antislavery forces rallied public opinion to support Lescene and Escoffery, who ultimately received a monetary award from Parliament as compensatory damages. The case helped to publicize the Abolitionists' complaint that "the power of slavery was in the colonies" of greater importance than the rights of British subjects.

Still another response to the public outcry against injustice in the West Indies was the Commission of Inquiry appointed by the government in 1822 to report on the administration of civil and criminal justice in the British West Indies. Three reports were made by the commission, containing a thorough analysis of the legal situation in the islands. The major finding was that there was a total lack of fixed principles of colonial jurisprudence. Some semblance of the English legal system did exist, but each colony had created its own traditions and distinctions. The commission did not recommend interfering with the existing systems, as they served the needs of each colony. Instead, it called upon the individual governments of all islands to alter their local laws to meet the demands of the times. One of its recommendations favoring the Abolitionist call for reform was that civil and political disabilities of free people of color be abolished. "It seems peculiarly hard utterly to exclude so large and opulent a class of freemen from the enjoyment of privileges which by British subjects is regarded as their most valuable inheritance."

The legislature of Jamaica had already disregarded these proposals. In 1823, "the free people of color" and the free Negroes had petitioned the assembly for equal rights. The request, the Assembly stated, was "incompatible with the subordination and tranquility of the different classes of the population." In rejecting it, the Assembly refused to heed the warnings of a white resident that "the time is not far distant when the free people of color, feeling their own weight in numbers, prosperity, and information, will not rest content with any qualification short of what the whites enjoy."

The Colonial Secretary, Lord Bathurst, in the fall of 1825 asked the island agent of Jamaica, who was "accredited to the Colonial Office in the same way in which a foreign minister is accredited to the Foreign Department," to convey to the Assembly the government's request that the free colored's condition be improved. When no change had been forthcoming, Bathurst warned the island agent that if privileges were not extended to the free colored, the issue would be brought before Parliament, and the government would have much trouble defending the "colonial point of view." Though Lord Bathurst had given his "final word" on the subject in February, 1826, it was not until June that the Jamaica Committee of Correspondence informed the island agent of the Assembly's decision. It held that no further privileges could be granted to the free colored "without at once admitting them to all the privileges of white persons." This the Assembly refused to do.

Stephen Lushington, however, since his defense of Lescene and Escoffery in 1825, had become very much involved in the problems of the free colored. It was his intention to bring before Parliament their plea for justice. His interest was aroused and his appetite whetted, he wrote to Buxton, "by all the follies and iniquities of the planters." He ultimately received the opportunity to present to Parliament a thorough account of the free Negroes' problems in Jamaican society. On June 26, 1826, Lushington presented their evidences to the House of Commons. This debate, however, proved of little immediate consequence to the Jamaican free Negroes. The efforts of the antislavery forces could be of little help to them as long as the government adhered to its position of nonintervention in the internal affairs of the self-governing colonies. In the Crown colonies, where the government had a long established legal precedent of direct intervention, the labors of the Abolitionists were not in vain. On March 13, 1829, an Order of the Privy Council for Trinidad proclaimed:

> Every law, ordinance, or proclamation in force within the island, whereby His Majesty's subjects of African birth or descent, being of free condition are subject to any disability, civil or military to which His Majesty's subjects of European birth or descent are not subject, shall be and the same for each of them are and is forever repealed and annulled.

By the end of 1830, similar orders had been issued for all of the Crown colonies of the empire.

Although it was the free colored of Jamaica who had borne the brunt of the struggle in England and who had first brought their plight to the attention of the antislavery forces, it was their counterparts in the Crown colonies who, by the summer of 1829, had received full civil rights. As the government failed to retreat from its "hands off" policy, the only alternative open to the free colored in Jamaica was to fight at home. Confining their efforts to peaceful means, they founded in 1829 a weekly newspaper, *The Watchman*. Its editor, Edward Jordon, had been secretary of a secret society that had championed the cause of the free colored since 1820. Closer in temperament to Martin Luther King than Booker T. Washington, Jordon in his weekly paper showed high indignation at the white minority's failure to aid the free colored.

Several delegations of white inhabitants from the island's heavily populated parishes sent petitions to the Assembly on behalf of the "colored natives of the island." The parishes of Saint James, Saint Catherine and Saint Thomas in the east were all represented, but word from Kingston was conspicuously absent. The substance of all three petitions was that "wealth, education, and property" had entitled them (the free colored) to participate with the white population in all rights, civil and political. To exclude them from offices of trust would be "at variance with the principle of good government and unsuitable to the present period."

Mindful of what would happen if the alliance between the two classes were broken, and aware that the magnitude of the material wealth of a large portion of the free colored population was to be respected, members of the white population in the three eastern parishes had by 1829 set aside many of their prejudices toward the free colored and found it expedient to strengthen the alliance between the free colored and the white groups. To weaken it by refusing concessions to the nonwhite citizens was seen as detrimental to the welfare of those whose interests traditionally received the greatest protection from government.

At the beginning of 1830, the forces that had long kept the free colored from assuming an equal part in the government and judiciary of Jamaica began to retreat into history. Their retreat was slow and gradual.

A bill of 1830 granted the right to vote to the wealthier segments of the peoples of free condition. The franchise was given to those in the towns who owned freeholds of 100 pounds or more in value. In the countryside, the franchise was granted to those who owned freeholds of 50 pounds or paid rents of 100 pounds. The discrepancy between the city and country requirements may have been a concession to the inhabitants of Kingston, who in 1813 had displayed a particular fear of the free Negroes and in 1829 had failed to present a petition in their favor, as other leading parishes had.

Once again, as was the case in 1795 and in 1813, the Assembly had granted the free Negroes a meager slice of the pie, hoping that the appetite for privileges would be appeased. But the public voice of the free colored quickly made it clear that only a full serving of civil liberties would satisfy them. If this was not forthcoming, other and more severe measures would be taken by the free colored to secure these privileges. *The Watchman*, in an editorial on the day the Assembly passed the privilege bill, stated that the free colored had been "taunted, tantalized, and insulted into a spirit which, if not met by measures of a direct kind, must produce serious consequences," for they had, for too long, "been made the dupes of an inhuman policy."

There was no reaction from the Assembly or the governor to this published threat, and in July the free colored petitioned the King to withhold his approval of the act of February, 1830, for if it were brought into operation the pretensions of the Assembly would be sanctioned. It was "expediency alone" that had "induced the appearance of liberality." The legislature had only "pretended to give" in order to stop "another higher power" from granting full privileges. Failing once again to abolish the entire system of exclusion, the free colored had turned to England for help.

Suddenly and dramatically, in the last month of 1830, the Assembly reversed its decision and passed an act granting the free colored full civil liberties. This bill, said W. Burge, the Attorney General, originated with and was not "suggested to" the legislature. It was passed by the Assembly, according to one newspaper, *"nemine dissentiente."* Concise in its phrasing, the law boldly but clearly stated:

All the free brown and black population of this island shall be entitled to enjoy all rights, privileges, immunities and advantages whatsoever to which they would have been entitled if born of or descended from white ancestors.

In the sweep of reform, in the following year, 1831, revisions were made in the Consolidated Slave Law. Major clauses of previous laws that had been rejected by the British Government were removed. Demands of reformers that slave evidence be admitted in all the courts of the island, that slaves be given jury trials, and that missionaries be allowed to work with the slaves without restriction were all accepted. The Assembly made it clear, however, that it could make no further concessions to reform demands. Their message to the British Government was "any further amelioration of the condition of our slave population must emanate from ourselves." The intransigent attitude of the Jamaican Government would not be shaken. On May 13, 1832, the Whig government offered the legislative colonies financial aid to the extent of half their respective annual revenues, provided the several legislatures would translate into law the government's program. Jamaica and the others flatly refused.

Of great concern to the Jamaica Assembly was a slave rebellion that broke out on the island in December, 1831. Reform was felt to be the cause of the rebellion. Extreme discontent swept through the island's white population, and, as in 1823, local parish meetings roundly condemned the Abolitionists and the British Government as responsible. They blamed the Abolitionists for inciting the slaves to rebellion. The governor, the Earl of Mulgrave, described the colonist's wrath in a letter to Lord Goderich.

> Yet in spite of all these reasons for moderation on their part they have shown such a reckless determination to defy the British Parliament, that it is quite impossible to hope that any measure in furtherance of the objects upon which England is so determined, can ever emerge spontaneously from them.

The objectives of the British Government, whether amelioration proposals or rules of law and order, were quickly put aside. Slaves were relentlessly shot down by both regular soldiers and militiamen. More than 100 Negroes were hanged, scores or others were severely flogged, and missionaries became the scapegoats of the white leaders. William Knibb and other Baptists were charged with inciting rebellion and jailed. Slurs in the local press against missionaries were common. "Ruffians," "preaching miscreants," and "vagabonding reverends" were common labels. The most vicious result of the fear, tension, and mistrust that seized the white population was the formation of the Colonial Church Union, which actively sought to persecute the missionaries. This Jamaican equivalent of the Ku Klux Klan rode through the countryside burning Methodist and Baptist chapels and the homes of missionaries. A value of 25,000 pounds was placed on the damaged property. The attempt on the part of local authorities to convict Knibb and his fellow Baptists of treason proved abortive, and at length they were reluctantly freed.

Meanwhile, the Colonial Church Union gained strength throughout 1832. Branches formed in each parish effectively checked Wesleyan and Baptist activities. A pledge made by every member "to obey promptly and implicitly all constitutional orders" of the union smacked of the worst kind of extremism. Official circles in England looked none too kindly on these developments, particularly after Knibb and a fellow missionary, Thomas Burchell, returned to England to tell the long, horrible tale. The British Government was soon convinced that the union was potentially a revolutionary organization, especially after the Earl of Mulgrave reported that some of its members proposed that Jamaica cut her ties with Britain and join forces with the United States or Spain. To support Mulgrave and considerably strengthen his forces the King, on the advice of the government, issued a proclamation in December, 1832, which was promulgated by the governor in January, 1833. The Royal Rescript, as it came to be called, upheld religious toleration in the islands and ordered the dissolution of the Colonial Church Union. Armed with the backing of the highest authority in the Empire, that of the King, Mulgrave moved swiftly to squelch the power of the union. Persons connected with it were removed from positions of prestige and power in government. To conciliate the colonials, the British Government offered an advance of 500,000 pounds in exchequer bills to the Jamaican treasury to be used by those who had suffered damages during the trouble. These measures achieved the desired results: By April, 1833, Governor Mulgrave could safely report that the Colonial Church Union was "quite suppressed." A Parliamentary grant of some 12,000 pounds made at that same time enabled the missionaries to rebuild their chapels so they could proceed with their educational work with a minimum delay.

A committee of the Assembly appointed to inquire into "the cause of, and the injury sustained by, the slave rebellion of 1831" reported that "the primary and most powerful cause" of the rebellion "arose from an evil excitement created in the minds of our slaves generally by the unceasing and unconstitutional interference of His Majesty's ministers with our local legislature." After the British Government, the Assembly committee blamed "the false and wicked reports of the Anti-Slavery Society industriously circulated, by the aid of the press, throughout this island as well as the British Empire" as a cause of the trouble. Missionaries, too, came in for a share of criticism; the report told of the

> preaching and teaching of the religious sects called Baptists, Wesleyans, Methodists, and Moravians which had the effect of producing in the minds of the slaves a belief that they could not serve both a spiritual and temporal master; thereby occasioning them to resist the lawful authority of their temporal masters under the delusion of rendering themselves more acceptable to a spiritual master.

Rebukes of the kind the Assembly inserted in its report could not be tolerated by the Abolitionist movement in England.

Experience had taught the Abolitionists that "the slow and silent course of temperate but authoritative admonition" (as the Colonial Secretary, The Earl of Bathurst, described the amelioration program), led nowhere. The system of slavery had proved incapable of being reformed; it therefore had to be abolished. Through the 1820's the leaders of the antislavery movement had been preparing the British people for this step by exposing the nature of the slave system, which they characterized as "not only beyond knowledge but beyond belief." Established in every city and town, large and small, were branches of the Society for the Mitigation and Gradual Abolition of Slavery Throughout the British Dominions, whose members disseminated information and organized petitions to be sent to Parliament in support of Abolitionist policies and programs. By 1830, antislavery forces had been successful in building heavy public support for their programs. In May, 1830, at a mass meeting, a resolution demanding that slavery be abolished "at the earliest possible period" was amended to read "immediately" and carried by a storm of applause. Further support came in 1831, when word reached England of the persecution of missionaries in Jamaica. "I have seen congregated masses . . . burning and almost raving with indignation of the system," was one man's description of an audience's reactions to a speech by William Knibb, the most famous of the persecuted missionaries. Leading newspapers in England, previously hostile to the antislavery cause, changed their position to one of support for the Abolitionists. In the churches and cathedrals throughout the land, sermons were preached in sympathy with the movement not only by Baptists and Methodists but by leading Anglican ministers, many of whom had only recently joined the Abolitionists' ranks. Sensitive to this renewed public support, the Abolitionists led a new assault on Parliament, not with arms but with petitions—one had almost a million and a half signatures—demanding immediate emancipation.

They also increased their activities among the public at large. A "speakers' bureau" known as the Agency Committee was organized by men who were imbued with a fiery vision of the righteousness of their cause. Their moral indignation and religious zeal won the hearts and souls of their pious audiences. The West India Committee, representing the planters and merchants, sent its own speakers into the countryside on a counter-offensive. The West India Committee was well financed and organized, but its spokesmen only served to aid the cause of emancipation; their defenses paled before the sins of slavery as portrayed by the Abolitionist orators. Henry Brougham described the mood of the times when he said that the people of Britain were "once more awake—awake to the conditions of Negro slavery. The same indignation kindles in the bosom of the same people, the same cloud is gathering which annihilated the slave trade." Stephen Lushington later analyzed the influence of the Abolitionists: "The hold of Wilberforce and the antislavery movement on the solid middle class in town and country was a thing entirely beautiful—English to the best and something new in the world."

An aroused public opinion in Great Britain demanded change, and Lord Goderich, the Foreign Secretary, in a circular dispatch to the governors of the colonies in the West Indies warned them in December, 1831, that concessions would have to be made. Not to do so would ultimately affect the political fortunes of the colonies. He deplored the continuance on the part of the West Indian colonists "of that insensibility to the influence of public opinion in the mother country by which they are daily bringing themselves more and more within the dangers of calamities far more grievous than any which can be caused by commercial reverses."

Some of the West Indian planters saw the handwriting on the wall. If emancipation was to become a reality, they were determined to salvage their investments in the slave system. A petition of planters and others interested in property in the West Indies was presented to the House of Commons at the end of 1830. It demanded that "any measure to be adopted should be on the principle of the fullest compensation for any loss or depreciation of property it might occasion."

In May, 1832, Commons adopted a motion presented by Buxton and amended by Lord Althrop that a committee be appointed to draw up plans "for the purpose of effecting the extinction of slavery throughout the British dominions, at the earliest period compatible with the safety of all classes in the colonies." On June 9, 1832, Lord Goderich, in a circular dispatch, informed the West Indian colonists that free labor would soon replace forced labor and that this would be effected "without any shock or convulsion." As a foreshadowing of things to come, the government freed all Crown slaves in August, 1832. And at the end of 1832, as a precautionary measure, Lord Goderich began assembling a list of proposals to create a government plan for emancipation of the slaves. Early in 1833 he asked the governor of Jamaica, the Earl of Mulgrave, for his comments on the scheme he had devised. The perspective and evaluation of someone directly involved in the day-to-day life of the colonies would be of utmost importance. Of all the proposals in Goderich's scheme—including immediate emancipation and compensation in the form of a 15-million-pound loan—the one Mulgrave most strenuously objected to was the proposal to allow each island to make up and pass its own emancipation act. The governor pointed out to Goderich that the reception given to emancipation would be far from cordial in the Assembly, for it was composed of men "from the management of a troublesome and precarious species of property." Because they were not planters and had no serious stake in the island, "the moment emancipation on any terms takes place, their occupation is gone." Mulgrave still further analyzed Jamaica's reaction to emancipation in terms of how it would affect the other classes. Neither the yeomen with their small freeholds; nor the tradesmen employed in different estates; nor the general storekeepers on the coast, who sold little luxuries; nor the Jews, who formed a "very influencial class," would support the emancipation idea. Mulgrave also favored compensation in the form of a gift rather than a loan. For Britain, emancipation would have to be "an expensive indulgence of good feeling." The principle of immediate emancipation was also questioned. The governor favored progressive rather than immediate emancipation, so that the slaves might share in the costs of emancipation and have a direct role in obtaining their freedom.

On May 14, 1833, a select committee established by Parliament in May, 1832, recommended to the House of Commons that "immediate and effectual measures be taken for the entire abolition of slavery throughout the colonies." On that same day, Edward Stanley, who had recently replaced Lord Goderich as Colonial Secretary, presented the government's emancipation program to Commons. It called for freedom for the slaves within a year's time and a twelve-year apprenticeship thereafter, during which the wages of the Negroes would be collected by the government as reimbursement for a 15-million-pound loan granted the slave-owners as compensation. Slave children under six years of age were to be freed immediately, as they were not economically valuable property.

Both sides in the dispute sought changes in the government plan. The proposals evoked lively debates among the government, the West Indians, and the antislavery forces. While the planters approved of a long apprenticeship period and of having the Negroes buy their own freedom, they opposed putting their monetary compensation in the form of a loan and clamored for an outright grant in lieu of the proposed advance. The antislavery forces behemently attacked the long apprenticeship and self-liberation through purchase. Radicals within the group were against payment of any kind, whether a loan or an outright grant. For a while it seemed that there would be no emancipation act in 1833 at all. Wearisome debates dragged on for several weeks. The antislavery forces worked in the background, organizing a United Committee to represent both provincial deputies and metropolitan committees in meetings with Members of Parliament to devise strategy for securing a better measure. Their efforts and Buxton's strong commitment to compensation (despite the disapproval of some leading Abolitionists) brought forth a compromise scheme. The final proposals included immediate freedom for the slaves as of one year after the passing of the act; their conversion into apprentices for a period of six years for field hands and four years for all others; the outright grant of 20 million pounds of compensation money to the planters; and a provision for 100 special magistrates appointed and supported by the King to be sent out to the colonies to insure proper treatment of the slaves. Finally, the law stipulated that each colony would draft and enact its own emancipation act, which would have to be acceptable to the British Government before compensation money could be given to that colony.

With the compromise worked out, it did not take long for emancipation to become a reality. On August 28, 1833, just a month before the death of Wilberforce, slavery was abolished forever in the British Empire.

Jamaica was among the first to send back its law, not to ensure speedy justice for the slaves but to get monetary compensation for the slave-owners more quickly. It was drafted, according to the historian Paul Knapland, with "the purpose of getting the maximum of slave compensation money with the minimum of observance in letter and spirit of the rules fixed by the Imperial Government." On January 31, 1834, Colonial Under Secretary James Stephen issued a long report on the deficiencies of the law. His greatest concern was the law's failure to give the Negroes safeguards for their rights as free men. Stephen strongly recommended disallowance. Not prepared to go that far, the Colonial Office sent Stephen's suggestions for amending the act back to Jamaica. By the close of 1834, the proposals had not been adopted. To Stephen, this was proof that the aim of the planters was merely to "re-establish under the shelter of new titles, the offices and much of the authority which are peculiar characteristics of slavery."

The emancipation act drawn up by the Jamaican legislature was but the first of many examples of the inability of the local population to put aside past attitudes and prejudices. The ruling classes of Jamaica were being asked to put aside their deep involvement and lifelong connections with slavery as an institution and to take a drastically different view of the relationship between themselves and the Negroes. Jamaican soil had never nurtured mutual respect between the races, and the ingredients for its growth were not there in significant quantities. Yet the British Government left wholly in the hands of these men the details of implementing a decision they had never made or been consulted about. It was the House of Assembly, as representatives of free Jamaicans, that was supposed to supply the leadership to reconstruct the new social order. Although on August 1, 1833, the old order was officially and legally dead, its values and attitudes would remain very much alive. And thus what W. E. H. Lecky called one of the "three or four perfectly virtuous pages comprised in the history of nations" was inserted in the history book of the British Empire. One chapter—bondage—was forever closed and a new one—freedom —was just beginning.

# 6. The Fate of the Freed Man

The newly emancipated slaves would find in the legislative establishment neither philosophical vision nor practical programs to ease the burdens they acquired with freedom. Masters remained masters and continued to insist that they would retain their all-powerful position. An Assembly composed for the most part of those who had been the direct beneficiaries of slavery was not inclined to help their former chattels by enacting beneficial social legislation.

To help the Negro, it was necessary to extend and enlarge the lines of communication between the masses and the elite groups. Instead, they were strained, truncated or completely ruptured. The self-righteous former slave owners stubbornly clung to the belief that the Negro was best off as a servant of the higher orders. Thus Jamaica was unable—because of its unwillingness—to cope with social change.

Most needed was a program that would provide for the formal education of the masses. Experience had shown that Jamaica and its sister colonies would not take the initiative in this area, so the Abolitionists had succeeded in having included in the act of emancipation a provision authorizing the British Government to "defray any such expense" as would be incurred in providing "for the religious and moral education of the Negro population to be emancipated." This resolution was warmly supported by British public opinion, which had come to recognize that emancipation would be meaningless unless it

121

was accompanied with education for the former slaves. Only through education could they learn to live by the principles that guided Christian society in England.

The system of mass education common in the Western world today had no counterpart in the nineteenth century. Even if Jamaica had looked to England for its institutional patterning, it would have found little guidance for the concept of mass compulsory education, as this principle was not yet accepted by the British people. Yet colonial officials held that, as the conditions of England and of the colonies were different, their needs were different. Thus, compulsory education for the masses was promoted in the colonies. This departure from tradition was explained in terms of the special circumstances in Jamaica. "Whatever objections may exist in more advanced societies," a dispatch from the Colonial Office in 1836 stated, "to the principle of compulsory education, they can have no place in reference to a colony in which the great mass of people have just emerged from slavery. . . . In such a case, it will be a substitution of the name for the substance of liberty if we should not hold ourselves bound to acknowledge and respect amongst the Negroes the freedom to choose between knowledge and ignorance."

An annual grant of 30,000 pounds was provided for five years to promote education in the West Indies. Besides the government grant, additional funds were made available from the charitable bequest made in 1690 by Lady Mico for the purpose of redeeming Christians captured and enslaved by the Barbary pirates. The money had not been used and the Abolitionists were instrumental in having the bequest reactivated for Negro education in the West Indies.

The staggering task of educating the large numbers of newly freed men was left largely to the Baptists, Methodists, Wesleyans, Moravians, and others who had been most active as missionaries among the slaves. The Church of England was responsible as well, but it had not been closely involved with the slaves, and its representatives in the colonies did not shoulder the major burden. It fell to those denominations that had actively proselytized among the slaves long before there was any prospect of their gaining freedom. The grants from the government were given directly to these groups rather than to the local government. Once again, the Abolitionists, doubtful of getting any meaningful leadership from the local ruling population, had succeeded in circumventing its authority.

With the ideal set clearly and forcefully before them, the missionaries planned ambitious education programs. The British Government grants were to provide two-thirds of the costs, while one-third was supplied by the missionary societies from their own funds. For the first two years, the government grants were earmarked for the construction of school buildings. The details of the curriculum were left to the missionary organizations. Instruction was to be on a full-time basis for children and on a part-time basis for adults. The curriculum was to include the three R's—reading, writing and arithmetic—and also instruction in the principles of religion. No provision was made for any kind of manual, mechanical, or technical education. Concerned with the spiritual rather than the material, the missionary organizations unwittingly laid the basis for the negative attitude toward "vocational" education that was, until modern times, characteristic of the Jamaican outlook.

It was not long before the missionary societies realized that they had taken on a financial burden too great for them to bear. Although the British Government contributed to the construction of buildings, all other expenses—salaries, books, and equipment—had to be met by the societies. The costs were so high that, in the words of a report of the Church Missionary Society, they could not be met "without seriously interfering with the just claims of other missions on our resources." Even after the imperial government directed that one-third of the annual grants be allocated for teachers' salaries, the missionary societies, because of their worldwide commitments, were still forced to cut back their operations in the West Indies.

After a few years, the British Government also cut down its grants. The amounts allotted for education were reduced after 1838 and completely terminated in 1845. Responsibility now rested with the local government to continue the work started with the help of England. A dispatch from the Colonial Office to the governor of Jamaica explained that "it was in the interest of all classes" for the task of education to be assigned to the colonists themselves, and the British Government expressed confidence that "it will engage their anxious attention."

The Jamaica legislature failed to turn its attention, anxious or otherwise, toward establishing a well-organized educational system on the island. Whenever possible, the colonists and their elected representatives sought to prevent any bridging of the chasm that separated the freed man from free society. After the termination of the grants, the schools in Jamaica were left to support themselves. Little was contributed by the Jamaican Goverment to the upkeep of the schools or to teachers' salaries. Nor did the legislature provide the leadership needed for an effective public educational system. The Board of Education, established in 1845, was given meager financial support. The Anglican Church, although most educational work was carried on by the other Christian denominations, received two-thirds of the small annual allotments made by the Assembly. Even more serious was the shortage of qualified personnel to work directly with the Negroes; the Jamaican Government did nothing to provide for the training of teachers. The only teacher training college in Jamaica was established by the Lady Mico Charity and was supported wholly by private funds. The majority of the native teachers who were recruited into the schools came from the 526 teachers trained in Mico College between 1835 and 1855. The Baptists, recognizing the dire need for more teachers, established, on a meager budget, Calabar College.

With little support from local government and limited contributions from abroad, the schools had to charge tuition to meet their operating expenses. As a result, a large majority of Negroes were excluded from the classroom. If lack of funds was not a sufficient cause to keep children away from school, the failure of the curriculum to include courses related to the practical problems of everyday life tended to discourage attendance. Droughts, hurricanes, and other natural disasters would often keep children away. In 1864 it was estimated that only one out of five school-age children was receiving full-time or part-time instruction on the island. Thirty years after emancipation, only 13 per cent of the adult population could read and write.

The vast majority of those who held the reins of power in Jamaica felt that the Negro should stay ignorant. That way, their expectations would not be great and they could still be exploited for the advantage of the few. What was most feared was that an educated Negro would have a high level of aspiration, which would make him discontented with his low position in society. The planters were ready to blame whatever the former slaves did wrong on the schools, especially as the schools closest to the masses were run by Baptist and Wesleyan missionaries who, many believed, preached a creed of insubordination to those in authority. Had not emancipation itself come about in large measure because of the campaign waged in England by sectarian groups? As a result, traditional authority had been destroyed. Because the schools established when freedom was declared were run by those associated with emancipation, they should not be supported. As one planter put it, the plantations would be productive "if religion would only protect agriculture and education and not unfit the peasantry for labor."

Social action was also needed to promote sanitation, hygiene, and other public health standards. In this area too, the Assembly did little. Sewage facilities were absent in the large towns, and systematic garbage disposal was unknown. Heaps of refuse were left to decay in the streets in the poorer quarters, while in the prosperous neighborhoods slaves carried open tubs to the waterfront and simply dumped them into the sea. Mosquito-breeding swamps were everywhere, with the result that malaria and yellow fever killed thousands. In 1850–51, cholera raged in Jamaica, killing 40,000 to 50,000. Smallpox followed the cholera, causing considerably more desolation.

Prevention of disease requires, besides forethought and planning, some sensitivity to the living conditions of the people. Jamaica had no food inspection or regulation of the water supply, and poor housing was chronic. With the end of slavery, Kingston and Spanish Town were overrun with squatters who lived in overcrowded shacks. As many as ten people might live in a dwelling eight or nine feet square with a thatched roof that was a magnet for infected mosquitoes. Estate workers lived in similar circumstances, hence the hired laborers, whether in town or in country, suffered the greatest losses from disease.

There was no organized medical service. During the period of slavery, doctors had been hired by estates and paid for every slave treated. Makeshift hospital facilities were also provided for serious illness. Health care was a business expense necessary to keep the tools of production—the slaves—in good shape so that they could perform well. With freedom, the planter was no longer so obligated. Doctors who had been assured a steady income from estate work could no longer depend on it. As a result, more and more doctors left the island, and it soon became apparent that the welfare of the middle and upper classes was also being affected. To keep some doctors on the island, the government enacted the Dispensary Act of 1846, which gave doctors a stipend of 40 pounds. The public was invited to subscribe in advance for the medical services, thus giving the doctor a guaranteed number of patients. It was hoped that some doctors, assured in advance of this income, would remain on the island. Nevertheless, the number of doctors rapidly declined from 200 in 1830 to 50 in 1860.

Only in the towns could doctors secure an adequate number of people who had the means to subscribe in advance. Though officially the government fee required the medical practitioner to run a public dispensary, obviously it was the private patient who came first. Rural areas, for the most part, had no medical personnel whatsoever, as there were not nearly enough people who could afford to subscribe in advance for medical service, and dispensaries rarely were opened there.

After the cholera epidemic of 1851, the British Government sent Dr. Gavin Milroy out to Jamaica to investigate its cause. His evaluation of the local government's efforts in the public health field was applicable to all areas where government intervention was needed. "The colonists, if left to themselves," the conscientious doctor declared, "will do little and that little badly."

The Jamaica legislature did little to help the Negroes and

proceeded, in the late 1840's and throughout the 1850's, to enact legislation that was in fact detrimental to their welfare and freedom. Of all the former slaves, those who had become independent farmers were most hated, and much of the legislation was specifically aimed against them. Boats, canoes, horses, and cattle that were used to bring their produce to market or to work their land were taxed at rates that favored the large planter over the "small settler." A new law broadened the definition of praedial larceny to include not only the theft of cultivated crops but the gathering, collecting, or picking of fruits and berries that grew wild. Still another law gave the local authorities the right to kill any stray goats and pigs that were found wandering away from their owners. The Jamaican planters and their allies were strongly opposed to an independent Negro peasantry, for they wanted a large pool of laborers available to work the estates. The greater the pool, the lower the wages. Thus they sought to squeeze the peasant out of existence.

Nor did they want him to share in the political life of the island. In 1841, paid-up taxes was made a condition for voting, and early in the 1850's the Assembly enacted an "hereditaments tax" of twelve shillings a year on freeholders whose land was valued at six pounds or more. This tax represented on the average 10 per cent of the annual income of the small settlers. The hereditaments tax, the poll tax, and the stamp tax, all of which had to be paid as a prerequisite for voting, effectively excluded the Negroes from the franchise. Similar laws to limit the franchise had been disallowed by the British Government in 1834 and 1836. By 1850, colonial officials in effect had given the Jamaican oligarchy a free hand, and it could call for support upon other segments of white society. A common fear and distrust of the Negro majority consolidated the white minority. Antagonisms between planter and merchant, city and country, northside and southside, were always submerged when it came to dealing with the Negro masses. In 1863, out of a population of 300,000, including 50,000 freeholders who met the property (but not the tax payment) qualifications for voting, only 1,457 exercised the franchise.

If the masses were to be uplifted, only those who thought of them as wholly human could reach them. The missionaries were best able to understand the shortcomings of the newly emancipated Negro.

In Jamaica, it was the Baptists who took the most active role in working with the former slaves on the island. They, along with the other sects, such as the Moravians and the Wesleyans, willingly and wholeheartedly accepted the task of leading what was thought would be a "great awakening," not only in the religious values of the Negro but also in every other aspect of his character. Not free from the racial prejudices of the day, the missionaries saw the Negro character in a negative light. It was made up, according to one, of a combination of "cunning, craft and suspicion" with "dark passions." Unlike many others in the West Indies, however, they did not think the Negro was beyond redemption, as they believed that all men were equal before God, regardless of race or color. Under their zealous leadership, he would be, in the words of William Knibb, transformed into "a noble, manly, and independent, yet patient and submissive spirit." The missionaries, in the process of converting the slaves into Christians, tried to teach them how to live with the society at large. This was indeed difficult to accomplish. It required zeal and an ability to surmount frustration; only those with a strong sense of "calling" were well equipped for the undertaking.

The former slave had many emotional scars as a result of the deprivations of his past, and these were not easily erased. The slave had lived in a Hobbesian world. At any time, he could be punished at will by those in authority. Early in life, he began to learn to adapt to this situation. Subversion of authority through lying, cheating, and stealing was common. These character traits were not well suited for the moral life prescribed by the missionaries. Many conflicts developed between them and the former slaves. The preachers, not fully understanding slavery's impact on the personality, could not quite understand why the Negroes would not shed their past. It was not easy to slough off the thick residue of accumulated habits acquired early in life by the slave child. In 1837, a teacher who worked with the former slaves in Jamaica and understood their problems commented that "the ignorance and evil which still exists so extensively amongst the young may clearly be traced to past neglect. The fountain of life is deeply tainted."

Communication with the former slaves was thus difficult, as the missionary spoke an unfamiliar "language," not easily understood. When the missionaries preached parental responsibility, it was an alien idea, while the concept of a Christian God was too abstract. Methods used by zealous men were not always suitable to translate the ideas of free society into terms the former slave could comprehend. Campaigns were launched against customs considered un-Christian, such as concubinage, drumming, dancing, and sabbath-breaking. In the hope of promoting permanent unions, marriages were performed *en masse*. Illegitimacy was condemned, and some ministers refused to baptize offspring born out of wedlock. The minister brought his message in his varied role as teacher, religious leader, and personal adviser. But even in his many roles he was often ineffective in changing all the ways of the former slaves.

Of all the Christian denominations in Jamaica at the time, the Baptists achieved the best results. Sir Charles Metcalfe, governor of Jamaica in the 1830's, remarked that they had a "greater influence than any other sect in the island." This was largely due to the leadership of William Knibb, who had great faith in the newly freed man. As he confessed, "to assist them in the attainment of their civil and religious liberties, is to me a source of pleasure only surpassed by the proclaiming of that mercy by which they are freed forever." To develop their potential, Knibb felt that the Negroes should be independent economically. If the Negro was to become a self-respecting man and a good Christian, he had to be free from the plantation— cut loose from the ties that bound him to those who would keep him dependent and ignorant. Toward this end, Knibb established the "free villages"—communities of former slaves who were settled as independent farmers on the land. Under Baptist leadership, these villages became self-governing, with the members responsible not only to themselves but to the rest of the community as well. Each village built its own chapel, school house, and community meeting hall and raised its own funds to support its own church and minister, school and teacher. Between 1837 and 1847 almost 200 villages were established. Knibb appropriately labeled these settlements the "germ of a noble free peasantry."

The creation of the free village system went hand in hand with Knibb's belief that only a native ministry could truly serve the needs of the people. While the Anglicans, Wesleyans, Moravians, and others thought of a local church under the leadership of English ministers, Knibb and the Baptists directed their efforts toward establishing a native leadership. Despite the opposition of the other Christian denominations working in Jamaica, Knibb went ahead with his program, bringing into the church many of the native religious leaders who were best able to communicate with the Negroes on their own terms and in their own language. Knibb established a theological college to train them in the Baptist tradition. A further radical move by Knibb was the changing of the status of the Baptists in Jamaica from a missionary outpost to a wholly local "national" church. In other areas of social action, the Baptists encouraged the plantation worker to hold out for higher wages and to support candidates who favored the peasantry. As a result, the Baptists had the largest following on the island—34,000. There were sixteen English-born ministers and a host of native preachers to run the thirty-one chapels established by the denomination.

Despite the often intensive educational campaigns conducted by the various missionary orders, the gaps between the slave culture and the Christian culture could not be closed. By the 1860's it was increasingly clear to all religious denominations that African mysticism was still very much a part of the religious views of the Negro. Two cults that had been outlawed under slavery—Myalism and Obeah—flourished. Obeah was essentially a private experience and Myalism took the form of open outbreaks of hysteria among fairly large groups of individuals who claimed to be seized by spirits. The obeah man continued to possess magical powers to ward off spirits or to bring them to people to do evil. The obeah man, it was believed, could call off or summon the spirits when called upon in times of fear or when revenge was sought.

The Myal religion developed to counter the obeah men. It claimed to remove the curse of the obeah through counterspells evoked by other spirits. Myal men had their own particular procedures and trances to ward off the spirits and were called upon whenever bad luck or illness was attributed to some unleashing of a wicked spirit by an obeah man. Dances and songs common to the secret societies of West Africa were employed in the rituals.

Though these cults continued to exist, the missionary teachings were not completely rejected. A curious blend of Africanisms and Christian religious practices evolved. Preaching and prophesying entered into Myalism, much to the horror of the organized groups. An evangelical revival sponsored by Christian denominations in Jamaica and designed to convert the masses to a legitimate form of Christianity took place in 1860. It proved a failure when Myal practices invaded the conversion ceremonies. The leaders of the Afro-Christian cults used the opportunity offered by the revival to recruit adherents.

A major adaptation from the Christian world was the belief that the Bible represented a major spiritual force that should be respected, worshiped, and feared. Believing in a world in which spirits predominated, the Negro easily adopted the fundamentalist faith that represented everything in the Bible as true. To the Negro, the Bible was justification for the importance of the spiritual world. The authenticity of spirit communications and possession could not be doubted after he had read or been told the Biblical stories.

Common to Christian teachings was the belief in supernatural intervention, and this went along well with the Negro's explanation of the real world as motivated by spirits. When sickness struck, it was attributed to a "bad" spirit. When a dear one was lost, it was because the spirit of God had come to get him. Revivalist meetings were openly embraced by the Negro, for to him they were wondrous occasions for warding off the spirits that would cause him harm or bad luck. Prophetic visions from the Bible were absorbed into the religious experience of the Jamaican revivalists. Native preachers, such as Alexander Bedward in the 1920's, who claimed to be the incarnation of Christ, promised salvation and freedom from the evil spirits that plagued man. Bible in hand, the native revivalist would claim to shut out the spirit when he closed the Good Book. Whooping, hollering, screaming, mystically clothed figures, and faint drum beats all added to the mysterious atmosphere of the revival meeting, which fed the hopes of men who wanted help in a world they found so harsh.

At the outset of emancipation, before the difficulties became apparent, missionaries had actively sought to bridge the chasm dividing Negro religion from their own. The ranks of organized religion were swollen with new members, and the missionaries thought they were well on the way to converting the heathen. The constant and continued appearance of African mystical beliefs, coupled with an absence of perceptible change in the character and habits of the former slaves, transformed optimism into pessimism. The missionaries found themselves alienated from the vast majority of Negroes in the same way as the elite middle-class colored and whites were.

The 1860 revival was final proof to many missionaries that they had not succeeded in transforming the great majority of heathen slaves into Christians. Relinquishing the hope of converting the masses, they too came to feel, as did the elite groups of society, that the distance between themselves and the masses could not be bridged. Except for the Baptists, who had begun to fashion their own native ministry and whose objectives were tailored to the realities of the situation, the Christian denominations curtailed their missionary programs.

Because of a reliance on magic and other mystical experiences to explain and cope with the realities of life, a dual set of values or alternative value systems became part of the Jamaican Negro's experience. His knowledge of the world came not only from the educational system, which was middle class in origin and ideas, but also from the worlds of miracle-working, faith healing, spiritual trances, and sorcery. Neither value system could claim the total commitment of the Jamaican Negro, but it is obvious that he was more at home with the world of the supernatural. Confusion and conflict between the two systems weakened the individual's effectiveness in areas outside his cultural milieu.

The events of the post-emancipation decades fostered the development of a set of common behavioral norms that were to become characteristic of Jamaican peasants and agricultural workers. They were described more than a century later by an English psychologist, Madeline Kerr, in her book *Personality and Conflict in Jamaica* (1952):

> The Jamaican personality tends to shift the blame for misfortune to other forces. Thus the individual himself never offends—it is always someone else who does something to him or "puts something on him." Disaster is never self-caused but always emanates from some external agency which most unfairly causes the trouble. From childhood on the child has never been taught to think causally; neither the significant adults in his life nor the school has instructed him on the variety of skills and methods associated with the physical and emotional manipulation of reality.

The plantation system and its institutions had left their mark on the freed men. The cultural traits that had been embedded in many generations were to a considerable degree self-perpetuating. In 1860, a local official commented:

> They have been cast adrift, and like gulf weeds float hither and thither without any fixed governing principle or acknowledged plan to meliorate their intellectual state, or elevate them one step above their African progenitors.

To the observer who possesses European values, the Jamaican peasant would thus often appear to be in a different world. Indeed, this was the judgment of the local elites of yesterday, if not today.

# 7. The Surrender
# of Self-Government, 1833–65

The record of the Jamaica legislature during the trying decades that immediately followed emancipation was not a distinguished one. The leadership needed to improve the economic and social conditions of the island was lacking and the stagnation of economic life was accepted as inevitable. All ills that befell society were considered by the oligarchy to be the results of emancipation and the decline of the sugar industry, both beyond its control. Obstruction, vacillation, and inaction marked the conduct of the legislature. The elite groups of Jamaica were expressing through the Assembly their anger toward government policies imposed upon them without their consent.

Great Britain and its colonial officials sought to direct Jamaica toward a dynamic course, but the "popular" branch of government, whenever it could, turned a deaf ear to its directives. Governors sent out to Jamaica during this period faced fierce battles with the Assembly when they sought to implement the directives of Her Majesty's Government. "Defiance" was the watchword of the politically articulate groups in Jamaica, and on many occasions the Assembly acted exactly opposite to the course advocated in England.

During the apprenticeship period, the Assembly had passed a resolution that reiterated its view of its own power. On May 31, 1836, it resolved:

> It is the undoubted birthright of Her Majesty's subjects of this island to have and enjoy all and every of the same rights, privileges and immunities as their fellow subjects in England, and that no

law or enactment affecting their lives or fortunes, their peace or happiness, is of any force or effect or can legally be acted upon by any authority in this island, unless such an enactment shall have been sanctioned by the people themselves through their representatives in Assembly.

This position was as old as representative government in Jamaica, and the tradition would not die.

The first major clash between the British Government and the Jamaican Assembly took place immediately following the abolition of apprenticeship in 1838. To insure meaningful prison reform, Parliament enacted legislation permitting the governors of the island to take over the management of penal institutions. The law gave them the power to legislate by proclamation without having to seek the consent of the local legislature. The Jamaican Assembly considered this an infringement of its constitutional rights. Prisons were an internal matter, and the power of the local legislature to deal with them could not be supplanted by an order of another legislature residing many thousands of miles away.

Though deprived of a voice on the issue of emancipation, the Jamaican legislature would not stand idly by on the prison reform issue. Here it would make a stand to retrieve its rights. Passive resistance was the technique employed. A month before the West Indies Prisons Law was enacted, the legislature had warned Parliament that, if it passed, "the popular branch of the legislature of Jamaica will cease to exist, and if any taxes are demanded, they must be levied at the point of a sword." The Assembly asked, "Can you make us do what we really don't want to do?" Its answer, in effect, was "no." Thus, in September, 1838, the Assembly ceased to conduct legislative business and refused to provide the funds to support public institutions, including the militia.

This deliberate defiance was met in England with severe measures. The Whig government led by Melbourne proposed to suspend the legislative powers of the Jamaican Assembly for five years, during which period the governor and his Advisory Council would carry on all legislative functions. Opposition to this measure was so strong in Parliament that the suspension of the Jamaica constitution was carried by only five votes in May of 1839. Support for a governmental resolution by such a small majority was tantamount to defeat, and Melbourne resigned. Thus, the Jamaican legislature achieved its purpose. It had successfully defied the British Government and had brought on the "bedchamber crisis."

The "bedchamber crisis" was so named because each time a new government came to power in England the monarch had to accept the recommendations of the new Prime Minister and replace the ladies of her household. To avoid this, Queen Victoria reappointed Melbourne. Restored to office, Melbourne nevertheless had to yield to Parliamentary opinion and rescinded the legislation stripping the Jamaican legislature of its power.

The "bedchamber crisis" was a test of the ability of the British Government to overrule a colonial government. The outcome was a victory for the colonies. Having failed to overrule a local legislature by a Parliamentary act, the authorities in England could not impose a program of domestic reform on Jamaica or any other colony that was ruled by a "representative" government. Thereafter, until the House of Assembly was abolished in 1865, the British Government might demand, but it was the local legislature that would ultimately decide. The British Government had found it in its power to break the iron-clad shackles of slavery but not the strength to make the social revolution that could—and should—have occurred. Successive British Governments, desiring peaceful relations with Jamaica, gradually gave up their vigorous support and promotion of programs that could have helped the newly freed man. When educational grants to the West Indies were abolished in 1845, Lord John Russell, Secretary of State for the Colonies, explained that "it must be left to the local legislature to consider the best mode of raising the necessary funds for public education." What was true for public education was true for everything else. So the oligarchy that made the policies in Jamaica could without further restraint reject legislative programs designed to improve the lot of the former slave.

In another area of reform, the British Government also took the path of least resistence. Judicial reform in all the West

Indian colonies had been strongly promoted by colonial officials, but when the local authorities in Jamaica refused to carry out the reform measures no pressure was put upon them to comply with official policy. Amicable relations were to be maintained at any cost. Sir Charles Metcalfe, sent out to Jamaica as governor in September, 1839, recognized this and requested that the Colonial Office not disallow legislation directed against the Negroes. Both Sir John Russell and James Stephen concurred. After the "bedchamber crisis" of 1839, this was the course of British-Jamaican relations for a decade.

The policy adopted by Britain in its relations with Jamaica represented much more than acquiescence. It was an example of the changing relationship between Britain and its colonial empire that was evolving during this period. Freedom from control was the "spirit of the age." Colonies, the fruits of power in one age, were the dregs in another. Trade was still fundamental to economic life, but trade with the entire world, not restricted to colonies. After the Corn Laws were repealed in 1846, the last vestige of the old mercantile system of preferential treatment to colonies was gone. England, by virtue of its strong industrial position, would supply the world with manufactured goods, while all nations would supply it with primary products and raw materials. "Freedom" was defined as self-help, self-development and self-government. Every colony, to paraphrase the poet, would be master of its fate and captain of its soul. The colonists, like other members of Her Majesty's dominions, had to look out for their own best interests. As the British Government discovered, for Jamaica this meant obstructionist acts against what was deemed unfair colonial policy.

When the sugar industry was deprived of preferential treatment in 1848, the Assembly boldly gambled as it had in 1838. By openly defying Britain, it hoped to get the preferential duties restored. Once again, public expenditure was the tool. In the summer of 1849, it adopted a "retrenchment" policy that considerably reduced the salaries of government officials, including the governor. No new appropriations were made for police and other public services. As a memorandum of the legislature explained, the island was in an "impoverished condition" with its agricultural economy in ruins. Consequently, Jamaica could no longer meet its expenses.

Learning a lesson from the past, the British Government did not answer in kind. Instead, it made a minor concession by extending the deadline for the abolition of the preferential tariffs to 1854. Glad for the extension, as it was hoping a Conservative government would come to power in the next general election of 1852 and restore the duties, the Jamaican Assembly ceased its obstructionism and voted for part of the annual revenues needed to support public services. Rum duties, however, were allowed to lapse, so that the public treasury lost more than 50,000 pounds.

The calculations of the Assembly proved false. When the Conservatives came to power in 1852 they did not re-establish a preferential tariff on sugar. Again, the Assembly went on a legislative "strike" as thorough as that of 1838. The British Government took practical measures to meet the problem. A large loan at low interest rates was offered to the Jamaican Government in reply to the Assembly's "impoverishment" plea. The loan was contingent upon the Assembly's revitilizing and reorganizing the Jamaican Government. Sir Henry Barky, the new governor, who was sent out in 1853 to institute the required changes, warned the assemblymen that they had to be made if the Assembly wished to survive. Barky insisted that "it would be vain to expect that a body so little in harmony with the spirit of the times as the Assembly of Jamaica can be long maintained in the exercise of irresponsible power." Individual assemblymen lost their power to initiate revenue bills, which passed to a newly established executive committee of three assemblymen, one councilman, and the governor. This inner council was to frame fiscal legislation for approval by the Assembly. It was also responsible for supervising the disbursement of public funds and the auditing of accounts.

During the twelve years of its existence (1853–65) the executive committee was not notably successful in gaining power, for the Assembly refused to yield to its leadership. The conflicts between the governor and the Assembly continued, and the executive committee never became a real decision-making body. The Assembly continued to guard its independence from intrusions.

Other political and governmental institutions on the island were not immune from oligarchic and irresponsible ways. On the local level, the parish boards and the judiciary operated for the benefit of the few rather than the many. Staffed for the most part by planters and others who had been intimately connected with slavery, local government had little understanding and even less sympathy for the freed man. In disputes that called for governmental intervention or judicial decision, the workers and small settlers were almost always at a decided disadvantage. On the local level, the slave-master relationship was never completely severed—at least in men's hearts and minds. Attitudes that were centuries old could not be done away with in a few short years.

The old plantocracy and its allies in the towns had been able, in the words of the American William Sewell, to perpetuate "things that were meant to die and ought to have died, as soon as the props of slavery . . . were removed." They were helped by allies from the large group of Negroes that had been free before 1833. These free Negroes, most of whom had some white blood, who in 1830 numbered from 10,000 to 20,000, had paid heavy penalties for generations because they were the descendants of slaves. Their skin color, a mark of their origins, had been an effective barrier to social and political equality with the white man. Many of them were landowners and skilled craftsmen, people of means who were, however, barred because of their color from an equal place in society. Sons and daughters and half-siblings of those who sought to exclude them, the free colored subjects had long been treated as if they had no right to be free.

They had received all civil rights by 1830, only a few years before emancipation, largely because their cause had been championed by the Abolitionists in England. It was thanks to Abolitionist influence that a Parliamentary debate on the civil rights of free Negroes had been held in 1827. The order of the Privy Council of 1829 putting free Negroes on an equal par with whites in all of the Crown colonies was also due to the Abolitionists' influence and led to the Jamaican Assembly's granting free Negroes all civil rights. Paradoxically, the goals of the Abolitionist movement were remote from the thinking of the free Negroes. In meetings held throughout the island in 1831, the year after they had been granted full civil rights, free Negroes affirmed that they were in the camp of the white residents. All slave-masters, regardless of color, displayed the same attitude toward their Negroes. Having acquired slaves under the same title as their fellow colonists, the free Negro inhabitants of the parish of Saint Elizabeth declared that "the interests" of the white settlers "were inseparably connected" with their own. A resolution from a meeting of still another group was unanimous in declaring that its members were "embodied with the white class of His Majesty's subjects and consequently their liberties, rights, and properties are identified with the whites and they are determined to repel any unconstitutional measures that may be taken against those rights and liberties."

Not only was there no bond between the free Negro (of whatever complexion) and the slaves; there was even conflict within the free Negro community. Those who were not full-blooded Negroes were by far the largest number. To the mulattoes, or "people of color," white blood was a great source of pride. Whereas black skin had been the badge of servitude associated with the contemptible "subhuman" state of slavery, the brown or "coffee-colored" skin was proof of white ancestry, giving those who possessed it claim to kinship with the white race. Degrees of complexion lightness became a significant distinction for the Negroes themselves. The lighter the complexion, the greater the pride. Mulattoes had, for the most part, only contempt for those who were darker than themselves. The governor reported in 1823, "the dark colored and black portions of the free people are highly indignant of the superiority which those of fairer complexion claim over them."

Racial distinctions and racial consciousness, a legacy of slavery, continued to be strong for many generations. Although more than 90 per cent of the people of Jamaica were full-blooded Negroes, black skin color was considered a stigma, a mark of shame. Habit and custom were very strong. The relationship between a dark skin and slavery might legally be sundered, but the effects of that relationship were to be felt long afterward. "Whiteness" always had been, and would continue to be, a sign of prestige, while "blackness" was the worst degradation. As a long-time resident in Jamaica explained to a Parliamentary committee in 1832, "the principal distinctions of society are founded on distinction of color," and the distinctions were to continue. Almost all—white, "mixed," and black—accepted the pigmentary values of whiteness as the ideal.

Those free people of color who had, over the years, acquired both education and wealth continued to be shut out from equal social relationships with white society. After gaining all civil rights in 1830, the prosperous among them hoped that it would not be long before they would win acceptance in the white community. They supported the white elite and looked to the white community for their own values. Thus they embraced the anti-Semitic attitudes that had long been popular with many white Christians in Jamaica. Like the ruling whites, the mulattoes also opposed the political and civil "emancipation" of the Jews. Anti-Semitic comments appeared from time to time in *The Watchman*, the newspaper of the free colored. Jews had received all the rights of free citizens at almost exactly the same time as free Negroes. The Jamaican legislature enacted a bill giving Jews the same rights as other white citizens in December, 1826. They had acted after being petitioned by the "Merchants and others Interested in Trade of this Island" who declared that, as the Jews possessed "no opinions that are destructive to civil society or prejudicial to their country's able attachment to King and Country," they were entitled to all the rights of Englishmen. As the Jews had not as yet received all the rights of subjects in Britain, the Jamaican legislature had included in this act a required clause that the bill was not to take effect until it had been approved by the King. A year went by without action by the Privy Council. The British Government inflicted on the Jamaican legislature the supreme insult of ignoring it. Finally, on December 4, 1827, the Assembly sent a petition to Great Britain requesting action. As at this time the free Negroes were exerting pressure at home and abroad to secure equal rights with whites, the Assembly's petition stressed that, "at a time when all classes in the community are seeking an opportunity to obtain an extension of civil liberties, the House would not refuse white fellow subjects." The "principal Christian merchants and other Christian inhabitants" felt the same way. Just a few days before, they had sent a petition to the Assembly declaring that it would be "degradation of a meritorious class of our own society" if civil liberties were not finally given to Jews at a time when the free colored were demanding these rights. It was not until July, 1831, six months after the Jamaican legislature had granted all civil rights to free Negroes, that the English Privy Council approved the law. Alluding to the political rights granted in 1830 to free Negroes, the Jamaican legislature had in February, 1831, sent a special message to the governor of the island requesting that he inform England of the "inconvenience and injury sustained by the Jews" because the act had not yet been approved. Because of the British Government's failure to sanction the bill, the lawmakers pointed out, the Jews were now "the only class of free men" without the franchise—a "peculiar situation" for the people who possess "a magnitude of property" and who had always conducted themselves as "good citizens and faithful and loyal subjects."

While hostile to both groups, the ruling elite had always feared, despised, and hated non-whites more than Jews. As long as it could restrict the rights of both, it was not ready to make concessions to either. When, however, it became clear that it would be most difficult to withstand, alone, the pressures from abroad to ameliorate the conditions of the free Negroes and the slaves, the white Christians made common cause with the Jews. By granting them the rights of subjects just four years before they were given to free Negroes, they made the Jews a part of a "united front" of white people on the island.

Free people of color, who had been agitating since 1816 to gain full citizenship, reacted with hostility when Jews (whom they considered heathen) were given, before they were, preferential treatment by the Jamaican legislature. Edward Jordan, an important leader of the free colored and editor of *The Watchman,* demonstrated this hostility in the first election in which both Negroes and Jews participated. This was the election of Kingston City Councilmen in the fall of 1831. The campaign waged by some members of the colored community had been bitter. *The Watchman* had openly attacked Jews, some of whom had competed in the election. Shocked and intimidated by the attack, Moses Delgado, a leading Jewish citizen, withdrew from the campaign, declaring that "deprived as Jews were of political rights," they in the past had never and would not now find fault with any other group.

The Jews were not the only group critical of the conduct of the free colored during the elections. A group of black freeholders expressed shock and surprise at the outcome. The free mulattoes had not supported their candidates either, though the blacks had cooperated with the mulattoes in the Assembly and municipal election. At a meeting held on January 25, 1832, the black freeholders of Kingston complained that, though they had manifested a genuine fraternal solicitude toward their colored brethren, "a prejudice still operates against us by men bound in honor to support us." They resolved "never to assist" the free colored again and to oppose all their "designs relative to the elective franchise." In allying themselves with the free colored, the black freeholders asserted, they had sacrificed their own interests "at the shrine of subservience and intolerance," tricked by the "false promises of the colored body."

It was not long before the Jews and black freeholders united against the colored. It was because of this alliance that the first Jew was elected to the Legislative Assembly. Daniel Hart won the election by almost the same plurality that had worked against the Jewish candidates in the municipal elections of 1831. The free blacks had not forgotten, stated an editorial in the *Kingston Chronicle,* how the mulattoes had opposed them in the past. They retaliated by shifting their strength to the Jewish candidate.

In subsequent decades, aided by their economic strength, Jews and colored, and more rarely blacks, gained political office. Of the forty-eight representatives in the Assembly in

1866, twelve were free colored and thirteen were Jews. Prominent government positions were held by individuals from both groups. Many Englishmen came and went, but Jews and colored, among the oldest groups of permanent settlers, stayed on to manage the destinies of the island population. The attorneys, estate managers, and other representatives of the absentee landlords, a significant group in an earlier period, became much less influential. The planter interest was still present, but now the planters were mostly permanent residents.

Although bigotry did not disappear, divisions in the Assembly were hardly ever along religious or racial lines. Saint James, a parish in the northwest, had a colored majority but a conservative white assemblyman. Many prominent colored were planters, and in parishes where they were dominant they often supported a white candidate or a colored representative who promoted the agrarian point of view. Coalitions built around economic interests did coalesce in the Assembly. A "country party" and a "town party" arose from time to time. What was lacking was a tightly knit party organization. Assemblymen could and did shift their votes from issue to issue. Whether planters or merchants, doctors or lawyers, their political loyalties were usually immediate and transitory rather than far-reaching. On one problem, however, there was almost unanimous agreement. The freed Negro—be he a small settler or estate worker—must be kept down. As Governor Lionel Smith said, "constituted as the popular branch of the legislature now is, no Governor will be permitted to do justice to the Negro."

For a brief moment in history, in the year 1865, a portion of the Jamaican masses made a passionate but futile effort to secure justice. Unusually hard times had come to the island in the 1860's. A series of droughts had ruined a large part of the crops, making scarce the staples that were the sustenance of the peasants and agricultural workers. Small settlers barely maintained themselves, and there was no surplus that could be sold. Salt fish and grain, the staple foods of the Negro masses, were in short supply and were sold for extremely high prices, as the Civil War in the United States had cut off a major source for Jamaica of these staples. Unemployment continued to rise on the estates as sugar production continued to slide downhill. Even when work was available, wages were low and were not paid regularly.

Characteristically, the island legislature turned its back on the problem. Nor did Governor Edward John Eyre, who had just come from Australia, intercede or even suggest that it do anything about alleviating conditions. Eyre failed to appreciate the grievances of the people and showed a marked dislike, if not hatred, for them. His remedy was punitive action, and he was instrumental in securing legislation prescribing harsh punishments, like flogging, for stealing fruits and vegetables and other petty offenses. Eyre, the local magistrates, and government officials ignored the prophecy of George W. Gordon, a mulatto champion of the blacks: "A ruler who does not assuage the sword with justice becomes distasteful, and instead of having the love and respect of the people, he becomes despised and hated."

The English Baptists, who had maintained close contact with the branch of their church in Jamaica and had taken more than a passing interest in the fate of its people, sought to have the British Government do something to alleviate the suffering in Jamaica. Dr. Edward B. Underhill, Secretary of the Baptist Missionary Society, who had received many reports from Baptists living in Jamaica, sent a letter to the Colonial Secretary warning that "it is more than time that the [lack of] wisdom that has governed Jamaica since emancipation should be brought to an end."

The Underhill Letter, as it came to be called, was given wide publicity in Jamaica. On the strength of the Underhill Letter, some peasants were inspired in June, 1865, to send an appeal directly to Queen Victoria for help. The Governor and Assembly had done nothing for them, but having found one friend abroad, the small settlers from the parish of Saint Ann believed that help might be at hand from the highest authority in the empire. Their image of the Queen was one of loving benevolence, and they appealed to her to help them in their poverty, made worse by recent droughts and rising unemployment. Their only specific request was that Crown lands that were not being used for any other purposes be released to them for settlement.

They were completely rebuffed. The Colonial Secretary, Edward Cardwell, replied that neither the Queen nor Her Majesty's government could do anything for the peasants of Saint Ann. The Queen's Letter, as it came to be known, stated that it was "from their own industry and prudence . . . that they [the peasants] must look for improvement in their condition." Poverty was the result of individual failing, it said, and the government could do nothing.

The Queen's Letter was a cruel blow to the masses, but to Governor Eyre and his supporters it was a vindication of their position. Eyre had 50,000 copies of the letter printed as a handbill, which he distributed throughout the island. Though the Queen's Letter was instrumental in bringing the anger of the masses to a fever pitch, the protest was directed not at the Queen and her advisers but at the governor, who was blamed for not advising the British Government about the true conditions in Jamaica. The monarch as monarch could do no wrong; the advisers were at fault.

After the demands of the small settlers had been rejected, Paul Bogle, himself a small farmer, and others decided to take the bull by the horns. At an open-air meeting in August, 1865, at Morant Bay, they resolved to send a deputation to the governor, hoping that a direct confrontation would force him to act in their favor. Eyre refused to see them. Understandably, they were bitter: They had tramped forty-five miles from their homes in Stony Gut to King's House in Spanish Town, all for nought. They had not, however, reached the stage as enunciated by Bogle when he was to tell his followers: "It is now time for us to help ourselves. . . . War is with us; black skin war is at hand."

There was no preconceived plan or sinister plot of revolt against authority. The Jamaican masses had, during centuries of oppression, learned to live with their discontent without exploding. Though alienated from the authority structure, the small settlers had learned to cope with it. They knew no other way. Almost by accident an explosion did, however, occur. The uprising at Morant Bay did not begin as an uprising at all. Bogle and his group did not wish to cause trouble when they went to the courthouse at Morant Bay on October 7, 1865. They had merely come to observe the trial of one of their fellows. Though they carried sticks and cutlasses, they remained peaceful until one of the group shouted at a defendant. The police immediately tried to arrest the man for disrupting the court, but Bogle and his band had fled, spiriting him away with them. This provided officials of Saint Thomas with what they had long wanted—an excuse for arresting Paul Bogle, upon whose activities they had looked with suspicion and alarm.

The incident at the courthouse provided the magistrates with the occasion to charge Bogle and his men with rioting and resisting and assaulting the police. The local militia was sent to Stony Gut and destroyed the village when they were unable to locate Bogle and his followers, who had fled. When the militia left, Bogle sent an appeal directly to Governor Eyre. It was a simply reasoned petition, which reaffirmed loyalty to the Queen —a loyalty that entitled the petitioners to protection from the Queen's representative in Jamaica—the governor. The petitioners called upon Eyre to grant them protection from the local government of Saint Thomas, which they felt had tried to seize them illegally. "We have been imposed upon for a period of twenty-seven years," stated the petition, "with due obeisance to the laws of our Queen and country and we can no longer endure the same." Having been harassed and oppressed by the parish authorities over the years, Bogle and his followers now were appealing to the British Government, believing that somehow the loyalty they felt for the Queen would be understood, accepted, and rewarded.

This was hardly to be the case. Eyre completely ignored the petition. His answer was to send troops to the parish to bolster the forces of the local militia. Meanwhile, Bogle and his followers waited two days for some word from the governor. When no reply came, they took the decision to march down to the town and openly confront the parish government with their demands. They knew that all other channels for appeal had been sealed off.

The local militia, lined up at the court house, was waiting for them, and the riot of October 10, 1865, began when the magistrate ordered the militia to fire directly into the crowd. Bogle and his men drove the militia into the courthouse and set fire to the building, the fire soon spreading to other parts of the town. In the subsequent violence and looting, fifteen white officials died and thirty-one were wounded or injured. Several plantations were attacked and three of the more unpopular planters were killed.

Governor Eyre immediately declared martial law and sent large detachments of soldiers to the parish. To prevent the rioters from escaping to other parts of the island, the troops surrounded the disturbed area. The Maroons, who Bogle believed would support him, sided with the government forces instead. Outnumbered and outarmed, the rioters were quickly rounded up; the government forces met with little resistance and suffered no casualties. Within ten days the disturbance had been brought completely under control.

The punishment meted out was severe. More than 1,000 peasant dwellings in Saint Thomas were burned. Eyre brought the peasants to trial in a series of courts martial in which 354 persons were sentenced to be executed. Wanton killing of other Negroes and the indiscriminate flogging of at least 600 persons of both sexes completed the reign of terror. Eyre seemed to delight in the cruel and excessive sentences of the courts and the barbarities of the soldiers. Just twelve days after the rioting had started, Bogle himself was captured and hanged from the yardarm of the H.M.S. *Wolverine,* an English battleship that had been summoned to Jamaica.

Needing a scapegoat on whom to blame the entire episode, Eyre found it in one of his severest critics, George W. Gordon, a mulatto who had championed the cause of the poor in the Assembly and who had on many occasions assailed Eyre, calling him a "cruel" and "voracious" animal. Eyre declared that Gordon's "seditious language addressed to the ignorant black people" was "the chief cause and origin of the whole matter." It was convenient and relatively simple for Eyre to assume that Gordon had preached insurrection.

Gordon, as a member of the Baptist church, had spoken several times at Bogle's church in Stony Gut and had ordained him as a Deacon. Gordon was arrested, court-martialed and hanged less than two weeks after the uprising, on the same yardarm of the H.M.S. *Wolverine*. With his death went one of the most articulate defenders of the Negro masses in Jamaica.

To the privileged minority, Eyre was a savior, and one by one—custos, magistrates (Justices of the Peace), assemblymen, journalists—they came forward to thank him for finding a solution to their problems. The Assembly enthusiastically endorsed Eyre's repressive tactics in speedily putting down the uprising at Morant Bay. The courts martial, floggings, and other atrocities were condoned.

The masses were taught an extremely important lesson by the events of 1865. It would be almost a century before they or their leaders would dare protest openly against their conditions. But the rising at Morant Bay also had its lesson for the ruling elites. It filled their minds and hearts with dread. Though most of them were never in any actual danger, as the rebellion was confined to the parish of Saint Thomas, the thought of a full-scale uprising was very vivid in their minds. An oligarchic minority among a vast sea of black faces, the whites and some of the colored of Jamaica viewed the uprising at Morant Bay as symbolic of the danger they had always feared and lived with—a vision of the black majority taking over the reins of government, with expropriation of property and wealth to follow. If the grip of the minority was to be loosened, all would be lost to those to whom they had denied everything.

Eyre played upon their fears when he declared, in the aftermath of the rebellion, that "the spirit of disaffection" was "widely spread" and "deeply rooted" so that one day Jamaica would become "a second Haiti," ruled by Negroes who would expel and kill the white people and destroy their property.

To keep the peace, and as a protective device against future rebellions, the oligarchy that ruled Jamaica did away with representative government on the island, willingly relinquishing their political power. By abolishing the Assembly, they hoped to close off the political channels that might be used at a fu-

ture time for the benefit of the masses. Governor Eyre drama-
tized the entire problem and played on the fears of the oligarchy by exaggerating the significance of the revolt. What was
needed, he declared, was "a strong government" and a "firm
hand to guide and direct."

The Assembly, hitherto so jealous of its powers, capitulated
completely when confronted by the specter of Paul Bogle, who
symbolized to them the angry Negro. Better to give up "representative" government than to have one that was vulnerable to
popular agitation and ultimately to mob rule.

Necessity and expediency dictated that the Assembly now be
abolished and a new form of government established in its
stead. On December 22, 1865, the Assembly enacted a law providing that "the present Legislative Council and House of Assembly, and all and every of the functions and privileges of
those two bodies shall cease" immediately and "absolutely."

Earlier in the month, the legislature had outlined the type
of government structure that should be instituted after it abolished itself. This would be a single-chamber legislative council
consisting of twenty-four members, twelve of whom would be
nominated by the governor and twelve of whom would be
elected. But the Colonial Office rejected such a plan and instead proposed a "Crown colony" form of government comprising a council whose membership would be determined by
the governor. As the horrors of Morant Bay still loomed large
in the minds of so many, a frightened Assembly gave in. In the
act of December 22, by which representative government in
Jamaica was abolished, the Assembly granted the British Government the right to "create and constitute a government for
this island . . . and from time to time to alter and amend such
a government." Jamaica received the official order for a new
government from the Queen in Council on June 11, 1866. After
almost two centuries of representative government, the transition to the Crown colony form was smooth and orderly, and
without violence on the part of those who lost their political
power.

The crushing of the rebellion resulted in the demise, by acquiescence and consent, of the independent political power so

long held by a small oligarchy. In surrendering that power—
and, of course, this was the reason—the oligarchy also delayed
the coming of a more truly representative government. It was
necessary, in Jamaica, for absolutism to precede democracy.

# 8. Economic Change
## and Development, 1833–1962

Whether or not the high cost of slaves and slave labor would have led ultimately to the end of slavery was never put to the test of time. Slavery in the British Empire did not "wither away"; it was ended because of the pressure of public opinion, organized and inflamed by zealous, religiously oriented humanitarians who held that the enslavement of man by man was morally reprehensible and could not be tolerated by any civilized government. In 1833, the British Parliament "abolished" slavery, though with compensation to the slave-owners.

Emancipation was both a great experiment and a daring adventure. It was recognized that more than a wave of the wand or even an act of Parliament was necessary if slavery was to be abolished in a society so long and so largely dependent on it. Fearful of the consequences of immediate freedom, the lawmakers provided for an intermediate stage or transition period between the abolition of slavery and the advent of total freedom. Called "apprenticeship," it was based on the premise that the former slave was not ready to assume full responsibility for himself as a free individual. Under apprenticeship, the former slave was required to work three-quarters of every week on the plantation of his former master. Otherwise, it was feared that if he was no longer bound by the coercive force of servitude, he would simply run away. The apprenticeship period guaranteed the planters seven more years of compulsory labor. At the same time, the Negro was given time in which to learn "how to act as a free man."

As an "apprentice" the former slave was allowed to become a free laborer for one-fourth of the work week. During this time he could earn wages by selling his labor or he could work on his provision grounds. Freedom might be secured before the end of the seven-year period by purchase, using the proceeds of the wages or profits from his own small holding. Because it was feared that the local judiciary would be less than fair in dealing with the former slaves, the British Government sent out from England special judges, known as stipendary magistrates, specifically for the purpose of adjudicating disputes over work, wages, and manumissions. They were paid by the British Government.

The apprenticeship period was designed to be a bridge for the slave to cross to freedom with a minimum of disturbance to the social fabric, but it did not provide a meaningful transition for the planter. Accustomed as he was to having complete control over hours and rules of work and discipline, the planter found it difficult to accept the halfway measures introduced in the apprenticeship scheme. He found it much easier to view his semifree labor force as still totally servile, and he made every effort to keep it that way.

In order to prevent the apprentices from accumulating a surplus, the planter charged high rents for the slaves' dwellings and provision grounds and payments for all food rations. All the time alloted the slave to work for himself as a free man was spent earning the subsistence that should have been provided by the planter, as the laborer was still giving, without pay, most of his working time to the plantation and was not otherwise being paid for it. In an effort to maintain the same labor force that they had during slavery, the planters tried to tie the apprentices to their service. Accustomed to the arbitrary powers of the past, they gave little heed to the newly acquired rights of the Negro under the law. As the Earl of Mulgrave, the governor of Jamaica, remarked in 1834, "persons who have been used to the diplomacy of the lash" are seldom "acquainted with the best method of influencing the human mind by persuasion."

From 1834 to the abolition of apprenticeship in 1838, dis-

putes over wages, hours of work, and the exhorbitant rents
and fees charged for food and shelter were common problems
throughout the island. Despite the presence of the stipendary
magistrates, conflicts were usually settled in favor of the planter.
At every turn the apprentice was dependent on the existing
judicial and governmental apparatus. Stipendary magistrates did
not have jurisdiction in all disputes, nor did they have control
over the workhouses and prisons to which laborers were committed for the slightest offense. Even when they did have jurisdiction, they easily assimilated the planter's point of view. Local prejudices and pressures powerfully supported the status
quo. As a leading Abolitionist bitterly remarked, apprenticeship
was "entirely inconsistent with the most limited degree of freedom." Still chained to the estate and subject to harsh punishments for all offenses, large and small, the Negro was free in
theory only.

Fearful that the ill working of the apprenticeship system
would in effect make emancipation a dead letter in the West
Indies, the Abolitionists pressed for its termination. Tempers
were particularly inflamed after 1836, when reports on the
treatment of the Negroes in Jamaica reached England. Public
opinion was marshaled once again.

The great Irish orator Daniel O'Connell, who was also a
member of Parliament, stirred crowds when he declared that
"you [the British nation] are cheated, you are humbugged,
you are bamboozled, you are swindled, cheated and swindled
every man, woman and child among you. It is not a petty larceny affair at all, it is not a matter of pounds, shillings and
pence, but you are cheated of 20,000,000 pounds sterling." In
August, 1838, Parliament abolished the Apprenticeship system
in the Crown colonies. Fearing Parliamentary intervention, the
Assembly abolished apprenticeship in Jamaica that same year.

The excessive demands of the Jamaican planters during the
apprenticeship period and the Negro's response were a foreshadowing of the future. Instead of submitting to unfair treatment, many former slaves drifted away from the estates and
established themselves on small freeholds. Those who were
treated fairly remained. Some years later, an outsider remarked

that "the history of estate abandonment in Jamaica is a history of systematic injustice and oppression on the part of the proprietary body, accompanied by a most fatal blindness to their own interests." This was indeed the case. After apprenticeship was abolished, the relationship that had been established in the past between planter and laborer was often an important factor working for or against an adequate labor supply. Workers offered their services to estates where they had been well treated and avoided planters known to be unjust or unfair.

Even more cogent than a reputation based upon past performance was the reality of present practices. Wages were crucial. To have an adequate labor supply, it was necessary to pay adequate wages; wages, however, were the greatest single production cost, and hard cash had always been a scarce commodity in a society that lived largely in a credit economy. Forced to work without wages when they had been slaves, the freedmen were under no such legal compulsion after emancipation. They could now settle and establish for themselves freeholds in the mountain areas of Jamaica, or on abandoned estates. It was no longer necessary for them to take orders.

The development of a native peasantry in Jamaica is the most unique and important of the post-emancipation developments. Truck farming was not a foreign skill to the former Jamaican slaves, many of whom had grown their own fruits and vegetables in slavery days when the practice had been encouraged by the planters because of the continued shortage of food supplies. The provision ground kept by slaves on the plantations were similar to truck gardens. Sometimes pigs, poultry, and other livestock were also raised. Bondsmen often bartered or sold their surpluses. At the time of emancipation, Jamaica had a well-developed internal marketing system run by slaves. They would mostly trade from estate to estate, but the more ambitious among them would go into the towns and sell in their markets. Market days would find both slaves and free men selling together, peddling fruit, poultry, river fish, and suckling pigs. Other products were made. "Panniers," the large twin baskets that were slung over the back of a mule for transport of produce were also made and sold by slaves, who engaged in other types of basket work as well. A most ambitious operation was reported by an English landscape painter, James Hakewell. He found that some Negroes belonging to the Holland Estate in Saint Thomas in the east kept a boat "which trades regularly between that place and Kingston." Observing the Negroes as they traded, Hakewell found them to be like English farmers. "The slaves," he reported, "grumble as much at the low price of yams and plaintains as an English farmer at the fall of corn."

With many former slaves becoming freehold farmers after emancipation, those who remained on the estates probably did so because they received good wages and paid cheap rents for houses and land. A great many, however, chose "to go it alone," and there was a spectacular increase, particularly in the eastern and western parishes, of freehold properties of ten acres or less. Some landowners divided their lands up into small parcels and sold them to the former slaves. Prices were cheap, as rising costs of production and falling market values for sugar forced many estates out of business. Negroes who had saved money acquired from marketing their products while still slaves, or who had worked a few years after freedom and saved their wages, eagerly bought up the land. Ready outlets for marketing their produce were found at the sugar estates that had managed to survive the agricultural depression of the 1820's as well as the changeover to the free labor system. Supplementary incomes could also be found for ambitious men in part-time employment on the estates. An industrious individual found that freedom was a meaningful experience; no longer exploited for the profit of another, he discovered the self-rewards of hard labor.

Besides growing provisions, many of the neophyte peasants engaged in cultivating coffee and selling it for export to the American market. The coffee plant had been first introduced in Jamaica about 1728 by the governor of the island, Sir Nicholas Lawes. At first it was produced on a plantation basis, but with emancipation it became more and more a crop grown by small farmers. A simple machine had been invented by a mechanic in Kingston to clean the beans so that the peasants could produce a marketable product.

So successful were the small farmers that Jamaica, in the period directly following the end of apprenticeship, had for the first time in its history sizable exports of such products as pimento, ginger, arrowroot, coconuts, and honey. Minor crops, such as beeswax, cassava, and fruit, never sold outside the island before emancipation, were also exported. Little wonder that local officials proudly reported to the Colonial Office in 1839 that "they [the peasants] are becoming what we all must, or shall rejoice to see, a yeomanry." They rejoiced because a backbone of a stable agricultural society had been fathered by emancipation.

The average farm was two and three-quarter acres. The majority of the peasants cultivated only one acre of their holdings, leaving the rest fallow or in pasture, but that one acre could produce sufficient potatoes, corn, yams, sugar, arrowroot, ginger, and other crops to provide subsistence and a surplus for the local market that had the cash value of approximately 15 pounds a year, sufficient for clothing for a family of seven in addition to allowing some savings.

The peasants who owned four or five acres usually set aside some portion of it as a "cane-piece." After harvesting the stalks of sugar from the plot, they would extract the cane juice by hand, using a primitive wooden instrument that looked, one observer said, like "a giant lemon squeezer." Many of them were able to extract a relatively large yield of raw sugar.

Forebodings that the freed Negroes would riot, live riotously, or both soon ceased to occupy the minds of responsible officials. As one observer put it, the change that the Negroes had undergone was "assuredly no sign of incapacity, no proof of indolence, no indication of unconquerable vice." Farming brought a respectable livelihood and a dignified existence to individuals who had not long before been subject to the absolute authority of others.

The small farmers became an essential part of the Jamaican economy. As the cultivation of sugar declined, more and more workers were attracted to the alternative of independent cultivation. The number of freeholders increased and so did their share of total agricultural output. The total number of landholdings of five acres or less went from 36,756 in 1880 to

108,943 in 1902. In 1930, 153,406 acres, or 82 per cent of all land settlements, were from one-half to five acres. The peasants' share in exports quadrupled from 1850 to 1890 and continued to grow afterward. By 1930, peasant holdings accounted for about 40 per cent of Jamaica's exports.

Some of the small landholders were "squatters," who had occupied and cultivated abandoned or unused land. Since the ownership of this land was not clear and the occupiers subject to being dispossessed, the possibilities of conflict were plentiful. To provide an element of stability, Crown colony governors made serious efforts to give the peasants a clear legal title to their land and to open up new lands for further settlement. If the lands had been abandoned, the government took over the title and sold the land to the squatters on an installment plan. In 1920, agricultural loan banks were established to provide credit for the purchase of lands by would-be settlers.

The decline of sugar in the nineteenth century had serious consequences for Jamaica's increasing population. Slavery had tended to hold down the growth of population; after emancipation population increased rapidly. There were, however, no new labor-intensive industries to absorb the increase. Unable to find work in sugar, those who were not small farmers or vagrants sought a livelihood as domestic servants or independent service personnel. Carpenters, blacksmiths, wheelwrights, and others who had been employed on the sugar properties were now also thrown on the labor market as estates were abandoned. As a result the market value of these jobs was lowered and wages and conditions of employment were very poor. If applicants were many, jobs were few. Some of the men found employment in households as butlers or handymen, worked as merchants, or became petty, most often itinerant, traders. Women had several paths they could follow, from cooking, cleaning, and baby-tending in households to working independently as dressmakers, washerwomen, or market hucksters. Providing the greatest security in a surplus labor market were domestic jobs. Few of these were available, even though it was a common practice for a government clerk to have "as many servants as a foreign ambassador." There was, as was pointed out in 1865 to E. Cardwell, the Secretary of State for the Colonies, "not enough work available for the people; neither work nor capital to employ them."

The labor requirements for the cultivation of land per acre sharply decreased. This was due chiefly to the decline of sugar cultivation and the rise of banana-growing, which was not a labor-intensive industry. It has been estimated that between 1871 and 1911 the total area of land under cultivation increased 250 per cent, but the labor requirements per acre halved.

It was during this period that Jamaicans in great numbers sought refuge in other lands of the hemisphere. Haiti, Colombia, British Guiana, British Honduras, and the United States all welcomed Jamaicans after 1880, but the efforts of first France and then the United States to build a canal across Panama gave Jamaicans their greatest opportunity. As early as 1853, almost 2,000 left the island to work on railway construction in Panama. With the arrival of the French company on the isthmus in 1880, more than 54,000 emigrated there. More than half of them returned within two years, either for a holiday or to invest their earnings in land or a small business. Ultimately, as a result of the failure of the French effort to build the canal in 1888, almost all the Jamaicans were repatriated. Despite the reverse flow, however, there were still some 6,000 Jamaicans left on the isthmus. Between 1890 and 1904, emigration to Panama was negligible, but in 1905 the United States played the piper's tune and Jamaicans were again lured by the canal project. More than 100,000 left during this period, and at least 36,000 of them never returned home. When the canal work ran out, there was banana-planting in Costa Rica and work on the more distant mainland, in the United States or Canada. From 1911 to 1921, there was a net total of 72,000 emigrants, which partially offset a natural increase of 104,000 in population. After World War I, a sugar boom in Cuba offered more jobs to the able-bodied, and by the early 1930's more than 60,000 Jamaicans were living there.

A large number of women joined the exodus to Cuba, not to do manual labor but to work in the service trades. Women, like men, were forced to seek a livelihood away from the island.

Like the Puerto Ricans of today, who are tempted to seek better opportunities in the United States, the Jamaicans of that era found Cuba and Central America a magnet.

The majority of those who left escaped a cruel reality. A stark picture of conditions in Jamaica as experienced by the poorer segments of the population was drawn by an official investigating commission in 1877. It investigated the existing destitution on the island and furnished a vivid picture of the condition of the masses. Witnesses before the committee distinguished between "two distinct classes of Negroes, the estates people and the mountain Negroes." The latter were the free peasants and were considered industrious and quite superior to the laborers. Their cultivation of ginger, arrowroot, and coffee had increased their material wealth. On the moral plane, the peasants were family-oriented and wished to give their children both a religious and a secular education.

It was from the other class of Negroes—the estate workers— that there was a constant drift into the towns, especially Kingston. With this came overcrowding and more unemployment. Poor living conditions, unwed mothers, fatherless children, and male drifters were conditions of life. No efforts were made by the local authorities to find employment opportunities for this group.

Vocational training and encouragement of the growth of the independent peasantry were some of the recommendations made by the commission. But no solution proposed could eliminate the conditions in the lowland sugar districts where employment was seasonal, wages were low, and estate managers exploited both male and female youths. That the royal commission of 1882, headed by Sir William Crossman, appointed to investigate finances, reported that the "great majority of the population does and will always seek a livelihood by any other means than by working on estates."

Adolescents threw off parental control and sought employment in the urban environment, further adding to the crowding. They survived by casual employment and theft. At fourteen or fifteen, boys commonly formed illicit relationships with girls and then abandoned mother and child. Children were then left in the care of other relatives, who taught the children to sustain themselves by stealing from neighbors. Roving gangs of adolescents—male and female—wandered from town to country picking up work where they could find it, either as estate laborers or in some service capacity. Stable family life was almost unknown. Women seem to have had more job opportunities than men. They could engage in a wide range of domestic chores, from seamstress to cook to maid to "nanny." They also worked on the wharves loading coal and bananas. Men and boys frequently lived off the earnings of the females and remained idle.

Hostility toward the estates would continue to manifest itself over successive generations. Because of the casual nature of employment and the instability of the work force, sugar producers could never count on the same group of workers from one season to the next or from one week to the next. There was no telling how long a worker would remain at his job, as he had not the least compunction about leaving it at any time. If the Negro could not control the sources of power, he could at least decide upon the limits of his participation. An odious connection between manual work and slavery lived on for many generations. Captain Lorenzo Baker, the founder of the banana industry in Jamaica, believed that Jamaicans worked harder and earned better wages in Costa Rica than they did on their own island, as they were averse to laboring with their hands in their native land. Lord Sidney Olivier, in evaluating this problem, once said about conditions early in the twentieth century that there was the "paradoxical coincidence of a shortage of labor on Jamaica estates with a constant immigration of laborers to work at wages abroad." Olivier also noted that, while most Negroes were viewed by officials as laborers or working men, it was "not the habit of the Jamaican so to think of himself. For him work was an instrument contributory to the primary affair of his personal or social life and it is largely within his power to determine on what conditions he will employ it."

At times, planters looked to Asia for disciplined and committed agricultural workers and made minor efforts to bring them into the island. Though large numbers of East Indians were imported into the West Indies as indentured servants, Jamaica received a very small proportion of the whole. Of the 38,681 immigrants that came to the island between 1845 and 1917 to work on sugar and banana plantations, 31 per cent, or 11,959, were repatriated. Offers of cash payments or land at the expiration of labor contracts did not attract sufficient numbers. Sickness, high mortality rates, and the preference of planters for males did not create an environment conducive to permanent settlement. In 1960 there were 26,500 Jamaicans who claimd East Indian descent, or approximately 2 per cent of the population.

Whereas the majority of East Indians came to Jamaica between 1860 and 1905, most Chinese immigrated between 1911 and 1921, and they came in far fewer numbers. In 1921 Chinese numbered 3,696, as compared to 18,600 East Indians. The East Indians by and large remained in agriculture, but the Chinese almost immediately sought commercial occupations. They dominated the grocery trade for many decades in North Kingston and the rural parts of the island. In 1943, more than 75 per cent of the Chinese population of 12,394 was engaged in trade, white-collar, manufacturing, and service occupations, more than half of them in trade alone. There were 12,409 Jamaicans that claimed Chinese descent in 1960, or approximately 1 per cent of the island's population.

At the end of the nineteenth century, the inspector of schools, J. R. Williams, said, "With us the difficulty is to make active and efficient and available the labor of a population of nearly 800,000 of mostly very poor people." In "improved education," Williams hoped to find "one of the avenues leading to a solution to the problem." Another leading citizen had a remedy. At the height of the economic crisis of 1865, Richard Hill, judge, naturalist, and author, advised Governor Eyre that "capital and new sources of productive industry and trade, are the only cure for this state of evil." What was needed was innovation in, and diversification of, the Jamaican economy so as to open up new areas of employment and business opportunities. Agricultural diversification could have been coupled with the creation of industries to supply the internal demand for consumer products. Fishing, dairy farming, cattle ranching, and large-scale vegetable and produce farming, already practiced on a minor scale on the island, could have been developed into profitable enterprises not only to serve the local market but also to provide a surplus for export.

Diversification and extension of the economy would also have been possible in the urban sectors. Many former slaves had learned trades on the plantations, and it was estimated that there were over 17,000 journeymen and master tradesmen on the island in 1861. A furniture industry might have been started to utilize the island's woods and its many carpenters, or a public works program could have been instituted by the government, utilizing the many bricklayers, masons, and builders. Some meager beginnings were made, but, as a magistrate commented, "they hardly deserve the name of industrial pursuits."

Certain "adventurous" men had started one or two handicraft operations. Working in their homes, peasants were provided with the raw materials needed to make such articles as mats, fans, baskets, and ornaments. But these endeavors, as compared to the need, were insignificant. In Spanish Town alone there were 127 tailors and 772 seamstresses, most of whom were very irregularly employed. Clothing manufacture might have been started with a pool of talent of this kind. Instead, these people, in the words of a Baptist mission report, lived "a very precarious existence . . . a life of poverty and almost necessary immorality." In 1848, the governor of the island lamented that "it would be a *mercy* to find some easy and healthy employment for the women and children, but they do not even make straw hats."

No mercies could be had from the most prosperous of all the occupational groups on the island—the large merchants—who had the highest annual income in the island. With most of their commercial contacts in North America, not with the sugar trade in Britain, they were not as severely affected by the decline of the sugar industry. As the only group on the island with real capital resources, many of the merchants had added to their wealth in land transactions, buying up bankrupt estates and reselling them. Still another source of income for them was lending to planters, who often were forced to rely on them when the traditional suppliers in England lost confidence in sugar.

It was only after new investment opportunities had been exploited by others and had become "sure things" that local initiative and capital came forth to claim the prizes. The role of innovator was reserved for outsiders. The most substantial investment of foreign capital was made in agriculture, and it was North American investors who brought a new agricultural industry to the island. Bananas had been introduced in Jamaica during the Spanish occupation and were later cultivated by slaves on their "provision grounds," but it had never been a commercial crop. In the days before refrigerated ships it had been thought impossible to ship bananas for export, but as early as 1869 an American sea captain, Lorenzo Baker, was successful in transporting bananas from the island in good condition. Baker's "find" came to the attention of one of the early founders of the United Fruit Company, Andrew W. Preston, who became convinced that there were promising investment opportunities on the island. So it came about that Jamaica, formed, along with Cuba, Santo Domingo, Hondurus, and Costa Rica, the foundations upon which United Fruit built its tropical empire.

Expansion of the industry was rapid as plantations were established, usually on abandoned sugar estates. Land was cheap, and relatively little capital equipment was required, making the initial investment low and rather suited to the taste of the conservative Jamaican businessmen. Wages were the largest current expense, and even these remained low, as the ever shrinking sugar industry and the continued population growth swelled the labor market to overflowing.

Banana-planting was ideally suited for the economic and social conditions of the island. No special skills or techniques were required to set up banana estates, and neither expensive capital equipment nor highly paid managerial skills were needed. All that was necessary was what Jamaica had in abundance—land and labor. By the turn of the century, bananas became almost what sugar had been in the past.

The small peasant was the greatest beneficiary of the new industry. In 1915 those producing and marketing bananas in Jamaica included one large producer, Sir John Pringle, who had 3,000 acres under cultivation; 400 planters with 100 or more acres in bananas; and more than 10,000 small growers, some of whom possessed no more than one or two dozen plants. The peasant was, however, put at a disadvantage by United Fruit's marketing practices in Jamaica. His products were purchased in the open market at low prices, while the large producers received contracts at a fixed price that was immune to market fluctuations. Regardless of marketing practices, the results were impressive. In 1914, Frederick W. Adams, in his book on the United Fruit Company, *Conquest of the Tropics,* called Jamaica "still by far the greatest banana producing section of the globe." The 1 million stems that were exported from the island in 1884 were increased to 24.5 million by 1930—57.3 per cent of the total exports of the island.

While quick to invest in the planting end of the banana business, the Jamaican businessmen did not venture out of the narrow confines of their local environment and left all the marketing and shipping of the fruit to the United Fruit Company and its competitor, the Di Giorgio Fruit Company, which moved into the island around 1890. Di Giorgio was able to make inroads in United Fruit territory by guaranteeing a fixed price for all fruit supplied by contracting growers, together with an additional share of 50 per cent of all profits realized by the corporation from the sale of the fruit. Di Giorgio Fruit further strengthened its ties on the island by forming an equal partnership with the Jamaica Banana Producers Association, established in 1927 to ship bananas directly to foreign markets.

The Banana Producers Association was a unique organization—a cooperative marketing association that helped not only the large producer but the small farmer as well. For the first time since emancipation, the peasant in agriculture was given protection on the open market. Contracts were made by producers with the association for a period of years, guaranteeing a minimum purchase price. United Fruit, however, could not be squeezed out. Nor could its control over the banana industry be totally broken. In an attempt to weaken the association, United Fruit offered higher minimum prices, but the cooperating members continued to support the association because of the contracts guaranteeing purchase over several years. As a result of these practices, the association handled more than 35 per cent of Jamaica's banana exports in 1932, and its 14,066 members together owned 62,776 acres.

Banana production reached its all-time high in 1937, after which there was a steady decline in output. By the close of World War II, Panama disease, and leaf spot disease had taken their toll on the banana crop, and the postwar high of 14 million stems in 1960 came nowhere near the 27 million stems exported in 1937. Despite the development of the disease-resistant Lacatan strain, introduced after World War II, bananas though important to the economy, ceased to be a major export item.

The significance of the banana trade was all the more marked because of the decline of sugar. A general mood of pessimism prevailed in the sugar industry in Jamaica.

Loss of preferential treatment in the British market hit the Jamaican planters hard. Estates formerly worth thousands of pounds were sold for a few hundred; in many cases, planters sold their machinery to their competitors in Cuba and abandoned their estates. Credit institutions that had been established since emancipation, like the Planter's Bank, collapsed. To encourage purchases of these estates, Parliament enacted the Encumbered Estates Act in 1854. Commissioners were appointed in both London and Jamaica to receive applications from those who wished to buy encumbered estates. When a purchaser was found, the commission arranged the sale and then distributed the proceeds among the creditors. A new grant of the land was issued, and the property was sold with a clear and unencumbered title. However, the act had no significant effect in arresting the decline of the sugar industry. By 1896 there were only half as many estates as there had been in 1869. It was apparent to even the most conservative owners and investors in the industry that a radical reorganization of production methods was necessary. But, while price declines were rapid, fundamental changes were slow in coming. Whereas on the other West Indian islands the sugar estates were owned by foreign companies that could finance a modernization program, in Jamaica, unlike in the days of slavery, the majority of the estates were owned by local individuals, who had considerable difficulty finding the capital for modernization. Financing came primarily from local sources. The most urgent need was for a central place for refining the sugar that would make use of modern machinery and replace the individual—and inefficient—refineries of the various estates. But the capital costs involved in establishing the central factory were great and the amount of cane supplied would have to be sufficient to keep the plant running at full capacity. Not until the turn of the century was there any really significant amalgamation of smaller plantation units into larger ones, making it possible to establish the central refineries. In order to encourage this trend, the Jamaican Government in 1902 guaranteed the interest on capital used for this purpose and empowered the larger companies to make binding contracts with smaller growers. From 1890 to 1910, the number of operating units was reduced by more than half. Even with these improvements, sugar exports after 1900 came nowhere near the prominent position they once held.

World War I and the ensuing rise of sugar prices on the world market stimulated the expansion of the industry for the first time in nearly a century. With expansion came still further increases in modernization and a growing number of amalgamations of estates, which increased the average size to 368 acres by 1920. A decade later, the average size was almost doubled.

The sugar industry took significant strides forward in the period immediately following World War II. In 1950, as a result of the Commonwealth Sugar Agreement, Jamaica was given preferential markets in Great Britain on a quota basis. With a ready market available, production was stimulated and acreage expanded. In 1960, Jamaican sugar production reached the highest peak in its history. Jamaica's crop accounted for 35 per cent of all sugar exported from the West Indies. Both the large estates and the small farmers contributed to Jamaica's cane production. Peasants contributed almost 45 per cent of the total crop in 1959, while twenty large estates contributed the rest. Today, sugar is Jamaica's largest agricultural export.

The citrus industry had its beginnings at the end of the nineteenth century. Oranges had always been indigenous to the island, but local businessmen had not sought export markets for them. Jamaica's potential for becoming an important citrus exporter was realized in 1898–99 when a failure of the Florida crop sent American purchasers to Jamaica and the other Caribbean islands. Florida's subsequent recovery brought some decline, but nevertheless a place had been carved out for oranges in Jamaica's export picture.

Coconuts were also grown for export. The export of pimento and ginger, both indigenous to Jamaica, increased rapidly after 1890. Jamaica ginger enjoyed a good reputation abroad and invariably comanded higher prices than ginger produced elsewhere, but the yield fluctuated sharply, as the delicate pimento plants are affected by hurricanes and variation in weather. Like bananas, oranges, coconuts, coffee, sugar, rum, and molasses, these spices, although they never accounted for more than 6 per cent of Jamaica's exports, became a permanent part of Jamaica's export picture.

Local businessmen and investors who had hesitated to enter into the marketing of bananas were just as reluctant to invest in the extension of railroads, which was made necessary by the development of banana plantations and the citrus industry. As of 1869, the only railroad in Jamaica ran some 30 miles from Kingston to Old Harbour, a town on the southwest coast. The extension of the railroad to Montego Bay in 1894 and to Port Antonio in the east in 1896 was made possible by North American investors. The railroad provided an essential link within the country and ran to the chief ports. The age of truck transport had not yet arrived, and island roads were hardly in proper condition to transport fruit. Bananas and citrus fruits were perishable commodities and bruised easily on long journeys. As railroad transport of products reduced the possibility of damage, its introduction on an extended scale aided the small as well as the large producer.

The rapidly expanding manufacturing and food-processing industries of the United States supplied Jamaica with such essentials as cereals, fish, dairy and meat products, wines, beer and ale, spirits, tobacco, cotton, linens, woolens, leather, soap, candles, hardware, stationary, and books. Besides consumer goods, materials necessary for agriculture and construction such as wood, cement, cord, sacks and machinery and agricultural implements were also supplied. From this long list, it is obvious that Jamaica's consumer lifeline was strongly tied to foreign markets. One agricultural product, bananas, had replaced another, sugar, as the leading money-maker, and bananas had found a ready outlet in the expanding markets of the United States—the "Giant of the North." When Great Britain abandoned free trade after World War I and gave preferential treatment to colonial imports, its share of Jamaica's trade increased somewhat, but the United States still remained Jamaica's major trading partner. Canada, however, took some share of the Jamaican export-import market after a reciprocal trade agreement was signed between the two countries in 1920. By 1930, most of the sugar and coffee exported from the island went to Canada in exchange for fish, flour, and condensed milk, which had been originally supplied by the United States.

Despite the reciprocal trade agreements and preferential duties within the empire, the United States in 1930 was still the largest single source of supply for Jamaica's imports, while providing the largest market for its exports, accounting for two-thirds of all its foreign trade. Lagging somewhat behind were Great Britain, with more than one-fourth of total imports and exports, and Canada, with more than one-fifth. Trade with the other European countries and with South America was almost negligible.

In the years immediately following World War II, reciprocal agreements between Great Britain and Jamaica made Britain Jamaica's leading trading partner in both imports and exports. The United States moved to second place and Canada remained third. This trend reversed the pattern of the Crown colony era. Then political ties had been strong and economic ties weaker; from 1944 on, economic ties were strong and political ties gradually dissolved.

Jamaica's past economic experience had left a permanent mark on all sectors of society. The plantation system was not noted for breeding a spirit of innovation. Lack of dynamic, imaginative, and enterprising leadership on the part of the monied and propertied classes helped to perpetuate Jamaica's economic doldrums. The rapid decline of the sugar industry from which most of them had directly or indirectly received a livelihood was a traumatic experience from which they never fully recovered. It would seem that the merchants were in an ideal position to take the economic risks needed to start new enterprises. Yet, this group, like the sugar planters, remained narrow and rigid in economic outlook, having as little confidence in Jamaica's economic potential as the gloomiest prophets in England. Safe in their own businesses, they wove invisible cocoons around themselves and their wealth. They had little interest in, or desire to explore, workable projects for the economic reconstruction of society. In 1861, an American newspaperman, William Sewell, after surveying conditions on the island, commented: "Lower still she [Jamaica] can sink—lower still must she sink,—if the governing classes are not stimulated to more energetic action, and are not guided by more unselfish counsels." Jamaica was ill-served because of the lack of leadership and public interest on the part of the local elites. The descendants of the earlier merchants and planters could not shake off the attitude that Jamaica was destined to play a distinctly secondary role to economic forces that were somehow out of its control. Outside forces had ruined its social order when slavery was abolished and its economic life when the preferential duties given West Indian sugar were dropped. Adopting a defeatist attitude, the elites thought of Jamaica's economic decline as inevitable. At home in what they felt to be the "realities" of Jamaican life, they were complacent as others floundered. Anthony Froude, who visited Jamaica in the 1870's, complained of the "want of spirit and of the despondency" which pervaded the island. The worst feature about them he said, was their loss of heart.

The worldwide depression that began in 1929 brought ever increasing hardship to Jamaica and the other West Indian colonies, forcing the British Government to intervene. A series of recommendations were made, and some were implemented, but it was not until the close of World War II that changes occurred in the economic outlook of Jamaica. Economic change was openly welcomed and intensely encouraged by the new political elites that were emerging to carry Jamaica forward to nationhood. To further these ends, economic planning was introduced for the first time in Jamaica's history. Between 1945 and 1946 a ten-year plan was instituted, which was mainly concerned with raising the level of social services and charting new areas of economic development.

When the ten-year plan ran out, a new one was instituted in 1957 to run for another ten years. However, with the coming of independence this plan was scrapped in 1963 and replaced by a five-year independence plan. The latest plans stressed foreign borrowing to finance development programs designed to raise living standards and promote economic development.

Industrial development was one of the major new avenues for exploration. In 1949 the Pioneer Industries Law gave tax incentives to fledgling industries and their local investors. To attract local capital, the law granted a 20 per cent write-off from income tax for capital investments and duty-free importation of all building materials and equipment. Still another spur to industrial development was the creation of the Jamaica Industrial Development Corporation in 1952, which provided administrative services and financial aid for the new industrialists on the island. In 1959 the Development Finance Corporation was established to make medium and long-term loans to industry. Manufacturing throughout the decade of the 1950's would add greatly to the over-all wealth of the island. By the end of 1961, more than seventy factories had been built as a result of the incentives provided by the government. A wide range of products was created for both the local market and for exports: pharmaceuticals, paints and varnishes, cosmetics, clothing, shoes, plastics, processed foods, and glassware, to mention a few. The largest contributions to industrial output were made by food-processing, furniture and fixtures, and cement and clay products. Certain adverse factors could have hindered Jamaica's industrial development: It had only a small home market to receive the products and uncertain world outlets. The International Bank for Reconstruction and Development recommended in 1952 that Jamaica concentrate on developing its agricultural sector rather than industry. But, as there is not enough land in Jamaica to support its expanding population, its leaders recognized that it had to industrialize to create new economic opportunities. Faith in industrial development could not be undermined despite the difficulties. The adversities were somehow overcome. By 1960 the contribution of manufacturing industries to the gross national product was equal to that of agriculture. For the first time in its history, Jamaica had developed an alternative form of economic endeavor.

In another area of economic development, Jamaica has been the beneficiary of the Jet Age. The tourist industry, which had meager beginnings in the 1920's and 1930's, underwent a tremendous expansion in the 1950's. By virtue of its climate, scenic beauty, and excellent beaches, Jamaica, particularly its northern coast, was a natural center for the tourist industry, offering a haven for escapees from winter cold in the United States and Canada. Between 1954 and 1960, the number of tourists visiting the island doubled. Since 1945 the number of hotels on the island has doubled. Besides the traditional center of tourism at Montego Bay, Ocho Rios, also on the north shore, has been developed. Most hotel-building has been financed by foreign capital—American, British, and Canadian. Hotels are owned by Jamaican or foreign owners or both. Orderly development of the tourist industry is made possible by the Jamaica Tourist Board, a statutory body appointed by the government to promote and expand tourism. As of 1959, tourism, along with sugar and bauxite, was among the top three money-earners of the island. Experts predict an even greater expansion of the industry over the next decade.

Still another area of development in the postwar decades was mining. Before the discovery of large deposits of bauxite, Jamaica was described as a country of samples. There were many kinds of useful minerals found in its soil, but they did not occur in large enough quantities to establish a profitable commerical enterprise.

"For two generations," *The Gleaner* reported in its special Independence Supplement of 1962, "the people of Jamaica sat on a source of wealth and merely grumbled about it. They complained of the poor soil of the central plateau, the red dirt which grew pimento, provided them pasture for cattle and produced oranges." That "red dirt" proved to bauxite, and after its discovery in the early 1940's Jamaica was to benefit enormously from this natural wealth. Rich deposits of this leading component of aluminum were a magnet, attracting the world's leading producers of the product—Reynolds, Kaiser, and Aluminium Ltd.—to establish mining operations on the island. In 1953 Jamaica produced 8.5 per cent of the world output; by 1960 it was 21.2 per cent. Jamaica had become the world's largest single producer of bauxite and the United States' and Canada's major supplier. Known reserves of bauxite in 1953 totaled 130 million tons, and there was a distinct possibility that more would be found. Jamaica can look forward to rich revenues in this area, provided the companies now operating in the island favor expansion locally instead of their other foreign holdings. Whatever the forecast, the mining industry is a permanent economic institution of the island.

There is no "loss of heart" among Jamaica's leaders, as there was in times gone by. Today the government strongly supports industrial and tourist development. However—except for immigrants like the Issas and the Matalons, who have been major entrepreneurs in the new postwar economic age—the role of innovator has again been left to outsiders. Still another trend from the past is Jamaica's export-geared economy. Though the development of consumer goods industries has cut down somewhat on imports, Jamaica still does not have adequate resources to meet the demands of its home market. Rapid economic growth has taken place, and consumer needs have expanded imports of food and other durables. Local production has not kept up with expanding market. With an ever growing population, it is not easy to determine whether Jamaica can ever really achieve the goal of self-sufficiency. But if it cannot, unlike in former eras, it won't be for want of trying.

# 9. The Crown Colony Era, 1865–1939

With the adoption of Crown colony government, the lawmaking apparatus in Jamaica was completely overhauled. The governor emerged as the chief repository of power in the Crown colony system. His voice replaced the Assembly's as the decisive one in all questions of public policy. Concentrated in his office were the chief executive and legislative functions of government. The governor made public policy, translated it into a "legislative" program, and was responsible for the implementation of that program. The weak executive of the old representative system was transformed into a strong head of state.

Aiding the governor were members of the Legislative Council, British officials, and other personal advisers who constituted an inner council or "privy council." Their function was, however, purely advisory. It was the governor alone who had the decisive voice, subject, of course, to the approval of the home government in Great Britain. Whereas in the past a measure became law only after it had the approval of an elected Assembly and an appointed Council, as well as the governor, in the new order of things it needed the approval of a Legislative Council and the governor. The old Council had been abolished along with the Assembly. The new organ—the Legislative Council—had none of its powers. In the new constitutional scheme of things, it was a legislature in name only.

Between 1865 and 1884, all members of the Council were appointed by the governor. Reforms in 1884 and 1895 enlarged the membership on the Council to include elected members along with the original fifteen, who were either appointees of the governor or *ex officio* members from the colonial civil service. After 1895 the Legislative Council had twenty-nine members, a majority of whom were not elected and owed their appointments to the governor.

By the standards of membership alone, the Legislative Council was not an independent lawmaking body, and its legislative powers made it no more of one. No member, elected or appointed. could introduce financial legislation. Councilmen merely had the right to vote "yes" or "no" to legislative proposals, which could originate only with the governor. In fact, it was almost wholly on his initiative that laws were made relating to every area of island life. Though the governor's proposals didn't become the law of the land until they were passed by the Council, there was little likelihood that it would counteract his wishes, as the majority of its members were part of his official establishment. The Council played the consultant's role in the legislative process, often questioning, sometimes challenging, but never overriding the governor's decisions.

As a public official, the governor was not responsible to those who were most affected by his decisions—the citizens of Jamaica. Only those who appointed him—the British Government—could veto any or all of his decisions, whether legislative or executive. The new, direct role the British Government played in island affairs through the governor's office was unchallenged.

The small portion of the population that had long held political power was not satisfied with the new state of affairs. In a moment of panic, they had abdicated the responsibility of governing. In subsequent moments of calm, they regretted what they had done. Many of the white merchants, planters, and professional men and their colored counterparts chafed at the bit of political containment.

Others were convinced, however, that the presence of an unchallenged British authority in the island would do much to pacify what they believed to be a restive Negro populace.

Another Morant Bay rebellion, they feared, might arise phoenix-like on the ashes of the old. To prevent this, the government needed to have the maximum authority.

Neither those who supported nor those who criticized the Crown colony scheme wished to return to the pre-1865 type of government. What was desired was a modification of the existing structure so that the local citizens would have some means to check the almost unlimited power of the governor and the English officials who advised him. One major reform suggested was enlargement of the Legislative Council to include an elected majority. As the Council's approval was needed for all programs proposed by the governor, the Jamaican ruling class could then have a countervailing power to offset that of the governor. Another area the former ruling elite felt needed reforming was that of government jobs. The highest ranks of the civil service were filled by Englishmen instead of local inhabitants. It was this group of Englishmen who served in the governor's privy council and advised him in the formulation of his programs. Creole participation in appointed positions in government was strongly desired. If both reforms were implemented, the local citizens would have a voice in government policy on both the executive and the legislative levels.

Some islanders were so dissatisfied with the Crown colony system that they petitioned the Colonial Office in the 1870's for changes, asserting that the existing form of government "strikes at the root of all manhood and self-reliance, and will end in making the inhabitants of the Colony weak, dependent, and childish." Those who supported Crown colony government, however, like W. Kelly Smith, a newspaper editor and a pure Negro, asserted:

> Crown Colony government has very happily produced peace and harmony among all classes of the community; each class has been duly separated and left to work out its respective destiny.

The old form of government—the representative Assembly—according to Mr. Smith, had never been beneficial to the Negroes. Under that regime, Negroes had been "isolated and kept apart from social or other intercourse." The great achievement of the present government was that it had "broken down disaffection, private interests and primitive oligarchism." Kelley Smith was convinced that "without the protection of the government our fellow colonists would not permit us [the Negroes] to enjoy the breath we breathe."

Some reform in Crown colony government took place after the *Florence* affair of 1882, which brought upper-class dissatisfaction with Crown colony government to its peak. The *Florence* was a ship that had been detained in Jamaica by order of the governor, Sir Anthony Musgrave, as it made its way from Colon to Saint Thomas. Part of its cargo of guns and munitions was taken off by order of the governor, and the consigner of the cargo sued Musgrave for damages. A costly judgment was made against the governor by the Jamaican courts. As he had acted in an official capacity, the Colonial Office instructed Musgrave to get half of the money he needed to pay the amount of the judgment from the Jamaican Government, while the other half would be paid by Britain.

If the plan seemed reasonable to the British, the Jamaicans did not agree. Even the wholly appointed Legislative Council balked at the proposal. Legal losses of this kind, it was felt, should be borne entirely by the imperial government, because Musgrave had acted in its behalf. The raid on the local treasury could not be countenanced by those members of the Legislative Council who were native Jamaicans. They resigned as a group, leaving the Colonial Office and the governor to rule.

The whole issue aroused hard feelings on the island. Communication between the governor and the local population broke down completely. Officials in England decided it was opportune to act on the complaints of the local citizens, so that good relations between them and the governor, along with his British advisers, might be restored. Constitutional reform became official with the Order of the Privy Council for May 19, 1884. By this order, the governor's powers remained the same, but, as a concession to the local elites, the Legislative Council was enlarged to include nine elected members (after 1895 the number was raised to fourteen) who served in the same advisory capacity as the governor's appointees. The chief executive officer, with the aid of civil servants who continued to be English appointees, drew up all governmental programs.

The elites of Jamaica had been given a consultant's role in government, but the governor's decisive role in policy formation, lawmaking and administrative implementation was left intact. The elected members, chosen for five-year terms, were severely handicapped in promoting policies that were at variance with the governor's own programs. They could merely criticize government policy and had no legal power to initiate legislation of their own. They had available to them only one method of making known their complete disagreement with government policy. The so-called "rule of the nine and fourteen" provided that financial measures could not be enacted if nine elected members voted against them. For nonfinancial legislation, the unanimous vote of all fourteen elected members was necessary for defeat. This veto of government policy was not necessarily the final word, however, for the governor had merely to declare that his legislative proposals were of "paramount importance to the public interest" and the measure in question would be passed, because the fifteen appointees on the Council were automatically obliged to vote with the governor when the "paramount importance" clause was invoked. Though it was not often used, the "paramount power" clause was another strong restraint against local representatives who might try to enlarge their powers by "bargaining" with the governor.

Most of the elected representatives accepted their membership in what amounted to a publicly supported debating society as right and proper. The elective voice in the Council rarely called for self-government, whether in the form of internal autonomy, dominion status, or independent nationhood. Rather, the elected members tried to enlarge their own powers on the Council and reduce those of administrative officialdom. They did not want popular government, for their fear of the black masses was as intense as ever. White and colored elites who had, since emancipation, showed little sympathy for, or interest in, the problems of the masses, sought to advise and influence the governor to promote measures suitable to their own interests. The best of the Crown colony governors succeeded, however, in looking beyond this group and developing some programs to help the masses. All of them tended to be influenced by the opinions of the white and colored elites; their ideas were the ones most readily available to the governor. English society had long believed that the voice of property and "intelligence" was superior, and its representatives in Jamaica were greatly influenced by this voice when making decisions concerning the welfare of Jamaican society.

The Crown colony era (1865–1944) may be conveniently divided into two major periods. The first, between 1866 and 1884, witnessed a wide range of administrative reforms on all levels of government and in the services that the government provided. The second, between 1884 and 1938, when elected representation was introduced into the Council saw no major changes, but there was some effort made to find solutions to problems in many areas, though in general the barest minimum of protection and assistance was accorded to the vast majority.

Sir John Peter Grant, who came to the island in 1866 as the first governor under the Crown colony regime, was instrumental in making many administrative reforms. The central government's operations were streamlined and modernized, considerably reducing operating costs. The Anglican Church ceased to be a financial burden on the central government when, because of Grant's recommendation, it was disestablished in 1870. Parish government was reorganized and greatly improved, reducing corruption. A centralized police force was formed to replace the county militias. Grant initiated many other schemes that, if subsequently developed and expanded, would have been even more beneficial to the island. He established trade schools, the first public works program in the island's history, and the Rio Cobre irrigation schemes, which made more land available for sugar and banana cultivation.

In the field of education, Grant took initial steps toward creating an efficient educational system on the island. Government grants were regularly made to schools that could demonstrate their ability to educate children. These grants were added to a "concurrent endowment" for the denominational schools, made with funds that had formerly gone to the Anglican Church before it was disestablished in 1870. Schools were examined regularly by an inspector, who certified them as eligible for grants. In 1871 there were only six elementary schools that qualified for the maximum amount of money given. The amount a particular school received was dependent upon the degree of excellence it achieved. "Payment for results" was the phrase applied to this financial arrangement, though in many places "results" were difficult to attain because of a grave shortage of qualified educational personnel. The staff-student ratio in the public schools was about one to ninety-seven.

Grant also reorganized the "endowed schools"—institutions that were started with legacies left by wealthy planters and merchants. Most of the endowments had been made in the eighteenth century, and over the years mismanagement of funds had taken a heavy toll of them. Now boards of trustees were appointed to handle the endowments and to oversee the curriculums. The new trustees held their jobs on government appointment and were obliged to perform their tasks in a responsible manner. Though no public funds were allocated to them, the endowed schools were assigned the task of secondary education. Not until the 1920's were grants in aid made regularly to support secondary schools.

Public health was another area severely neglected in the past where Grant instituted reforms. A government-supported medical service was organized in 1869, and doctors were sent to some forty districts of the island, making physicians available at least to those who could afford to pay for their services. Vaccinations were available to all.

Governor Grant was also responsible for the first public utility program in the island's history when supervision of the water supply was taken over by the government in 1871. The Kingston and Liguanea water works were bought and completely rebuilt to ensure a sufficient and safe supply for the city.

Reforms during the Grant era also included the reorganization of the administrative structure of the island government. In 1870 a local law established the office of colonial secretary, who, after the governor, became the chief administrative officer of the island. Under him were established six departments, which had staffs of between five and ten clerks. They included the Internal Revenue Office, the Medical and Hospital offices, the Inspector of Schools Office, the Treasury Department, and the Audit Office. Except for minor clerks, who were appointed on the basis of open competition from 1885 on, all positions in the civil service were filled by appointments made by the British Colonial Office or the governor; most were filled by Englishmen sent from abroad. Not until 1942 would the local civil service be liberalized in favor of Jamaicans.

Grant also made changes in the judicial structure of the island to improve efficiency and reduce corruption. District courts on the model of the English county courts were established. The system was further centralized in 1888 when district courts were abolished and replaced by resident magistrates. In still another effort to bring impartiality to the court system, government funds were allocated to pay the subordinate court officers, thus eliminating the practice of having them depend on fees. In 1879 the jurisdiction of the Supreme Court of Jamaica was extended to include a wide variety of courts, including Chancery, Encumbered Estates, and Bankruptcy.

Another governor, Sir Henry Norman, introduced further reforms. During his tour of service (1883–89), local govenment was reformed so that parish boards were elected rather than appointed by the governor. He hoped that these reforms would enable the peasants and agricultural workers to secure a voice in their local government. The requirement for voting for delegates to the newly enlarged Legislative Council was reduced so that citizens who paid 10 shillings a year in taxes or received an annual income of 50 pounds a year were able to vote.

Grant's and Norman's accomplishments exemplify the constructive role the governor could play under the Crown colony system. Succeeding governors did not do quite as much, but most of them made some contribution toward strengthening the government's operations on the island, adding to the foundations so carefully constructed by Grant. By the late 1870's, Kingston had its first gas works and central slaughterhouse. Public markets were built, and after 1899 the sale of fresh meat, poultry, and game was confined only to them. In 1895 the island's first modern sewerage system was installed in Kingston.

Preventive medicine was another area where the government continued to play a leading role. Treatment for yaws and malaria was provided after 1910 and continued to be a service open to all inhabitants of the island. Several epidemic areas of malaria were brought under control in 1928. Administrative innovations like the Bureau of Public Health instituted in 1926, and the establishment of a program for training health inspectors for rural areas in 1919 further enhanced the government's role. Between 1870 and 1930, expenditures for health services rose sevenfold.

The rudimentary educational system fashioned by Grant was not neglected by subsequent governors, most of whom turned their attention to improving the elementary schools, which had earlier been left to the religious denominations to organize and run. High costs were met partially through government subsidy and partially by student tuition. Nevertheless, the schools were handicapped by shortages in funds, as most of them received very small subsidies because of their low level of excellence. Added to this was the difficulty of collecting fees from parents, most of whom barely had the means of subsistence. Governor Henry Norman appointed a commission to investigate these problems in 1886 and took some small steps to alleviate matters. Acting upon the recommendations of the commission, he abolished elementary school tuition and ordered the first government elementary schools to be built. Norman, however, advised against a government takeover of the schools, as the costs would be prohibitive.

Norman established a precedent that would set the pattern for operating the public school system on the island. A balance was struck between public support and private management whereby denominational groups continued to run their local schools while the government paid teachers' salaries. Clerical managers hired and fired their staff and were responsible for the day-to-day running of the schools. The government also supported and maintained two teacher training colleges, Mico College for men and Shortwood College (founded in 1885) for women.

There were, however, many hurdles to overcome. The problem of finance was the most difficult. Educational expenditures, which had increased by more than 5 per cent between 1870 and 1890, increased by only slightly more than 2 per cent from 1890 to 1930. A severe financial crisis in the 1890's forced the government to cut expenditures. Denominational groups were prohibited from building new schools, and the government did not step in to fill the gap. Grants in aid to the existing schools were drastically cut, which means that teachers' salaries were at new low levels. Neither personnel ratios nor school facilities could keep up with the expanding population. The early decades of the new century witnessed no real progress in education on the island.

Secondary education, left to the endowed schools, was still more neglected. After Grant's reorganization and consolidation of their facilities, ten remained, with a student body of 878. This meant that only one in a hundred received a high school education. After the turn of the century there was a gradual increase in the number of secondary schools, and beginning in 1920 the government began to finance the endowed schools, using the "payment for results" criteria—the long-established system used for the elementary schools. By 1929 there were twenty-five high schools. One child out of fifty received a secondary education, as tuition fees still had to be paid.

Vocational education was difficult to establish. Agricultural education was looked upon with hostility even on the primary level. The initial experience of those who sought education after emancipation was through the missionaries, who thought of education as book learning to improve the soul and mind. Everyday problems were outside of their range of instruction, hence the Jamaicans' concept of what an education should be was confined to the knowledge acquired from books. At the turn of the century, Inspector of Schools J. R. Williams, reported that "our attempts in 1895 to secure practical work in elementary schools was to all intents and purposes a failure." Parents objected to the soiling of the children's clothes in practical work, contending that book learning and nothing else was what they had sent the children to school for. The heritage of slavery—the association of manual labor with slave labor—could not be easily forgotten.

An important educational and cultural innovation created during the Crown colony era was the Institute of Jamaica, founded in 1879 during the governorship of Sir Anthony Musgrave. Its purpose, according to its founders, was to encourage "literature, science and art." From its founding the institute served as both a museum and a library. Its original collections contained the libraries of the old Assembly and Council, while the foundations for a museum were acquired from the old Royal Society of Arts and Agriculture, which had been founded in the 1840's.

During the Crown colony era, the institute was instrumental in promoting public education through lectures and publications. Its board drafted the rules for Jamaican scholarship, and because of its efforts the Senior Cambridge Examination was established in Jamaica in 1882. The West India Reference Library, as it came to be known, owes much of its growth from those early beginnings to the work of Frank Cundall, who served as secretary and librarian of the institute from 1891 to 1937. Cundall built up the library's collection of historical documents and books as well as its unique collection of old West Indian and Jamaican newspapers. Cundall also wrote several books on Jamaican history and compiled several bibliographies. The institute, throughout the Crown colony period, came to be associated with a latent cultural nationalism, supported by the elites who were rooted historically in the islands.

Lady Musgrave, the governor's wife, was instrumental in founding the first social service organization in Jamaican society —the "Self Help" Organization—which enabled women who sewed and embroidered to sell their handwork. It was the beginning of a craft industry, which was to be encouraged later by the Jamaican Government.

Sir Henry Blake, the last governor of the nineteenth century, is remembered for having been instrumental in establishing the Jamaica Agricultural Society. In communication among the classes, this organization proved to be a catalyst. J. R. Williams, Inspector of Schools for Jamaica, reported to the Conference on West Indian Agriculture held in Trinidad in January, 1905, that the new organization

> shows the beginnings of cooperation amongst people whose inability to cooperate and lack of public spirit have been amongst their most discouraging characteristics. The service, social and political, which they render in offering opportunity to representatives of every class in the district to meet and talk over matters of common interest, and to get to know each other is exceedingly valuable. Not a little of the improved popular attitude to agriculture is due to these societies.

Supported by annual grants from the Legislative Council, the formation of the society was the first government program to aid the small settlers.

As its instrument of popular education, the society chose a journal whose circulation at the turn of the century was 3,250. It also sponsored local and island-wide shows and sent agricultural instructors to various parts of the island to lecture to local branches and to give individual farmers help. That the society's help was aimed toward small settlers can be seen by the fact that it offered, starting in 1903, prizes for the best kept holdings of under 20 acres, 10 acres, and 5 acres.

Blake was the first governor to consider in a fundamental way the immediate needs of the small settlers. Besides helping them to produce better products he adopted a program of road improvement so that peasants could get their products to market. It was hoped that they would be stimulated to produce more.

Thus, by the close of the nineteenth century, judicious and paternalistic guidance by some of the more enlightened Crown colony governors had helped to provide Jamaica with a working administrative system, a health service, and a rudimentary educational system.

Even with these innovations and changes, most Negroes viewed the government as an alien authority wholly unsympathetic to them. If it touched their lives at all, it was usually in a negative way, in the form of either the tax collector or the policeman. And even if they wished to vote, the requirements for exercising the franchise were prohibitive for most of them. Besides the usual requirements of age, residence, citizenship, and sex (women were excluded until 1919, one year after they were granted the vote in Britain), a prospective voter had to pay at least 10 shillings a year in property taxes. Thus the small settlers would be automatically excluded, as annual taxes on property of 10 acres or less was a little over 2 shillings. So, too, would the estate workers and domestics be excluded from the franchise, as only those earning 50 pounds in annual wages had the right to vote.

Clearly, the qualifications for exercising the franchise suited the purposes of the upper classes in Jamaica, which, despite their relatively small numbers, exerted both directly and indirectly a major influence on government policy, through their representatives in the Legislative Council and because the governor relied on their advice in formulating his programs. While their influence remained, their numbers declined. The white share of the population declined steadily from 1866 on so that it was only 1.7 per cent of the total population in 1921, though the colored or mulatto portion of the population remained at about 18 per cent of the total throughout the Crown colony period.

Jamaican elites might have differed among themselves, but there was no discord when it came to dealing with the masses. This unity is reflected in the record of the Legislative Council during the Crown colony era. Especially prejudicial to the interests of the masses were the methods and programs of public finance, which taxed the rich but "soaked" the poor, as they were not structured around the principle of "ability to pay."

The chief source of revenue from 1843 on was import duties, which accounted for 60 per cent of total government income. Whereas in slavery days the major source of revenue was a property tax confined to a small portion of the population, now an excise tax forced the entire community to shoulder the burden. These duties raised the prices of staples such as cod-fish, herring, cured beef and pork, flour, and rice by as much as 30 per cent. Regardless of income, all had to pay the same prices for essential consumer goods. As a concession to the rich, many items normally not purchased by most of the population were exempt from import duties. These included books, carriages, fresh meat and fish, apples, grapes, peaches, and strawberries. Carts and wagons used on the sugar estates were exempted from taxes, but a peasant who owned a vehicle used on public roads to carry provisions to market had to pay taxes on it.

After import taxes, other excise taxes were the second source of government revenues. This too affected all regardless of ability to pay. Property taxes, the third most important source of revenue, were also so designed that the heaviest burdens fell on the poorest classes. Besides the basic taxes on houses and land, there were additional house taxes to support local relief and education. Even the land taxes were not equitably assessed. Peasants owning up to ten acres paid from 4 to 5 pence per acre while landowners with holdings of more than 1,000 acres paid about one quarter of a pence per acre. In 1901, because of the difficulties connected with collecting a multiple set of taxes, new rolls were prepared and a single assessment was made based on the real value of all property. After 1903 a single sum was collected from all property-owners. In 1918, new excise taxes were collected on packaged liquor and entertainments. A small income tax was introduced in 1920—the only levy that placed the burden of taxation on incomes of 100 pounds per year or more. Nevertheless, this tax provided only 5 per cent of the government revenue in 1930, as compared with more than 75 per cent from indirect taxes.

Equally prejudicial to the masses were the public safety laws of Jamaica during the Crown colony period, as they were almost as harsh as in the days of slavery. Whippings for petty larceny were common, and a more stringent criminal code was put into effect. Loiterers and vagrants could be fined. Tread-mills were in common use in all prisons. Police were instructed to fire directly into crowds that appeared ready to riot. As late as 1942, flogging was used to punish those who stole growing crops. In 1912 an American visitor to the colonies summed up the feelings of both races: "The spirit which manifest itself at the close of the Sepoy Rebellion in India has not died out in the minds of the present white rulers of Jamaica and the black men are convinced of this by their experience with minor breaches of the law."

The problem was not to be easily solved. Slave society was based on the gulf that separated the slaves from free men. Even when all were free, the separation, if not fixed, was continued. The "classes," whether white or black, felt no empathy with the masses. Dark-skinned legislators acted no differently from their light-skinned predecessors. Until 1900, the Legislative Council was composed predominantly of whites from the landed and mercantile interests, with a sprinkling of professional men. In 1901 the first black man, the schoolmaster Alex Dixon, was elected to the Council, to be followed in 1906 by Dr. Robert Love. By 1935 there were eight Negro members. Most were as conservative in their thinking as the white members. Members of the Council had to have an annual income of at least 150 pounds from landed property, or 300 pounds if a businessman with no income from real property. Thus they felt distinguished not because they had black skins but because they had risen to an economic position far above that of the masses. Having made the great leap to the middle class, many of them, like the mulattoes of the post-emancipation period, had only contempt for those who remained behind. Seeking recognition from those who had long been the eminent members of Jamaican society, the successful black man easily adopted their values and beliefs, feeling the same cultural distance from the masses. Besides, his constituents were of the middle class, so the black Council member was not responsible to the masses as an elected official. Out of a population of slightly more than 1 million in 1935, only 68,636 were registered to vote.

Of all the black members of the Legislative Council, Dr. Robert Love was the only one to hold a distinctly Negro attitude. He was a great exponent of racial pride, or negritude. The young Marcus Garvey (1887–1940) was apprenticed to a printer in Kingston at the time Love was urging the full-blooded Negroes to throw off their lethargy and step forward and claim their political rights. Garvey took elocution lessons from Love and no doubt was seriously influenced by his ideas. It was Love who declared that "We love the white man because he is a brother; we love the colored man because he is a son; we love the black man because we love ourselves." Garvey organized his United Negro Improvement and Conservation Association and African Communities League in Jamaica in 1914. Some of the words contained in the manifesto written by Garvey at the founding of the organization sound very much like Love's own pronouncements: "To establish a Universal Cofraternity among the race; to promote the spirit of race pride and love." Garvey went to the United States to raise money for his organization in 1916, intending to return to Jamaica to build his association.

Finding the Negro community in Harlem receptive to his ideas, Garvey remained in the United States. He spent some time in jail. After part of his prison term for fraud was served, Garvey's sentence was commuted and he was deported from the United States. After touring in Central America and Europe, he returned to Jamaica.

In 1930, Garvey is reputed to have proclaimed, "Look to Africa where the black king is crowned, for the day of deliverance is near." When Haile Selassie became King of Ethiopia that year, certain native preachers interpreted Garvey's words to mean that the salvation of the black man was near and would come about through repatriation to Africa. Here was the black king whom Garvey proclaimed the Savior. Followers of these teachings became known as Ras Tafarians (another name for Haile Selassie). To them Selassie was a living God, the returned Messiah. As Selassie claims descent from Solomon and the ancient people of Israel and is known as the Lion of Judah, Ras Tafarians claim the same descent for all black people. They, like their Messiah, are among God's chosen people. And as their Savior resides in Africa, this is their Zion, rather than ancient Israel. Drawn mainly from the depressed and lower classes, these Jamaicans have found a way of gaining self-esteem through a unique combination of both African and Western traditions.

Garvey tried to launch a political revival as well. He organized a local political arm, the People's Political Party, and a daily newspaper called *The Blackman,* which was to last but two years, from 1929 to 1931. During the general election of 1930, Garvey used his organization to sponsor candidates to run for elective office in the various parishes for seats in the Legislative Council and for positions in the Kingston–Saint Andrew municipal government. The political platform of his party sounded very much like the nationalist aspirations of other Jamaicans who within a decade would create new political organizations to make their demands known. The program stated that Jamaicans should "be represented in the Imperial Parliament" and called for "a larger modicum of self-government in Jamaica" and social security, a minimum wage, and workmen's compensation laws. Promotion of native industries, improvement of "city, town and urban areas" and the establishment of a "Jamaica University and Polytechnic," as well as a "public library in the capital town of each parish" were some other proposals. Still others were legal, judicial, and prison reform; legal aid for the poor; land reform with government loans; free medical aid; health and sanitation instruction; and a National Opera House with an Academy of Music and Art. Published in January, 1930, in *The Blackman,* this platform was a remarkable forecast of things that later came about and that are still to come in Jamaica.

However, it wasn't thought of in that way in 1930. There were two black men on the Legislative Council who were difficult to defeat. As Garvey could not win over the mulatto and white populations who formed the majority of qualified voters, he and the other candidates of his party were defeated in the election for the Legislative Council. Garvey did win a seat in the Kingston municipal council, but the complexities and budgetary maneuverings of local politics were not for him. His Peoples' Political Party died as quickly as it had come to life. After this experience, Garvey lost all faith in Jamaicans.

On February 1, 1930, *The Blackman* carried a front page head-line, "The People Sold Themselves for Mess of Pottage—Fortune Spent to Corrupt Them—Made Drunk For Their Votes." Discouraged and hounded by creditors, who eventually deprived him of his printing press, Garvey left Jamaica for England in 1935, to die there in 1940.

Garvey was the first Jamaican political leader openly to espouse the regeneration of society. He was symbolic of a new age—the age of nationalism and self-government—which was about to be born. At an end was a period of history in which Jamaica was an administered territory subject to and governed by directives from outside itself. About to start was a period in which those who governed would respond to demands from within, from the masses of the people.

In the Crown colony period, no local leaders had emerged who were sensitive to the needs of the people. Improvements in the lot of the masses were sporadic. No guiding philosophy to improve conditions or effect social change existed, nor did anyone in the ruling group in Jamaica think this was essential and necessary. Subsequent events would shape the attitudes of a group of newly emerging leaders who would seek achievements that to the Crown colony society would have seemed revolutionary.

# 10. From Crown Colony
# to Independent Nation, 1938–62

The Depression, which began in 1929, had an impact on the entire world. Jamaica was not exempt: As a producer of "primary" products, prices of which fell more sharply than those of manufactured goods, it was more severely affected than industrial countries, and no class in Jamaican society was immune to the Depression's consequences.

The 1930's were difficult years everywhere; in Jamaica they seemed even more so. It was not that the unrest there took a more violent form than in other parts of the world; it was rather that the relative tranquility of the past and the fears of the white minority combined to make a series of "disturbances" and strikes seem almost revolutionary. The basic causes of the "disturbances" of the 1930's, which seemed to fan out with the speed of fire, was discontent, long latent but now intensified and brought to the surface by the economic shocks of the Depression. Though unemployment, underemployment, low wages, and bad conditions had been endemic in Jamaica, the people, despite their outward placidity, apparently had not become inured to them, and certainly not when the bad conditions intensified.

Up to now, emigration had helped to act as a safety valve. From 1883 to 1935, an average of 10,000 Jamaicans emigrated each year. Many of them sent money home. They had left Jamaica to find a better life elsewhere, but some were forced to return because of the worldwide Depression—only to encounter even worse conditions. The shock was too great to bear with equanimity. Some leaders of the discontented were repatriated emigrants from the United States and the Latin American countries.

A violent strike at the Frome Estate of the West Indies Sugar Company began in May, 1938, and soon spread. Strikes and riots occurred throughout Jamaica. These developments came largely as a surprise to local officials and to the Colonial Office in London. There had been no severe popular disturbances since 1865, and by 1938 Jamaica had experienced some ten years of Depression and its effects without any large-scale articulate discontent. Little wonder that Jamaica had developed a reputation in the Colonial Office as a "model colony," unlike some of the other West Indian islands. Stability in Jamaican society was attributed to its substantial number of small peasant proprietors who were almost entirely black—a facsimile of England's "happy yeomanry." What was overlooked was that in the middle 1930's the average weekly income of the bulk of the employed population fell to new lows, and many others were unemployed.

When the riots broke out in several parts of the island, Jamaica had gone for more than seventy years without a system of self-government. The 1938 disturbances signified the beginning of a new period in the history of modern Jamaica. Lord Olivier, a former governor of the island, exclaimed on June 2, 1938: "All over Jamaica, in places where one would least expect it, the worm is beginning to turn." Hedley P. Jacobs, an English-born resident of Jamaica and one of a handful of white men associated with the reform movement, characterized the disturbances as not a "widening of cleavages, but the discovery of them." As an expression of discontent, it was more than a mere blind protest. There was a positive demand for the creation of better conditions.

The outburst of discontent did not at the outset center upon political demands. The strikes and riots growing out of it were more spontaneous reactions to appalling economic and social conditions and were not at their initial stages politically motivated or organized. They proved, however, to be a leaven for the rise of trade unions and political parties. The discontent and the demand for changes was now focused on the working class. As Arthur Lewis, a future vice-chancellor of the University of the West Indies, which was established a decade later, asserted in 1939: "The major issues discussed today no longer revolve around the aspirations of the middle classes but are working class demands. Initiative has passed into the hands of trade union leaders and the new working class bodies."

These bodies, including trade unions, were on a scale new to Jamaica. Modern trade unionism in Jamaica dates, for all practical purposes, from 1938. Although there had been a few small craft unions before that, their membership was very small and their power not much greater. Marcus Garvey, born in Jamaica, lost his job when he joined a strike of printers in 1907. Many skilled craftsmen emigrated to other lands, as did Garvey himself. A number of strikes occurred in 1918, but these were, as was true of the early 1930's, spontaneous rather than organized. The governor opposed the strikes but sought concessions from the employers. Not until 1922 did a union—the Longshoremen's Union—apply for recognition under a union registration law passed in 1919. Labor organization in Jamaica was still in an embryonic state, and the local press, which paid much attention to trade union developments elsewhere, had little to report on the situation at home. In 1938 large-scale changes were made in government policy. Although the Government of Jamaica in 1937–38 was still Crown colony in form, the "climate of opinion" had changed—largely owing to the "disturbances" in the West Indies and later in Jamaica. Acting on the recommendations of Orde Brown, who had been sent by the Colonial Office to investigate labor conditions, a relatively impressive program of social legislation was enacted by the Government of Jamaica in the area of wages and hours and in permitting, legally, the development of trade unions.

A Shop Assistants Law of 1937, revised in 1938, regulated the hours of store and clerical personnel. In 1938, a Minimum Wage Law provided for the establishment of advisory boards to recommend wage rates for certain specified industries. The 1919 law on trade unions was amended in 1938 to permit peaceful picketing and to remove union liability for breach of contract in strikes. Provisions were also made for arbitration, conciliation, and mediation of employer-employee disputes. Thereafter, the Jamaican labor movement was not faced with any formidable legal or even ideological barriers to its growth and expansion. The impact of events had been felt in the government as well as in society.

The man who emerged as the leader of the masses in Jamaica was a somewhat mysterious character of mixed Irish and Indian descent. Alexander Bustamante, a one-time money-lender, made himself their spokesman during the disorders of 1938. He was, according to his own testimony, born Alexander Clark, in 1884, the son of an Irish planter and a part-Indian mother. At the age of fifteen, he was adopted and taken to Spain, where he received his education and took the name Bustamante. He served in the Spanish Army and worked and traveled in South America, in the United States, and in Cuba, Canada, and England. Returning to Jamaica, he became a successful money-lender.

Bustamante filled what might be called the void that was created by seventy years of Crown colony government. Unable to cast ballots at the polling booths, deprived of political power, the mass of people had developed no political leaders. When, finally, they were goaded by conditions to express their sentiments, they were able to do so only in overt—and sometimes violent—action. Still without leadership, they eagerly accepted Bustamante, who strode forth on the scene, dramatic and dynamic. Bustamante held out the promise of a better life here and now. With "his towering height, shock of greying hair, emphatic stride and unquestioned verbal flair"—and his energy and fearlessness—Bustamante became the leader of the desperate unemployed and underemployed, sorely in need of a bold, self-confident, and aggressive spokesman. The chief figure to emerge from the disorders which began in sugar estates, Bustamante was a flamboyant, messianic leader with a great ability to articulate the grievances of the discontented.

In an article published in the island's leading newspaper, *The Gleaner*, immediately after the 1938 riot at Frome, Bustamante explained his motives. He wanted "to prevent workers of all classes from being trampled upon as they have been in the past," like "footmats belonging to no one, not even the British Government." He was not modest about proclaiming that he would be the voice and the instrument for change. "I want power, sufficient power to be able to defend those weaker than I am; those less fortunate, and that's what I have today, power." He promised to use that power. As he considered himself the true representative of the people, there was no need for popular votes or majorities. "I want to dictate the policy of the unions; the minority have had their dictators too long." He would, he said, replace a minority dictatorship with a dictatorship that claimed to represent the workers.

To further Bustamante's image as a popular leader, only a degree of martyrdom was required to bring him closer to the suffering masses; conveniently, Governor Denham of Jamaica rushed to complete the scenario. Just after the Frome riot, he clapped Bustamante in jail on charges of sedition and unlawful assembly. Thereafter, Bustamante was the unquestioned leader of the masses, now growing more "visible" as they became more demanding.

Bustamante's imprisonment hastened the pace of developments. The longshoremen, so vital in an island economy, refused to report to work until Bustamante was released. This was accomplished a short time later at the intercession of Norman Manley, a first cousin of Bustamante, a leading lawyer in Jamaica. Bustamante and Manley then traveled to various areas in Jamaica to negotiate on behalf of the strikers, who had no other leaders. Manley was quick to acknowledge Bustamante's charismatic appeal. On August 27, 1938, he declared, "Mr. Bustamante is Jamaica's leader by the only test that matters and that is the support and confidence of labor." Encouraged by the success of his negotiation, Manley decided to organize a political party. In September, 1938, in cooperation with other middle-class leaders, Manley, a former Rhodes Scholar, entered the life of politics and launched what proclaimed itself a "party for all the people"—the People's National Party, or PNP, as it was popularly called. One of its chief planks was a call for universal suffrage. In this, the organizers were capitalizing on a changed public opinion that had seemingly arisen almost overnight. A former trade union official turned educator, Hugh Springer, was to write, "For the first time the people as a whole were politically awakened." Soon, for many Jamaicans, the cry for a greater voice in ruling themselves became the *sine qua non*.

Manley's political action in 1938 was matched by trade union organization. Bustamante announced plans for organizing five unions under the rubric "Bustamante Industrial Trade Union." He abandoned his original concept of separate unions based on industries and organized all workers, regardless of industry, together, in an adaptation of the "one big union" of the Knights of Labor and its earlier counterparts in Great Britain. The Bustamante Industrial Trade Union or BITU, registered as required under the law in January, 1939. It claimed the membership of 2,000 longshoremen and 4,000 agricultural workers, mostly in sugar. Bustamante became "Founder and Life President."

In his efforts at organizing the workers, he was obstreperous and refused to cooperate with government agencies that sought to create more peaceful employer-employee relations. Bustamante was loved by the masses, but his deliberate sabotage of the government's efforts during the war aroused the ire of Governor Arthur Richards, who had Bustamante interned in September, 1940.

During the seventeen months that Bustamante was interned, Manley, who was seeking a trade union base for his fledgling political party, took it upon himself to become overseer of the BITU. Manley showed great organizing ability and used his lawyer's talents to revitalize and reorganize the union, believing that it would be the other side of the coin to the People's National Party. Manley proved most successful in his organizing effort. Within little more than a year, membership rose from 8,000 to 20,000. In negotiations skillfully guided by Manley, the union was also able to negotiate, in March, 1941, the first all-island sugar agreement. This was the first time collective bargaining had taken place in the sugar industry, and the new contract set the pattern for future large-scale wage agreements in other industries. A distinctive feature of the contract was that wages for workers were to be determined by the cost-of-living index.

Not only did the British Government institute immediate reforms in 1937 and 1938, it also looked to the future. A commission was appointed in 1938 under Lord Moyne to report on the problems of Jamaica and other colonies hard-hit by the Depression. The commission concerned itself with the twin problems of social welfare and political reform. The full report was not published until after the end of World War II out of fear that the description of the situation in the British Caribbean territories would provide propaganda for the Axis Powers, but a summary of the recommendations was published in 1940.

The commission conducted a thorough investigation of conditions, made extensive recommendations for badly needed welfare programs, and dealt with the problems of political reform. It was pointed out that the masses now demanded the creation of conditions that would render possible a "better and less restricted" life.

The commission recognized the demand for more self-government. In a Crown colony, it pointed out, the elected members of the Legislative Council are "compelled through that system to resort to permanent opposition to the government." They were forced "into a position of being vehement and continual critics." With no power to convert their criticisms into practical measures, they become "irresponsible." The system, the commission noted, also tended to arouse mutual suspicions of motives as between the appointed and the elected members of the Council; likewise, "white Englishmen" and the "brown elected" representatives confronted each other with fear and suspicion.

The commission held that the "existing circumstances" limited the degree of political autonomy that could be granted. Jamaica needed substantial assistance from the United Kingdom to develop its economy and to promote social reforms. In recognition of this need, the commission refused to go along with traditional British policy that each administrative unit was expected financially to stand on its own feet. The commission, in effect, recognized what had been pointed out by an editorial in the Conservative *Daily Telegraph and Morning Post* at the time of the Jamaican strikes:

> A great deal is amiss with the economic and social conditions in Jamaica. . . . The truth is that we are now reaping the harvest of a century's neglect. . . . The time has come when it is incumbent upon Britain . . . to apply herself earnestly to the task of redressing the more fundamental causes of West Indian discontent.

The Moyne commission recommended a more representative Legislative Council, counterbalanced by somewhat increased powers for the governor. It further recognized that political reform was essential, as economic and social reform would not be enough. The "growing political consciousness" made it "doubtful" that any schemes of social reform, however wisely conceived and efficiently conducted, would be completely successful unless they were accompanied by the largest measure of constitutional development deemed to be judicious in the "existing circumstances."

Reform was essential. In the words of the commission, "There are in Jamaica, as indeed throughout the West Indies, social conditions and problems of living that one does not care to think exist in any part of the British Empire." The Caribbean colonies were indeed, in the words of David Lloyd George, "slums of the Empire." The eighteenth-century phrase "as rich as a West Indian planter" was no longer used to describe the richest individuals in Britain and its Empire, but it was still true, as the commission discovered, that any study of Jamaica was a study in poverty. Jamaica was still, in the words of Dr. Samuel Johnson, a "place of dreadful wickedness and a dungeon of slaves," even if it were somewhat less a "place of great wealth and a den of tyrants." The Caribbean Commission in 1943 called it a "social and economic anachronism in a progressing Western Hemisphere." The contrast, and the knowledge of better conditions elsewhere, made the situation more serious. Compounding the seriousness and the difficulty was the fact that the demand for a better life was becoming increasingly insistent at a time when world economic conditions were seriously endangering even the maintenance of existing standards.

If the rich of Jamaica were not as rich as they had once been, by the standards of the great majority of Jamaicans they were rich indeed. Two-thirds of the total farm land was in holdings of 200 acres or more in size. This land was held by 900 holders or less than 1 per cent of those owning farms. About 330,000 persons, including dependents, were directly associated with land-ownerships. Most of them were peasant holdings smaller than 10 acres (many of them 1 acre or less) and were too small to support a family at a minimum standard of living. Almost 1 million people did not own any land.

The importance of welfare assistance had been brought dramatically before the British Government. As a result, the Colonial Development and Welfare Act was passed by Parliament in 1940. The responsibility of the British Government to its colonies was given clear recognition, even if the colonies found that the sums allotted were pitifully small as measured against the vast needs. On the other hand, there was a realization that Great Britain alone could not begin to foot all the bills. There was even some objection in Britain to the principle of the Colonial Development and Welfare Act, but on the whole public opinion accepted it. The British public was resigned to the fact that "in the past the white man's burden was on his shoulder," but now it was "in his pocket."

The Moyne recommendations for limited political reform seemed to win favor at first. When, however, the elected members of the Legislative Council went to the constituencies to discuss the proposals and to ascertain the wishes of the people, considerable opposition was encountered at the grass roots level. The PNP opposed the Moyne recommendations as too restrictive and demanded full self-government and dominion status by 1948 instead. Lord Moyne countered criticism by threatening: "If the proposals are fundamentally rejected, then universal suffrage, local government reform, taking a census, and allied changes would be definitely postponed."

Rising to the challenge, the Legislative Council rejected the Moyne recommendations as not going far enough in the direction of self-government and suggested that universal suffrage be adopted immediately. For Moyne, however, this offered the prospect that the polls might be "swamped" by a new and in-experienced electorate that might elect inexperienced and poorly qualified legislators. He advocated, instead, that the legislature should also consist of appointed, experienced members. The elected representatives would ultimately get more power, but he held that the Jamaican population was not yet "ready" to control completely its own destiny. He did, however, recommend gradual increases in suffrage with the ultimate goal of universal suffrage. The concept of tutelage was still strong in British Government circles.

The commission recommendation that future colonial policy not be based on the doctrine that a colony could have only those economic and social sources that it could finance itself found supporters in England. Many of the Jamaican intellectuals and professionals concurred, but they went farther. For them, economic and social problems should be taken up by a government that represented the Jamaican people. And it would be the obligation of the British Government to assist to the extent that the Jamaican people needed help.

The approach of World War II, which caused the British Government not to publish the report lest it be used for propaganda purposes by the Nazis, was to delay reforms, but it also stimulated the demands for change enormously. As in many other areas, there were visions of a "new society" that would emerge out of the war. An increasing number of Jamaicans began to view political reform as a vehicle for economic and social improvement. British control had led to little improvement; it was necessary for the people of Jamaica to control their own destiny. In October, 1942, a proposal for a new constitution was put forward in a joint memorandum by three groups, including all fourteen of the elected members of the Legislative Council, three representatives from the People's National Party, and three representatives from the Federation of Citizens' Associations (now constituted as a second political party).

The Three Party Agreement was, in the words of a contemporary observer, a "miracle" in that it was a unanimous agreement. It called for a bicameral legislature—an elected lower house or House of Assembly, and an upper house to consist of nominated and *ex officio* members. The reserve powers of the governor were to be limited. The governor would not have any power of certification by paramount power, and his veto power, which was characterized as "obnoxious" could be exercised only under limited specified conditions. Of an Executive Committee of ten, seven were to be elected by the lower house and three were to be officials nominated by the governor. The Committee was to be "the principal instrument of policy," with "power to initiate all laws, financial and otherwise." It was expected that the Executive Committee would develop into a Cabinet along British lines, and that subsequently its name would be changed to Council of Ministers. To further this end, the members of the Executive Committee who came from the lower house were to be placed in charge of specific administrative departments, and their authority gradually extended. One resolution called for the setting up of a Jamaican civil service.

The PNP took a leading role in politically activating the general public. The local newspaper, *The Gleaner*, described a meeting on November 16, 1942, when the party leaders demanded self-government for Jamaica. "A crowd which occupied all seats at Edelweiss Park last night passed a resolution demanding self-government, then swarmed forward as one man, to affix their names to the document."

Fearful of persistent and possibly dangerous agitation, prodded also by demands in the United States that Britain introduce democratic reforms in its Caribbean empire, the British Government yielded, and in a dramatic rejection of the Moyne commission's recommendations, the Colonial Office agreed to most of the Jamaican demands. Colonel Stanley, Secretary of State for Colonies, on February 23, 1943, stated that Britain was now ready to introduce "far reaching constitutional advances" in Jamaica. A new chapter in Jamaican history was initiated with the inauguration of a new constitution in 1944.

The British Government was not yet prepared to give up what amounted in the last analysis to its complete control over a colony. In the new constitution it therefore reserved the power, when it deemed it necessary to exercise that control. The governor was "the single and supreme authority responsible to, and representative of, His Majesty," in a Crown colony. The "paramount power" of the governor was retained with respect to the power of veto, reservation, and certification, to be exercised when it became expedient in the interests of "public order, public faith, or good government." And the definition of the terms was, of course, left to the governor. He could thus "certify" bills that he deemed necessary, without the consent of the legislature, and he had, also, the negative power of veto and disallowance. Despite the promise of far-reaching constitutional advances, the British Government did not give up all control.

It was further provided in the new constitution that the lower house, the House of Representatives, was to comprise thirty-two members, elected by universal suffrage, with no literacy or property requirement. As was true of the British House of Commons, the maximum duration of the House of Representatives was five years. A plurality was necessary for election. The upper house, the Legislative Council, comprising official and nominated members, had deliberative and delaying powers. The Executive Council, later called Ministers, was to be the "principal instrument of policy" under the Constitution. There was also a Privy Council, or advisers to the governor, whose main function was to advise the governor on matters of discipline and the exercise of his judicial prerogative.

Thus, although under unusual circumstances complete and unrestricted power could be exercised by the governor (as the representative of the British Government), the Jamaican citizens, through the House of Representatives, and indirectly through the members of the Executive Council designated by the House of Representatives, had a considerable degree of self-government. It became known among the Jamaicans as the "half-and-half government." The Executive Council was the principal and, in effect, the sole instrument of policy. It had, however, no individual party functions or responsibility, nor any direct executive authority. Its members were, it was said, "dukes without kingdoms." Under these conditions, orderly organization and planning and efficient administration were impossible. The central secretariat was headed by the Colonial Secretary.

It was stated in the British House of Commons that the Jamaica Constitution of 1944 "was largely suggested by the people of Jamaica themselves." Literally, this was true, but it was also true that the people of Jamaica objected to the restrictions on their own power to govern. Theirs was only a "semi-responsible" government, but the way was paved for complete self-government. The constitution went into effect on November 20, 1944, and a general election was held on December 14. The new legislature held its first session on December 9, 1945, with Colonel Stanley present. The new constitution was hailed as a "great experiment."

To opponents of self-government—although their members and influence tended to diminish—the constitution of 1944 seemed like a "slippery slope" that would lead to complete self-government. Just eight years later, in 1952, the popularly elected House of Representatives unanimously supported a resolution calling for self-government.

The political parties that captured political power in the wake of the 1944 constitution came to life as a result of a split between Alexander Bustamante and Norman Manley. Ever jealous of his own prerogatives and power, Bustamante, when released from prison in February, 1942, immediately broke with Manley and ordered the BITU to have nothing to do with the PNP. A year later Bustamante formed the Jamaica Labor Party (JLP) to oppose the PNP. Critics of Bustamante and of the government charged that the release of Bustamante was part of a bargain allowing Bustamante to attempt to sabotage the People's National Party, which the government had begun to view as a threat. Heated charges were made both by Bustamante and Manley.

In the first elections held under the 1944 constitution, the Jamaica Labor Party won an overwhelming majority in the House of Representatives. It won twenty-three seats to five for the People's National Party and four for independent candidates. Manley failed to win a seat. While it was a sharp setback for the People's National Party with its socialist program, a middle-class, private enterprise organization fared even worse: The Jamaica Democratic Party did not even gain one seat and failed to survive the election.

When universal suffrage came into effect, the majority of the electorate had participated in no organizations expressive of their demands other than the fledgling unions, largely under Bustamante. In the general election the electorate voted for their union leader and the political party he headed. Bustamante's success made it clear that mass electoral support could not be achieved without a well-organized trade union base. In an electorate dominated by propertyless wage earners, trade unions are the largest single organized group of the voting population. Above all, the election of 1944 marked the emergence of a vigorous two-party system, which became stable by 1949. A relatively large number of voters—59 per cent of those eligible—went to the polls. Suffrage gave the hitherto submerged black laboring population a sense of self-assurance and self-respect. No longer could it be asserted that the Jamaican masses were politically apathetic.

The years following the 1944 election marked the development of political parties in the "modern" sense. When the People's National Party and the Jamaica Labor Party were first established, there was a lack of solid organization around a definite set of principles or objectives. Over the years, the parties became more coherent and better organized, and the small independent groups lost popular support. Minor parties that had participated in the first general election had been obliterated by the time of the second general election. In 1954, all of the minor parties of the 1949 election had disappeared. The total vote cast for independent candidates was 30 per cent in 1944 and 13 per cent in 1949. The emergence of a well-defined two-party system came to many as a happy surprise, but the institutional forms adopted in Jamaica were an important contributing factor. The election of representatives in the single-member districts encouraged the growth of the two-party system and discouraged the rise and continuation of third parties.

Faced with a loss of popular support after the 1944 elections, the PNP sought to organize workers who were discontent with or had not come under the umbrella of the BITU. Manley had as his aids in this endeavor four dedicated men—the four H's, as they came to be called. Richard Hart, Arthur Henry, Frank Hill, and his brother, Ken Hill, were successful in organizing the civil servants and skilled workers, and a new labor federation—the Trades Union Congress, an affiliate of the People's National Party, was formed. The middle-class and "intellectual" leadership of the PNP had a far greater appeal to the better-educated worker than did Bustamante. As a result, Manley and his party sank political roots into some of the largest unions in the island. The public workers, the railway workers, the postal and telegraph workers, and the government auxiliary workers all came under PNP control. With both parties now having solid trade union support, the two-party system was a reality in Jamaica. Subsequent elections would prove this to be so.

In 1951, a split developed in the Trades Union Congress. One faction, headed by Thossie Kelley and Wellington McPherson, resigned and formed a rival union, the National Labor Congress. This group attacked the "4H's" and the PNP for supporting Communism. To forestall the disintegration of his party, Manley appointed a tribunal of top-ranking members to investigate the subversive charges against the Hills, Hart, and Henry. Although the evidence against them was not conclusive, the investigating tribunal recommended their expulsion from the PNP. Manley openly supported this recommendation at the PNP conference summoned to clarify the issue in April, 1952. Manley became convinced that in order to win greater public support for the PNP, it was necessary to purge it of what was publicly being attacked as the "red fringe." After ten hours of bitter debate, the recommendation for expulsion was approved, though not by an overwhelming majority. The expelled leaders formed a separate political party based on their control of the Trades Union Congress, but both the political party and the union were soon to wither. The PNP formed a new labor organization, the National Workers' Union, which gained the support of Trades Union Congress affiliates. The NWU was also successful in organizing the hotel and bauxite industries, which were developing at the time.

Rewritten after the 1952 purge, the PNP program abandoned

its former socialist orientation, although it called for economic reform as well as self-government. The trend toward a more conservative approach was also evidenced in the JLP, which in 1954 revised its constitution so that power was more widely distributed. This reform had the effect of making the party more than just a rubber stamp of Bustamante. Wealthy businessmen and many professionals, still unhappy with the PNP and its advocacy of greater economic and social reform, joined the JLP, thus merging business and labor politically. Despite the change in the JLP, in the election of January, 1955—the third under the 1944 constitution—the PNP emerged the victor.

The JLP's public image had become stale after its ten years in power. There was a growing desire for change. A "time for a change" slogan became especially effective after the imprisonment of two of the JLP's ministers for bribery. The election of 1955 was evidence of the clear emergence of a strong two-party system and of the lively interest of the Jamaican electorate. Of the more than 750,000 eligible voters, almost 500,-000 went to the polls. The PNP received more than 50 per cent of the vote, as against 40 per cent for the JLP, and won eighteen seats in the House of Representatives, as against fourteen won by the JLP. The minor parties failed to win any seats. Though his party lost the election, Alexander Bustamante, or "Busta," as he was popularly called, was knighted by Queen Elizabeth and became Sir Alexander Bustamante.

The election of 1955 removed any remaining doubts as to the working of the Jamaica party system and the stability of government—regardless of which party ruled. By 1955, three general elections had been held and Jamaica had had twelve years of democratic government.

When Manley took office in 1955, he established an extra-constitutional body called the Ministers Conference. The members of the conference were drawn from a group that had been formed in 1952 as a result of the recommendations of Governor Hugh Foote. Governor Foote had proposed that a ministerial system be established within the Executive Council in which individual members would also be heads of administrative departments. These fledgling cabinet ministers were to be appointed by the governor on the recommendation of the Chief Minister. They were drawn from the House of Representatives and would preside over the ministries of Local Government, Finance, Agriculture and Lands, Education and Social Welfare, Trade and Industry, and Communications. These reforms were largely sanctioned by the British Government in 1953.

As a further advance toward independent, national control, the governor was removed from the Executive Council in 1957. The Chief Minister was to preside over this body, a large majority of which consisted of members of the House of Representatives appointed to the Council by the Chief Minister. In 1959, the Council became, in name as well as in fact, a Cabinet, and the Chief Minister became Prime Minister. The governor's veto power was limited to bills affecting the royal prerogative, international relations, and any laws inconsistent with the constitution. Thus Jamaica became entirely self-governing except in certain matters of foreign policy. Manley, the Chief Minister, whose party had won the general election of 1955 and who was to become Premier, declared, "We will cut ourselves entirely free of the Colonial Office overlordship . . . and the constitution, to take Jamaica as far as she can go until we have complete nationhood."

A year before, in 1958, Jamaica had become part of the Federation of the West Indies. Conceived largely by the British Government as a way of reducing the costs of governing its possessions in the Caribbean and of making a viable state out of scattered islands, the federation was, in 1958, backed strongly by political leaders in all the islands. It was believed that each of the individual islands had insufficient area, population, and wealth to create a viable economy. Some union of the various islands would tend to avoid duplication of offices and services and, in addition to saving costs, would create a stronger and more unified administration. Although the British Government had begun to recognize that these territories would have to receive foreign aid, it was obvious that Great Britain sought, as much as possible, to minimize their demands.

The original idea of federation was not rooted in the West Indies. Its impetus was largely from Great Britain. Throughout the nineteenth century, the federation idea was conceived by the Colonial Office as a panacea for the West Indies and as a means of reducing the costs of the Caribbean territories.

After World War I, West Indian businessmen became interested in the possibility of some form of closer association among the various Caribbean territories. Nevertheless, a British official sent to investigate conditions in West Indian Islands reported that public opinion was opposed to federation and that it was therefore "both inopportune and impracticable to attempt amalgamation of existing units of Government into anything approaching a federal system." In 1926, a West Indian Conference was held in London, attended by representatives of the British Government and most of the colonies. (It must be emphasized, of course, that it did not represent most of the people in the colonies, who were at the time without political rights.) Though there was some talk of federation, nothing was done to bring the idea to fruition.

The sharp fall in prices as a result of the Great Depression stimulated efforts to achieve some sort of closer association of the various colonies. The burdens of the costs of government were particularly heavy in the impoverished economies. The British Government responded in 1933 by appointing a Closer Union Committee, but the committee, after extensive hearings, concluded that public opinion was not prepared for federation and rejected it.

The Moyne Commission, appointed in 1938 to investigate conditions in the West Indies, also found the time "not yet ripe" for federation but suggested attempts to "overcome local prejudice against Federation, both by exposition of its theoretical advantages and by testing these in practice through amalgamation of some of the smaller units." The ideal aimed at was the "combination into one political entity of all British possessions in the area."

Because of World War II, nothing was done until March, 1945, when Oliver Stanley, Colonial Secretary of the War Cabinet, in a circular dispatch, proposed discussion on the question of federation and political reform. The goal, as he put it forth, was self-government, but because the individual units were too small and too weak to be independent nations, federation became a practical requirement. A majority in the colonies were in favor of self-government, but they were much less enthusiastic about federation. West Indian nationalism was local, not "West Indian." The various territories had no sense of community, and only a few intellectuals saw merit in the creation of a West Indian community. For the great majority, who had no personal contact with the populations in territories other than their own, those populations were "foreign."

As it became apparent that, in the British view, increasing self-government could come only with federation, the colonial legislatures decided to investigate the possibility. In February, 1947, when the Secretary of State for the Colonies, Arthur Creech Jones, asked the various legislatures to send representatives to a conference to be held in Montego Bay, Jamaica, in July, 1947, there was, with the exception of the Bahamas, a unanimous response. The Montego Bay Conference seemed like a great success. The representatives of nine British West Indian colonies, including Jamaica, unanimously adopted a resolution "recognizing the desirability of a political federation of the British Caribbean territories." Taking Australia as a model, the conference adopted the principle of a federation in which each constituent unit would retain complete control over all matters except those specifically assigned to the federal government. A Standing Closer Association Committee was organized to supervise and direct future planning. The committee held a number of meetings and recommended that the federation be given only very limited powers; police, education, and agriculture were to be controlled by the unit governments. The federation was not to have the power of taxation, but it could raise money through "loans," and its finances were to be based largely on customs duties. Although the lower house of the legislature was to be popularly elected, the governor-general (as representative of the sovereign) could select six of the fourteen members of the executive body, the Council of State. The governor-general also retained a wide range of "reserve" powers. Thus, in the view of many West Indians, the effect of the proposed constitution was not to promote self-government but simply to recast

British power over the individual colonies into a unified system of control.

Lord Listowel, Minister of State for the Colonies, after a visit to the Caribbean in 1950, said that, although the political thought of the West Indian leaders had "matured" rapidly in recent years, public opinion was not yet prepared for political union. "I confess that I returned in grave doubt whether the word 'federation' is in the mind or even in the vocabulary of the ordinary estate worker, peasant or townsman." A year later, R. L. M. Kirkwood, a highly respected representative of the sugar "interest," commented that "the West Indian peoples as a whole have no idea or aspirations with regard to federations whatsoever. It is not even a political topic. Not a topic on which an election could be fought at all." At the end of the century, the idea waned. The West Indian Royal Commission, reported in 1898 that, because it seemed no kind of unified government could be introduced, there would be no advantage in federation or even in a unified civil service.

The next conference was held in London in April, 1953. Some changes in the proposed constitution were suggested, but the major difficulty arose over central control of the movement of peoples and goods. Jamaica was opposed to giving up its control over tariffs. There was a need in Jamaica for customs duties for revenue, as well as for the purpose of protecting its own new industries. Though the issues were not resolved, more conferences were held and the necessary legislation was passed in Great Britain, and in January, 1958, the new constitution took effect. The lack of enthusiasm for federation in Jamaica became very clear when some of the opponents of federation emerged victorious in the election.

Political realities, as well as the structure and forms of the new Jamaican Government, made the organization of a viable confederation a most difficult task. The federation did not become the "expression of the aspirations of the area towards fuller national status." It failed to develop into an organization dealing with the common social and economic problems of the area. Jamaica, growing ever more confident of its own destiny, was opposed even to the very limited powers granted to the federal government.

Adam Smith, in proposing that colonial representatives be incorporated into Parliament, had argued that the result would be to provide new vistas for representatives who would see the possibility of drawing "some of the great prizes which sometimes come from the wheel of the great state lottery of British politics." But the prizes offered by the new federal government lay in an uncertain future. Most of the politicians, and those of Jamaica in particular, acted more like pragmatic Englishmen than starry-eyed visionaries. Jamaica feared that federalism would be "a clog" on independence. Nationalism did not result in support of the federation but rather served to bolster Jamaican loyalties and act against federation.

Larger in area than the other constituent territories combined, Jamaica also contained more than one-half the population. Manley, one of the chief architects of union, began to heed advice that he be a "good Jamaican" rather than a federalist. This was especially necessary because Bustamante, who had earlier favored federation, had now decided to oppose it and stated that he opposed the making of "sacrifices" by Jamaica for the sake of the other West Indian islands. He looked upon federation as "devastation" for Jamaica.

The development of bauxite mining, the growth of manufacturing enterprises, and the growing prospects of tourism dazzled Jamaican businessmen and politicians who had previously been among the leading exponents of federation. There was now a growing fear that federation would prove a drag on the economy of Jamaica. Manley pointed out that Jamaica was "driving ahead economically" and that it would be "just plumb crazy" to "hand over the whole development to a new entity." In September, 1959, the Jamaican legislature, by unanimous vote, threatened secession from the federation unless concessions demanded by Jamaica were granted. These included a revision of the federal constitution to give Jamaica half of the membership in the federal House of Representatives. These demands were never acted upon. On January 9, 1960, Manley went to London to find out if it was possible for Jamaica to leave the federation and seek dominion status on its own, should it fail to find satisfaction in the federal arrangements. On returning to Jamaica on January 18, 1960, Manley reported that if Jamaica was unable to reach early agreement with the other members of the federation, "Jamaica will leave the Federation and will seek independence on her own." Following this, Manley, who had previously ruled out a referendum on the question of whether Jamaica could withdraw from the federation, now authorized it. In September, 1961, a referendum on federation was held in Jamaica. By a small majority the island citizens voted against it. On March 21, 1962, Jamaica withdrew from the federation.

Federation, largely a British import with no roots in Jamaica, had been accepted because the British insisted on it as the only way of achieving independence. When it became clear, however, that independence could be attained without federation, the people of Jamaica opposed it. They would face the future as a free people, "unhampered" by other West Indian islands, which might weaken Jamaica. Jamaica's three centuries of colonial status came to an end on August 6, 1962. In less than twenty-five years (1939–62), Jamaica had been transformed in peaceful and gradual stages from a Crown colony to an independent nation. It now proudly faced the future. In the words of former Governor Foote, who had been in favor of both federation and independence, "we in this small island will help to show the world that free institutions are not the preserve and privilege of a few great nations. We shall help show the world that democracy knows no frontier of race or creed or color."

# 11. The New Nation, 1962–71

## Cultural Nationalism

A uniquely Jamaican national outlook has developed since in-dependence to instill a sense of pride and confidence in the individual's identity as a Jamaican. The national motto, "Out of Many, One People," rejects the notion of black separatism and black nationalism, embracing instead the notion of diversity in peoples and cultures. When the forces of Jamaican nationalism achieved independence, the leaders rallied the peoples of the island behind a new self-image. A new look was taken at the island's past. Archaeological teams, supported by the Institute of Jamaica have, since 1966, established such target projects as the excavations of Port Royal (the infamous city of pirates and wicked traders that was destroyed by an earthquake in 1692) and the Indian burial grounds at White Marl, outside of Kingston. Most recently the Spanish city of Sevilla Nueva, built on the site where Columbus spent his first full year on the island, has been marked for archaeological excavation. Colonial notions of history, starting with English rule and revolving around it, are being challenged by archaeological finds. New textbooks for children have been written to tell the story of Jamaica not from the English or colonial point of view, but from the standpoint of an island citizen. The broad streams of history have been brought together and consolidated in terms of the new cultural nationalism.

Colonial attitudes, which created negative value judgments on one set of customs and ideas inherent in the human fabric of the island, are being re-examined and challenged. The culture of the lower class, long considered inferior, has been given new status and recognition by the government. This new outlook has found expression in government plans to reform the laws relating to illegitimacy. The large number of children born out of wedlock among the lower classes has, throughout history, been the object of scorn and shame. In May, 1968, the government pledged itself to remove discriminatory clauses against illegitimate offspring in all existing legislation. It also plans to introduce legislation giving illegitimate children the right to inherit property.

On still another front, a Folklore Research Program has been established by the Institute of Jamaica, with the help of government funds. Inaugurated by the Minister of Finance and Planning, Edward Seaga, in 1967, the program aims, according to the 1969 report of the Institute of Jamaica, "to gather our cultural heritage through the simple folk of our country, many of whom are still illiterate." Between 1967 and 1969, the researcher assigned to the project traveled throughout the island collecting riddles, proverbs, ring games, names of people and places, legends, "big boy" stories, sayings, verses, and street cries, and recording recollections of dreams and other psychic experiences. Defining folklore as the "feeling and thinking of a people and how they behave in groups," the researcher also attended folk dances; ceremonial rituals; revival cult meetings of Rastafarians and Bewardites; and "Nine Night" celebrations. Ring plays "strikingly African in origin" were also found. Ultimately, the project's results will be published in a book or a series of books on folklore in Jamaica. It is expected that the folk cultures of other settlers—the Muslims, the Hindus, the Chinese, and the Germans—will also be incorporated into the project.

Another prejudice inherited from the colonial past is the contempt in which the English dialect spoken by a good portion of Jamaican population was once held. Today, these attitudes are very much in the process of changing. The popularity of the entertainer Louise Bennett, who has sung and written in dialect, reached a new high in 1966 with the publication of a full length book of her songs. *Jamaica Labrish* carried an introducton by a prominent university cultural leader, Rex Nettleford, who explained the use of dialect as opposed to dictionary English as the "free expression of the people." Miss Bennett, he wrote, is the "only poet who has really hit the truth about her society through its own language." She has "well earned a place in the infant nation's cultural history."

Jamaican leaders have been quick to give status to the nationalism and the nationalist movement, which legitimized their power. In 1968, again through the Institute and with the backing of the Minister of Finance and Planning, a Historical Research Project was established. The project's aim was to computerize information on "social, economic and political events within the period 1938 to Independence in 1962." Early in 1971 the Prime Minister, Hugh Shearer, called on Jamaicans in the creative arts to turn their attention increasingly to national themes.

In 1968, British honors, long the coveted goal of leaders in all areas of Jamaican life, were abolished. Other former colonies in the Caribbean took similar steps, but Jamaica's action was the most sweeping: It was the only former colony to do away with knighthood. National or Jamaican honors replaced the British honors. Knighthood was replaced by the Order of Jamaica, while lesser ranks were the Order of Merit and Order of Distinction. A new rank, National Hero, was created and placed above other honors. It was awarded posthumously to Marcus Garvey and to the leaders of the Morant Bay Rebellion of 1865, Paul Bogle and George William Gordon. In 1969, Alexander Bustamante and Norman Washington Manley were made National Heroes. National Heroes Day, celebrated on the third Monday in October each year, is preceded by National Thanksgiving the day before. Prime Minister Shearer gave this holiday religious significance by signing the proclamation establishing the holiday before the heads of the churches of Jamaica. Though the religious leaders of Jamaica have always had some role in developing nationalist pride, as of 1970, that role has been made official. They cannot be more useful for molding public opinion than on the most important national holiday of the year.

The new nationalism has put aside the Western cultural tradition as the only standard of value. In its place the groundwork is being laid for a uniquely Jamaican culture. As the British culture served the colonial image, the new Jamaican culture serves the nationalist. The intensity of Jamaica's interest in cultural nationalism is further demonstrated by the leadership it has given to the world community in this area. At a UNESCO intergovernmental conference on cultural policies held in Venice in September, 1970, the proposal put forth by Jamaica that a culture conservation bank be set up was adopted. The idea originated with Edward Seaga, Jamaica's Minister of Finance and Planning, who felt that UNESCO should give financial support to member countries for the development and preservation of areas of their culture that might be lost through lack of means to conserve them in the face of demands on government finances for programs of more immediate practical importance. Jamaica's proposal found wide support among African, Asian, and Latin American countries that are facing the same problems. The nationalist chord sent vibrations throughout the conference, echoing the words of Jamaica delegate, Senator Hector Wynter:

> We who are from newly independent countries after a long period of colonization have had by necessity to adopt an aggressive policy of discovery and identification of our cultural heritage in order to gain its recognition, first nationally, then regionally, and then internationally.

Though territorially one of the smallest of new nations, Jamaica has cultural ambitions to match those of the largest nations. Its "aggressive policy of discovery and identification" is shared by all.

### Political Developments

About the time of Jamaica's fifth anniversary as an independent nation, a political commentator in the island's newspaper, *The Gleaner*, declared: "Jamaica is 'party controlled' rather than 'parliamentary controlled.'" The political events of

Jamaica's first seven years of independence are solidly anchored in the two political parties that collected the support of disparate sections of the colony in 1941, providing them with the leadership to unify and make an independent nation. The Jamaica Labor Party and the Peoples' National Party continued to have the undivided support of their loyal constituencies. The structures of the parties, firmly rooted in their trade union organizations, remained viable and secure. The JLP, under the leadership of Alexander Bustamante from 1942 until his retirement in 1967, maintained political control. The PNP, under its founder, Norman Washington Manley, played a significant role as loyal opposition to the government and a constant goad. The party was quick to criticize any and all government action that it found undemocratic or detrimental to the interests they represented. The PNP could do little to stop government action in the legislature, where the JLP had a large majority. It could only offer an alternative point of view to the Jamaican public.

There were several issues during the first years of independence that created party differences. Tensions were aggravated by the distribution of wealth and income among the constituent elements of the nation. This brought forth various proposals for the development of both the industrial and the agricultural sectors. The PNP was radically different from the Jamaica Labor Party in calling for "common ownership" of large agricultural industries like sugar and for the nationalization of utilities. In 1965 the PNP advocated the immediate nationalization of the Jamaica Public Service Company while declaring that enterprises like wharves, the telephone service, and cement and textile production "should not be regarded as legitimate sources of private profit." The nationalization theme was a feature of the PNP "Plan for Progress," featured in the 1967 general election. Nationalization of all public utilities, as well as cement production and transportation, was demanded in the name of government of and for the people.

Most recently, in July, 1970, Michael Manley, who succeeded his father as head of the PNP in 1969, enlarged the concept of public ownership to include a share for Jamaicans in the ownership of the bauxite companies. In a Parliamentary debate on the budget, Manley declared that all phases of the aluminum industry operating in Jamaica should be owned by government, workers, and private shareholders together. The younger Manley's speech might imply that the PNP is moving away from a program of public ownership toward a new concept of partnership between public and private sectors. Another difference between the PNP and the JLP is in their tax policies. Party planners of the PNP have consistently declared that income tax laws are "over-generous at levels where no national purpose is served." This position was maintained during the 1967 elections. On the matter of tax reforms, Michael Manley recently proposed that additional taxes be levied on the bauxite industry.

With regard to programs of economic development, the parties are not far apart. Both are committed to land reform. The PNP originally called for the restructuring of land ownership in 1964, but by 1969 a policy of rezoning and greater land use was favored. Both the JLP and PNP favor a policy of economic development that stresses ownership by Jamaicans and employment of Jamaicans in industrial, agricultural, and financial enterprises, both large and small. The PNP, like the JLP, gives top priority to agriculture. Michael Manley, has declared that more national resources must be diverted to agriculture, although PNP programs once favored industry. When Manley was asked in 1969 whether the party was shifting away from its emphasis on industrialization as a major goal for Jamaica, he answered "positively yes." Throughout the 1960's, the JLP government implemented a wide variety of agricultural programs aimed at the small and middle-sized farmers.

Though economic differences exist, there have been no outright political conflicts over these issues. It has been in the area of civil liberties that the stands taken by the parties have reflected more serious differences. On the administrative level, the PNP program has called for the creation of an ombudsman in Jamaica. This is a particularly ingenious stroke for the PNP, as its trade union affiliate, the National Workers Union, contains many of the civil service unions. Teachers and postal workers have been embroiled in conflict with the government over wage and personnel matters. During the 1960's there were costly strikes. In 1966, a month-long strike of the postal workers caused the then acting Prime Minister, Donald Sangster, to blame the inefficiencies of the post offices on the "uncontrollable postal employees and the union" representing them. There was also in 1966 a three-day, all-island teachers' strike to protest clauses in the new education code giving the Minister of Education the final authority on all teacher appointments. The PNP had voted against the code in the House of Representatives. There were also strikes by other NWU affiliates—hospital workers, bus drivers, Public Service Company employees, Jamaica Broadcasting Company employees, and doctors. An impartial ombudsman could have an important role in investigating government practices and might help to alleviate internal strife. Fearing encroachment on its political power, the JLP-controlled Senate turned down the PNP's motion for the creation of an ombudsman in 1966.

In Jamaica, as elsewhere, political patronage is an important area of party conflict. In a country with a high unemployment rate, the government's power to allocate jobs is an especially powerful weapon. Leslie Ashenheim, a JLP supporter and brother of the leading JLP politician Neville N. Ashenheim, remarked soon after the 1967 elections that there was a "widespread feeling that the government had carried the victimization of PNP supporters in the matters of public appointments, employment, and government contracts to a hitherto unknown high point . . . to the detriment of the unity of the country." In 1968, Michael Manley declared that "the very concept of human rights was being trampled underfoot in Jamaica" because of "government victimization" of PNP supporters who sought jobs, particularly in public works projects. Manley called for the negotiation of a joint agreement between the parties about work distribution, threatening PNP sit-ins in the absence of such an agreement. The ethic of party patronage, as opposed to nonpartisan appointments, is the orientation of Jamaica's political culture. In a region where government power is very highly centralized, this means that JLP leaders, as long as the party is in power, can manipulate the agencies of government to their own advantage with little obstruction.

The general elections of 1967 were held during the fifth anniversary year of Jamaican independence, and the political parties engaged in an intense contest for power. The JLP used its position as the party in power to maneuver constituency boundaries in its favor. One representative was taken away from Kingston, and the districts were redrawn so that sections supporting the JLP in neighboring Saint Andrew were given an extra representative. The parishes of Saint Thomas, Saint Mary, Saint James, Westmoreland, Manchester and Clarendon, and Saint Catherine were also given an additional representative each. The House of Representatives Delimitation Committee, which drew up the new boundaries and added the new representatives, submitted its report to the House on December 7, 1966. After a debate in which the PNP strongly protested the changes, declaring that "their action could cause a major rupture between political parties," the new districts were approved on December 27, 1966. Well prepared, the JLP called the general election. On February 1, 1967, Acting Prime Minister Donald Sangster declared that elections would be held in three weeks. The date was February 21, and it was chosen, according to Sangster, because February 24 was the birthday of Alexander Bustamante and the party wanted to give its beloved leader a birthday present—an election victory. Political custom and tradition usually allowed the opposition party eight weeks' notice before an election. On January 25, 1967, *The Gleaner* had reported that elections would be held within the next eight weeks —probably on March 28. The JLP, stretching its political power to its absolute limit, called the election in a hurry, catching the opposition off guard and with very little time to mount an election campaign. Norman Manley angrily denounced the move. It was a "rape of democracy," he declared, "to hold a snap election in three weeks."

On the basis of the popular vote, the election was very close indeed. With 446,815 ballots cast, the JLP received 224,180, or 50.65 per cent of the popular vote, while the PNP received 217,207, or 49.08 per cent. However, in the new House of

Representatives, the JLP received 33 seats to the PNP's 20. The results of the election show that the JLP gerrymandering had been successful. With voting in the House almost always along party lines, the JLP attained an impregnable majority. Once again, the JLP showed its strength in rural areas, though the PNP had made small inroads there. Comparing the results with the vote in 1962 elections, the JLP lost more than 48,000 votes outside Kingston, as against a more than 27,000-vote loss for the PNP. The figures—171,705 for JLP, 161,830 for the PNP—according to PNP analysts represented a 3 per cent gain in their favor. The PNP held its own in the urban areas, where most of the white-collar and civil service workers live. They are largely members of the NWU-affiliated unions. Michael Manley edged out his JLP opponent in central Kingston. Hugh Shearer, contesting Bustamante's old seat in West Clarendon (his retirement was announced before the election), won.

The PNP blamed a new system of registration for its losses in the election. The PNP had opposed passage of the law in 1964 on the grounds that it was costly to operate and difficult to administer and that it was discriminatory because it created two different registration procedures. The law, the PNP charged, was also responsible for the decline in the number of eligible voters between 1962 and 1967. There were 100,000 fewer people on the voter rolls in 1967 than in 1944, although the population had increased by at least 500,000. There was a drop in the number of voters since the 1962 election of 130,000. Between 1965 and 1966, an additional 50,000 who had already registered under the new law had been taken off the eligible list. A kind of selective disenfranchisement had taken place under the 1964 law. Solicitor Leslie Ashenheim, a JLP stalwart, criticized his own party just a week after the election. "Registration work was shockingly badly carried out," he charged. "There are too many cases of persons who struggled hard to get on the list and failed." Whether the system will be changed by the 1972 elections is still in doubt. Since the election of 1967, the registration system instituted at a cost of 1 million pounds has not been made a major political issue. What

Michael Manley once called the "Machiavellian system of registration" is still the law of the land.

Some of the sting of the 1967 defeat of the PNP was relieved
by the considerable gains made by the party in the local elections of March 18, 1969. Besides gaining control of the municipal
council of the corporate area (Kingston–Saint Andrew) the
PNP won an important Parliamentary by-election in the constituency of South East Saint Ann. Both parties had considered
this contest a significant test of strength and popularity. The
JLP lost by a wide margin, 5,605 to 2,474. On an all-island basis,
the JLP captured control of seven local governing boards, compared to five for the PNP. The intense political competition
between the two parties continues unabated.

The 1967 election was significant in terms of the emergence
of two new political leaders to take charge of their parties'
destinies. Hugh Lawson Shearer, who, according to *The Gleaner*,
rose from "obscurity to stardom" as "Sir Alexander's apprentice,"
became the new Prime Minister. A distant cousin of both Bustamante and Manley, Shearer began his political career in 1940 as
a staff member of the newspaper of the Bustamante Industrial
Trade Union. By 1942 he had become editor of the newspaper,
but his responsibilities ranged from newspaper work, to speaking at workers' meetings, to formulation of general union
strategy. After the success of the JLP in the first countrywide
election of 1944, Shearer used the power base Bustamante had
established in West Kingston to gain a seat in the Kingston–
Saint Andrew Parish Council in 1947. All the while, he continued
to edit the union newspaper and devote himself to union problems. Shearer acquired a reputation during the 1940's as a
shrewd negotiator, assisting Bustamante in the formulation of
collective bargaining agreements. West Kingston in 1949 became a PNP stronghold, and Shearer failed in his bid then and
in 1955 to gain a Parliamentary seat. This did not cause Bustamante to change his high opinion of Shearer. In 1951 he
designated him his "heir apparent," and in 1955 Shearer was
given the top post in the BITU, that of Island Supervisor. In
1962 Shearer was appointed a Senator. He also served as gov-

ernment spokesman and troubleshooter for foreign affairs and as chief of the Jamaican delegation to the United Nations.

Sir Donald Sangster's sudden death set off a power struggle. Even with Bustamente's support, Shearer was not the overwhelming choice of his party colleagues in the government. Voting through secret ballot, the JLP Parliamentary group was severely split. On the first ballot, Robert Lightbourne, the Minister of Trade and Development, received eight votes; D. C. Tavres, the party leader in the House and Acting Prime Minister, received twelve; and Shearer received ten. On a second ballot, Shearer narrowly squeezed through, sixteen to fifteen. That was in March, 1967. Since then, D. C. Tavres has died, while Robert Lightbourne continues to be a tough competitor. At the annual conference of the JLP in December, 1968, Lightbourne was elected Second Deputy Leader by a large majority. In the past, Lightbourne had depended on either Bustamante or Sangster for support, but in this first conference since their departure from political activity he showed great popular strength. Mr. Lightbourne, the political analyst in *The Gleaner* wrote, has "an unrelenting ambition to become Prime Minister of Jamaica," whereas Mr. Shearer "is not firmly entrenched in his leadership of the Jamaica Labor Party," for he "lacks the forcefulness of a Bustamante or the political velvet-gloved toughness of a Sangster." By the close of 1970, Shearer had sharpened his political skills. Still holding his own as Prime Minister, he kept Lightbourne from gaining the spotlight. In April, 1969, Lightbourne was forced to resign from his hard-won post as Second Deputy Leader of the JLP. As Shearer completed three years as Prime Minister of Jamaica, he had snuffed out, at least temporarily, his leading rival.

In 1969 Shearer reshuffled his Cabinet and reorganized some of the government departments. In key positions were his staunch supporters—Edward Seaga, Minister of Finance and Planning, and Edwin Allen, Minister of Education. Newly created departments went to Wilton Hill, Minister of Public Utilities and Housing, and William McLaren, Minister of Rural Land Development. The Cabinet also included many hold-overs from previous JLP governments. Robert Lightbourne re-

mained as Minister of Trade and Industry, as did Roy McNeil
as Minister of Home Affairs. Victor Grant retained his post as
Attorney General, and John P. Gyles stayed on as Minister of
Agriculture and Lands. Cleve Lewis joined the Cabinet as
Minister of Communication and Works, while Herbert Eldemire
retained his post as Minister of Health. Hector Wynter, former
Minister of Education, was transferred to the Ministry of Youth
and Community Development to work with Allan Douglas in
order to give that department more dynamism. A final member
of the Cabinet was Sir Neville Ashenheim, Minister Without
Portfolio. Prime Minister Shearer, who had also retained the
portfolio of Minister of External Affairs, put the Jamaica Information Service and the Jamaica Broadcasting Service under his
direct control. Firmly entrenched, Prime Minister Shearer has
enhanced his power by his ministerial appointments and his
administrative changes.

The PNP also changed leaders. A split in the party over
ideology, called by *The Gleaner* political reporter "fundamental
as was the crisis of 1952," was smoothed over by Norman Manley's diplomacy. After the defeat of 1967, David Coore, who
had headed the more radical faction in the party, was put in
charge of party policy, appeasing the radical elements. At the
same time Michael Manley, who, like Shearer, had been both a
journalist and all-island union superviser, in his case for the
NWU, became First Vice President of the party and the obvious
heir to his ailing father's position. Like Shearer, he had been a
senator since 1962, while continuing his trade union activities.
His election to the House of Representatives in 1967 strengthened
his hold on the party helm. After the retirement of Norman
Manley in February, 1969, Michael Manley was elected Party
chief by an overwhelming majority of 221 votes. The PNP is no
longer plagued by factional rivalries, as is so often the case with
political parties out of power. Michael Manley is in a good
position to provide the dynamic leadership the party needs.
Upon his retirement as party chairman, Norman Manley declared that the PNP had a tradition of collective leadership by
men with strong views and character. Michael Manley, an
honors graduate of the University of London, a former Canadian

Air Force pilot, and a leading trade unionist, has the qualifications and the personality to do the job. He has the support and help of other young party leaders. Wills O. Isaacs, Florizel Glasspole, and Allan Isaacs, veterans of the PNP since its founding, have retired as party vice presidents in favor of younger men–Vivian Blake, David Coore, and Dudley Thompson. Ken Hill, ousted from the PNP in 1952, has returned to the party, serving as senator and trade union leader.

In both the JLP and PNP, a governing elite has been created that makes use of political power in a creative and responsible manner. The question of political succession, so often a problem among parties in newly emerging nations, has been already solved in Jamaica. A second generation of leaders has emerged possessing the talent and expertise of the founders.

Norman Manley stepped aside at the end of 1968, as had Alexander Bustamante in 1967. Hugh Shearer, a contemporary of Michael Manley, is the leader of his party, as the younger Manley is. And farther down in the ranks, within the union structures, there are young men, some of them graduates of the University of the West Indies, who are becoming effective leaders within the organization. As heads of their respective parties, Manley and Shearer had to relinquish their posts as Island Supervisers of the NWU and the BITU, respectively, to younger officials. Like the democratic leadership that emerged in 1944, at the beginning of Jamaica's gradual road to independence, these men have met the test of leadership by accepting and meeting the challenges of responsibility. With the emergence of a new leadership since independence, dedicated to the principles of the old, Jamaica's stability as a nation is assured.

## Foreign Policy

Like other independent nations, Jamaica received its baptism into the world of national states when, soon after independence, it became a member of the United Nations. Despite this identification with the international community of nation-states, Jamaica's foreign policy was, during the years immediately following independence, oriented toward its traditional allies—Great Britain, the Commonwealth states, the United States, and Canada. "I am with the West," Bustamante declared and, in a gesture of friendship, offered the United States the opportunity to establish military bases on the island. The United States declined the invitation, but the loan agreements and the economic and technical aid given by the United States, Great Britain, and Canada seemed sufficient proof that amicable relations with these powers would take care of Jamaica's needs. During these years, Jamaica's foreign policy jelled in this traditional mold.

After the break-up of the West Indian Federation, regional ties picked up again. There were frequent summit conferences of Caribbean heads of state. And, for the first time in history, there was discussion of forming closer alliances with South American and non-British island neighbors. It was not until Hugh Shearer became Prime Minister and Minister of External Affairs that action was taken. Shearer's world outlook had been considerably enriched during his stint as Jamaica's delegate to the United Nations. He toured four Caribbean and South American countries in 1968—Netherlands Antilles, Surinam, Guyana, and Trinidad. He was the first Jamaican head of state to do so. Further efforts were made to promote regional ties when Shearer led Jamaica into the Organization of American States on July 2, 1969.

Jamaica sought the friendship of the African nations during the late 1960's. Haille Selassie and other African leaders made state visits to Jamaica. Ties between Ethiopia and Jamaica were further strengthened in 1970, when the first ambassador to an African country appointed by the government was sent to Ethiopia. In making the appointment, the government hoped to establish a point of contact with the Organization of African Unity, which has its headquarters in Addis Ababa. It was envisioned, as negotiations were completed, that the Ambassador would be accredited to other African nations. Reaching out to other "third world" nations, Jamaica participated in the summit meeting of heads of government of nonaligned countries held in Lusaka, Zambia, in September, 1970.

In Europe, under Prime Minister Shearer's direction, Jamaica forged ties beyond England with the Common Market States of France, West Germany, and the Netherlands. Shearer toured these nations in 1968, and by 1970 Jamaica had appointed its first ambassador on the European continent. With headquarters in Bonn, Vincent McFarland was also accredited to the Netherlands, Belgium, and Luxembourg. Shearer also created a "first" by making Jamaica, in 1968, the first Commonwealth country in the Caribbean region to establish diplomatic relations with Yugoslavia. Taking advantage of Yugoslavia's nonaligned position in Eastern Europe, Jamaica created the potential for increasing communication with a part of the world that has, outside of Cuba, little contact with the Caribbean. Jamaica has already imported crude material and household appliances from Yugoslavia, and since diplomatic relations were established the way has been left open for Jamaica to export rum, bananas, and coffee.

Jamaica has played an active role in the United Nations. For the twenty-fifth anniversary session of the General Assembly, a Jamaican was elected to be one of the seventeen vice-presidents of the Assembly. Along with Brazil, Chad, China, Ecuador, France, Iraq, Kenya, Malta, Mauritius, Nepal, Philippines, Senegal, the Ukrainian Socialist Soviet Republic, the United Kingdom, the U.S.S.R., and the United States, Jamaica, elected by 103 votes, will, in rotation, assume the functions of President of the Assembly. Jamaica is also a member of the Human Rights Commission, the Inter-Governmental Committee of the World Food Program, the Economic and Social Council, the Social Development Commission, the Commission on Narcotic Drugs, and the Executive Board of the World Health Organization. Jamaica's intensive efforts to assume an important position in the world of nations have been successful at the United Nations.

Prime Minister Shearer strikes a judicial balance between Jamaica's ties to its older allies and its newer involvements with the other members of the world community. A state visit to Canada in September, 1968, brought assurances of friendship and continued aid from Prime Minister Pierre Trudeau. Still solidly anchored, as it has been for centuries, on the rock of the Commonwealth and North American ties, Jamaica, in diversifying its foreign involvements, is taking advantage of its independent status as a new nation. ·

## Developments in Education

At the time of independence, Jamaica's school system was already established as a viable, working institution. Crown colony government supported a primary and secondary school system run for the most part by sectarian groups. Alongside this was a wholly public school system that, after 1962, underwent a tremendous expansion. In January, 1963, Bustamante declared that "illiteracy and independence are at variance and incompatible." The Jamaica Labor Party government has since put into operation a number of programs to make the public school system more efficient and effective.

In 1966 the Minister of Education, Edwin Allen, issued a ministry paper outlining the government objectives, "The New Deal for Education in Independent Jamaica." It addressed itself to the major problem—the provision of primary and secondary education. The government called for the enrollment of all children between the ages of six and fifteen in school by 1970. It hoped in 1971 to make attendance compulsory at both the elementary and secondary levels. Technical and high school education would also be expanded. The government's Five-Year Development Plan called for 100 per cent literacy for all children. Expansion of existing facilities were necessary to achieve this goal. With 18,000 new places needed every year in primary schools, the ministry paper acknowledged that so many places "have never been built in Jamaica in one year." Staggered attendance and the upgrading of old facilities, along with the building of new ones, are the means by which the ministry hopes to solve these problems. Also on the primary level, the government's long-range plan called for the reduction of class size from one teacher to every fifty pupils in 1970 to one to forty-five by 1975, and one to forty by 1980. In 1965 the Jamaica Teachers Association reported that there was a shortage in graduate teachers and a 44 per cent shortage in nongraduate teachers throughout the island. Government projections call for full staffing by trained primary school teachers and secondary school teachers by 1980. The teachers needed for this program would come from expanded teacher-training programs. Whereas at the time of independence teacher-training schools produced 200 to 300 new graduates each year, by 1969 it was projected that they would produce 1,000 trained teachers annually. Government projections were right on the mark. In September, 1970, an exam was given to recruit 1,200 secondary school students into teacher-training colleges for 1971. Free tuition plus room and board, when necessary, is provided by the government.

The major emphasis in the 1966 plan was on the expansion of secondary school facilities. The construction of sixty-six junior secondary schools by 1970 was an immediate target. The importance of the junior secondary school to Jamaica's educational planners can be seen by the goals: 93 junior secondary schools are projected for 1975. Unlike the high schools, which require admissions tests, the junior secondary schools are open to all children between the ages of 12 and 15. It is projected that 36 per cent of this open admissions group will go on to some form of higher education. While the majority of these junior secondary schools would provide candidates for high school and advanced technical schools, some of them would be developed into comprehensive schools. Five other secondary schools would also become comprehensive schools, providing both technical and academic education in separate programs.

In 1970 a vocational training program was established, designed to help youths who did not have the academic qualifications to be admitted to the technical schools. Ten training institutes were established in various parts of the island to give the idle but physically fit an opportunity to acquire skills needed for employment. The United Nations Development Program and the International Labor Organization have provided assistance to Jamaica. Plans also emphasize the expansion of technical education at the advanced level. Jamaica's equivalent to a technical institute—the College of Arts, Science, and Technology (CAST)—had an enrollment jump from 400 to 780 between 1966 and 1970. The Jamaica School of Agriculture underwent a similar expansion. On the secondary level, the government hoped to have a total of twenty-four comprehensive schools and twenty-three vocational schools by 1975.

This ambitious expansion program is financed by the World Bank, U.S. AID, and Canadian loans and grants. Loan funds would provide 60 per cent of the cost, and the government would provide the balance. The government expected to receive a World Bank loan at the end of 1966, but it was not until 1968 that the funds were allocated. With the AID loan and the World Bank loan, the government announced that there would be 4,500 additional places in junior schools by the beginning of 1969, with the completion of twenty-nine new junior secondary schools. In 1970 it was announced that Jamaica had begun negotiations with the World Bank for a new loan to continue the expansion of the junior secondary school program. On March 25, 1971, an agreement was signed for a loan of $11 million. Minister of Finance and Development Edward Seaga called this development a "major breakthrough" in Jamaican education. Thousands who might never have more than a primary education would now have the opportunity to advance to higher education.

At the university level, the Jamaican Government contributes $3.5 million to the expenses of the UWI. This amount does not include the subsidies given to 82 per cent of the Jamaican nationals. There are plans for the expansion of the professional schools of the university. There are proposals for an engineering college and for a faculty of agriculture to be established in Jamaica at some time between 1972 and 1975. Provision has been made for the training of lawyers beginning in 1970. Government projections that Jamaica will need three times as many university graduates as it now has led Edward Seaga to declare in 1968 that Jamaica may need its own national university. Jamaica's growth rate is faster, and its need for more graduates greater, than any other nation's in the region. Nevertheless, Jamaica has not pulled out of the multinational UWI. In 1969 an agreement was reached among all governments involved to continue the UWI as a multinational institution at least until 1981.

The imperial system of education, Prime Minister Shearer declared, had "trained clerks crammed with impersonal knowledge," while the new education system would "meet the challenges which technology is creating." The government's "New Deal for Education" program, Prime Minister Shearer added, "is a complete and exhaustive reconstruction of the system of education" in the interest of national development.

## The Expanding Economy

The legacy of the past did not disappear when Jamaica became independent in August, 1962. Along with the hopes for the future and the needs of the present remained the problems of the past. A small island with limited natural resources, it had made what to some seemed like phenomenal progress in less than two decades, but it was now faced with the task of continuing and even accelerating the pace of its economic and social development.

Politically, Jamaica had proved itself prior to independence. A two-party democratic system was firmly entrenched and universal suffrage was operating successfully. This political stability was to continue to be a major asset. Jamaica established missions abroad and applied for and was accepted for membership in the United Nations and other international bodies. It decided to participate in the General Agreement on Tariffs and Trade, but its application for membership in the European Common Market was blocked by France. Steps were taken for the continued operation of the common services in the Caribbean that had continued after the break-up of the Federation of the West Indies. These included the British Caribbean Meteorological Service, the Regional Shipping Service, the University of the West Indies, and the Regional Research Center. Directly or indirectly, these affected the economy of Jamaica.

Independence was a source of renewed hope and confidence; nevertheless, at the start it created a climate of economic uncertainty, especially among foreign investors. The newly established nation assured the world and its own citizens that it would continue to promote economic and social development and that foreign investments were welcome and necessary for Jamaica to achieve its goals. The government, now responsible

only to the citizens of Jamaica, promised to increase its efforts
to promote the economic and social welfare of the people. It
announced a budget of nearly 14 million pounds (almost $40
million) for capital development expenditures and promised
that its long-term program would be presented in 1963. However, there was a lag in construction because of an award of
higher wages to construction workers, which increased costs,
and because industry awaited developments under independence. Tourism, which was becoming increasingly important to
the Jamaican economy, also decreased by 8 per cent. These
slowdowns were viewed as temporary, and the government, in
an effort to encourage the expansion of tourism, announced
plans for the establishment of a national airline.

Hoping to increase home investments as well as foreign investments, and seeking to involve a larger number of its own
people in the further development of the country, Jamaica
introduced, in November, 1962, a National Savings Bond program to induce investments by small savers in a government
security. No interest was to be paid but holders of the bonds
were eligible for monthly prize drawings.

The trends already evident in the past continued. There was
increased trade with the United States, which provided a
greater market for Jamaica's exports than did the United
Kingdom and was also the largest source of Jamaica's imports.
Jamaica, along with other West Indian sugar producers, continued to benefit from the embargo imposed in 1960 by the
United States on Cuban sugar. The United Fruit Company,
through a British subsidiary, entered into an agreement to
renew cultivation of bananas.

The problem of a growing population in a land of limited
resources continued. In the 1951–62 period there was a natural
increase of population of more than a half-million, offset in part
by a net emigration of 191,000, or about 37 per cent of the
natural increase. Net emigration, which had averaged more than
30,000 per year during the preceding three years, was expected
to decrease because of the sharp curtailment of immigration
into the United Kingdom by the Commonwealth Immigration
Act, which came into effect in July, 1962, and which drastically

limited the number of immigrants entering the United Kingdom from the countries of the British Commonwealth of Nations. With emigration limited, the only hope of easing the population pressure was in the reduction of the birth rate. And, indeed, the birth rate, which had reached 42.9 per thousand in 1960, had fallen by 2.3 per cent. But it was still very high, and there was little prospect of a sharp reduction.

As the months went by in 1963, there were clear signs of a definite economic upturn despite damage caused by flood rains carried along by a hurricane, which, happily, did not hit Jamaica directly. Agricultural activities were adversely affected, but the year was nevertheless marked by increases in exports of sugar, bananas, citrus products, pimento, and ginger. Increases in building construction and the tourist trade also helped the economy. Most noticeable was the increase in manufacturing. Manufacturing became (and continues to be) the largest contributor to the gross domestic product, surpassing agriculture, mining, construction, and distribution.

The budget announced in April, 1963, called for an expenditure of 51 million pounds, with 14 million of this total allocated for development projects. The budget provided for some tax increases, and higher tariffs were imposed for the purpose of stimulating local production. The confidence of the financial world in the future of Jamaica was demonstrated by the oversubscription, within five minutes, of a loan of 1.5 million pounds in London. Jamaica was also able to meet the requirements of the International Monetary Fund and borrowed 1 million pounds from the World Bank.

The Five-Year Independence Plan, as promised in 1962, was presented to the Jamaican Parliament in July, 1963. Faced with the need for development and plagued by increasing social discontent, the government sought to bring about a balance between economic growth and immediate social improvement. The plan called for a combination of private and public enterprises which, it was hoped, would contribute to both the economic development of the Jamaican economy and the welfare of the people. Based on an assessment of the economic and social problems of the country and of its resources, the plan called for a total expenditure of 91 million pounds on development projects over the next five years.

In a speech announcing the plan, Prime Minister Alexander Bustamante took note of the demands of the people for an improvement in their condition. Jamaica could not overlook the rising expectations of its people. The "energy and vitality of its people" were Jamaica's most precious asset, but this same energy "imbues the community with a restless, questing spirit, steadily seeking for higher standards of living, better amenities, and a fuller life for the individual, his family, and for the community." It was, Bustamante said, the government's responsibility to ensure that Jamaica's limited resources were fully exploited and that living standards and the economic and social opportunities of the people were increased to the greatest possible extent. The government could not, however, do everything; it would lay the foundations, but it was for the people to set their hands to the task of building the society. Striking a theme that was to recur very frequently in speeches and statements by public officials during the decade, the Prime Minister stressed that "every person, man or woman, must be prepared to work hard."

Edward Seaga, Minister of Development and Welfare, emphasized that "we must fashion our country with the mold of our own deliberate wish and not as others wish us to be. This right and exercise of it, in the final analysis, is the essence of independence." He stressed that the plan was not a rigid instrument, since it involved forecasts into a future hedged by uncertainties. It was a "five-year plan" with a long-term development program. It projected an annual economic growth of 5 per cent.

Recognizing that agriculture was still the largest single source of employment, and in an effort to retain the population on the land and check its influx into the slums of Kingston, the government undertook a program to improve conditions in the rural areas. The Farmers Production Program of 1964 provided for various housing plans, construction of schools and other educational facilities, and improved water supply and drainage. Legislation was enacted providing for greater security for small tenant farmers. It would now be necessary for the owner to give a tenant five years' notice before eviction from all lands except bauxite land, where only two years' notice was required. However, the program could not hope to achieve any widespread improvements because of budgetary limitations.

The budget for the fiscal year 1964–65 totaled 64 million pounds, including 17 million, or more than 25 per cent, for development programs. About 14 per cent was allocated for education; about 10 per cent for health services; 8 per cent for agriculture; and about the same amount for improvements in transportation. In order to increase the employment opportunities for the local population, foreigners were required to have work permits, which would be issued only when local labor was not available to fill the vacancy. Work permits were issued on a liberal basis to skilled workers and managers, who were in scarce supply in an expanding economy.

In 1964, Jamaica became a member of the International Finance Corporation, established under the aegis of the World Bank. Adding to the other incentive programs, the government sought to encourage additional capital investment by foreigners by providing for income tax exemptions for nonresidents investing in building associations and housing schemes and granted depreciation allowances for commercial buildings built since 1961. The government bought or leased land, which it then leased or sold for industrial development purposes. The Jamaica Industrial Development Corporation reported that more than 100 new manufacturing companies had been established under the Industrial Incentives Law, The Export Industry (Encouragement) Law, the Cement Industry (Encouragement) Law, and the Textile Industry (Encouragement) Law.

Increases in production and employment were made even more necessary by the rise in population. In 1963 the net increase in population was 44,000; in 1964 there was a further increase of 42,000, or 2.4 per cent over 1963. The birth rate rose in 1964 and the death rate declined, while the average net emigration for 1963 and 1964 was 10,000, or only about one-third of the net emigration during the years 1960–63. The Five-Year Independence Plan had proclaimed that Jamaica would "encourage the spread of information on the techniques for the spacing or limitation of families for the benefit of those persons who desire them." In the absence of large-scale publicity and facilities, the program was hardly adequate and had little effect on the birth rate. The Jamaica Family Planning Association conducted a more intensive campaign to encourage the use of birth control methods, but it was not until later years, with the opening of rural clinics and additional facilities, that the campaign to reduce the birth rate showed some signs of success.

The economy as a whole continued to expand at a significant pace in 1965, though it showed a relative decline as compared to the growth during the 1960–64 period. Although the output of agriculture increased substantially, there was, because of lower prices, no corresponding increase in earnings. Construction increased by 9 per cent, and the Esso Oil refinery completed its first full year of operation, providing Jamaica with most of its needs for refined oil and gasoline. (Crude oil had to be imported, as no oil deposits had been discovered in and around Jamaica). A new cigaret factory was opened, and imports of cigarets greatly reduced. Tourism rose during the year. Tourists numbered 317,000, an increase of 39 per cent over the previous year, and tourist expenditures rose at an even greater rate. To further encourage tourism by affording some protection to visitors and to encourage the upgrading of facilities, the Jamaica Tourist Board issued a "Hotel Value Guide" based on the report of a United States team of hotel specialists.

The rate of total economic growth was 7.5 per cent over 1964, but this was partially offset by an increase in prices of about 3 per cent. Total income increased by 3.6 per cent to provide a per capita income of 145.6 pounds. Visible exports declined by 2 per cent in 1965 as compared to a 12.9 per cent increase in 1963 (in part due to a sharp increase in sugar prices) and an 8.5 per cent increase in 1964.

Governmental measures were taken to increase control of trading companies. The Companies Act, modeled on the United Kingdom Companies Act of 1948, provided for the registration and regulation of trading companies. Although there was no attempt to restrict the bulk of imports, which consisted of capital goods essential for economic development, there were continued efforts to cut down on imports of food and other consumer goods by placing additional restrictions and taxes on imported consumer goods.

To stimulate domestic production, a food crops subsidy was introduced for garden vegetables. At the same time, there was a promising increase in the number of food-processing plants to handle the increased production. A loan of almost 1.5 million pounds was received from the United States Agency for International Development for further expansion of the dairy industry.

To aid agriculture, the government guaranteed loans up to three thousand pounds (amended in 1968 to ten thousand pounds) made by commercial banks to farmers for specific projects. As part of the land reform program, it was announced that 27,500 acres would be distributed to farmers by March 31, 1966, on a five-year lease. If occupiers developed the land satisfactorily, they would be given the option to buy it at the end of the rental period.

The income tax was amended to provide concessions to sugar manufacturers for capital write-off for the years 1965–67 in order to encourage investment in a projected 5 per cent expansion of factory capacity to provide for a planned increase in sugar cane over the period. In 1965 Jamaica attained the highest sugar production in its history.

Unfortunately, this record was not repeated in the next year, especially with respect to prices. In 1966 the economy was affected by a continued decline in sugar prices. Other sectors of the economy fared better. Manufacturing and processing rose to 47 million pounds, almost 15 per cent of the gross domestic product, for an increase of 7.5 per cent over 1965 at current prices. During the year new plants were opened under various "incentive" programs, particularly with the stimulus of tax exemption. A basic feature of the industrialization program had been to encourage new industries to locate in rural area. By the end of 1966, twenty-three firms were operating in the countryside, and negotiations had been completed for the establishment of nine more plants. The government promised to encourage the decentralization of industry.

Construction remained good, and it was announced that the major aluminum companies had joined a consortium to build a 62.5-million-pound aluminum plant in Saint Elizabeth, one of the poorer areas of Jamaica. The plant, scheduled to go into production in 1969, would provide employment at the peak of construction for about 2,000 workers and, when completed, would employ 800 Jamaicans. The project would use local materials where possible and employ and train Jamaican personnel in the construction and operation of the plant. It would more than double the existing production of aluminum and would increase the bauxite and aluminum payroll by more than one-fourth.

The tourist trade prospered. The number of tourists totaled almost 350,000, for a 15 per cent increase over the previous record of 1965. Total tourist expenditures increased by 20 per cent to a total of 28 million pounds. The port facilities of Kingston were in the process of transfer to a new location nearby, Newport West, a portion of which had been completed early in the year. In February, the *United States* docked there, the first large cruise passenger ship to do so. Tourism was further encouraged by the inauguration of Air Jamaica service between Jamaica, Miami, and New York. Lufthansa, the West German airline, began operating to New York, Jamaica, and several South American cities.

Government expenditures continued to rise. The 1966–67 budget totaled more than 70 million pounds, about 20 per cent of it for capital works. Almost 30 per cent of the total was for various social services.

The single most difficult problem facing the Jamaican economy and people was that of agriculture. Although agriculture remained the largest employer of labor and there was a marked growth over the years, it accounted for less than 12 per cent of the gross domestic product in 1966. The value of agricultural products had increased from less than 26 million pounds in 1959 to more than 37 million pounds in 1966, but the increase was insufficient. Conditions in the rural areas, if better than in the Kingston slums, called for major improvements. As the population increased and the standard of living of segments of the population benefiting from the over-all improvement in Jamaican economy rose, there was an increase in imported food. Jamaica's total gross domestic product during the same period had increased from less than 200 million pounds in 1959 to 317 million pounds in 1967. In an effort to increase agricultural production, a Land Development and Utilization Commission was established to compel the cultivation of idle or under-utilized land of 50 acres or more. It had been estimated in 1963 that between 150,000 to 200,000 acres of land in farms of 100 acres or more in size were idle or under-utilized. Taxes on unimproved land had failed to encourage cultivation, and by 1966 the government decided on more direct action.

Arable lands of 50 or more acres now idle or under-utilized had to be put into acceptable cultivation by their owners. If the owners failed to do so, the commission was empowered to buy or lease the land and then rent it to farmers, who would, after a period of years, if they had proved efficient cultivators, be able to purchase the land. As the commission would first have to survey the land, there would be little immediate effect, but the legislation was symbolic of the announced intention of the government to bring all sectors of the economy to the fullest possible production.

Though there was a large increase in net capital growth in 1967, the year was marked by a relative slowdown in economic growth. However, there was an improvement in agriculture. Despite a severe drought, which began in 1966 and continued through 1967, agricultural production increased by more than 8 per cent. Riots in West Kingston sparked by student protests at the University of the West Indies, the retirement of Sir Alexander Bustamante as Prime Minister, and the early and unexpected death of his successor, Sir Donald Sangster, who had formerly been the Deputy Prime Minister, all within the first four months of the year, combined to retard the growth of other sectors of the economy. In addition, the economic situation was worsened by international monetary uncertainties, which culminated in the devaluation of the British pound in

November. Jamaica, along with other countries, was forced to follow suit, and the Jamaican currency was reduced to a par with the British pound (from $2.80 United States to $2.40 United States).

The gross domestic product rose 4.4 per cent to 336.5 million pounds, about one-half the rate of the previous year. Per capita income rose by 2.7 per cent to 156.7 pounds, but when allowance is made for price increases, the growth was only about 1 per cent. Manufacturing, including clothing and footwear, was the largest contributor to the gross domestic product, accounting for more than 50 million pounds, or 15 per cent of the total. The number of tourists decreased by 3.6 per cent (largely because of a sharp reduction in armed forces visitors), but expenditures increased by 2.5 per cent to 28.7 million pounds. Tourism was deemed essential to help overcome, in part, a balance of payments deficit of 26 million pounds. Legislation was enacted providing for a new Hotel Law Incentive Program, as well as a 50 per cent increase in government expenditures to encourage tourism. A Hotel Training School was also approved. It was designed to train local personnel and minimize the need for foreign workers and managerial personnel.

In addition to incentives for the development of tourist facilities, Jamaica continued its direct and indirect aid to encourage other economic development. The Kingston Waterfront Redevelopment Company, a government-organized and -owned venture, was established. Development corporations for other areas like Ocho Rios were also organized. The Jamaica Institute of Management was organized to train local personnel for managerial positions. The Industrial Incentives Act of 1966 was amended to provide for ten years' income tax relief, and up to fifteen years' relief in new areas. There was an emphasis on governmental capital investment to augment private investment.

In October, it was announced that a Jamaica Development Bank would be established, with the existing Development and Financial Corporation, in operation since 1959, to serve as its nucleus. Capitalized at 5 million pounds, it was designed to provide short-term and medium-term loans at commercial rates of interest for the development of housing, tourism, agriculture, and industry. Among its functions was the creation of discount facilities and the stimulation of exports. Two United States banks immediately made substantial loans to the Development Bank to assist in its organization.

Foreign trade in 1967 was in line with the trend already established. Over the years, an increasing share of Jamaica's trade was with the United States. In 1959 Jamaica had exported goods valued at 13 million pounds to the United States. By 1964 exports had more than doubled to a total of 28 million pounds. The value of exports to Canada during this period had increased from 11.5 million pounds to 16 million pounds. For the United Kingdom, the rate of growth was considerably smaller, rising from 16 million pounds in 1959 to 22 million pounds in 1964. About half of Jamaica's exports to the United Kingdom was sugar. Bananas accounted for another 25 per cent. Imports from the sterling area supplied 34 million pounds, or 27 per cent of the total imports. Imports from the dollar areas were more than 72 million pounds, or more than 57 per cent. Exports to the dollar areas were more than 50 per cent of the total exports of Jamaica. The exports to the United States, Canada, and the United Kingdom were valued at 65 million pounds, or 80 per cent of the total export earnings. The major exports to the United Kingdom were sugar, bananas, citrus, and tobacco. Exports to the United States were largely bauxite and aluminum. Bauxite, aluminum, sugar, and bananas accounted for more than 60 per cent of the total exports. Agricultural exports totaled 30 million pounds, of which 20 million, or nearly 64 per cent, went to the United Kingdom; 3 million, or 9 per cent, was shipped to Canada; and 6 million, or 19 per cent, to the United States.

Jamaica joined the Caribbean Free Trade Association, and its exports to the members of the association amounted to 2.4 million pounds. It was hoped that within a few years these countries would be able to absorb about 10 per cent of Jamaica's total exports.

At the end of 1967, population totalled 1,893,000, an increase of 1.9 per cent over 1966, as against increases of 2.6 per cent in

1968 and 2.8 per cent over 1965. The birth rate fell sharply to about thirty-six per thousand, and this matched a decline in the death rate to seven per thousand. The infant mortality rate dropped to thirty per thousand, as compared to at least twice that rate a decade before. Net emigration, largely to the United States but also to Canada rose, from less than 9,000 in 1966 to 20,000 in 1967.

The effects of the drought of the two previous years remained, but the economy advanced in 1968. Two favorable factors were the continued decline in the birth rate and the high level of emigration to the United States. The gross domestic product rose 9 per cent, or double the increase of 1967. From 1962 to 1967 there had been an average annual increase of 7 per cent. The tourist trade increased by 16 per cent, and the export of manufactured goods by 27 per cent. The economy was also aided by private remittances of almost 1.5 million pounds sent by Jamaicans in the United States. The per capita income was 160 pounds a year.

The population at the end of 1968 was 1,923,000. About 750,000 people fourteen years of age and over were in the labor force, of which about 20 per cent were unemployed or underemployed. About 63,000 were employed in the sugar industry, 43,000 in manufacturing, and about 15,000 in the tourist trade. A total of twenty-two new factories went into operation, representing an investment of 4 million pounds, as against twenty factories in 1967 with an investment of 3 million pounds. Investments undoubtedly would have been higher but for the stringency of the United States' balance of payments and a relatively large number of strikes in Jamaica, which also served as a restraining influence on would-be foreign investors.

During 1968, to counter the inflationary effects of devaluation, price controls and subsidies held down the consumer price index. Prices of all commodities increased at a more rapid rate, because many items that were imported (now at higher prices) had little effect on the consumer price index. For example, the rise in prices of imported capital goods was not reflected in the consumer price index.

With the expiration of the Five-Year Plan for 1963–68, which,

it was estimated, had fallen short of the 1963 projections by
2.4 per cent, the government announced a new "flexible" planning program under which every year the goals for the fifth
year thereafter would be reviewed in the light of changing conditions. Of course, the government reserved the right to make
changes at any time, but the plan was designed to furnish "tar-
gets" to be aimed at.

To encourage new planting of sugar, bananas, coffee, citrus,
cocoa, and other crops, cultivators were permitted to exempt
40 per cent of their investment from taxation, and new crops
were to be tax-free for five years. Subsidies for fertilizers and
for poultry, pig, and dairy feeds were continued at a cost to the
government of 1.4 million pounds a year.

In an effort to exercise more control over some of the gov-
ernment-sponsored development programs for the urban areas,
an Urban Development Corporation was established to take
over the general supervision of the three development companies already in operation—the Kingston Waterfront Redevelopment Company, the Saint Ann Development Company,
and the Saint Catherine Redevelopment Company—as well as
any others that might be created in the future. Although each
of the "subsidiary" companies would act as a limited liability
company, with its own board of directors, the Urban Development Corporation would serve as a clearing house and, if necessary, as a source of governmental directives.

The Kingston Waterfront Redevelopment Company had been
founded in 1966 for the purpose of undertaking the renewal
and rehabilitation of downtown Kingston. The area had long
been in need of rebuilding and this was now made more necessary because of the completion in 1966 of new docks in Newport West (in Kingston Harbor). The plans of the Kingston
Waterfront Redevelopment Company called for the tearing
down of most of the existing (and obsolescent) buildings, the
construction of new roads, and the erection of hotels, apart-
ments, office buildings, and garages, and a modern shopping
center, as well as an adjoining recreational and park area.

The Saint Ann Development Company was established in
1967 for the purpose of reclaiming almost 2 million feet of

beach land and the building of a resort town, but its progress had been slower than in Kingston. The announced aim of the Saint Catherine Redevelopment Company was to develop the area so that it would, in time, become as large and important as Kingston. These projects were financed mostly by commercial banks, but always in the background, and sometimes taking a more active part, was the Development Finance Corporation.

The year was also marked by the inauguration of a national system of old age and disability insurance. In April, 1968, the first stage of the National Insurance Law, to be financed by employers and workers, came into effect. Contributions were to be made by employers and employees, but not by the government. All workers earning less than 6 pounds a week were to contribute 1 shilling, 6 pence per week, and the employer was to pay 2 shillings, 6 pence. For those earning 6 to 20 pounds a week, additional payments of 6 pence per pound were to be made by both employer and employee. No additional contributions were to be made on earnings in excess of 20 pounds per week. Domestic workers in private households were also covered and were to pay a flat rate of 1 shilling a week, with the employer paying 2 shillings a week. Benefits provided under the law included old age pensions, medical care, and cash payments of 50 per cent of earnings for disabilities incurred by workers while on the job. Benefits were also provided for widows and orphans. It was estimated that for most workers employed for thirty years, the old age pensions would amount to 30 per cent of the insurable wage or salary.

In 1969, G. Arthur Brown, Governor of the Bank of Jamaica, characterized 1968 as "the year of missed opportunities." The "basic ingredients for growth, availability of market outlets, low interest rates, large capital inflows, a banking system highly liquid with available funds were all there, but for one reason or another, many within our own control, those favorable factors were not fully used." Mr. Brown did not expand on these comments, but it was clear that Jamaica would have to take more drastic action to seize, if not to create, opportunities for economic and social development. Others, including Robert

Lightbourne, Minister of Trade and Industry and President of the Jamaica Chamber of Commerce and the Jamaica Manufacturers Association, agreed that 1968 was a year of "problems and difficulties." It had been a slightly better year economically than 1967, but all agreed that it had somehow failed to live up to its possibilities. They agreed that the effects of devaluation had been, on balance, beneficial. All agreed, too, that the prospects for 1969 were favorable.

A major change in 1969, though achieved with little difficulty and no discernible economic effects, was the conversion to a decimal currency system. The Jamaican pound, devalued from $2.80 to $2.40 (in United States currency) in November, 1967, following the devaluation of the British pound sterling, was now converted to Jamaican dollars ($1.20 United States) to simplify the conversion of shillings (12 cents United States currency and formerly twenty to a pound) into "dollars."

The economic picture that emerged at the end of 1969 was mixed. The gross domestic product grew almost 10 per cent in 1969 and totaled 24.3 million pounds. Exports of goods and services rose by more than 11 per cent. The national income rose by 8.4 per cent, but the net balance of payments deficit in terms of Jamaican dollars was $100 million.

Despite the fact that the year was a "boom" year in development, there was a sharp decline in private investments to about one-half the 1968 total. To offset this, the government announced more plans for public investment to encourage the growth of industry, agriculture, and housing. In August, 1969, Edward Seaga, Minister of Finance and Planning, announced an additional development plan for the Ochus Rios Area, which would include housing for 35,000 people and would encourage industry and create new jobs over a ten-year period. One of the projects planned by the government was to establish modern townships with accompanying facilities. Additional housing developments were also planned for the Kingston suburbs and for other areas.

The 1969 population was 1,954,000, representing an increase of 1.6 per cent. A declining birth rate and a higher level of net emigration, mainly to the United States and Canada, was responsible for the relatively small increase. The government was stepping up its activities in encouraging birth control.

Imports and exports, although both increased in value, in part because of an increase in the level of prices, followed in large measure the pattern of the recent past. Total domestic exports increased from $150 million to $207 million, more than half of this total being the value of bauxite and aluminum exports. Other important exports were sugar, rum, and molasses, which fell slightly from $35 million to $32 million; bananas, which remained at the previous year's level of $32 million: and citrus, cocoa, and coffee and their products, which rose slightly from $10 million to $11 million, after a decline in the years 1965–69. Exports to the members of the Caribbean Free Trade Association (CARIFTA) rose from $4.8 to $7.2 million. The total trade of Jamaica with the CARIFTA members was $12 million. In December, Jamaica joined the Inter-American Development Bank.

Imports rose to a total of $369 million in 1969 as against $320 million the previous year, but the percentages of the types of goods imported remained remarkably stable. Consumer goods accounted for slightly more than one-third of the total, raw materials about 27 per cent, and capital goods one-third of the total.

Tourism continued to grow, with a total of almost 375,000 tourists in 1969 as compared to 300,000 in 1965. Feeling confident that prospective tourists would not be deterred by a tax, Jamaica for the first time levied a tourist accommodation tax to provide additional revenues. It was also announced that the airports were being enlarged to accommodate the new jumbo jets. By the end of the year, hotel accommodations for 11,000 visitors at any one time were available, and the rate of building was accelerated.

There was a general decline in agriculture. In an attempt to bolster the sagging sugar industry—suffering from both lower production and lower prices—increased loans were granted, prices on the local market were raised, and there was an extension of fertilizer subsidies to some farmers. A 40 per cent investment allowance was granted for expenditure for training programs.

Training programs for industry were also increased. To further the development of industrial training, schools were to be established, financed jointly by Jamaica and the United Nations Development Program Special Fund.

It was clear by the opening of the year 1970 that the economy of Jamaica would be affected by the economic "slowdown" in most of the world. At the same time, prices in Jamaica—as everywhere else in the world—had risen and were continuing to rise. In November, 1969, the Bank of Jamaica had issued directives to commercial banks to restrict credit, especially for consumer goods.

Jamaica could not, however, slacken its efforts to improve the economic and social conditions of its people. The budget of 1970–71 called for an expenditure of $250 million, of which $38.5 million was to be raised by loans. In part the higher budget was the result of inflation, but the increase also reflected the determination of the government to attempt to bolster a sector of the economy that was becoming an increasing cause of concern—agriculture. Thus, the amount allocated to agriculture increased from $4.5 million the previous year to $21.5 million. There were also increased expenditures for education and social services. In announcing the budget, the government hailed it as a "share-the-wealth" budget.

Although the birth rate during 1969 had fallen for the third consecutive year, from 3.9 per cent in 1966 to 3.3 per cent in 1969, population was approaching the 2 million mark and additional steps were taken to increase educational efforts and facilities for encouraging family planning. The Family Planning Board had been established in 1967, and by the beginning of 1970 more than ninety family planning clinics had been established all over the island. But they had been badly administered, and in July, 1970, Jamaica received a loan of more than 1.5 million dollars from the World Bank for family planning. By the end of the year there were one hundred fifty family planning clinics in operation. An innovation was the opening of the clinics at night to facilitate their use by employed women. All services, including the examination of women for possible cervical cancer, were free, although a nominal charge of 10 cents was made for a month's supply of oral contraceptives.

Although industry and tourism continued to receive assistance and encouragement, the government placed great emphasis on the need for increasing agricultural productivity by helping to promote greater efficiency and promoting the welfare of the agricultural population. Jamaica received a World Bank loan of $3.5 million to help finance mixed farming of major crops on holdings of 100 acres and more, and the Prime Minister announced production targets for a wide range of both domestically consumed and export crops over the next five years. Corn production, which had totaled 5,000 tons in 1969, was scheduled to increase to 70,000 tons in 1975. This would, of course, have a major effect on the livestock industry by supplying it with home-grown food. The Minister of Agriculture and Fisheries announced that beef production, which had risen from 4.7 million pounds in 1965 to 6.8 million pounds in 1969, would be sufficient to supply the domestic market even earlier —by 1972 or 1973.

Farm production was increased by the activities of the Land Utilization Commission, charged with the responsibility of putting idle or under-utilized land into full production. By July, 1969, the commission had inspected 913,000 acres of land and had adjudged more than 10 per cent of it as idle or under-utilized. More than 30,000 acres were already under full cultivation, with more planned. Full production on other land not completely utilized had already been begun by owners who sought to avoid government intervention. Reynolds Jamaica Mines owned a total of 62,000 acres, of which 11,000 were unused. The company had been developing this land at a rate of 500 acres a year, but it now agreed to step up its development to 2,000 acres a year.

Despite the increased utilization of land, agriculture as a whole was in an unsatisfactory state. This was especially true of the two major crops—bananas and sugar. Efforts were made to make banana-growing more profitable. On Christmas Eve,

1969, the Banana Board was replaced by a new body to be headed by Sir Neville Ashenheim, one of the most successful industrialists of the island, who had been the first Ambassador from Jamaica to the United States. The grower was to be guaranteed basic minimum prices; 10,000 acres of banana lands were replanted by the Banana Board with government assistance; and measures were taken for quality inspection of banana exports and for improvement in the packaging of bananas for export. Fertilizer subsidies were continued, and loans extended and increased.

The sugar industry was a particular source of trouble. Price increases announced in December, 1969, had not served to rescue the ailing industry. The sugar companies had long been advocating mechanization, but this had been resisted by the government because it would result in increased unemployment. Not only were the large estates affected, but the small sugar cane farmers, who had been a major source of strength in the economy and produced about half of the crop, had been hard hit. Many of them had discontinued production in the past two years. In four years the production of cane farmers had gone down from 255,000 tons to 180,000 tons. The sugar estates had either closed down or announced their intention to discontinue sugar production. In December, 1969, Sir Robert Kirkwood, Chairman of the Sugar Manufacturers Association, asserted that the sugar producers had lost $7 million in the past two years. The government had been forced, in 1969, to permit mechanization by the threat of the largest sugar producer, Tate and Lyle, to close down its Monymusk factory if it were not permitted. It was estimated that mechanization would increase efficiency and lower production costs on about 100,000 acres of the 160,000 acres utilized for sugar cultivation. On the other hand, the sugar industry employed about 60,000 workers with an average wage of about $6 per week and was thus a major source of employment. It was estimated that with their families, the total number of people dependent upon the sugar industry was more than 300,000.

Sugar was a labor-intensive industry as compared to bauxite and manufacturing, and in a land with a high rate of unemployment it was an important asset as such, besides being one of the major exports of Jamaica. Nevertheless, faced with no alternatives, the government had to capitulate. In November, 1968, in answer to demands of the Banana Growers Association for mechanization of loading at the docks and other changes that would result in higher unemployment, the Prime Minister had flatly overruled the recommendations of his own appointed committee. "To preside over the liquidation of the work force is not one of the planks on which I was elected," he had proclaimed. Now, faced with no alternative in the sugar industry, he was forced to capitulate again. In any event, the full effects of mechanization would not be felt for a number of years, as it would be introduced gradually and on an experimental basis.

Other export crops, though hardly of the importance of sugar and bananas, had also decreased during the past few years. Exports of coffee were down, mainly because of increased domestic demand, and in 1968–69 Jamaica had been able to take up only 40 per cent of its quota under the International Coffee Agreement. Much of the coffee was produced by 53,000 small farmers, most of whom grew not more than half a bag of coffee per crop. Cocoa exports, too, were down because of decreased production and increased domestic demand.

Agriculture was not the only cause for concern. The need for additional foreign investment to sustain and promote economic growth—and the welfare of the inhabitants of Jamaica—was a continuing preoccupation. The Prime Minister reiterated that foreign investments were necessary and that investors were welcome. Jamaica, with its limited capital resources, had to look to other countries for financial assistance with which to develop its economy. At the same time, to avoid becoming a mere satellite, Jamaica demanded that operations be on a basis of "partnership," with full opportunity for Jamaican investors to participate in the development and expansion of the economy and to provide additional employment on all levels.

The increasing participation of Jamaican nationals in the industrial economy was becoming evident. At the beginning of 1970, 24 per cent of industry was wholly owned by Jamaicans, as against 10 per cent in 1962, and about 40 per cent of all industrial firms were owned by Jamaicans and foreigners on an equal partnership basis. Nevertheless, more than one-third of the industry in Jamaica was owned by foreign nationals exclusively, with the balance owned in part by Jamaicans but with foreigners exercising majority control.

Sensitive to the requirement of partnership, foreign-owned enterprises sought to assist the direct and indirect efforts of Jamaica to promote local enterprise. Thus, the Kaiser Aluminum and Chemical Company of California, which was a major United States company engaged in the mining of bauxite and the production of alumina, set up a subsidiary, the Kaiser Development Corporation of Jamaica, designed to provide venture capital financing to Jamaican-owned and Jamaican-managed small and medium-sized businesses. The Kaiser Company was also prepared to help the firms in locating and in obtaining technical and management assistance. Emphasis would be placed on enterprises to produce items for export or goods that would reduce the need for imports.

In addition to private investments by foreign nationals and loans and grants, including about $5 million (Canadian) annually to Jamaica from foreign governments, the Jamaica Development Bank announced that for the twelve months ending September, 1970, it had approved loans for more than $4.1 million for twenty-eight development projects in industry, tourism, agriculture, and housing. Industry accounted for more than one-half of the total: about $2.5 million for fifteen projects. What was officially described as a "significant break-through" came in the field of agriculture. A limited number of loans were granted and a large number of applications were received, some of which were expected to be approved.

Industrial development and construction continued. As part of the renewal project for downtown Kingston, the first shopping center complex was opened and additional buildings were in various stages of construction. Tourism continued to expand at a rate double that of 1969, and additional facilities were completed; others were in the process of completion or being planned. It was estimated that tourist facilities would by 1972 be double those available in 1967.

In August, the Jamaica National Export Corporation was opened, and the Prime Minister promised that the government would do everything it could to provide incentives to facilitate and encourage exports by providing loans and other assistance. He exhorted all parties to cooperate and to do their "part towards making our country a better place."

In building and extending industrial enterprises, Jamaica was able to take advantage of the latest technological advances. Caribbean Asbestos Products, a Jamaica concern with 70 per cent local capital, was able—with the assistance of an Italian firm, which supplied the machinery and undertook to train Jamaicans to run the enterprise—to build the most up-to-date asbestos cement plant in the Western Hemisphere. The new plant, which cost $2.5 million, was an addition to a plant already established by the company in Montego Bay, for which machinery and initial personnel had been supplied by the same Italian firm. After a two-year training period, the entire operation at the older plant had been taken over by Jamaicans, and the same plan was now to be followed. The entire project called for the spending by the company of $12 million for expansion over a five-year period.

To increase and develop Jamaican banking facilities, the Government Savings Bank was to be reconstituted and would, in the future, operate along more commercial lines. The new bank would be formed with capital of $2.5 million, subscribed by the government, and would extend and expand its services. Having operated before the change through 255 branches in post offices, it would also establish its own branches in the principal cities and towns in Jamaica. It would offer loan facilities to compete with building societies and credit unions.

The need for additional employment opportunities was clear, but if the government found it impossible to reduce the unemployment rate by any significant amount, it could provide increased welfare provisions for those who were unemployed, as well as benefits for those employed.

Public assistance to more than 14,000 indigents, classified as "out-door paupers," who had been receiving annual allowances at a cost to the government of more than $570,000, was to be raised after July 1, 1970, to 2 dollars a week, which would raise government costs almost threefold. Benefits were also provided for 28,000 persons classified by the Minister of Local Government, Leopold Lynch, as the "respectable poor," who were experiencing economic hardship but were too proud to register as paupers and therefore had not been receiving any public assistance. Other forms of assistance were continued or extended, but on a very modest scale. Legislation was enacted providing that beginning on July 1, 1970, sick leave and paid vacations would be provided for some 500,000 workers. Employers were required to give their employees two weeks' vacation with pay and two weeks of paid sick leave after the first two days of illness. Workers who had been employed less than a full year were to be given paid vacations and sick pay in the ratio of 1:22 for each day of work beyond the 110-day qualifying period.

In addition, legislation was enacted to broaden the coverage and increase the benefits formerly provided by the Workmen's Compensation Act. The National Insurance Act was amended to include persons previously covered by the Workmen's Compensation Act. The changes, at an estimated cost to the government of $2 million annually, were to provide additional benefits. About 500,000 people were now to be provided with protection for injury or disability resulting from industrial accidents or disease. Medical treatment, invalid benefits, payments for disabilities, and death benefits were provided for, in addition to the other benefits, including old-age pensions, already provided for under the National Insurance Act. Actuarial studies were also to be undertaken with the help of the International Labor Office to review progress under the National Insurance Act and to investigate the possibility of extending the act.

Government workers received a pay increase that would cost more than $10 million in 1970 and $54 million over the next three years. At the same time, all workers earning less than $1,000 a year were exempted from income taxes (the previous exemption had been $600). It was estimated that 20,000 workers would benefit by this change. As for workers earning more than $1,000, allowances were permitted for working wives and the amount exempted from the surtax was increased.

Jamaica continued to receive aid and loans from various international agencies and foreign governments. The United States continued to send members of the Peace Corps to Jamaica to assist in various ways, but the shortage of teachers in Jamaica forced a concentration on teaching. Canada had been extending loans and assistance since 1964, which were sharply increased in 1970. The largest single package of loans, aid, and technical assistance ever to be negotiated by the Government of Jamaica, more than $35.6 million Canadian (approximately $28.5 million in Jamaican currency) was concluded with the Canadian International Development Agency. In announcing this agreement, the Minister of Finance and Planning, Edward Seaga, said that it "represents a critical break-through in Jamaica's external financing strategy not only by virtue of its record size, but because of certain other unique features."

The package, which covered the five-year period 1970–75, included $27.6 million (Canadian) in loan funds at 3 per cent interest for thirty years and $8 million (Canadian) in grants. One of the main features of the agreement was the integration of technical assistance with loans and grants, thus matching capital with manpower resources. The Canadian program for the first time included operational personnel, which would, Seaga asserted "fill the need for skilled professional manpower." Further, the five-year period enabled Jamaica to regulate the flow of funds in accordance with Jamaica's long-term planning.

The advantages of a low interest rate with payment extended over thirty years were emphasized by the ministry. The Canadian funds "have the easiest repayment terms which make them suitable for social development" and for roads, bridges, education, and water supplies, "all of which have a long-term gestation period before generating sufficient economic impact on the economy."

The size and terms of the Canadian loan and assistance grants would aid Jamaica in its goals of providing for economic and social development, but the answer to the question raised in the First Five-Year Independence Plan—whether a small country with limited natural resources could achieve and maintain "democracy, economic viability and social justice"—was not yet fully answered. Jamaica had undoubtedly maintained parliamentary democracy; its "viability" without continuous infusions of foreign loans and investments was open to question.

On the whole, the Five-Year Plan of Independence and the subsequent development plan had met their goals. Yet to many it seemed that the major problems of developing the economy and of simultaneously providing increased employment, higher wages, and better housing and educational facilities was still far from solved. The task of making Jamaica a viable economy and providing for the welfare of its people on the scale of the "developed" nations had not yet been achieved, although the Minister of Health, Herbert Eldemire, declared in 1968 that Jamaica could no longer be considered an "underdeveloped" nation.

Although social services had been greatly expanded, a large number of unemployed and underemployed, estimated at from 15 to 20 per cent of the population, and a high rate of "functional illiteracy" that left a large number of people who were, because of their lack of the most elementary skills, unemployable, demonstrated that the road to "social justice" was not easy to follow.

Unemployment, in the words of one of the ministers, remained "the cancer of our society," and, although there was no doubt that the government was, in the words of Minister of Local Government Leopold Lynch, striving not only to relieve the poor but "to stamp out the curse of poverty," the goal still seemed far off. That the development of the Jamaican economy had increased rather than decreased the gap between the rich and the poor was acknowledged by one of the island's leading developers, Sir Isaac Matalon, who declared that 5 per cent of the population earned 27 per cent of the country's total income, while the poorest 20 per cent of the population was earning only 5 per cent of the national income.

Jamaica, like much of the world, was experiencing the tide of "rising expectations." The Prime Minister had publicly voiced the conviction that "we are living in times when it must be recognized that we must have changes in our society." Robert Lightbourne, Minister for Trade and Economic Development, publicly recognized that it was necessary for economic and social developments to proceed "hand in hand." The alternative, he admitted, was to court political disorder and "inevitable disaster."

The goal was clear; how it was to be realized was much less so. Jamaica's natural resources were limited. It had no coal or oil; though sporadic drilling for oil had been going on since 1955, and in 1970 a serious effort was made to discover offshore oil deposits, the outlook was not promising. Perhaps at some future date Jamaica could achieve a power breakthrough by means of nuclear energy, but the needs were immediate. In the absence of vastly increased power sources, provided at low cost, Jamaica could not hope to reach the stage of converting its bauxite into aluminum.

Paradoxically, despite a high rate of unemployment and underemployment, Jamaica had a substantial shortage of skilled and semiskilled workers and of managerial personnel. The government had sought to alleviate this by providing training facilities, but it was evident that a massive increase in vocational and technical education would be necessary in the 1970's if Jamaica was to meet the demands of an expanding economy, especially as it was also trying to "Jamaicanize" its economy.

As Jamaica faced the future it could not rely upon its past achievements to overcome the hurdles presented by the present and the future. In the words of Robert Lightbourne to the Jamaican-American Chamber of Commerce in New York in July, 1970, it was necessary for Jamaica not only to continue and accelerate its economic development but also to provide the people of Jamaica with a "better quality of life—a resolve rooted not merely in our desire to benefit our country but also to reinforce the belief" that Jamaica could make "a contribution to the world of new developing nations by proving that a small nation, predominantly colored, can properly run its affairs and achieve viability." With pride and pardonable exaggeration, he asserted that Jamaica had set about "to create in a decade what the United States took over a century to attain."

While there was, on the basis of past performance, no reason for pessimism, the problems of the future were formidable, and their solution would require intelligence and dedication. There is no doubt that Jamaica had made great progress, but the fate of the future rested on more than the achievements of the past.

# Selected Bibliography

## Bibliographies

Boston College Library. *Catalogue of Books, Manuscripts, Etc. in the Caribbeana Section: Specializing in Jamaicana of the Nicholas M. Williams Memorial Ethnological Collection.* Boston, 1932.

Comitas, L. *Caribbeana 1900–1965: A Topical Bibliography.* Seattle, 1968.

Cundall, F. *Bibliographia Jamaicensis.* Kingston, 1902; Supplement, 1908; reprint, Philadelphia, 1967.

Ragatz, L. *Guide to the Study of British Caribbean History.* Washington, D.C., 1932.

## Public Documents

Calendar of State Papers, Colonial Series. *America and the West Indies.* London, 1880–1938.

Government of Jamaica. *Laws.* Spanish Town, Jamaica: Public Record Office.

Great Britain, House of Commons, *Reports and Papers.*

Jamaica, Council. *Minutes.* Spanish Town, Jamaica: Jamaica Government Archives.

Jamaica, Government of, *A National Plan for Jamaica 1957–1967.* Kingston, 1957.

Jamaica, Government of, *Annual Reports on Jamaica 1958–1969.* Kingston, 1959–70.

Jamaica, Government of, *Five Year Independence Plan.* Kingston, 1963.

Jamaica, Government of, *Report of the Returning Officer for the Election of 1962.*

Jamaica, Government of, *Report of the Returning Officer for the Election of 1967.*

Jamaica, House of Assembly. *Journals.* 14 vols. *Jamaica 1797–1829.*

Jamaica, House of Assembly. *Letter Book.* Spanish Town, Jamaica: Jamaica Government Archives.

Jamaica, House of Assembly. *Votes, Jamaica 1785–1866.*

Jamaica, House of Assembly, Committee of Correspondence. *Letter Book.* Kingston, Jamaica: Institute of Jamaica.

Jamaica Island Agent. *Letter Book to the Committee of Correspondence.* Kingston, Jamaica: Institute of Jamaica.

West India Royal Commission, Report–1938–1939. Comd. 6607. London, 1945.

### General Literature on Jamaica and the West Indies

ABRAHAMS, P. *Jamaica.* London, 1958.

BAXTER, I. *The Arts of an Island.* Metuchen, N.J., 1970.

BEMANS, E. A., ROSE J. HOLLAND, and A. P. NEWTON, eds. *The Growth of the New Empire 1783–1870.* Cambridge, England, 1940.

BENT, R. *A Complete Geography of Jamaica.* London, 1966.

BLACK, C. *History of Jamaica.* 3d rev. ed. London, 1965.

BRIDGES, G. *Annals of Jamaica.* 2 vols. London, 1826; New York, 1968.

BROWNE, P. *Civil and Natural History of Jamaica.* London, 1756.

BURN, W. L. *The British West Indies.* London, 1951.

BURNS, A. *History of the British West Indies.* London, 1954.

CASSIDY, F. G. *Jamaica Talk: Three Hundred Years of English Language in Jamaica.* London, 1961.

CUNDALL, F. *Historic Jamaica.* London, 1915.

DEER, N. *The History of Sugar.* 2 vols. London 1949–50.

GARDNER, W. J. *History of Jamaica.* London, 1873.

GORDON, S., ed. *A Century of West Indian Education.* London, 1963.

HENRIQUES, F. *Jamaica, Land of Wood and Water.* London, 1957.

HILL, R. *Eight Chapters in the History of Jamaica.* Jamaica, 1868.

———. *Lights and Shadows of Jamaican History.* Jamaica, n.d.

PARRY, J. H., and P. M. SHERLOCK. *Short History of the West Indies.* New York, 1956; London, 1956.

ROBERTS, G. W. *The Population of Jamaica.* Cambridge, 1957.

ROBERTS, W. A. *Jamaica: The Portrait of an Island.* New York, 1955.

———. *Six Great Jamaicans.* Kingston, 1951.

SHERLOCK, P. *West Indies.* New York, 1966; London, 1966.

WRONG, H. *Government of the West Indies.* London, 1923.

### The Spanish Period and Early English Settlement

BLOME, R. *Description of the Island of Jamaica.* London, 1672.

COLUMBUS, C. *The Journal of Christopher Columbus.* Trans. by C. JANE. London, 1960.

CRUIKSHANK, E. A. *The Life of Sir Henry Morgan.* Toronto, 1935.
CUNDALL, F. *Governors of Jamaica in the First Half of the Eighteenth Century.* London, 1937.
———. *Jamaica Under the Spaniards.* Kingston: Institute of Jamaica, 1919.
CUNDALL, F., and P. M. SHERLOCK. *The Aborigines of Jamaica.* Kingston: Institute of Jamaica, 1939.
DE LEEUM, H. *Crossroads of the Buccaneers.* New York, 1957.
HAKLUYT, R. *The Principal Navigations, Voyages, Traffiques and Discoveries of the English Nation* (1589). 12 vols. New York, 1903–5; Glasgow, 1903–5.
HARING, C. H. *The Spanish Empire in America.* New York, 1948.
*Interesting Tracts Relating to the Island of Jamaica.* Jamaica, 1800.
LARABEE, L. W. *Royal Instructions to British Colonial Governors 1670–1776,* 2 vols. London, 1935.
MORALES, PADRON, F. *Jamaica Espanola.* Sevilla, 1952.
MORISON, S. E. *Admiral of the Ocean Sea.* Boston, 1942.
———. *Christopher Columbus, Mariner.* Boston, 1955; London, 1956.
NEWTON, A. P. *The European Nations in the West Indies, 1493–1688.* New York, 1933; London, 1933.
PARRY, J. H. *Europe and the Wider World.* London, 1949; New York, 1956.
ROBERTS, W. A. *Sir Henry Morgan, Buccaneer and Governor.* New York, 1933.
SPURDLE, F. M. *Early West Indian Government.* London, 1962.
TAYLOR, S. A. G. *The Capture of Jamaica.* Kingston, 1951.
———. *The Western Designs: An Account of Cromwell's Expedition to the Caribbean.* London, 1969.
THORNTON, A. P. *British West India Policy Under the Restoration.* Oxford, 1956.
WHITSUN, A. M. *The Constitutional Development of Jamaica.* London, 1929.
WRIGHT, IRENE A. *The English Conquest of Jamaica.* London, 1923.

## Slavery and the Plantation Society

BECKFORD, W. *Descriptive Account of Jamaica.* 2 vols. London, 1790.
BEER, G. L. *British Colonial Policy 1754–1765.* New York, 1907.
BICKELL, R. *The West Indies as They Are.* London. 1825.
COKE, THOMAS. *History of the West Indies.* London, 1810.
CUNDALL, F. *History of Printing in Jamaica 1717–1834.* Kingston: Institute of Jamaica, 1935.
DALLAS, R. C. *History of the Maroons.* 2 vols. London, 1803; New York, 1969.

DAVIES, K. G. *The Royal African Company*, London, 1957; New York, 1970.

DICKSON, W. *Letters On Slavery*. London, 1789.

EDWARDS, B. *Historical Survey of the Island of St. Domingo Together with an Account of the Maroon Negroes in the Island of Jamaica.* London, 1801.

————. *The History, Civil and Commercial, of the British West Indies.* 2 vols. London, 1794; 5 vols. New York, 1819.

FORTESCUE, SIR J. W. *History of the British Army.* 13 vols. London, 1898–1930; reprint, New York, 1970.

GOVEIA, E. *Slave Society in the British Leeward Islands at the End of the Eighteenth Century.* New Haven, 1965.

————. *A Study on the Historiography of the British West Indies.* Mexico City, 1956.

HAKEWILL, JAMES. *Picturesque Tour of the Island of Jamaica.* London, 1825.

*Historical Account of the Assembly Sessions of the Island of Jamaica 1755.* London, 1757.

*Jamaican Almanacks 1780–1832.*

LESLIE, C. *A New and Exact Account of Jamaica.* Edinburgh, 1739.

*Letters from Jamaica to a Friend.* London, 1748.

LEWIS, M. G. *Journal of a West India Proprietor, Kept During Residence in the Island of Jamaica.* Boston, 1929.

LONG, E. *History of Jamaica.* 3 vols. London, 1774.

MANNING, H. T. *British Colonial Government After the Revolution, 1782–1820.* New Haven, 1933; reprint, 1966.

*Marly* (anonymous novel). Glasgow, 1828.

METCALF, G. *Royal Government and Political Conflict in Jamaica 1729–1783.* London, 1965.

"Notes on Reports of a Committee of the House of Assembly of Jamaica Appointed to Answer Allegations of Several Petitions Made to the English Parliament." England, 1799.

PARES, R. "Merchants and Planters," *Economic History Review*, Supplement No. 4. Cambridge, England, 1960.

————. *War and Trade in the West Indies 1739–1763.* Oxford, 1936; New York, 1963.

PATTERSON, O. *The Sociology of Slavery.* London, 1967; Rutherford, N.J., 1970.

PENSON, L. M. *Colonial Agents of the British West Indies.* London, 1924.

PITMAN, F. *The Development of the British West Indies 1700–1763.* New Haven, 1917; 1967.

RAGATZ, L. J. *The Fall of the Planter Class in the British Caribbean, 1763–1833.* Washington, D.C., 1928; New York, 1963.

RENNY, R. *History of Jamaica.* London, 1807.

ROBINSON, C. *The Fighting Maroons of Jamaica.* Jamaica, 1969.

ROUGHLEY, T. *Jamaica Planters Guide.* London, 1823.

SENIOR, B. *Jamaica, as It Was, as It Is, and as It May Be.* London, 1835.

SIBERT, W. H. *The Legacy of the American Revolution to the British West Indies and the Bahamas.* Columbus, 1913.

SMITH, R. W. "The Conflict Between Planter and Parliament over the Slave Laws of Jamaica." Unpublished Ph.D. dissertation, University of California, Los Angeles, 1942.

SOUTHEY, T. *Chronological History of the West Indies.* 3 vols. London, 1827; New York, 1967.

STEWART, J. *View of the Past and Present State of the Island of Jamaica.* Edinburgh, 1823.

WILLIAMS, C. R. *Tour Through Jamaica In 1823.* London, 1827.

WRIGHT, R. *Revels in Jamaica 1682–1838.* New York, 1937.

WYNDHAM, H. A. *The Atlantic and Slavery.* Oxford, 1935.

YOUNG, SIR WILLIAM. *The West Indian Common Place Book.* London, 1807.

## Emancipation and the Postemancipation Period

*Addresses and Memorials to His Majesty from the House of Assembly at Jamaica in the Years 1821–1826 Inclusive: And Which Have Been Presented to His Majesty by the Island Agent.* London, n.d.

BLEBY, H. *Death Struggles in Slavery.* London, 1853.

BROUGHAM, HENRY. *An Inquiry into the Colonial Policy of the European Powers.* Edinburgh, 1803; reprint, New York, 1969.

BUCHNER, J. H. *The Moravians in Jamaica.* London, 1854.

BURN, W. L. *Emancipation and Apprenticeship in the British West Indies.* London, 1937.

BUXTON, CHARLES. *Slavery and Freedom in the British West Indies.* London, 1860.

COUPLAND, R. *The British Anti-Slavery Movement.* 2d ed. New York, 1964.

CUNDALL, F., ed. *Lady Nugent's Journal.* London, 1907.

CURTIN, P. *Atlantic Slave Trade: A Census.* Madison, 1969.

CURTIN, P. *Two Jamaicas: The Role of Ideas in a Tropical Colony.* Cambridge, 1955.

DUTTON, G. *The Hero as Murderer.* London, 1967.

GRIGGS, E. *Thomas Clarkson: The Friend of the Slaves.* Ann Arbor, 1936.

HALL, D. *Free Jamaica.* New Haven, 1959.

HARLOW, V., and F. MADDEN, eds. *British Colonial Developments, 1763–1793.* New York and London, 1953.

HARVEY, THOMAS. *Jamaica in 1866.* London, 1867.

HINTON, J. *Memoir of William Knibb, Missionary in Jamaica.* London, 1847.

HUME, H. *Life of Edward John Eyre.* London, 1867.

KLINGBERG, F. *The Anti-Slavery Movement in England: A Study in English Humanitarianism.* New Haven, 1968.

KNAPLUND, PAUL. *James Stephen and the British Colonial System 1813–1847.* Madison, Wis., 1953.

LONG, A. *Jamaica and the New Order.* Kingston, Jamaica, 1956.

McCULLOCH, S. C., ed. *British Humanitarianism: Essays Honoring Frank J. Klingberg.* Philadelphia, 1950.

MADDEN, R. R. *A Twelvemonth's Residence in the West Indies, During Transition from Slavery to Apprenticeship.* Philadelphia, 1835.

MATHIESON, W. L. *British Slavery and its Abolition, 1834–1838.* London, 1926; New York, 1967.

MELLOR, G. R. *British Imperial Trusteeship.* London, 1951.

MURRAY, D. *The West Indies and the Development of Colonial Government 1801–1834.* New York and London, 1965.

NEW, C. W. *Life of Henry Brougham to 1830.* New York and London, 1961.

*Papers Relating to the Case of Lescene and Escoffery.* Kingston: Institute of Jamaica, n.d.

PHILLIPPO, JAMES M. *Jamaica: Its Past and Present State.* London, 1843.

SEWELL, WM. *The Ordeal of Free Labour in the West-Indies.* New York, 1861.

SLIGO, MARQUESS OF. *A Letter to the Marquess of Normandy Relative to the Present State of Jamaica.* London, 1839.

STEPHEN, G. *Anti-Slavery Recollections.* London, 1854.

STEPHEN, JAMES. *Reasons for Establishing a Registry of Slaves in the British Colonies.* London, 1814.

THOMPSON, EDWARD JOHN. *The Life of Charles, Lord Metcalfe.* London, 1937.

WADDELL, H. M. *Twenty Nine Years in the West Indies and Central Africa 1829–1858.* London, 1863.

YOUNG, D. M. *The Colonial Office in the Early Nineteenth Century.* New York, 1961; London, 1961.

### From Crown Colony to Independent Nation

ADAMS, F. U. *Conquest of the Tropics: The Story of the Creative Enterprises Conducted by the United Fruit Company.* New York, 1914.

AYEARST, M. *The British West Indies: The Search for Self-Government.* New York, 1960.

BACON, C., and A. AARON. *New Jamaica*. Kingston, 1890.

BECKWITH, M. *Black Roadways: A Study of Jamaican Folk Life*. Chapel Hill, N.C., 1929.

BELL, W. *Jamaican Leaders: Political Attitudes in a New Nation*. Berkeley and Los Angeles, 1964.

BIGELOW, J. *Jamaica in 1850*. London, 1851.

BLANCHARD, P. *Democracy and Empire in the Caribbean*. New York, 1952.

BROOKS, A. A. *History of Bedwardism or The Native Baptist Free Church*. Kingston, 1917.

BRUCE, SIR CHARLES. *The Broad Stone of Empire: Problems of Crown Colony Administration*. 2 vols. London, 1910.

BURT, A. E. *The Development of Self-Government in Jamaica 1884–1913*. Toronto, 1960.

CRONON, E. D. *Black Moses*. Madison, Wis., 1955.

CUMPER, G. *The Social Structure of Jamaica*. Kingston, 1949.

DeLISSER, H. G. *Twentieth Century Jamaica*. Kingston, 1913.

EISNER, G. *Jamaica 1830–1930*. Manchester, 1961.

ELLIS, REV. J. B. *The Diocese of Jamaica*. London, 1913.

FORREST, A. S., and J. HENDERSON. *Jamaica*. London, 1906.

FOX, A. B. *Freedom and Welfare in the Caribbean*. New York, 1949.

FROUDE, J. A. *The English in the West Indies*. New York, 1888.

HARVEY, T., and WM. BREWIN. *Jamaica in 1866*. London, 1867.

HURSTON, Z. N. *Voodoo Gods*. London, 1937.

International Bank for Reconstruction and Development. *The Economic Development of Jamaica*. Baltimore, 1952.

Jamaica Agricultural Society. *Journal*, 1895.

KEPNER, C. D. and J. H. SOOTHILL. *The Banana Empire: A Case Study of Economic Imperialism*. New York, 1935, 1967.

KERR, M. *Personality and Conflict in Jamaica*. London, 1952.

LEWIS, G. *The Growth of the Modern West Indies*. New York, 1968.

LIVINGSTONE, W. P. *Black Jamaica*. London, 1899.

MacFARLANE, W. *The Birth of Self-Government in Jamaica, 1937–1944*. Brooklyn, 1957.

MacMILLAN, W. M. *Warning from the West Indies*. London, 1938.

MARIER, R. *Social Welfare Work in Jamaica*. Paris: UNESCO, 1959.

MORDECAI, SIR JOHN. *The West Indies: The Federal Negotiations*. London, 1968.

NEBHARD, L. S. L. *Trials and Triumphs of Marcus Garvey*. Rev. ed. Kingston, 1953.

OLIVIER, SIR. S. *Jamaica the Blessed Land*. London, 1937.

SHERLOCK, P. M. *Caribbean Citizen*. London, 1957.

SIMEY, T. S. *Welfare and Planning in the West Indies*. Oxford, 1946.

SMITH, M. G., R. AUGIER, and R. NETTLEFORD. *The Ras Tafari Movement in Kingston, Jamaica*. Kingston, 1960.

TROLLOPE, A. *The West Indies and the Spanish Main.* London, 1860, reprint, 1968.

WARTEL, A. *Jamaica: Modified Crown Colony Government and the Crisis of 1938.* College of Social Sciences, Univ. of Puerto Rico, mimeographed, 1965.

### The New Nation 1962–71

BENNETT, L. *Jamaican Labrish.* Kingston, 1966.

CARLEY, M. M. *Jamaica: The Old and the New.* London, 1963.

CORKRAN, H. *Patterns of International Cooperation in the Caribbean 1942–1959.* Dallas, 1970.

ERICKSON, E. G. *The West Indies Population Problem.* Lawrence, Kans., 1962.

GREEN, I. *The Effects of the Population Explosion on Jamaica's International Relations.* Johannesburg, 1966.

HAMILTON, B. J. St. John. *Problems of Administration in an Emergent Nation: A Case Study of Jamaica.* New York, 1967.

HOETNIK, H. *The Two Variants in Caribbean Race Relations.* London and New York, 1967.

MAU, J. *Social Change and Images of the Future: A Study of the Pursuit of Progress in Jamaica.* Cambridge, 1968.

NORRIS, K. *Jamaica: The Search for an Identity.* London, 1962.

PALMER, R. W. *The Jamaican Economy.* New York, 1968.

SINGHAM, A. *The Hero and the Crowd in Colonial Polity.* New Haven, Conn., 1968.

### Periodicals

The periodical literature on Jamaica and the West Indies is too extensive to be cited in a selected bibliography.

### Newspapers

*The Gleaner*
*Jamaica Courant and Public Advertiser*
*Kingston Chronicle*
*The Royal Gazette*
*The Trifler*
*The Watchman*

# Index

# LEAF STORM AND OTHER STORIES

*Books by Gabriel García Márquez*

Leaf Storm and Other Stories
One Hundred Years of Solitude
No One Writes to the Colonel and Other Stories

*Gabriel García Márquez*

# LEAF STORM

## AND OTHER STORIES

Translated from the Spanish by Gregory Rabassa

HARPER & ROW, PUBLISHERS
New York, Evanston, San Francisco, London

*Leaf Storm* was originally published in Spanish under the title *La Hojarasca*.
"The Handsomest Drowned Man in the World" originally appeared in *Playboy Magazine*.
"A Very Old Man with Enormous Wings" originally appeared in *New American Review*.
"Blacamán the Good, Vendor of Miracles" was first published in *Esquire Magazine*.

Grateful acknowledgment is given to the University of Chicago Press for Sophocles' *Antigone*, translated by Elizabeth Wyckoff, which appears in *Sophocles I*, edited by David Greene and Richard Lattimore. Copyright 1954 by The University of Chicago. Reprinted by permission.

FIRST U.S. EDITION

STANDARD BOOK NUMBER: 06-012779-1

LIBRARY OF CONGRESS CATALOG CARD NUMBER: 76-138784

But Polyneices' corpse who died in pain
they say he has proclaimed to the whole town
that none may bury him and none bewail,
but leave him unwept, untombed, a rich sweet sight
for the hungry birds' beholding.
Such orders they say the worthy Creon gives
to you and me—yes, yes, I say to me—
and that he's coming to proclaim it clear
to those who know it not.
Further: he has the matter so at heart
that anyone who dares attempt the act
will die by public stoning in the town.
                                                    Antigone

# Contents

*Leaf Storm*

—Suddenly, as if a whirlwind had set down roots in the center of the town, the banana company arrived, pursued by the leaf storm. A whirling leaf storm had been stirred up, formed out of the human and material dregs of other towns, the chaff of a civil war that seemed ever more remote and unlikely. The whirlwind was implacable. It contaminated everything with its swirling crowd smell, the smell of skin secretion and hidden death. In less than a year it sowed over the town the rubble of many catastrophes that had come before it, scattering its mixed cargo of rubbish in the streets. And all of a sudden that rubbish, in time to the mad and unpredicted rhythm of the storm, was being sorted out, individualized, until what had been a narrow street with a river at one end and a corral for the dead at the other was changed into a different and more complex town, created out of the rubbish of other towns.

Arriving there, mingled with the human leaf storm, dragged along by its impetuous force, came the dregs of warehouses, hospitals, amusement parlors, electric plants; the dregs made up of single women and men who tied their mules to hitching posts by the hotel, carrying their single piece of baggage, a wooden trunk or a bundle of clothing, and in a few months each had his own house, two mistresses, and the military title that was due him for having arrived late for the war.

Even the dregs of the cities' sad love came to us in the whirlwind and built small wooden houses where at first a corner and a half-cot were a dismal home for one night, and then a noisy clandestine street, and then a whole inner village of tolerance within the town.

In the midst of that blizzard, that tempest of unknown faces, of awnings along the public way, of men changing clothes in the street, of women with open parasols sitting on trunks, and of mule after abandoned mule dying of hunger on the block by the hotel, the first of us came to be the last; we were the outsiders, the newcomers.

After the war, when we came to Macondo and appreciated the good quality of its soil, we knew that the leaf storm was sure to come someday, but we did not count on its drive. So when we felt the avalanche arrive, the only thing we could do was set a plate with a knife and fork behind the door and sit patiently waiting for the newcomers to get to know us. Then the train whistled for the first time. The leaf storm turned about and went out to greet it, and by turning it lost its drive. But it developed unity and mass; and it underwent the natural process of fermentation, becoming incorporated into the germination of the earth.

Macondo, 1909

I've seen a corpse for the first time. It's Wednesday but I feel as if it was Sunday because I didn't go to school and they dressed me up in a green corduroy suit that's tight in some places. Holding Mama's hand, following my grandfather, who feels his way along with a cane with every step he takes so he won't bump into things (he doesn't see well in the dark and he limps), I went past the mirror in the living room and saw myself full length, dressed in green and with this white starched collar that pinches me on one side of the neck. I saw myself in the round mottled looking glass and I thought: *That's me, as if today was Sunday.*

We've come to the house where the dead man is.

The heat won't let you breathe in the closed room. You can hear the sun buzzing in the streets, but that's all. The air is stagnant, like concrete; you get the feeling that it could get all twisted like a sheet of steel. In the room where they've laid out the corpse there's a smell of trunks, but I can't see any anywhere. There's a hammock in the corner hanging by one end from a ring. There's a smell of trash. And I think that the things around us, broken down and almost falling apart, have the look of things that ought to smell like trash even though they smell like something else.

I always thought that dead people should have hats on. Now I can see that they shouldn't. I can see that they have a head like wax and a handkerchief tied around their jawbone. I can see that they have their mouth open a little and that behind the purple lips you can see the stained and irregular teeth. I can see that they keep their tongue bitten over to one side, thick and sticky, a little darker than the color of their face, which is like the color of fingers clutching a stick. I can see that they have their eyes open much wider than a man's, anxious and wild, and that their skin seems to be made of tight damp earth. I thought that a dead man would look like somebody quiet and asleep and now I can see that it's just the opposite. I can see that he looks like someone awake and in a rage after a fight.

Mama is dressed up as if it was Sunday too. She put on the old straw hat that comes down over her ears and a black dress closed at the neck and with sleeves that come down to her wrists. Since today is Wednesday she looks to me like someone far away, a stranger, and I get the feeling that she wants to tell me something when my grandfather gets up to receive the men who've brought the coffin. Mama is sitting beside me with her back to the closed door. She's breathing heavily and she keeps pushing back the strands of hair that fall out from under the hat that she put on in a hurry. My grandfather has told the men to put the coffin down next to the bed. Only then did I realize that the dead man could really fit into it. When the men brought in the box I had the impression that it was too small for a body that took up the whole length of the bed.

I don't know why they brought me along. I've never been in this house before and I even thought that nobody lived here. It's a big house, on the corner, and I don't think the door has ever been opened. I always thought that nobody lived in the house. Only now, after my mother told me, "You won't be going to school this afternoon," and I didn't feel glad because she said it with a serious and reserved voice, and I saw her come back with my corduroy suit and she put it on me without saying a word and we went to the door to join my grandfather, and we walked past the three houses that separated this one from ours,

4

only now do I realize that someone lived on the corner. Someone who died and who must be the man my mother was talking about when she said: "You have to behave yourself at the doctor's funeral."

When we went in I didn't see the dead man. I saw my grandfather at the door talking to the men, and then I saw him telling us to go on in. I thought then that there was somebody in the room, but when I went in I felt it was dark and empty. The heat beat on my face from the very first minute and I got that trash smell that was solid and permanent at first and now, like the heat, comes in slow-spaced waves and disappears. Mama led me through the dark room by the hand and seated me next to her in a corner. Only after a moment could I begin to make things out. I saw my grandfather trying to open a window that seemed stuck to its frame, glued to the wood around it, and I saw him hitting his cane against the latches, his coat covered with the dust that came off with every blow. I turned my head to where my grandfather was moving as he said he couldn't open the window and only then did I see there was someone on the bed. There was a dark man stretched out, motionless. Then I spun my head to my mother's side where she sat serious and without moving, looking off somewhere else in the room. Since my feet don't touch the floor and hang in the air half a foot away, I put my hands under my thighs, placing the palms on the chair, and I began to swing my legs, not thinking about anything until I remembered that Mama had told me: "You have to behave yourself at the doctor's funeral." Then I felt something cold behind me. I turned to look and I only saw the wall of dry and pitted wood. But it was as if someone had said to me from the wall: *Don't move your legs. The man on the bed is the doctor and he's dead.* And when I looked toward the bed I didn't see him the way I had before. I didn't see him lying down, I saw him dead.

From then on, as much as I try not to look, I feel as if someone is forcing my face in that direction. And even if I make an effort

5

to look at other places in the room, I see him just the same, everywhere, with his bulging eyes and his green, dead face in the shadows.

I don't know why no one has come to the wake. The ones who came are us, my grandfather, Mama, and the four Guajiro Indians who work for my grandfather. The men brought a sack of lime and emptied it inside the coffin. If my mother hadn't been strange and far away I would have asked her why they did it. I don't understand why they have to sprinkle lime inside the box. When the bag was empty one of the men shook it over the coffin and a few last flakes fell out, looking more like sawdust than lime. They lifted the dead man by the shoulders and feet. He's wearing a pair of cheap pants tied at the waist by a wide black cord, and a gray shirt. He only has his left shoe on. As Ada says, he's got one foot a king and the other one a slave. The right shoe is at one end of the bed. On the bed the dead man seemed to be having trouble. In the coffin he looks more comfortable, more peaceful, and his face, which had been like the face of a man who was alive and awake after a fight, has taken on a restful and secure look. His profile is softer. It's as if in the box there he now felt he was in his proper place as a dead man.

My grandfather's been moving around the room. He's picked up some things and put them in the box. I look at Mama again hoping that she'll tell me why my grandfather is tossing things into the coffin. But my mother is unmoved in her black dress and she seems to be making an effort not to look where the dead man is. I try to do the same thing but I can't. I stare at him. I examine him. My grandfather throws a book inside the coffin, signals the men, and three of them put the lid over the corpse. Only then do I feel free of the hands that were holding my head toward that side and I begin to look the room over.

I look at my mother again. For the first time since we came to the house she looks at me and smiles with a forced smile, with nothing inside; and in the distance I can hear the train whistle as

6

it disappears around the last bend. I hear a sound from the corner where the corpse is. I see one of the men lift one edge of the lid and my grandfather puts the dead man's shoe into the coffin, the shoe they had forgotten on the bed. The train whistles again, farther off, and suddenly I think: *It's two-thirty.* I remember that it's the time (when the train whistles at the last bend in town) when the boys line up at school to go in for the first class in the afternoon.

*Abraham,* I think.

I shouldn't have brought the child. A spectacle like this isn't proper for him. Even for myself, turning thirty, this atmosphere thinned out by the presence of the corpse is harmful. We could leave now. We could tell Papa that we don't feel well in a room where the remains of a man cut off from everything that could be considered affection or thanks have been accumulating for seventeen years. My father may be the only one who's ever shown any feeling for him. An inexplicable feeling that's been of use to him now so he won't rot away inside these four walls.

I'm bothered by how ridiculous all of this is. I'm upset by the idea that in a moment we'll be going out into the street following a coffin that won't inspire any feeling except pleasure in anyone. I can imagine the expression on the faces of the women in the windows, watching my father go by, watching me go by with the child behind a casket inside of which the only person the town has wanted to see that way is rotting away, on his way to the cemetery in the midst of unyielding abandonment, followed by three people who decided to perform a work of charity that's been the beginning of his own vengeance. It could be that this decision of Papa's could mean that tomorrow there won't be anyone prepared to walk behind our funeral processions.

Maybe that's why I brought the child along. When Papa told me a moment ago: "You have to go with me," the first thing that occurred to me was to bring the child so that I would feel protected. Now here we are on this suffocating September afternoon, feeling that the things around us are the pitiless agents of our enemies. Papa's got no reason to worry. Actually, he's spent his whole life doing things like this; giving the town stones to chew on, keeping his most insignificant promises with his back turned to all convention. Since that time twenty-five years ago when this man came to our house, Papa must have imagined (when he noticed the visitor's absurd manners) that today there wouldn't be a single person in the whole town prepared even to throw his body to the buzzards. Maybe Papa foresaw all the obstacles and measured and calculated the possible inconveniences. And now, twenty-five years later, he must feel that this is just the fulfillment of a chore he's thought about for a long time, one which had to be carried out in any case, since he would have had to haul the corpse through the streets of Macondo by himself.

Still, when the time came, he didn't have the courage to do it alone and he made me take part in that intolerable promise that he must have made long before I even had the use of reason. When he told me: "You have to go with me," he didn't give me time to think about how far his words went; I couldn't calculate how much shame and ridicule there would be in burying this man whom everyone had hoped to see turn to dust inside his lair. Because people hadn't just expected that, they'd prepared themselves for things to happen that way and they'd hoped for it from the bottom of their hearts, without remorse, and even with the anticipated satisfaction of someday smelling the pleasant odor of his decomposition floating through the town without anyone's feeling moved, alarmed, or scandalized, satisfied rather at seeing the longed-for hour come, wanting the situation to go on and on until the twirling smell of the dead man would satisfy even the most hidden resentments.

Now we're going to deprive Macondo of its long-desired pleasure. I feel as if in a certain way this determination of ours has

8

given birth in the hearts of the people not to a melancholy feeling of frustration but to one of postponement.

That's another reason why I should have left the child at home; so as not to get him mixed up in this conspiracy which will center on us now the way it did on the doctor for ten years. The child should have been left on the sidelines of this promise. He doesn't even know why he's here, why we've brought him to this room full of rubbish. He doesn't say anything, sitting, swinging his legs with his hands resting on the chair, waiting for someone to decipher this frightful riddle for him. I want to be sure that nobody will, that no one will open that invisible door that prevents him from going beyond the reach of his senses.

He's looked at me several times and I know that he finds me strange, somebody he doesn't know, with this stiff dress and this old hat that I've put on so that I won't be identified even by my own forebodings.

If Meme were alive, here in the house, maybe it would have been different. They might have thought I came because of her. They might have thought I came to share in a grief that she probably wouldn't have felt, but which she would have been able to pretend and which the town could have explained. Meme disappeared about eleven years ago. The doctor's death has ended any possibility of finding out where she is or, at least, where her bones are. Meme isn't here, but it's most likely that if she were— if what happened and was never cleared up hadn't happened—she would have taken the side of the town against the man who warmed her bed for six years with as much love and humanity as a mule might have had.

I can hear the train whistling at the last bend. *It's two-thirty*, I think; and I can't get rid of the idea that at this moment all of Macondo is wondering what we're doing in this house. I think about Señora Rebeca, thin and looking like parchment, with the touch of a family ghost in her look and dress, sitting beside her electric fan, her face shaded by the screens in her windows. As she hears the train disappearing around the last bend Señora Rebeca leans her head toward the fan, tormented by the heat and her resentment, the blades in her heart spinning like those on the fan (but in an opposite direction), and she murmurs: "The devil has a hand in all of this," and she shudders, fastened to life by the tiny roots of everyday things.

And Águeda, the cripple, seeing Solita coming back from the station after seeing her boyfriend off; seeing her open her parasol as she turns the deserted corner; hearing her approach with the sexual rejoicing that she herself once had and which changed inside her into that patient religious sickness that makes her say: "You'll wallow in your bed like a pig in its sty."

I can't get rid of that idea. Stop thinking that it's two-thirty; that the mule with the mail is going by cloaked in a burning cloud of dust and followed by the men who have interrupted their Wednesday siesta to pick up the bundles of newspapers. Father Ángel is dozing, sitting in the sacristy with an open breviary on his greasy stomach, listening to the mule pass and shooting away the flies that are bothering his sleep, belching, saying: "You poisoned me with your meatballs."

Papa's cold-blooded about all this. Even to the point of telling them to open the coffin so they could put in the shoe that was left on the bed. Only he could have taken an interest in that man's meanness. I wouldn't be surprised if when we leave with the corpse the crowd will be waiting for us with all the excrement they could get together overnight and will give us a shower of filth for going against the will of the town. Maybe they won't do it because of Papa. Maybe they will do it because it's something as terrible as frustrating a pleasure the town had longed for over so many years, thought about on stifling afternoons whenever men and women passed this house and said to themselves: "Sooner or later we'll lunch on that smell." Because that's what they all said, from the first to the last.

It'll be three o'clock in a little while. The Señorita already knows it. Señora Rebeca saw her pass and called her, invisible behind the screen, and she came out from the orbit of the fan for a moment and said to her: "Señorita, it's the devil, you know." And tomorrow it won't be my son who goes to school but some other, completely different child; a child who will grow, reproduce, and die in the end with no one paying him the debt of gratitude which would give him Christian burial.

I'd probably be peacefully at home right now if twenty-five years ago that man hadn't come to my father's home with a letter of recommendation (no one ever knew where he came from), if he hadn't stayed with us, eating grass and looking at women with those eyes of a lustful dog that popped out of their sockets. But my punishment was written down from before my birth and it stayed hidden, repressed, until that fateful leap year when I would turn thirty and my father would tell me: "You have to go with me." And then, before I had time to ask anything, he pounded the floor with his cane: "We have to go through with this just the way it is, daughter. The doctor hanged himself this morning."

The men left and came back to the room with a hammer and a box of nails. But they hadn't nailed up the coffin. They laid the things on the table and they sat on the bed where the dead man had been. My grandfather seems calm, but his calmness is imperfect and desperate. It's not the calmness of the corpse in the coffin, it's the calmness of an impatient man making an effort not to show how he feels. It's a rebellious and anxious calm, the kind my grandfather has, walking back and forth across the room, limping, picking up the clustered objects.

When I discover that there are flies in the room I begin to be tortured by the idea that the coffin's become full of flies. They still haven't nailed it shut, but it seems to me that the buzzing I thought at first was an electric fan in the neighborhood is the swarm of flies beating blindly against the sides of the coffin and the

11

face of the dead man. I shake my head; I close my eyes; I see my grandfather open a trunk and take out some things and I can't tell what they are; on the bed I can see the four embers but not the people with the lighted cigars. Trapped by the suffocating heat, by the minute that doesn't pass, by the buzzing of the flies, I feel as if someone is telling me: *That's the way you'll be. You'll be inside a coffin filled with flies. You're only a little under eleven years old, but someday you'll be like that, left to the flies inside of a closed box.* And I stretch my legs out side by side and look at my own black and shiny boots. *One of my laces is untied,* I think and I look at Mama again. She looks at me too and leans over to tie my shoelace.

The vapor that rises up from Mama's head, warm and smelling like a cupboard, smelling of sleeping wood, reminds me of the closed-in coffin again. It becomes hard for me to breathe, I want to get out of here; I want to breathe in the burning street air, and I use my last resort. When Mama gets up I say to her in a low voice: "Mama!" She smiles, says: "Umm?" And I lean toward her, toward her raw and shining face, trembling. "I feel like going out back."

Mama calls my grandfather, tells him something. I watch his narrow, motionless eyes behind his glasses when he comes over and tells me: "That's impossible right now." I stretch and then remain quiet, indifferent to my failure. But things start to pass too slowly again. There's a rapid movement, another, and another. And then Mama leans over my shoulder again, saying: "Did it go away yet?" And she says it with a serious and solid voice, as if it was a scolding more than a question. My stomach is tight and hard, but Mama's question softens it, leaves it full and relaxed, and then everything, even her seriousness, becomes aggressive and challenging to me. "No," I tell her. "It still hasn't gone away." I squeeze in my stomach and try to beat the floor with my feet (another last resort), but I only find empty space below, the distance separating me from the floor.

Someone comes into the room. It's one of my grandfather's men, followed by a policeman and a man who is wearing green denim pants. He has a belt with a revolver on it and in his hand he's holding a hat with a broad, curled brim. My grandfather goes over to greet him. The man in the green pants coughs in the darkness, says something to my grandfather, coughs again; and still coughing he orders the policeman to open the window.

The wooden walls have a slippery look. They seem to be built of cold, compressed ash. When the policeman hits the latch with the butt of his rifle, I have the feeling that the shutters will not open. The house will fall down, the walls will crumble, but noiselessly, like a palace of ash collapsing in the wind. I feel that with a second blow we'll be in the street, in the sunlight, sitting down, our heads covered with debris. But with the second blow the shutter opens and light comes into the room; it bursts in violently, as when a gate is opened for a disoriented animal, who runs and smells, mute; who rages and scratches on the walls, slavering, and then goes back to flop down peacefully in the coolest corner of the cage.

With the window open things become visible, but consolidated in their strange unrealness. Then Mama takes a deep breath, takes me by the hand, and tells me: "Come, let's take a look at our house through the window." And I see the town again, as if I were returning to it after a trip. I can see our house, faded and run down, but cool under the almond trees; and I feel from here as if I'd never been inside that green and cordial coolness, as if ours were the perfect imaginary house promised by my mother on nights when I had bad dreams. And I see Pepe, who passes by without seeing us, lost in his thoughts. The boy from the house next door, who passes whistling, changed and unknown, as if he'd just had his hair cut off.

Then the mayor gets up, his shirt open, sweaty, his expression completely upset. He comes over to me all choked up by the excitement brought on by his own argument. "We can't be sure that he's dead until he starts to smell," he says, and he finishes buttoning up his shirt and lights a cigarette, his face turned toward the coffin again, thinking perhaps: *Now they can't say that I don't operate inside the law.* I look into his eyes and I feel that I've looked at him with enough firmness to make him understand that I can penetrate his deepest thoughts. I tell him: "You're operating outside the law in order to please the others." And he, as if that had been exactly what he had expected to hear, answers: "You're a respectable man, colonel. You know that I'm within my rights." I tell him: "You, more than anyone else, know that he's dead." And he says: "That's right, but after all, I'm only a public servant. The only legal way would be with a death certificate." And I tell him: "If the law is on your side, take advantage of it and bring a doctor who can make out the death certificate." And he, with his head lifted but without haughtiness, calmly too, but without the slightest show of weakness or confusion, says: "You're a respectable person and you know that it would be an abuse of authority." When I hear him I see that his brains are not addled so much by liquor as by cowardice.

Now I can see that the mayor shares the anger of the town. It's a feeling fed for ten years, ever since that stormy night when they brought the wounded men to the man's door and shouted to him (because he didn't open the door, he spoke from inside); they shouted to him: "Doctor, take care of these wounded men because there aren't enough doctors to go around," and still without opening (because the door stayed closed with the wounded lying in front of it). "You're the only doctor left. You have to do a charitable act"; and he replied (and he didn't open the door then either), imagined by the crowd to be standing in the middle of the living room, the lamp held high lighting up his hard yellow eyes: "I've forgotten everything I knew about all that. Take them somewhere else," and he kept the door closed (because from that time on the door was never opened again) while the anger grew, spread out, turned into a collective disease which gave no respite to Macondo for the rest of his life, and in every ear the sentence shouted that night—the one that condemned the doctor to rot behind these walls—continued echoing.

Ten years would still pass without his ever drinking the town water, haunted by the fear that it would be poisoned; feeding himself on the vegetables that he and his Indian mistress planted in the courtyard. Now the town feels that the time has come when they can deny him the pity that he denied the town ten years ago, and Macondo, which knows that he's dead (because everyone must have awakened with a lighter feeling this morning), is getting ready to enjoy that longed-for pleasure which everyone considers to be deserved. Their only desire is to smell the odor of organic decomposition behind the doors that he didn't open that other time.

Now I can begin to believe that nothing can help my promise in the face of the ferocity of a town and that I'm hemmed in, surrounded by the hatred and impatience of a band of resentful people. Even the church has found a way to go against my determination. Father Ángel told me a moment ago: "I won't let them bury in consecrated ground a man who hanged himself after having lived sixty years without God. Our Lord would look upon you with good eyes too if you didn't carry out what won't be a work of charity but the sin of rebellion." I told him: "To bury the dead, as is written, is a work of charity." And Father Ángel said: "Yes. But in this case it's not up to us to do it, it's up to the sanitary authorities."

I came. I called the four Guajiros who were raised in my house. I made my daughter Isabel go with me. In that way the act becomes more family, more human, less personal and defiant than if I dragged the corpse to the cemetery through the streets of the town myself. I think Macondo is capable of doing anything after what I've seen happen in this century. But if they won't respect me, not even because I'm old, a Colonel of the Republic, and, to top it off, lame in body and sound in conscience, I hope that at least they'll respect my daughter because she's a woman. I'm not doing it for myself. Maybe not for the peace of the dead man either. Just to fulfill a sacred promise. If I brought Isabel along it wasn't out of cowardice but out of charity. She brought the child (and I can see that she did it for the same reason), and here we are now, the three of us, bearing the weight of this harsh emergency.

We got here a moment ago. I thought we'd find the body still hanging from the ceiling, but the men got here first, laid him on the bed, and almost shrouded him with the secret conviction that the affair wouldn't last more than an hour. When I arrive I hope they'll bring the coffin, I see my daughter and the child sitting in the corner and I examine the room, thinking that the doctor may have left something that will explain why he did it. The desk is open, full of a confusion of papers, none written by him. On the desk I see the same bound formulary that he brought to my house twenty-five years ago when he opened that enormous trunk which could have held the clothing of my whole family. But there was nothing else in the trunk except two cheap shirts, a set of false teeth that couldn't have been his for the simple reason that he still had his own, strong and complete, a portrait, and a formulary. I open the drawers and I find printed sheets of paper in all of them; just papers, old, dusty; and underneath, in the last drawer, the same false teeth that he brought twenty-five years ago, dusty, yellow from age and lack of use. On the small table beside the un-lighted lamp there are several bundles of unopened newspapers. I examine them. They're written in French, the most recent ones three months old: *July, 1928.* And there are others, also unopened: *January, 1927; November, 1926.* And the oldest ones: *October, 1919.* I think: *It's been nine years, since one year after the sentence had been pronounced, that he hadn't opened the newspapers. Since that time he's given up the last thing that linked him to his land and his people.*

The men bring the coffin and lower the corpse into it. Then I remember the day twenty-five years ago when he arrived at my house and gave me the letter of recommendation, written in Panama and addressed to me by the Intendant General of the Atlantic Coast at the end of the great war, Colonel Aureliano Buendía. I search through various trifles in the darkness of the bottomless trunk. There's no clue in the other corner, only the same things he brought twenty-five years ago. I remember: *He had two cheap shirts, a set of teeth, a portrait, and that old bound formulary.* I go about gathering up these things before they close the coffin and I put them inside. The portrait is still at the bottom of the trunk, almost in the same place where it had been that time. It's the daguerreotype of a decorated officer. I throw the picture into the box. I throw in the false teeth and finally the formulary. When I finish I signal the men to close the coffin. I think: *Now he's on another trip. The most natural thing for him on his last trip is to take along the things that were with him on the next to the last one. At least that would seem to be the most natural.* And then I seem to see him, for the first time, comfortably dead.

I examine the room and I see that a shoe was forgotten on the bed. I signal my men again with the shoe in my hand and they lift up the lid at the precise moment when the train whistles, disappearing around the last bend in town. *It's two-thirty,* I think. *Two-thirty on September 12, 1928; almost the same hour of that day in 1903 when this man sat down for the first time at our table and asked for some grass to eat.* Adelaida asked him that time: "What kind of grass, doctor?" And he in his parsimonious ruminant voice, still touched by nasality: "Ordinary grass, ma'am. The kind that donkeys eat."

## II.

The fact is that Meme isn't in the house and that probably no one could say exactly when she stopped living here. The last time I saw her was eleven years ago. She still had the little *botiquín* on this corner that had been imperceptibly modified by the needs of the neighbors until it had become a variety store. Everything in order, neatly arranged by the scrupulous and hard-working Meme, who spent her day sewing for the neighbors on one of the four Domestics that there were in town in those days or behind the counter attending to customers with that pleasant Indian way which she never lost and which was at the same time both open and reserved; a mixed-up combination of innocence and mistrust.

I hadn't seen Meme since the time she left our house, but actually I can't say exactly when she came here to live with the doctor on the corner or how she could have reached the extreme of degradation of becoming the mistress of a man who had refused her his services, in spite of everything and the fact that they shared my father's house, she as a foster child and he as a permanent guest. I learned from my stepmother that the doctor wasn't a good man, that he'd had a long argument with Papa, trying to convince him that what Meme had wasn't anything serious, not even leaving his room. In any case, even if what the Guajiro girl had was only a passing illness, he should have taken a look at her, if only because of the consideration with which he was treated in our house during the eight years he lived there.

I don't know how things happened. I just know that one morning Meme wasn't in the house anymore and he wasn't either. Then my stepmother had them close up his room and she didn't mention him again until years later when we were working on my wedding dress.

Three or four Sundays after she'd left our house, Meme went

to church, to eight o'clock mass, with a gaudy silk print dress and a ridiculous hat that was topped by a cluster of artificial flowers. She'd always been so simple when I saw her in our house, barefoot most of the time, so that the person who came into church that Sunday looked to me like a different Meme from the one we knew. She heard mass up front, among the ladies, stiff and affected under that pile of things she was wearing, which made her new and complicated, a showy newness made up of cheap things. She was kneeling down up front. And even the devotion with which she followed the Mass was something new in her; even in the way she crossed herself there was something of that flowery and gaudy vulgarity with which she'd entered the church, puzzling people who had known her as a servant in our home and surprising those who'd never seen her.

I (I couldn't have been more than thirteen at the time) wondered what had brought on that transformation, why Meme had disappeared from our house and reappeared in church that Sunday dressed more like a Christmas tree than a lady, or with enough there to dress three women completely for Easter Sunday and the Guajiro girl even had enough drippings and beads left over to dress a fourth one. When mass was over the men and women stopped by the door to watch her come out. They stood on the steps in a double row by the main door, and I think that there might even have been something secretly premeditated in that indolent and mockingly solemn way in which they were waiting, not saying a word until Meme came out the door, closed her eyes and opened them again in perfect rhythm to her seven-colored parasol. That was how she went between the double row of men and women, ridiculous in her high-heeled peacock disguise, until one of the men began to close the circle and Meme was in the middle, startled, confused, trying to smile with a smile of distinction that was as gaudy and false on her as her outfit. But when Meme came out, opened her parasol, and began to walk, Papa, who was next to me, pulled me toward the group. So when the men began closing the circle, my father opened a way out for Meme, who was hurriedly trying to get away. Papa took her by the arm without looking at the people there, and he led her through the center of the square with that haughty and challenging expression he puts on when he does something that other people don't agree with.

Some time passed before I found out that Meme had gone to live with the doctor as his mistress. In those days the shop was open and she still went to Mass like the finest of ladies, not bothered by what was thought or said, as if she'd forgotten what had happened that first Sunday. Still, two months later, she wasn't ever seen in church again.

I remember the doctor when he was staying at our house. I remember his black and twisted mustache and his way of looking at women with his lustful, greedy dog eyes. But I remember that I never got close to him, maybe because I thought of him as the strange animal that stayed seated at the table after everyone had gotten up and ate the same kind of grass that donkeys eat. During Papa's illness three years ago, the doctor didn't leave his corner the same as he hadn't left it one single time after the night he refused to attend to the wounded men, just as six years before that he'd denied the woman who two days later would be his concubine. The small house had been shut up before the town passed sentence on the doctor. But I do know that Meme was still living here for several months or several years after the store was closed. It must have been much later when people found out that she'd disappeared, because that was what the anonymous note tacked on this door said. According to that note, the doctor had murdered his mistress and buried her in the garden because he was afraid the town would use her to poison him. But I'd seen Meme before I was married. It was eleven years ago, when I was coming back from rosary and the Guajiro woman came to the door of her shop and said to me in her jolly and somewhat ironic way: "Chabela, you're getting married and you didn't even tell me."

"Yes," I tell him, "that's how it must have been." Then I tug on the noose, where on one of the ends the living flesh of the newly cut rope can be seen. I retie the knot my men had cut in order to take the body down and I toss one of the ends over the beam until the noose is hanging, held with enough strength to contribute many deaths just like this man's. While he fans himself with his hat, his face altered by shortness of breath and liquor, looking at the noose, calculating its strength, he says: "A noose as thin as that couldn't possibly have held his body." And I tell him: "That same rope held up his hammock for many years." And he pulls a chair over, hands me his hat, and hangs from the noose by his hands, his face flushed by the effort. Then he stands on the chair again, looking at the end of the hanging rope. He says: "Impossible. That noose doesn't reach down to my neck." And then I can see that he's being illogical deliberately, looking for ways to hold off the burial.

I look at him straight in the face, scrutinizing him. I tell him: "Didn't you ever notice that he was at least a head taller than you?" And he turns to look at the coffin. He says: "All the same, I'm not sure he did it with this noose."

I'm sure it was done that way. And he knows it too, but he has a scheme for wasting time because he's afraid of compromising himself. His cowardice can be seen in the way he moves around in no direction. A double and contradictory cowardice: to hold off the ceremony and to set it up. Then, when he gets to the coffin, he turns on his heels, looks at me, and says: "I'd have to see him hanging to be convinced."

I would have done it. I would have told my men to open the coffin and put the hanged man back up again the way he was until a moment ago. But it would be too much for my daughter. It would be too much for the child, and she shouldn't have brought him. Even though it upsets me to treat a dead man that way, offending defenseless flesh, disturbing a man who's at rest for the first time; even though the act of moving a corpse who's lying peacefully and deservedly in his coffin is against my principles, I'd hang him up again just to see how far this man will go. But it's impossible. And I tell him so: "You can rest assured that I won't tell them to do that. If you want to, hang him up yourself, and you can be responsible for what happens. Remember that we don't know how long he's been dead."

He hasn't moved. He's still beside the coffin, looking at me, then looking at Isabel and then at the child, and then at the coffin again. Suddenly his expression becomes somber and menacing. He says: "You must know what can happen because of this." And I can see what he means by his threat. I tell him: "Of course I do. I'm a responsible person." And he, his arms folded now, sweating, walking toward me with studied and comical movements that pretend to be threatening, says: "May I ask you how you found out that this man had hanged himself last night?"

I wait for him to get in front of me. I remain motionless, looking at him until my face is hit by his hot, harsh breath, until he stops, his arms still folded, moving his hat behind one armpit. Then I say to him: "When you ask me that in an official capacity, I'll be very pleased to give you an answer." He stands facing me in the same position. When I speak to him he doesn't show the least bit of surprise or upset. He says: "Naturally, colonel, I'm asking you officially."

I'll give him all the rope he wants. I'm sure that no matter how much he tries to twist it, he'll have to give in to an ironclad position, but one that's patient and calm. I tell him: "These men cut the body down because I couldn't let it stay hanging there until you decided to come. I told you to come two hours ago and you took all this time to walk two blocks."

He still doesn't move. I face him, resting on my cane, leaning forward a little. I say: "In the second place, he was my friend." Before I can finish speaking he smiles ironically, but without changing position, throwing his thick and sour breath into my face. He says: "It's the easiest thing in the world, isn't it?" And

22

suddenly he stops smiling. He says: "So you knew this man was going to hang himself."

Tranquil, patient, convinced that he's only going on like that to complicate things, I say to him: "I repeat. The first thing I did when I found out he'd hanged himself was to go to your place and that was two hours ago." And as if I'd asked him a question and not stated something, he says: "I was having lunch." And I say to him: "I know. I even think you took time out for a siesta."

Then he doesn't know what to say. He moves back. He looks at Isabel sitting beside the child. He looks at the men and finally at me. But his expression is changed now. He seems to be looking for something to occupy his thought for a moment. He turns his back on me, goes to where the policeman is, and tells him something. The policeman nods and leaves the room.

Then he comes back and takes my arm. He says: "I'd like to talk to you in the other room, colonel." Now his voice has changed completely. It's tense and disturbed now. And while I walk into the next room, feeling the uncertain pressure of his hand on my arm, I'm taken with the idea that I know what he's going to tell me.

This room, unlike the other one, is big and cool. The light from the courtyard flows into it. In here I can see his disturbed eyes, the smile that doesn't match the expression of his eyes. I can hear his voice saying: "Colonel, maybe we can settle this another way." And without giving him time to finish, I ask him: "How much?" And then he becomes a different man.

Meme had brought out a plate with jelly and two salt rolls, the kind that she'd learned to make from my mother. The clock had struck nine. Meme was sitting opposite me in the back of the store and was eating listlessly, as if the jelly and rolls were only something to hold together the visit. I understood that and let her lose herself in her labyrinths, sink into the past with that nostalgic and sad enthusiasm that in the light of the oil lamp burning on the

23

counter made her look more withered and old than the day she'd come into church wearing the hat and high heels. It was obvious that Meme felt like recalling things that night. And while she was doing it, one had the impression that over the past years she'd held herself back in some unique and timeless static age and that as she recalled things that night she was putting her personal time into motion again and beginning to go through her long-postponed aging process.

Meme was stiff and somber, talking about the picturesque and feudal splendor of our family during the last years of the previous century, before the great war. Meme recalled my mother. She recalled her that night when I was coming back from church and she told me in her somewhat mocking and ironic way: "Chabela, you're getting married and you didn't even tell me." Those were precisely the days when I'd wanted my mother and was trying to bring her back more strongly in my memory. "She was the living picture of you," she said. And I really believed it. I was sitting across from the Indian woman, who spoke with an accent mixed with precision and vagueness, as if there was a lot of incredible legend in what she was recalling but also as if she was recalling it in good faith and even with the conviction that the passage of time had changed legend into reality that was remote but hard to forget. She spoke to me about the journey my parents had made during the war, about the rough pilgrimage that would end with their settling in Macondo. My parents were fleeing the hazards of war and looking for a prosperous and tranquil bend in the road to settle down in, and they heard about the golden calf and came looking for it in what was then a town in formation, founded by several refugee families whose members were as careful about the preservation of their traditions and religious practices as the fattening of their hogs. Macondo was my parents' promised land, peace, and the Parchment. Here they found the appropriate spot to rebuild the house that a few years later would be a country mansion with three stables and two guest rooms. Meme recalled the details without repentance, and spoke about the most extravagant things with an irrepressible desire to live them again or with the pain that came from the fact that she would never live them again. There was no suffering or privation on the journey, she said. Even the horses slept under mosquito netting, not because my father was a spendthrift or a madman, but because my mother had a strange sense of charity, of humanitarian feelings, and thought that the eyes of God would be just as pleased with the act of protecting an animal from the mosquitoes as protecting a man. Their wild and burdensome cargo was everywhere; the trunks full of clothing of people who had died before they'd been on earth, ancestors who couldn't have been found twenty fathoms under the earth; boxes full of kitchen utensils that hadn't been used for a long time and had belonged to my parents' most distant relatives (my father and mother were first cousins), and even a trunk filled with the images of saints, which they used to reconstruct their family altar everywhere they stopped. It was a strange carnival procession with horses and hens and the four Guajiro Indians (Meme's companions) who had grown up in the house and followed my parents all through the region like trained circus animals.

Meme recalled things with sadness. One had the impression that she considered the passage of time a personal loss, as if she noticed in that heart of hers, lacerated by memories, that if time hadn't passed she'd still be on that pilgrimage, which must have been a punishment for my parents, but which was a kind of lark for the children, with strange sights like that of horses under mosquito netting.

Then everything began to go backward, she said. Their arrival in the newborn village of Macondo during the last days of the century was that of a devastated family, still bound to a recent splendid past, disorganized by the war. The Indian woman recalled my mother's arrival in town, sidesaddle on a mule, pregnant, her face green and malarial and her feet disabled by swelling.

Perhaps the seeds of resentment were maturing in my father's soul but he came ready to sink roots against wind and tide while he waited for my mother to bear the child that had been growing in her womb during the crossing and was progressively bringing death to her as the time of birth drew near.

The light of the lamp outlined her profile. Meme, with her stiff Indian expression, her hair straight and thick like a horse's mane or tail, looked like a sitting idol, green and spectral in the small hot room behind the store, speaking the way an idol would have if it had set out to recall its ancient earthly existence. I'd never been close to her, but that night, after that sudden and spontaneous show of intimacy, I felt that I was tied to her by bonds tighter than those of blood.

Suddenly, during one of Meme's pauses, I heard coughing in the next room, in this very bedroom where I am now with the child and my father. It was a short, dry cough, followed by a clearing of the throat, and then I heard the unmistakable sound that a man makes when he rolls over in bed. Meme stopped talking at once, and a gloomy, silent cloud darkened her face. I'd forgotten about him. During the time I was there (it was around ten o'clock) I had felt as if the Guajiro woman and I were alone in the house. Then the tension of the atmosphere changed. I felt fatigue in the arm with which I'd been holding the plate with the jelly and rolls, without tasting any. I leaned over and said: "He's awake." She, expressionless now, cold and completely indifferent, said: "He'll be awake until dawn." And suddenly I understood the disillusionment that could be seen in Meme when she recalled the past of our house. Our lives had changed, the times were good and Macondo was a bustling town where there was even enough money to squander on Saturday nights, but Meme was living tied to a past that had been better. While they were shearing the golden calf outside, inside, in the back of the store, her life was sterile, anonymous, all day behind the counter and spending the night with a man who didn't sleep until dawn, who spent his time walking about the house, pacing, looking at her greedily with those lustful dog eyes that I've never been able to forget. It saddened me to think of Meme with that man who refused his services one night and went on being a hardened animal, without bitterness or compassion, all day long in ceaseless roaming through the house, enough to drive the most balanced person out of his mind.

Recovering the tone of my voice, knowing that he was in his room, awake, maybe opening his lustful dog eyes every time our words were heard in the rear of the store, I tried to give a different turn to the conversation.

"How's business been for you?" I asked.

Meme smiled. Her laugh was sad and taciturn, seeming detached from any feeling of the moment, like something she kept in the cupboard and took out only when she had to, using it with no feeling of ownership, as if the infrequency of her smiles had made her forget the normal way to use them. "There it is," she said, moving her head in an ambiguous way, and she was silent, abstract again. Then I understood that it was time for me to leave. I handed Meme the plate without giving any explanation as to why it was untouched, and I watched her get up and put it on the counter. She looked at me from there and repeated: "You're the living picture of her." I must have been sitting against the light before, clouded by it as it came in the opposite direction and Meme couldn't see my face while she'd been talking. Then when she got up to put the plate on the counter she saw me frontward, from behind the lamp, and that was why she said: "You're the living picture of her." And she came back to sit down.

Then she began to recall the days when my mother had arrived in Macondo. She'd gone directly from the mule to a rocking chair and stayed seated for three months, not moving, taking her food listlessly. Sometimes they would bring her lunch and she'd sit halfway through the afternoon with the plate in her hand, rigid, not rocking, her feet resting on a chair, feeling death growing inside of them until someone would come and take the plate from her hands. When the day came, the labor pains drew her out of her abandonment and she stood up by herself, although they had to help her walk the twenty steps between the porch and the bedroom, martyrized by the occupation of a death that had taken her over during nine months of silent suffering. Her crossing from the rocker to the bed had all the pain, bitterness, and penalties that had been absent during the journey taken a few months before, but she arrived where she knew she had to arrive before she fulfilled the last act of her life.

My father seemed desperate over my mother's death, Meme said. But according to what he himself said afterward when he was alone in the house, "No one trusts the morality of a home where the man doesn't have a legitimate wife by his side." And since he'd read somewhere that when a loved one dies we should set out a bed of jasmine to remember her every night, he planted a vine against the courtyard wall, and a year later, in a second marriage, he was wedded to Adelaida, my stepmother.

Sometimes I thought that Meme was going to cry while she was speaking. But she remained firm, satisfied at expiating the loss of having been happy once and having stopped being so by her own free will. Then she smiled. Then she relaxed in her chair and became completely human. It was as if she'd drawn up mental accounts of her grief when she leaned forward and saw that she still had a favorable balance in good memories left, and then she smiled with her old wide and teasing friendliness. She said that the other thing had started five years later, when she came into the dining room where my father was having lunch and told him: "Colonel, colonel, there's a stranger to see you in your office."

## III.

Behind the church, on the other side of the street, there was once a lot with no trees. That was toward the end of the last century, when we came to Macondo and they hadn't started to build the church yet. It was a dry, bald plot of land where the children ·played after school. Later on, when construction on the church began, they set up four beams to one side of the lot and it could be seen that the encircled space was just right for building a hut. Which they did. Inside they kept the materials for the construction of the church.

When the work on the church came to an end, someone finished putting adobe on the walls of the small hut and opened a door in the rear wall, which faced the small, bare, stony plot where there was not even a trace of an aloe bush. A year later the small hut was finished, big enough for two people. Inside there was a smell of quicklime. That was the only pleasant odor that had been smelled for a long time inside that enclosure and the only agreeable one that would be smelled ever after. When they had whitewashed the walls, the same hand that had completed the construction ran a bar across the inside door and put a padlock on the street door.

The hut had no owner. No one worried about making his rights effective over either the lot or the construction materials. When the first parish priest arrived he put up with one of the well-to-do families in Macondo. Then he was transferred to a different parish. But during those days (and possibly before the first priest had left) a woman with a child at her breast had occupied the hut, and no one knew when she had come, nor from where, nor how she had managed to open the door. There was an earthen crock in a corner, black and green with moss, and a jar hanging from a nail. But there wasn't any more whitewash left on the walls. In the yard a crust of earth hardened by the rain had formed over the stones. The woman built a network of branches to protect herself from the sun. And since she had no means to put a roof of palm leaves, tile, or zinc on it, she planted a grapevine beside the branches and hung a clump of *sábila* and a loaf of bread by the street door to protect herself against evil thoughts.

When the coming of the new priest was announced in 1903, the woman was still living in the hut with her child. Half of the population went out to the highway to wait for the priest to arrive. The rural band was playing sentimental pieces until a boy came running, panting to the point of bursting, saying that the priest's mule was at the last bend in the road. Then the musicians changed their position and began to play a march. The person assigned to give the welcoming speech climbed up on an improvised platform and waited for the priest to appear so that he could begin his greeting. But a moment later the martial tune was suspended, the orator got down off the table, and the astonished multitude watched a stranger pass by, riding a mule whose haunches carried the largest trunk ever seen in Macondo. The man went by on his way into town without looking at anyone. Even if the priest had been dressed in civilian clothes for the trip, it would never have occurred to anyone that the bronzed traveler in military leggings was a priest dressed in civilian clothes.

And, in fact, he wasn't, because at that very same moment, along the shortcut on the other side of town, people saw a strange priest coming along, fearfully thin, with a dry and stretched-out face, astride a mule, his cassock lifted up to his knees, and protected from the sun by a faded and run-down umbrella. In the neighborhood of the church the priest asked where the parish house was, and he must have asked someone who didn't have the least idea of anything, because the answer he got was: "It's the hut behind the church, father." The woman had gone out, but the child was playing inside behind the half-open door. The priest dismounted, rolled a swollen suitcase over to the hut. It was unlocked, just barely held together by a leather strap that was different from the hide of the suitcase itself, and after he examined the hut, he brought up the mule and tied it in the yard in the shade of the grape leaves. Then he opened up the suitcase, took out a hammock that must have been the same age and had seen the same use as the umbrella, hung it diagonally across the hut, from beam to beam, took off his boots, and tried to sleep, unconcerned about the child, who was looking at him with great frightened eyes.

When the woman returned she must have felt disconcerted by the strange presence of the priest, whose face was so inexpressive that it was in no way different from the skull of a cow. The woman must have tiptoed across the room. She must have dragged her folding cot to the door, made a bundle of her clothes and the child's rags, and left the hut without even bothering about the crock and the jar, because an hour later, when the delegation went back through town in the opposite direction preceded by the band, which was playing its martial air in the midst of a crowd of boys who had skipped school, they found the priest alone in the hut, stretched out in his hammock in a carefree way, his cassock unbuttoned and his shoes off. Someone must have brought the news to the main road, but it occurred to no one to ask what the priest was doing in that hut. They must have thought that he was related to the woman in some way, just as she must have abandoned the hut because she thought that the priest had orders to occupy it, or that it was church property, or simply out of fear that they would ask her why she had lived for more than two years in a hut that didn't belong to her without paying any rent or without anyone's permission. Nor did it occur to the delegation to ask for any explanation, neither then nor any time after, because the priest wouldn't accept any speeches. He laid the presents on the floor and limited himself to greeting the men and women coldly and quickly, because according to what he said, he hadn't shut his eyes all night.

The delegation dissolved in the face of that cold reception by the strangest priest they'd ever seen. They noticed how his face looked like the skull of a cow, with closely cropped gray hair, and he didn't have any lips, but a horizontal opening that seemed not to have been in the place of his mouth since birth but made later on by a quick and unique knife. But that very afternoon they realized that he looked like someone. And before dawn everyone knew who it was. They remembered having seen him with a sling and a stone, naked, but wearing shoes and a hat, during the time when Macondo was a humble refugee village. The veterans remembered his activities in the civil war of '85. They remembered that he had been a colonel at the age of seventeen and that he was intrepid, hardheaded, and against the government. But nothing had been heard of him again in Macondo until that day when he returned home to take over the parish. Very few remembered his given name. On the other hand, most of the veterans remembered the one his mother had put on him (because he was willful and rebellious) and that it was the same one that his comrades in arms would call him by later on. They all called him the pup. And that was what he was always called in Macondo until the hour of his death:

"Pup, Puppy."


So it was that this man came to our house on the same day and almost at the same hour that the pup reached Macondo. The former along the main road, unexpected and with no one having the slightest notion of his name or profession; the priest by the shortcut, while the whole town was waiting for him on the main road.

I returned home after the reception. We had just sat down to the table—a little later than usual—when Meme came over to tell me: "Colonel, colonel, colonel, there's a stranger to see you in your office." I said: "Tell him to come in." And Meme said: "He's in the office and says that he has to see you at once." Adelaida stopped feeding soup to Isabel (she couldn't have been more than five at the time) and went to take care of the newcomer. A moment later she came back, visibly worried:

"He's pacing back and forth in the office," she said.

I saw her walk behind the candlesticks. Then she began to feed Isabel her soup again. "You should have had him come in," I

32

said, still eating. And she said: "That's what I was going to do. But he was pacing back and forth in the office when I got there and said good afternoon, but he didn't answer me because he was looking at the leather dancing girl on the shelf. And when I was about to say good afternoon again, he wound up the dancing girl, put her on the desk, and watched her dance. I don't know whether it was the music that prevented him from hearing when I said good afternoon again, but I stood there opposite the desk, where he was leaning over watching the dancing girl, who was still wound up a little." Adelaida was feeding Isabel her soup. I said to her: "He must be very interested in the toy." And she, still feeding Isabel her soup: "He was pacing back and forth in the office, but then, when he saw the dancing girl, he took her down as if he knew beforehand what it was for, as if he knew how it worked. He was winding it up when I said good afternoon to him for the first time, before the music began to play. Then he put it on the desk and stood there watching it, but without smiling, as if he weren't interested in the dance but in the mechanism."

They never announced anyone to me. Visitors came almost every day: travelers we knew, who left their animals in the stable and came in with complete confidence, with the familiarity of one who always expects to find an empty place at our table. I told Adelaida: "He must have a message or something." And she said: "In any case, he's acting very strangely. He's watching the dancing girl until it runs down and in the meantime I'm standing across the desk without knowing what to say to him, because I knew that he wouldn't answer me as long as the music was playing. Then, when the dancing girl gave the little leap she always gives when she runs down, he was still standing there looking at her with curiosity, leaning over the desk but not sitting down. Then he looked at me and I realized that he knew I was in the office but that he hadn't worried about me because he wanted to know how long the dancing girl would keep on dancing. I didn't say good afternoon to him again, but I smiled when he looked at me because I saw that he had huge eyes, with yellow pupils, and they look at a person's whole body all at the same time. When I smiled at him he remained serious, but he nodded his head very formally and said: 'The colonel. It's the colonel I have to see.' He has a deep voice, as if he could speak with his mouth closed. As if he were a ventriloquist."

She was feeding Isabel her soup, and she said: "At first he was pacing back and forth in the office." Then I understood that the stranger had made an uncommon impression on her and that she had a special interest in my taking care of him. Nevertheless, I kept on eating lunch while she fed Isabel her soup and spoke. She said: "Then, when he said he wanted to see the colonel, what I told him was 'Please come into the dining room,' and he straightened up where he was, with the dancing girl in his hand. Then he raised his head and became as rigid and firm as a soldier, I think, because he's wearing high boots and a suit of ordinary cloth, with the shirt buttoned up to his neck. I didn't know what to say when he didn't answer anything and was quiet, with the toy in his hand, as if he were waiting for me to leave the office in order to wind it up again. That was when he suddenly reminded me of someone, when I realized that he was a military man."

And I told her: "So you think it's something serious." I looked at her over the candlesticks. She wasn't looking at me. She was feeding Isabel her soup. She said:

"When I got there he was pacing back and forth in the office and so I couldn't see his face. But then when he stood in the back he had his head held so high and his eyes were so fixed that I think he's a military man, and I said to him: 'You want to see the colonel in private, is that it?' And he nodded. Then I came to tell you that he looks like someone, or rather, that he's the same person that he looks like, although I can't explain how he got here."

I kept on eating, but I was looking at her over the candlesticks. She stopped feeding Isabel her soup. She said:

"I'm sure it's not a message. I'm sure it's not that he looks like someone but that he's the same person he looks like. I'm sure, rather, that he's a military man. He's got a black pointed mustache and a face like copper. He's wearing high boots and I'm sure that it's not that he looks like someone but that he's the same person he looks like."

She was speaking in a level tone, monotonous and persistent. It was hot and maybe for that reason I began to feel irritated. I said to her: "So, who does he look like?" And she said: "When he was pacing back and forth in the office I couldn't see his face, but later on." And I, irritated with the monotony and persistence of her words: "All right, all right, I'll go to see him when I finish my lunch." And she, feeding Isabel her soup again: "At first I couldn't see his face because he was pacing back and forth in the office. But then when I said to him: 'Please come in,' he stood there silent beside the wall with the dancing girl in his hand. That was when I remembered who he looks like and I came to tell you. He has huge, indiscreet eyes, and when I turned to leave I felt that he was looking right at my legs."

She suddenly fell silent. In the dining room the metallic tinkle of the spoon kept vibrating. I finished my lunch and folded the napkin under my plate.

At that moment from the office I heard the festive music of the windup toy.

## IV.

In the kitchen of the house there's an old carved wooden chair without crosspieces and my grandfather puts his shoes to dry next to the stove on its broken seat.

Tobías, Abraham, Gilberto, and I left school at this time yesterday and we went to the plantations with a sling, a big hat to hold the birds, and a new knife. On the way I was remembering the useless chair placed in the kitchen corner, which at one time was used for visitors and which now is used by the dead man who sits down every night with his hat on to look at the ashes in the cold stove.

Tobías and Gilberto were walking toward the end of the dark nave. Since it had rained during the morning, their shoes slipped on the muddy grass. One of them was whistling, and his hard, firm whistle echoed in the vegetable cavern the way it does when someone starts to sing inside a barrel. Abraham was bringing up the rear with me. He with his sling and the stone, ready to shoot. I with my open knife.

Suddenly the sun broke the roof of tight, hard leaves and a body of light fell winging down onto the grass like a live bird. "Did you see it?" Abraham asked. I looked ahead and saw Gilberto and Tobías at the end of the nave. "It's not a bird," I said. "It's the sun that's just come out strong."

When they got to the bank they began to get undressed and gave strong kicks in that twilight water, which didn't seem to wet their skin. "There hasn't been a single bird all afternoon," Abraham said. "There aren't any birds after it rains," I said. And I believed it myself then. Abraham began to laugh. His laugh is foolish and simple and it makes a sound like that of a thread of water from a spigot. He got undressed. "I'll take the knife into the water and fill the hat with fish," he said.

Abraham was naked in front of me with his hand open, waiting for the knife. I didn't answer right away. I held the knife tight and I felt its clean and tempered steel in my hand. *I'm not going to give him the knife*, I thought. And I told him: "I'm not going to give you the knife. I only got it yesterday and I'm going to keep it all afternoon." Abraham kept his hand out. Then I told him:

"*Incomploruto.*"

Abraham understood me. He's the only one who can understand my words. "All right," he said and walked toward the water through the hardened, sour air. He said: "Start getting undressed and we'll wait for you on the rock." And he said it as he dove in and reappeared shining like an enormous silver-plated fish, as if the water had turned to liquid as it came in contact with him.

I stayed on the bank, lying on the warm mud. When I opened the knife again I stopped looking at Abraham and lifted my eyes up straight toward the other side, up toward the trees, toward the furious dusk where the sky had the monstrous awfulness of a burning stable.

"Hurry up," Abraham said from the other side. Tobías was whistling on the edge of the rock. Then I thought: *I'm not going swimming today. Tomorrow.*

On the way back Abraham hid behind the hawthorns. I was going to follow him, but he told me: "Don't come back here. I'm doing something." I stayed outside, sitting on the dead leaves in the road, watching a single swallow that was tracing a curve in the sky. I said:

"There's only one swallow this afternoon."

Abraham didn't answer right away. He was silent behind the hawthorns, as if he couldn't hear me, as if he were reading. His silence was deep and concentrated, full of a hidden strength. After a long silence he sighed. Then he said:

"Swallows."

I told him again: "There's only one swallow this afternoon." Abraham was still behind the hawthorns but I couldn't tell anything about him. He was silent and drawn in, but his silence wasn't static. It was a desperate and impetuous immobility. After a moment he said:

"Only one? Ah, yes. You're right, you're right."

I didn't say anything then. Behind the hawthorns, he was the one who began to move. Sitting on the leaves, I could hear the sound of other dead leaves under his feet from where he was. Then he was silent again, as if he'd gone away. Then he breathed deeply and asked:

"What did you say?"

I told him again: "There's only one swallow this afternoon." And while I was saying it I saw the curved wing tracing circles in the sky of incredible blue. "He's flying high," I said.

Abraham replied at once:

"Ah, yes, of course. That must be why then."

He came out from behind the hawthorns, buttoning up his pants. He looked up toward where the swallow was still tracing circles, and, still not looking at me, he said:

"What were you telling me a while back about the swallows?"

That held us up. When we got back the lights in town were on. I ran into the house and on the veranda I came on the fat, blind women with the twins of Saint Jerome who every Tuesday have come to sing for my grandfather since before I was born, according to what my mother says.

All night I was thinking that today we'd get out of school again and go to the river, but not with Gilberto and Tobías. I want to go alone with Abraham, to see the shine of his stomach when he dives and comes up again like a metal fish. All night long I've wanted to go back with him, alone in the darkness of the green tunnel, to brush his thigh as we walk along. Whenever I do that I feel as if someone is biting me with soft nibbles and my skin creeps.

If this man who's come to talk to my grandfather in the other room comes back in a little while maybe we can be home before four o'clock. Then I'll go to the river with Abraham.

He stayed on to live at our house. He occupied one of the rooms off the veranda, the one that opens onto the street, because I thought it would be convenient, for I knew that a man of his type wouldn't be comfortable in the small hotel in town. He put a sign on the door (it was still there until a few years ago when they whitewashed the house, written in pencil in his own hand),

and on the following week we had to bring in new chairs to take care of the demands of his numerous patients.

After he gave me the letter from Colonel Aureliano Buendía, our conversation in the office went on so long that Adelaida had no doubts but that it was a matter of some high military official on an important mission, and she set the table as if for a holiday. We spoke about Colonel Buendía, his premature daughter, and his wild firstborn son. The conversation had not gone on too long when I gathered that the man knew the Intendant General quite well and that he had enough regard for him to warrant his confidence. When Meme came to tell us that dinner was served, I thought that my wife had improvised some things in order to take care of the newcomer. But a far cry from improvisation was that splendid table served on the new cloth, on the chinaware destined exclusively for family dinners on Christmas and New Year's Day.

Adelaida was solemnly sitting up straight at one end of the table in a velvet dress closed up to the neck, the one that she wore before our marriage to attend to family business in the city. Adelaida had more refined customs than we did, a certain social experience which, since our marriage, had begun to influence the ways of my house. She had put on the family medallion, the one that she displayed at moments of exceptional importance, and all of her, just like the table, the furniture, the air that was breathed in the dining room, brought on a severe feeling of composure and cleanliness. When we reached the parlor, the man, who was always so careless in his dress and manners, must have felt ashamed and out of place, for he checked the button on his shirt as if he were wearing a tie, and a slight nervousness could be noticed in his unworried and strong walk. I can remember nothing with such precision as that instant in which we went into the dining room and I myself felt dressed too domestically for a table like the one Adelaida had prepared.

39

There was beef and game on the plates. Everything the same, however, as at our regular meals at that time, except for the presentation on the new china, between the newly polished candlesticks, which was spectacular and different from the norm. In spite of the fact that my wife knew that we would be having only one visitor, she had set eight places, and the bottle of wine in the center was an exaggerated manifestation of the diligence with which she had prepared the homage for the man whom, from the first moment, she had confused with a distinguished military functionary. Never before had I seen in my house an environment more loaded with unreality.

Adelaida's clothing would have been ridiculous had it not been for her hands (they were beautiful, really, and overly white), which balanced, along with her regal distinction, the falsity and arrangement of her appearance. It was when he checked the button on his shirt and hesitated that I got ahead of myself and said: "My second wife, *doctor*." A cloud darkened Adelaida's face and turned it strange and gloomy. She didn't budge from where she was, her hand held out, smiling, but no longer with the air of ceremonious stiffness that she had had when we came into the dining room.

The newcomer clicked his heels like a military man, touched his forehead with the tips of his extended fingers, and then walked over to where she was.

"Yes, ma'am," he said. But he didn't pronounce any name.

Only when I saw him clumsily shake Adelaida's hand did I become aware that his manners were vulgar and common.

He sat at the other end of the table, between the new crystal ware, between the candlesticks. His disarrayed presence stood out like a soup stain on the tablecloth.

Adelaida poured the wine. Her emotion from the beginning had been changed into a passive nervousness that seemed to say: *It's all right, everything will be done the way it was laid out, but you owe me an explanation.*

And it was after she served the wine and sat down at the other end of the table, while Meme got ready to serve the plates, that he leaned back in his chair, rested his hands on the tablecloth, and said with a smile:

"Look, miss, just start boiling a little grass and bring that to me as if it were soup."

Meme didn't move. She tried to laugh, but she couldn't get it out; instead she turned toward Adelaida. Then she, smiling too, but visibly upset, asked him: "What kind of grass, doctor?" And he, in his parsimonious ruminant voice:

"Ordinary grass, ma'am. The kind that donkeys eat."

## V.

There's a moment when siesta time runs dry. Even the secret, hidden, minute activity of the insects ceases at that precise instant; the course of nature comes to a halt; creation stumbles on the brink of chaos and women get up, drooling, with the flower of the embroidered pillowcase on their cheeks, suffocated by temperature and rancor; and they think: *It's still Wednesday in Macondo*. And then they go back to huddling in the corner, splicing sleep to reality, and they come to an agreement, weaving the whispering as if it were an immense flat surface of thread stitched in common by all the women in town.

If inside time had the same rhythm as that outside, we would be in the bright sunlight now, in the middle of the street with the coffin. It would be later outside: it would be nighttime. It would be a heavy September night with a moon and women sitting in their courtyards chatting under the green light, and in the street, us, the renegades, in the full sunlight of this thirsty September. No one will interfere with the ceremony. I expected the mayor to be inflexible in his determination to oppose it and that we could have gone home; the child to school and my father to his clogs, the washbasin under his head dripping with cool water, and on the left-hand side his pitcher with iced lemonade. But now it's different. My father has once more been sufficiently persuasive to impose his point of view on what I thought at first was the mayor's irrevocable determination. Outside the town is bustling, given over to the work of a long, uniform, and pitiless whispering; and the clean street, without a shadow on the clean dust, virgin since the last wind swept away the tracks of the last ox. And it's a town with no one, with closed houses, where nothing is heard in the rooms except the dull bubbling of words pronounced by evil hearts. And in the room, the sitting child, stiff, looking at his shoes; slowly his eyes go to the lamp, then to the newspapers, again to his shoes, and now quickly to the hanged man, his bitten tongue, his glassy dog eyes that have no lust now; a dog with no appetite, dead. The child looks at him, thinks about the hanged man lying underneath the boards; he has a sad expression and then everything changes: a stool comes out by the door of the barbershop and inside the small altar with the mirror, the powder, and the scented water. The hand becomes freckled and large, it's no longer the hand of my son, it's been changed into a large, deft hand that coldly, with calculated parsimony, begins to strop the razor while the ear hears the metallic buzzing of the tempered blade and the head thinks: *Today they'll be coming earlier because it's Wednesday in Macondo.* And then they come, sit on the chairs in the shade and the coolness of the threshold, grim, squinting, their legs crossed, their hands folded over their knees, biting on the tips of their cigars; looking, talking about the same thing, watching the closed window across from them, the silent house with Señora Rebeca inside. She forgot something too: she forgot to disconnect the fan and she's going through the rooms with screened windows, nervous, stirred up, going through the knickknacks of her sterile and tormented widowhood in order to be convinced by her sense of touch that she won't have died before the hour of burial comes. She's opening and closing the doors of her rooms, waiting for the patriarchal clock to rise up out of its siesta and reward her senses by striking three. All this, while the child's expression ends and he goes back to being hard and stiff, not even delaying half the time a woman needs to give the last stitch on the machine and raise her head full of curlers. Before the child goes back to being upright and pensive, the woman has rolled the machine to the corner of the veranda, and the men have bitten their cigars twice while they watch a complete passage of the razor across the cowhide; and Águeda, the cripple, makes a last effort to awaken her dead knees; and Señora Rebeca turns the lock again and thinks: *Wednesday in Macondo. A good day to bury the devil.* But then the child moves again and there's a new change in time. When something moves you can tell that time has passed. Not till then. Until something moves time is eternal, the sweat, the shirt drooling on the skin, and the unbribable and icy dead man, behind his bitten tongue. That's why time doesn't pass for the hanged man: because even if the child's hand moves, he doesn't know it. And while the dead man doesn't know it (because the child is still moving his hand), Águeda must have gone through another bead on her rosary; Señora Rebeca, lounging in her folding chair, is perplexed, watching the clock remain fixed on the edge of the imminent minute, and Águeda has had time (even though the second hasn't passed on Señora Rebeca's clock) to go through another bead on her rosary and think: *I'd do that if I could get to Father Ángel.* Then the child's hand descends and the razor makes a motion on the strop and one of the men sitting in the coolness of the threshold says: "It must be around three-thirty, right?" Then the hand stops. A dead clock on the brink of the next minute once more, the razor halted once more in the limits of its own steel; and Águeda still waiting for a new movement of the hand to stretch her legs and burst into the sacristy with her arms open, her knees moving again, saying: "Father, Father." And Father Ángel, prostrate in the child's immobility, running his tongue over his lips and the viscous taste of the meatball nightmare, seeing Águeda, would then say: "This is undoubtedly a miracle," and then, rolling about again in the sweaty, drooly drowsiness: "In any case, Águeda, this is no time for saying a mass for the souls in Purgatory." But the new movement is frustrated, my father comes into the room and the two times are reconciled; the two halves become adjusted, consolidate, and Señora Rebeca's clock realizes that it's been caught between the child's parsimony and the widow's impatience, and then it yawns, confused, dives into the prodigious quiet of the moment and comes out afterward dripping with liquid time, with exact and rectified time, and it leans forward and says with ceremonious dignity: "It's exactly two forty-seven." And my father, who, without knowing it, has broken the paralysis of the instant, says: "You're lost in the clouds, daughter." And I say: "Do you think something might happen?" And he, sweating, smiling: "At least I'm sure that the rice will be burned and the milk spilled in lots of houses."

The coffin's closed now, but I can remember the dead man's face. I've got it so clearly that if I look at the wall I can see his open eyes, his tight gray cheeks that are like damp earth, his bitten tongue to one side of his mouth. This gives me a burning, restless feeling. Maybe if my pants weren't so tight on one side of my leg.

My grandfather's sat down beside my mother. When he came back from the next room he brought over the chair and now he's here, sitting next to her, not saying anything, his chin on his cane and his lame leg stretched out in front of him. My grandfather's waiting. My mother, like him, is waiting too. The men have stopped smoking on the bed and they're quiet, all in a row, not looking at the coffin. They're waiting too.

If they blindfolded me, if they took me by the hand and walked me around town twenty times and brought me back to this room I'd recognize it by the smell. I'll never forget how this room smells of trash, piled-up trunks, all the same, even though I've only seen one trunk, where Abraham and I could hide and there'd still be room left over for Tobías. I know rooms by their smell.

Last year Ada sat me on her lap. I had my eyes closed and I saw her through my lashes. I saw her dark, as if she wasn't a woman but just a face that was looking at me and rocking and bleating like a sheep. I was really going to sleep when I got the smell.

There's no smell at home that I can't recognize. When they leave me alone on the veranda I close my eyes, stick out my arms, and walk. I think: *When I get the smell of camphorated rum I'll be by my grandfather's room.* I keep on walking with my eyes closed and my arms stretched out. I think *Now I've gone past my mother's room, because it smells like new playing cards. Then it will smell of pitch and mothballs.* I keep on walking and I get the smell of new playing cards at the exact moment I hear my mother's voice singing in her room. Then I get the smell of pitch and mothballs. I think: *Now I'll keep on smelling mothballs. Then I'll turn to the left of the smell and I'll get the other smell of underwear and closed windows. I'll stop there.* Then, when I take three steps, I get the new smell and I stop, with my eyes closed and my arms outstretched, and I hear Ada's voice shouting: "Child, what are you walking with your eyes closed for?"

That night, when I began to fall asleep, I caught a smell that doesn't exist in any of the rooms in the house. It was a strong and warm smell, as if someone had been shaking a jasmine bush. I opened my eyes, sniffing the thick and heavy air. I said. "Do you smell it?" Ada was looking at me but when I spoke to her she closed her eyes and looked in the other direction. I asked her again: "Do you smell it? It's as if there were some jasmines somewhere." Then she said:

"It's the smell of the jasmines that used to be growing on the wall here nine years ago."

I sat on her lap. "But there aren't any jasmines now," I said. And she said: "Not now. But nine years ago, when you were born, there was a jasmine bush against the courtyard wall. It would be hot at night and it would smell the same as now." I leaned on her shoulder. I looked at her mouth while she spoke. "But that was before I was born," I said. And she said: "During that time there was a great winter storm and they had to clean out the garden."

The smell was still there, warm, almost touchable, leading the other smells of the night. I told Ada: "I *want* you to tell me that." And she remained silent for an instant, then looked toward the whitewashed wall with moonlight on it and said:

"When you're older you'll learn that the jasmine is a flower that *comes out*."

I didn't understand, but I felt a strange shudder, as if someone had touched me. I said: "All right," and she said: "The same thing happens with jasmines as with people who come out and wander through the night after they're dead."

I stayed there leaning on her shoulder, not saying anything. I was thinking about other things, about the chair in the kitchen where my grandfather puts his shoes on the seat to dry when it rains. I knew from then on that there's a dead man in the kitchen and every night he sits down, without taking off his hat, looking at the ashes in the cold stove. After a moment I said: "That must be like the dead man who sits in the kitchen." Ada looked at me, opened her eyes, and asked: "What dead man?" And I said to her: "The one who sits every night in the chair where my grandfather puts his shoes to dry." And she said: "There's no dead man there. The chair's next to the stove be- cause it's no good for anything else anymore except to dry shoes on."

That was last year. Now it's different, now I've seen a corpse and all I have to do is close my eyes to keep on seeing him inside, in the darkness of my eyes. I was going to tell my mother, but she's begun to talk to my grandfather: "Do you think something might happen?" she asks. And my grandfather lifts his chin from his cane and shakes his head. "At least I'm sure that the rice will be burned and the milk spilled in lots of houses."

# VI.

At first he used to sleep till seven o'clock. He would appear in the kitchen with his collarless shirt buttoned up to the neck, his wrinkled and dirty sleeves rolled up to the elbows, his filthy pants at chest level with the belt fastened outside, well below the loops. You had the feeling that his pants were about to fall down, slide off, because there was no body to hold them up. He hadn't grown thinner, but you didn't see the military and haughty look he had the first year on his face anymore; he had the dreamy and fatigued expression of a man who doesn't know what his life will be from one minute to the next and hasn't got the least interest in finding out. He would drink his black coffee a little after seven and then go back to his room, passing out his inexpressive "Good morning" along the way.

He'd been living in our house for four years and in Macondo he was looked upon as a serious professional man in spite of the fact that his brusque manner and disordered ways built up an atmosphere about him that was more like fear than respect.

He was the only doctor in town until the banana company arrived and work started on the railroad. Then empty seats began to appear in the small room. The people who visited him during the first four years of his stay in Macondo began to drift away when the company organized a clinic for its workers. He must have seen the new directions that the leaf storm was leading to, but he didn't say anything. He still opened up the street door, sitting in his leather chair all day long until several days passed without the return of a single patient. Then he threw the bolt on the door, bought a hammock, and shut himself up in the room.

During that time Meme got into the habit of bringing him breakfast, which consisted of bananas and oranges. He would eat the fruit and throw the peels into the corner, where the Indian woman would pick them up on Saturdays, when she cleaned the bedroom. But from the way he acted, anyone would have suspected that it made little difference to him whether or not she would stop cleaning some Saturday and the room would become a dungheap.

He did absolutely nothing now. He spent his time in the hammock, rocking. Through the half-open door he could be seen in the darkness and his thin and inexpressive face, his tangled hair, the sickly vitality of his hard yellow eyes gave him the unmistakable look of a man who has begun to feel defeated by circumstances.

During the first years of his stay in our house, Adelaida appeared to be indifferent or appeared to go along with me or really did agree with my decision that he should stay in the house. But when he closed his office and left his room only at mealtime, sitting at the table with the same silent and painful apathy as always, my wife broke the dikes of her tolerance. She told me: "It's heresy to keep supporting him. It's as if we were feeding the devil." And I, always inclined in his behalf out of a complex feeling of pity, amazement, and sorrow (because even though I may try to change the shape of it now, there was a great deal of sorrow in that feeling), insisted: "We have to take care of him. He's a man who doesn't have anybody in the world and he needs understanding."

Shortly afterward the railroad began to operate. Macondo was a prosperous town, full of new faces, with a movie theater and several amusement places. At that time there was work for everyone, except for him. He kept shut up, aloof, until that morning when, all of a sudden, he made an appearance in the dining room at breakfast time and spoke spontaneously, even with enthusiasm, about the magnificent prospects for the town. That morning I heard the words for the first time. He said: "All of this will pass when we get used to the *leaf storm.*"

Months later he was frequently seen going out into the street before dusk. He would sit by the barbershop until the last hours of daylight, taking part in the conversation of the groups that gathered by the door, beside the portable dressing table, beside the high stool that the barber brought out into the street so that his customers could enjoy the coolness of dusk.

The company doctors were not satisfied with depriving him of his means of life and in 1907, when there was no longer a single patient in Macondo who remembered him and when he himself had ceased expecting any, one of the banana company doctors suggested to the mayor's office that they require all professionals in town to register their degrees. He must not have felt that he was the one they had in mind when the edict appeared one Monday on the four corners of the square. It was I who spoke to him about the convenience of complying with the requirement. But he, tranquil, indifferent, limited himself to replying: "Not me, colonel. I'm not going to get involved in any of that again." I've never been able to find out whether his papers were really in order or not. I couldn't find out if he was French, as we supposed, or if he had any remembrance of a family, which he must have had but about which he never said a word. A few weeks later, when the mayor and his secretary appeared at my house to demand of him the presentation and registration of his license, he absolutely refused to leave his room. That day—after five years of living in the same house—I suddenly realized that we didn't even know his name.

One probably didn't have to be seventeen years old (as I was then) in order to observe—from the time I saw Meme all decked out in church and afterward, when I spoke to her in the shop— that the small room in our house off the street was closed up.

Later on I found out that my stepmother had padlocked it, was opposed to anyone's touching the things that were left inside: the bed that the doctor had used until he bought the hammock; the small table with medicines from which he had removed only the money accumulated during his better years (which must have been quite a bit, because he never had any expenses in the house and it was enough for Meme to open the shop with); and, in addition, in the midst of a pile of trash and old newspapers written in his language, the washstand and some useless personal items. It seemed as if all those things had been contaminated by something my stepmother considered evil, completely diabolical.

I must have noticed that the room was closed in October or November (three years after Meme and he had left the house), because early in the following year I began to dream about Martín staying in that room. I wanted to live in it after my marriage; I prowled about it; in conversation with my stepmother I even suggested that it was already time to open the padlock and lift the unbreakable quarantine imposed on one of the most intimate and friendly parts of the house. But before the time we began sewing my wedding dress, no one spoke to me directly about the doctor and even less about the small room that was still like something of his, a fragment of his personality which could not be detached from our house while anyone who might have remembered him still lived in it.

I was going to be married before the year was up. I don't know if it was the circumstances under which my life had developed during childhood and adolescence that gave me an imprecise notion of happenings and things at that time, but what was certain was that during those months when the preparations for my wedding were going forward, I still didn't know the secret of many things. A year before I married him, I would recall Martín through a vague atmosphere of unreality. Perhaps that was why I wanted him close by, in the small room, so that I could convince myself that it was a question of a concrete man and not a fiancé I had met in a dream. But I didn't feel I had the strength to speak to my stepmother about my project. The natural thing would have been to say: "I'm going to take off the padlock. I'm going to put the table next to the window and the bed against the inside wall. I'm going to put a pot of carnations on the shelf and an aloe branch over the lintel." But my cowardice, my absolute lack of decision, was joined by the foggy image of my betrothed. I remembered him as a vague, ungraspable figure whose only concrete elements seemed to be his shiny mustache, his head tilting slightly to the left, and the ever-present four-button jacket.

He had come to our house toward the end of July. He spent the day with us and chatted with my father in the office, going over some mysterious business that I was never able to find out about. In the afternoon Martín and I would go to the plantations with my stepmother. But when I looked at him on the way back in the mellow light of sunset, when he was closer to me, walking alongside my shoulder, then he became even more abstract and unreal. I knew that I would never be capable of imagining him as human or of finding in him the solidity that was indispensable if his memory was to give me courage, strengthen me at the moment of saying: "I'm going to fix the room up for Martín."

Even the idea that I was going to marry him seemed odd to me a year before the wedding. I had met him in February, during the wake for the Paloquemado child. Several of us girls were singing and clapping, trying to use up every drop of the only fun allowed us. There was a movie theater in Macondo, there was a public phonograph, and other places for amusement existed, but my father and stepmother were opposed to girls my age making use of them. "They're amusements from out of the leaf storm," they said.

Noontime was hot in February. My stepmother and I were sitting on the veranda, backstitching some white cloth while my father took his siesta. We sewed until he went by, dragging along in his clogs, to soak his head in the washbasin. But February was cool and deep at night and in the whole town one could hear the voices of women singing at wakes for children.

The night we went to the Paloquemado child's wake Meme Orozco's voice was probably louder than ever. She was thin, graceless, and stiff, like a broom, but she knew how to make her voice carry better than anyone. And in the first pause Genoveva García said: "There's a stranger sitting outside." I think that all of us stopped singing except Remedios Orozco. "Just think, he's wearing a jacket," Genoveva García said. "He's been talking all night and the others are listening to him without saying a peep. He's wearing a four-button jacket and when he crosses his legs you can see his socks and garters and his shoes have laces." Meme Orozco was still singing when we clapped our hands and said: "Let's marry him."

Afterward, when I thought about it at home, I couldn't find any correspondence between those words and reality. I remembered them as if they had been spoken by a group of imaginary women clapping hands and singing in a house where an unreal child had died. Other women were smoking next to us. They were serious, vigilant, stretching out their long buzzard necks toward us. In the back, against the coolness of the doorstep, another woman, bundled up to her head in a wide black cloth, was waiting for the coffee to boil. Suddenly a male voice joined ours. At first it was disconcerted and directionless, but then it was vibrant and metallic, as if the man were singing in church. Veva García nudged me in the ribs. Then I raised my eyes and saw him for the first time. He was young and neat, with a hard collar and a jacket with all four buttons closed. And he was looking at me.

I heard about his return in December and I thought that no place would be more appropriate for him than the small locked room. But I hadn't thought of it yet. I said to myself: "Martín, Martín, Martín." And the name, examined, savored, broken down into its essential parts, lost all of its meaning for me.

When we came out of the wake he put an empty cup in front of me. He said: "I read your fortune in the coffee." I was going to the door with the other girls and I heard his voice, deep, convincing, gentle: "Count seven stars and you'll dream about me." When we passed by the door we saw the Paloquemado child in his small coffin, his face powdered, a rose in his mouth, and his eyes held open with toothpicks. February was sending us warm gusts of death, and the breath of the jasmines and the violets toasted by the heat floated in the room. But in that silence of a dead person, the other voice was constant and different: "Remember. Only seven stars."

He came to our house in July. He liked to lean back against the flowerpots along the railing. He said: "Remember, I never looked into your eyes. That's the secret of a man who's begun to sense the fear of falling in love." And it was true, I couldn't remember his eyes. In July I probably couldn't have said what color the eyes of the man I was going to marry in December were. Still, six months earlier, February was only a deep silence at noontime, a pair of congorocho worms, male and female, coiled on the bathroom floor, the Tuesday beggar woman asking for a branch of lemon balm, and he, leaning back, smiling, his jacket buttoned all the way up, saying: "I'm going to make you think about me every minute of the day. I put a picture of you behind the door and I stuck two pins in your eyes." And Genoveva García, dying with laughter: "That's the kind of nonsense men pick up from the Guajiro Indians."

Toward the end of March he would be going through the house. He would spend long hours in the office with my father, convincing him of the importance of something I could never decipher. Eleven years have passed now since my marriage; nine since the time I watched him say good-bye from the window of the train, making me promise I would take good care of the child until he came back for us. Those nine years would pass with no one's hearing a word from him, and my father, who had helped him get ready for that endless trip, never said another word about his return. But not even during the two years that our marriage lasted was he more concrete and touchable than he was at the wake for the Paloquemado child or on that Sunday in March when I saw him for the second time as Veva García and I were coming home from church. He was standing in the doorway of the hotel, alone, his hands in the side pockets of his four-button jacket. He said: "Now you're going to think about me for the rest of your life because the pins have fallen out of the picture." He said it in such a soft and tense voice that it sounded like the truth. But even that truth was strange and different. Genoveva insisted: "That's silly Guajiro stuff." Three months later she ran away with the head of a company of puppeteers, but she still seemed scrupulous and serious on that Sunday. Martín said: "It's nice to know that someone will remember me in Macondo." And Genoveva García, looking at him with a face that showed exasperation, said:

"*Airyfay!* That four-button coat's going to rot with you inside of it."

## VII.

Even though he hoped it would be the opposite, he was a strange person in town, apathetic in spite of his obvious efforts to seem sociable and cordial. He lived among the people of Macondo, but at a distance from them because of the memory of a past against which any attempt at rectificaion seemed useless. He was looked on with curiosity, like a gloomy animal who had spent a long time in the shadows and was reappearing, conducting himself in a way that the town could only consider as superimposed and therefore suspect.

He would come back from the barbershop at nightfall and shut himself up in his room. For some time he had given up his evening meal and at first the impression at home was that he was coming back fatigued and going directly to his hammock to sleep until the following day. But only a short time passed before I began to realize that something extraordinary was happening to him at night. He could be heard moving about in his room with a tormented and maddening insistence, as if on those nights he was receiving the ghost of the man he had been until then, and both of them, the past man and the present one, were locked in a silent struggle in which the past one was defending his wrathful solitude, his invulnerable standoffish way, his intransigent manners; and the present one his terrible and unchangeable will to free himself from his own previous man. I could hear him pacing about the room until dawn, until the time his own fatigue had exhausted the strength of his invisible adversary.

I was the only one who noticed the true measure of his change, from the time he stopped wearing leggings and began to take a bath every day and perfume his clothing with scented water. And a few months later his transformation had reached the level where my feelings toward him stopped being a simple understanding tolerance and changed into compassion. It was not his new look on the street that moved me. It was thinking of him shut up in his room at night, scraping the mud off his boots, wetting a rag in the washstand, spreading polish on the shoes that had deteriorated through many years of continuous use. It moved me to think of the brush and box of shoe polish kept under the mattress, hidden from the eyes of the world as if they were the elements of a secret and shameful vice contracted at an age when the majority of men were becoming serene and methodical. For all practical purposes, he was going through a tardy and sterile adolescence and, like an adolescent, he took great care in his dress, smoothing out his clothing every night with the edge of his hand, coldly, and he was not young enough to have a friend to whom he could communicate his illusions or his disillusions.

The town must have noticed his change too, for a short time

later it began to be said about that he was in love with the barber's daughter. I don't know whether there was any basis for that, but what was certain was that the bit of gossip made me realize his tremendous sexual loneliness, the biological fury that must have tormented him in those years of filth and abandonment.

Every afternoon he could be seen passing by on his way to the barbershop, more and more fastidious in his dress. A shirt with an artificial collar, gold cuff links, and his pants clea¬ and pressed, except that he still wore his belt outside the loops. He looked like an afflicted suitor, enveloped in the aura of cheap lotions; the eternal frustrated suitor, the sunset lover who would always lack the bouquet of flowers on the first visit.

That was how he was during the first months of 1909, with still no basis for the gossip in town except for the fact that he would be seen sitting in the barbershop every afternoon chatting with strangers, but with no one's having been able to be sure that he'd ever seen him a single time with the barber's daughter. I discovered the cruelty of that gossip. Everyone in town knew that the barber's daughter would always be an old maid afer going through a year of suffering, as she was pursued by a *spirit*, an invisible lover who spread dirt on her food and muddied the water in the pitcher and fogged the mirrors in the barbershop and beat her until her face was green and disfigured. The efforts of the Pup, with a stroke of his stole, the complex therapy of holy water, sacred relics, and psalms administered with dramatic solicitude, were useless. As an extreme measure, the barber's wife locked her bewitched daughter up in her room, strewed rice about the living room, and turned her over to the invisible lover in a solitary and dead honeymoon, after which even the men of Macondo said that the barber's daughter had conceived.

Not even a year had passed when people stopped waiting for the monstrous event of her giving birth and public curiosity turned to the idea that the doctor was in love with the barber's daughter, in spite of the fact that everyone was convinced that the bewitched girl would lock herself up in her room and crumble to pieces in life long before any possible suitors would be transformed into marriageable men.

That was why I knew that rather than a supposition with some basis, it was a piece of cruel gossip, maliciously premeditated. Toward the end of 1909 he was still going to the barbershop and people were talking, organizing the wedding, with no one able to say that the girl had ever come out when he was present or that they had ever had a chance to speak to each other.

One September that was as broiling and as dead as this one, thirteen years ago, my stepmother began sewing on my wedding dress. Every afternoon while my father took his siesta, we would sit down to sew beside the flowerpots on the railing, next to the burning stove that was the rosemary plant. September has been like this all of my life, since thirteen years ago and much longer. As my wedding was to take place in a private ceremony (because my father had decided on it), we sewed slowly, with the minute care of a person who is in no hurry and has found the best measure of her time in her imperceptible work. We would talk during those times. I was still thinking about the street room, gathering up the courage to tell my stepmother that it was the best place to put up Martín. And that afternoon I told her.

My stepmother was sewing the long train of lace and it seemed in the blinding light of that intolerably clear and sound-filled September that she was submerged up to her shoulders in a cloud of that very September. "No," my stepmother said. And then, going back to her work, feeling eight years of bitter memories passing in front of her: "May God never permit anyone to enter that room again."

Martín had returned in July, but he didn't stay at our house. He liked to lean against the railing and stay there looking in the opposite direction. It pleased him to say: "I'd like to spend the rest of my life in Macondo." In the afternoon we'd go out to the plantations with my stepmother. We'd come back at dinnertime, before the lights in town went on. Then he'd tell me: "Even if it hadn't been for you, I'd like to live in Macondo in any case." And that too, from the way he said it, seemed to be the truth.

Around that time it had been four years since the doctor had left our house. And it was precisely on the afternoon we had begun work on the wedding dress—that suffocating afternoon when I told her about the room for Martín—that my stepmother spoke to me for the first time about his strange ways.

"Five years ago," she said, "he was still there, shut up like an animal. Because he wasn't only that, an animal, but something else: an animal who ate grass, a ruminant like any ox in a yoke. If he'd married the barber's daughter, that little faker who made the whole town believe the great lie that she'd conceived after a murky honeymoon with the spirits, maybe none of this would have happened. But he stopped going to the barbershop all of a sudden and he even showed a last-minute change that was only a new chapter as he methodically went through with his frightful plan. Only your father could have thought that after all that a man of such base habits should still stay in our house, living like an animal, scandalizing the town, giving people cause to talk about us as people who were always defying morals and good habits. His plans would end up with Meme's leaving. But not even then did your father recognize the alarming proportions of his mistake."

"I never heard any of that," I said. The locusts had set up a sawmill in the courtyard. My stepmother was speaking, still sewing without lifting her eyes from the tambour where she was stitching symbols, embroidering white labyrinths. She said: "That night we were sitting at the table (all except him, because ever since the afternoon he came back from the barbershop for the last time he wouldn't take his evening meal) when Meme came to serve us. She was different. 'What's the matter, Meme?' I asked her. 'Nothing, ma'am. Why?' But we could see that she wasn't right because she hesitated next to the lamp and she had a sickly look all over her. 'Good heavens, Meme, you're not well,' I said. But she held herself up as best she could until she turned toward the kitchen with the tray. Then your father, who was watching all the time, said to her: 'If you don't feel well, go to bed.' But she didn't say anything. She went out with the tray, her back to us, until we heard the noise of the dishes as they broke to pieces. Meme was on the veranda, holding herself up against the wall by her fingernails. That was when your father went to get that one in the bedroom to have a look at Meme.

"During the eight years he spent in our house," my stepmother said, "we'd never asked for his services for anything serious. We women went to Meme's room, rubbed her with alcohol, and waited for your father to come back. But they didn't come, Isabel. He didn't come to look at Meme in spite of the fact that the man who had fed him for eight years, had given him lodging and had his clothes washed, had gone to get him in person. Every time I remember him I think that his coming here was God's punishment. I think that all that grass we gave him for eight years, all the care, all the solicitude was a test of God's, teaching us a lesson in prudence and mistrust of the world. It was as if we'd taken eight years of hospitality, food, clean clothes, and thrown it all to the hogs. Meme was dying (at least we thought she was) and he, right there, was still shut up, refusing to go through with what was no longer a work of charity but one of decency, of thanks, of simple consideration for those who were taking care of him.

"Only at midnight did your father come back. He said weakly: 'Give her some alcohol rubs, but no physics.' And I felt as if I'd been slapped. Meme had responded to our rubbing. Infuriated, I shouted: 'Yes! Alcohol, that's it! We've already rubbed her and she's better! But in order to do that we didn't have to live eight years sponging off people!' And your father, still condescending, still with that conciliatory nonsense: 'It's nothing serious. You'll realize that someday.' As if that other one were some sort of soothsayer."

That afternoon, because of the vehemence of her voice, the exaltation of her words, it seemed as if my stepmother were seeing again, what happened on that remote night when the doctor refused to attend to Meme. The rosemary bush seemed suffocated by the blinding clarity of September, by the drowsiness of the locusts, by the heavy breathing of the men trying to take down a door in the neighborhood.

"But one of those Sundays Meme went to mass all decked out like a lady of quality," she said. "I can remember it as if it were today. She had a parasol with changing colors.

"Meme. Meme. That was God's punishment too. We'd taken her from where her parents were starving her to death, we took care of her, gave her a roof over her head, food, and a name, but the hand of Providence intervened there too. When I saw her at the door the next day, waiting for one of the Indians to carry her trunk out for her, even I didn't know where she was going. She was changed and serious, right over there (I can see her now), standing beside the trunk, talking to your father. Everything had been done without consulting me, Chabela; as if I were a painted puppet on the wall. Before I could ask what was going on, why strange things were happening in my own house without my knowing about them, your father came to tell me: 'You've nothing to ask Meme. She's leaving, but maybe she'll come back after a while.' I asked him where she was going and he didn't answer me. He was dragging along in his clogs as if I weren't his wife but some painted puppet on the wall.

"Only two days later," she said, "did I find out that the other one had left at dawn without the decency of saying good-bye. He'd come here as if the place belonged to him and eight years later he left as if he were leaving his own house, without saying good-bye, without saying anything. Just the way a thief would have done. I thought your father had sent him away for not attending to Meme, but when I asked him that on the same day, he limited himself to answering: 'You and I have to have a long talk about that.' And four years have passed without his ever bringing up the subject with me again.

"Only with your father and in a house as disordered as this one, where everybody does whatever he wants to, could such a thing have happened. In Macondo they weren't talking about anything else and I still didn't know that Meme had appeared in church all decked out, like a nobody raised to the status of a lady, and that your father had had the nerve to lead her across the square by the arm. That was when I found out that she wasn't as far away as I'd thought, but was living in the house on the corner with the doctor. They'd gone to live together like two pigs, not even going through the door of the church even though she'd been baptized. One day I told your father: 'God will punish that bit of heresy too.' And he didn't say anything. He was still the same tranquil man he always was, even after having been the patron of public concubinage and scandal.

"And yet I'm pleased now that things turned out that way, just so that the doctor left our house. If that hadn't happened, he'd still be in the little room. But when I found out that he'd left it and that he was taking his trash to the corner along with that trunk that wouldn't fit through the street door, I felt more peaceful. That was my victory, postponed for eight years.

"Two weeks later Meme opened the store, and she even had a sewing machine. She'd bought a new Domestic with the money she put away in this house. I considered that an affront and that's what I told your father. But even though he didn't answer my protests, you could see that instead of being sorry, he was satisfied with his work, as if he'd saved his soul by going against what was proper and honorable for this house, with his proverbial tolerance, his understanding, his liberality. And even a little empty-headedness. I said to him: 'You've thrown the best part of your beliefs to the swine.' And he, as always:

" 'You'll understand that too someday.' "


## VIII.

December arrived like an unexpected spring, as a book once described it. And Martín arrived along with it. He appeared at the house after lunch, with a collapsible suitcase, still wearing the four-button jacket, clean and freshly pressed now. He said nothing to me but went directly to my father's office to talk to him. The date for the wedding had been set since July. But two days after Martín's arrival in December, my father called my stepmother to the office to tell her that the wedding would take place on Monday. It was Saturday.

My dress was finished. Martín had been to the house every day. He spoke to my father and the latter would give us his impressions at mealtime. I didn't know my fiancé. I hadn't been alone with him at any time. Still, Martín seemed to be linked to my father by a deep and solid friendship, and my father spoke of him as if it were he and not I who was going to marry Martín.

I felt no emotion over the closeness of the wedding date. I was still wrapped up in that gray cloud which Martín came through, stiff and abstract, moving his arms as he spoke, closing and opening his four-button jacket. He had lunch with us on Sunday. My stepmother assigned the places at the table in such a way that Martín was next to my father, separated from me by three places. During lunch my stepmother and I said very little. My father and Martín talked about their business matter; and I, sitting three places away, looked at the man who a year later would be the father of my son and to whom I was not even joined by a superficial friendship.

On Sunday night I tried on the wedding dress in my stepmother's bedroom. I looked pale and clean in the mirror, wrapped in that cloud of powdery froth that reminded me of my mother's ghost. I said to myself in front of the mirror: "That's me. Isabel. I'm dressed as a bride who's going to be married tomorrow morning." And I didn't recognize myself; I felt weighted down with the memory of my dead mother. Meme had spoken to me about her on this same corner a few days before. She told me that after I was born my mother was dressed in her bridal clothes and placed in a coffin. And now, looking at myself in the mirror, I saw my mother's bones covered by the mold of the tomb in a pile of crumpled gauze and compact yellow dust. I was outside the mirror. Inside was my mother, alive again, looking at me, stretching her arms out from her frozen space, trying to touch the death that was held together by the first pins of my bridal veil. And in back, in the center of the bedroom, my father, serious, perplexed: "She looks just like her now in that dress."

That night I received my first, last, and only love letter. A message from Martín written in pencil on the back of a movie program. It said: *Since it will be impossible for me to get there on time tonight, I'll go to confession in the morning. Tell the colonel that the thing we were talking about is almost set and that's why I can't come now. Are you frightened? M.* With the flat, floury taste of that letter in my mouth I went to my bedroom, and my palate was still bitter when I woke up a few hours later as my stepmother shook me.

Actually, many hours passed before I woke up completely. In the wedding dress I felt again as if I were in some cool and damp dawn that smelled of musk. My mouth felt dry, as when a person is starting out on a trip and the saliva refuses to wet the bread. The bridal party had been in the living room since four o'clock. I knew them all but now they looked transformed and new, the men dressed in tweeds and the women with their hats on, talking, filling the house with the dense and enervating vapor of their words.

The church was empty. A few women turned around to look at me as I went down the center aisle like a consecrated youth on his way to the sacrificial stone. The Pup, thin and serious, the only person with a look of reality in that turbulent and silent nightmare, came down the altar steps and gave me to Martín with four movements of his emaciated hands. Martín was beside me, tranquil and smiling, the way I'd seen him at the wake of the Paloquemado child, but wearing a short collar now, as if to show me that even on his wedding day he'd taken pains to be still more abstract than he already was on ordinary days.

That morning, back at the house, after the wedding party had eaten breakfast and contributed the standard phrases, my husband went out and didn't come back until siesta time. My father and stepmother didn't seem to notice my situation. They let the day pass without changing the order of things, so that nothing would make the extraordinary breath of that Monday felt. I took my wedding gown apart, made a bundle of it, and put it in the bottom of the wardrobe, remembering my mother, thinking: *At least these rags can be my shroud.*

The unreal groom returned at two in the afternoon and said that he had had lunch. Then it seemed to me as I watched him come with his short hair that December was no longer a blue month. Martín sat down beside me and we remained there for a moment without speaking. For the first time since I had been born I was afraid for night to begin. I must have shown it in some expression, because all of a sudden Martín seemed to come to life; he leaned over my shoulder and asked: "What are you thinking about?" I felt something twisting in my heart: the stranger had begun to address me in the familiar form. I looked up toward where December was a gigantic shining ball, a luminous glass month; I said: "I was thinking that all we need now is for it to start raining."

The last night we spoke on the veranda it was hotter than usual. A few days later he would return for good from the barbershop and shut himself up in his room. But on that last night on the veranda, one of the hottest and heaviest I can remember, he seemed understanding as on few occasions. The only thing that seemed alive in the midst of that immense oven was the dull reverberation of the crickets, aroused by the thirst of nature, and the tiny, insignificant, and yet measureless activity of the rosemary and the nard, burning in the middle of the deserted hour. Both of us remained silent for a moment, exuding that thick and viscous substance that isn't sweat but the loose drivel of decomposing living matter. Sometimes he would look at the stars, in a sky desolate because of the summer splendor; then he would remain silent, as if completely given over to the passage of that night, which was monstrously alive. That was how we were, pensive, face to face, he in his leather chair, I in the rocker. Suddenly, with the passage of a white wing, I saw him tilt his sad and lonely head over his left shoulder. I thought of his life, his solitude, his frightful spiritual disturbances. I thought of the tormented indifference with which he watched the spectacle of life. Previously I had felt drawn to him out of complex feelings, sometimes contradictory and as variable as his personality. But at that moment there wasn't the slightest doubt in me that I'd begun to love him deeply. I thought that inside of myself I'd uncovered the mysterious force that from the first moment had led me to shelter him, and I felt the pain of his dark and stifling room like an open wound. I saw him as somber and defeated, crushed by circumstances. And suddenly, with a new look from his hard and penetrating yellow eyes, I felt the certainty that the secret of his labyrinthine solitude had been revealed to me by the tense pulsation of the night. Before I even had time to think why I was doing it, I asked him:

"Tell me something, doctor. Do you believe in God?"

He looked at me. His hair fell over his forehead and a kind of inner suffocation burned all through him, but his face still showed no shadow of emotion or upset. Having completely recovered his parsimonious ruminant voice, he said:

"It's the first time anyone ever asked me that question."

"What about you, doctor, have you ever asked it?"

He seemed neither indifferent nor concerned. He only seemed interested in my person. Not even in my question and least of all in its intent.

"That's hard to say," he said.

"But doesn't a night like this make you afraid? Don't you get the feeling that there's a man bigger than all of us walking through the plantations while nothing moves and everything seems perplexed at the passage of that man?"

He was silent then. The crickets filled the surrounding space, beyond the warm smell which was alive and almost human as it rose up from the jasmine bush I had planted in memory of my first wife. A man without dimensions was walking alone through the night.

"I really don't think any of that bothers me, colonel." And now he seemed perplexed, he too, like things, like the rosemary and the nard in their burning place. "What bothers me," he said, and he kept on looking into my eyes, directly, sternly, "what bothers me is that there's a person like you capable of saying with such certainty that he's aware of that man walking in the night."

"We try to save our souls, doctor. That's the difference."

And then I went beyond what I had proposed. I said: "You don't hear him because you're an atheist."

And he, serene, unperturbed:

"Believe me, colonel, I'm not an atheist. I get just as upset thinking that God exists as thinking that he doesn't. That's why I'd rather not think about it."

I don't know why, but I had the feeling that that was exactly what he was going to answer. *He's a man disturbed by God*, I thought, listening to what he'd just told me spontaneously, with

66

clarity, precision, as if he'd read it in a book. I was still intoxicated with the drowsiness of the night. I felt that I was in the heart of an immense gallery of prophetic images.

Over there on the other side of the railing was the small garden where Adelaida and my daughter had planted things. That was why the rosemary was burning, because every morning they strengthened it with their attention so that on nights like that its burning vapor would pass through the house and make sleep more restful. The jasmine gave off its insistent breath and we received it because it was the same age as Isabel, because in a certain way that smell was a prolongation of her mother. The crickets were in the courtyard, among the bushes, because we'd neglected to clean out the weeds when it had stopped raining. The only thing incredible, miraculous, was that he was there, with his enormous cheap handkerchief, drying his forehead, which glowed with perspiration.

Then after another pause, he said:

"I'd like to know why you asked me that, colonel."

"It just came to me all of a sudden," I said. "Maybe after seven years I wanted to know what a man like you thinks about."

I was mopping my brow too. I said:

"Or maybe I'm worried about your solitude." I waited for an answer that didn't come. I saw him across from me, still sad and alone. I thought about Macondo, the madness of its people, burning banknotes at parties; about the leaf storm that had no direction and was above everything, wallowing in its slough of instinct and dissipation where it had found the taste it wanted. I thought about his life before the leaf storm had struck. And his life afterward, his cheap perfume, his polished old shoes, the gossip that followed him like a shadow that he himself ignored. I said:

"Doctor, have you ever thought of taking a wife?"

And before I could finish asking the question, he was giving an answer, starting off on one of his usual long meanderings:

"You love your daughter very much, don't you, colonel?"

I answered that it was natural. He went on speaking:

"All right. But you're different. Nobody likes to drive his own nails more than you. I've seen you putting hinges on a door when there are several men working for you who could have done it. You like that. I think that your happiness is to walk about the house with a toolbox looking for something to fix. You're even capable of thanking a person for having broken a hinge, colonel. You thank him because in that way he's giving you a chance to be happy."

"It's a habit," I told him, not knowing what direction he was taking. "They say my mother was the same way."

He'd reacted. His attitude was peaceful but ironclad.

"Fine," he said. "It's a good habit. Besides, it's the cheapest kind of happiness I know. That's why you have a house like this and raised your daughter the way you have. I say that it must be good to have a daughter like yours."

I still didn't know what he was getting at in his long, round-about way. But even though I didn't know, I asked:

"What about you, doctor, haven't you ever thought about how nice it would be to have a daughter?"

"Not I, colonel," he said. And he smiled, but then he immediately became serious again. "My children wouldn't be like yours."

Then I didn't have the slightest trace of doubt: he was talking seriously and that seriousness, that situation, seemed frightful to me. I was thinking: *He's more to be pitied for that than for anything else.* He needed protection, I thought.

"Have you heard of the Pup?" I asked him.

He said no. I told him: "The Pup is the parish priest, but more than that he's a friend to everybody. You should get to know him."

"Oh, yes, yes," he said. "He has children *too*, right?"

"That's not what interests me right now," I said. "People invent bits of gossip about the Pup because they have a lot of love for him. But you have a point there, doctor. The Pup is a long way from being a prayermonger, sanctimonious, as we say. He's a whole man who fulfills his duties as a man."

Now he was listening with attention. He was silent, concentrating, his hard yellow eyes fastened on mine. He said: "That's good, right?"

"I think the Pup will be made a saint," I said. And I was sincere in that too. "We've never seen anything like him in Macondo. At first they didn't trust him because he comes from here, because the older people remembered him from when he used to go out hunting birds like all the boys. He fought in the war, he was a colonel, and that was a problem. You know how people are, no respect for veterans, the same as with priests. Besides, we weren't used to having someone read to us from the Bristol Almanac instead of the Gospels."

He smiled. That must have sounded as odd to him as it had to us during the first days. He said: "That's strange, isn't it?"

"That's the way the Pup is. He'd rather show people by means of atmospheric phenomena. He's got a preoccupation with storms that's almost theological. He talks about them every Sunday. And that's why his sermons aren't based on the Gospels but on the atmospheric predictions in the Bristol Almanac."

He was smiling now and listening with a lively and pleased expression. I felt enthusiastic too. I said: "There's still something else of interest for you, doctor. Do you know how long the Pup has been in Macondo?"

He said no.

"It so happens that he arrived the same day as you," I said. "And what's even stranger still, if you had an older brother, I'm sure that he'd be just like the Pup. Physically, of course."

He didn't seem to be thinking about anything else now. From his seriousness, from his concentrated and steady attention, I sensed that I had come to the moment to tell him what I wanted to propose:

"Well, then, doctor," I said. "Pay a call on the Pup and you'll find out that things aren't the way you see them."

And he said yes, he'd visit the Pup.


## IX.

Coldly, silently, progressively, the padlock gathers rust. Adelaida put it on the room when she found out that the doctor had gone to live with Meme. My wife considered that move as a victory for her, the culminaton of a systematic, tenacious piece of work she had started the first moment I decided that he would live with us. Seventeen years later the padlock is still guarding the room.

If there was something in my attitude, unchanged for eight years, that may have seemed unworthy in the eyes of men or ungrateful in those of God, my punishment has come about a long time before my death. Perhaps it was meant for me to expiate in life for what I had considered a human obligation, a Christian duty. Because the rust on the lock had not begun to accumulate when Martín was in my house with a briefcase full of projects, the authenticity of which I've never been able to find out, and the firm desire to marry my daughter. He came to my house in a four-button jacket, exuding youth and dynamism from all his pores, enveloped in a luminous air of pleasantness. He married Isabel in December eleven years ago. Nine have passed since he went off with the briefcase full of notes signed by me and with the promise to return as soon as the deal he was working on and for which he had my financial backing came through. Nine years have gone by but I have no right to think he was a swindler because of that. I have no right to think his marriage was only a pretext to convince me of his good faith.

But eight years of experience have been of some use. Martín could have occupied the small room. Adelaida was against it. Her

70

opposition was adamant, decisive and irrevocable. I knew that
my wife wouldn't have been bothered in the least to fix up the
stable as a bridal chamber rather than let the newlyweds occupy
the small room. I accepted her point of view without hesitation.
That was my recognition of her victory, one postponed for eight
years. If both of us were mistaken in trusting Martín, it was a
mistake that was shared. There was neither victory nor defeat for
either one of us. Still, what came later was too much for our
efforts, it was like the atmospheric phenomena the almanac fore-
tells, ones that must come no matter what.

When I told Meme to leave our house, to follow the direction
she thought best for her life, and afterward, even though Adelaida
threw my weaknesses and lack of strength up to me, I was able
to rebel, to impose my will on everything (that's what I've always
done) and arrange things my way. But something told me that I
was powerless before the course that events were taking. It wasn't
I who arranged things in my own home, but some other mysterious force, one which decided the course of our existence and of
which we were nothing but docile and insignificant instruments.
Everything seemed to obey the natural and linked fulfillment of
a prophecy.

Since Meme was able to open the shop (underneath it all everybody must have known that a hard-working woman who becomes
the mistress of a country doctor overnight will sooner or later
end up as a shopkeeper), I realized that in our house he'd accumulated a larger sum of money than one might have imagined,
and that he'd kept it in his cabinet, uncounted bills and coins
which he tossed into the drawer during the time he saw patients.

When Meme opened the shop it was supposed that he was here,
in back of the store, shut up because of God knows what bestial
and implacable prophecies. It was known that he wouldn't eat
any food from outside, that he'd planted a garden and that during the first months Meme would buy a piece of meat for herself,
but that a year later she'd stopped doing that, perhaps because

direct contact with the man had made a vegetarian of her. Then the two of them shut themselves up until the time the authorities broke down the door, searched the house, and dug up the garden in an attempt to find Meme's body.

People imagined him there, shut in, rocking in his old and tattered hammock. But I knew, even in those months during which his return to the world of the living was not expected, that his impenitent enclosure, his muted battle against the threat of God, would reach its culmination much sooner than his death. I knew that sooner or later he would come out because there isn't a man alive who can live a half-life, locked up, far away from God, without coming out all of a sudden to render to the first man he meets on the corner the accounts that stocks and pillory, the martyrdom of fire and water, the torture of the rack and the screw, wood and hot iron on his eyes, the eternal salt on his tongue, the torture horse, lashes, the grate, and love could not have made him render to his inquisitors. And that time would come for him a few years before his death.

I knew that truth from before, from the last night we talked on the veranda, and afterward, when I went to get him in the little room to have a look at Meme. Could I have opposed his desire to live with her as man and wife? I might have been able before. Not now, because another chapter of fate had begun to be fulfilled three months before that.

He wasn't in his hammock that night. He'd lain down on his back on the cot and had his head back, his eyes fixed on the spot on the ceiling where the light from the candle must have been most intense. There was an electric light in the room but he never used it. He preferred to lie in the shadows, his eyes fixed on the darkness. He didn't move when I went into the room, but I noticed that the moment I crossed the threshold he felt that he wasn't alone. Then I said: "If it's not too much trouble, doctor, it seems that the Indian girl isn't feeling well." He sat up on the bed. A moment before he'd felt that he wasn't alone in the room.

72

Now he knew that I was the one who was there. Without doubt they were two completely different feelings, because he underwent an immediate change, he smoothed his hair and remained sitting on the edge of the bed waiting.

"It's Adelaida, doctor. She wants you to come look at Meme," I said.

And he, sitting there, gave me the impact of an answer with his parsimonious ruminant voice:

"It won't be necessary. The fact is she's pregnant."

Then he leaned forward, seemed to be examining my face, and said: "Meme's been sleeping with me for years."

I must confess that I was surprised. I didn't feel any upset, perplexity, or anger. I didn't feel anything. Perhaps his confession was too serious to my way of seeing things and was out of the normal course of my comprehension. I remained impassive and I didn't even know why. I was motionless, standing, immutable, as cold as he, like his parsimonious ruminant voice. Then, after a long silence during which he still sat on the cot, not moving, as if waiting for me to take the first step, I understood what he had just told me in all of its intensity. But then it was too late for me to get upset.

"As long as you're aware of the situation, doctor." That was all I could say. He said:

"One takes his precautions, colonel. When a person takes a risk he knows that he's taking it. If something goes wrong it's because there was something unforeseen, out of a person's reach."

I knew that kind of evasion. As always, I didn't know where he was leading. I brought over a chair and sat down opposite him. Then he left the cot, fastened the buckle of his belt, and pulled up his pants and adjusted them. He kept on talking from the other end of the room. He said:

"Just as sure as the fact that I took my precautions is the fact that this is the second time she's got pregnant. The first time was a year and a half ago and you people didn't notice anything."

73

He went on talking without emotion, going back to the cot. In the darkness I heard his slow, firm steps against the tiles. He said:

"But she was ready for anything then. Not now. Two months ago she told me she was pregnant again and I told her what I had the first time: 'Come by tonight and be ready for the same thing.' She told me not that day, the next day. When I went to have my coffee in the kitchen I told her that I was waiting for her, but she said that she'd never come back."

He'd come over by the cot, but he didn't sit down. He turned his back on me again and began to walk around the room once more. I heard him speaking. I heard the flow of his voice, back and forth, as if he were rocking in the hammock. He was telling things calmly, but with assurance. I knew that it would have been useless to try to interrupt him. All I could do was listen to him. And he kept on talking:

"Still, she did come two days later. I had everything ready. I told her to sit down there and I went to my table for the glass. Then, when I told her to drink it, I realized that this time she wouldn't. She looked at me without smiling and said with a touch of cruelty: 'I'm not going to get rid of this one, doctor. This one I'm going to have so I can raise it.'"

I felt exasperated by his calmness. I told him: "That doesn't justify anything, doctor. What you've done is something that's twice unworthy: first, because of your relations inside my house, and then because of the abortion."

"But you can see that I did everything I could, colonel. It was all I could do. Afterward, when I saw there was no way out, I got ready to talk to you. I was going to do it one of these days."

"I imagine you know that there is a way out of this kind of situation if you really want to erase the insult. You know the principles of those of us who live in this house," I said.

And he said:

"I don't want to cause you any trouble, colonel. Believe me. What I was going to tell you is this: I'll take the Indian woman and go live in the empty house on the corner."

"Living together openly, doctor?" I asked him. "Do you know what that means for us?"

Then he went back to the cot. He sat down, leaned forward, and spoke with his elbows on his legs. His accent became different. At first it had been cold. Now it began to be cruel and challenging. He said:

"I'm proposing the only solution that won't cause you any distress, colonel. The other thing would be to say that the child isn't mine."

"Meme would say it was," I said. I was beginning to feel indignant. His way of expressing himself was too challenging and aggressive now and I couldn't accept it calmly.

But he, hard, implacable, said:

"You have to believe me absolutely when I say that Meme won't say it is. It's because I'm sure of that that I say I'll take her to the corner, only so I can avoid distress for you. That's the only reason, colonel."

He was so sure that Meme would not attribute the paternity of her child to him that now I did feel upset. Something was making me think that his strength was rooted much deeper than his words. I said:

"We trust Meme as we would our own daughter, doctor. In this case she'd be on our side."

"If you knew what I know, you wouldn't talk that way, colonel. Pardon me for saying it this way, but if you compare that Indian girl to your daughter, you're insulting your daughter."

"You have no reason to say that," I said.

And he answered, still with that bitter hardness in his voice: "I do. And when I tell you that she can't say that I'm the father of her child, I also have reasons for it."

He threw his head back. He sighed deeply and said:

"If you took time to spy on Meme when she goes out at night, you wouldn't even demand that I take her away with me. In this case I'm the one who runs the risk, colonel. I'm taking on a dead man to avoid your having any distress."

Then I understood that he wouldn't even go through the doors of the church with Meme. But what was serious was that after his final words I wouldn't have dared go through with what could have been a tremendous burden on my conscience later on. There were several cards in my favor. But the single one he held would have been enough for him to win a bet against my conscience.

"All right, doctor," I said. "This very night I'll make arrangements to have the house on the corner fixed up. But in any case, I want you to be aware of the fact that I'm throwing you out of my house. You're not leaving of your own free will. Colonel Aureliano Buendía would have made you pay dearly for the way you returned his trust."

And when I thought I'd roused up his instincts and was waiting for him to unleash his dark, primal forces, he threw the whole weight of his dignity on me.

"You're a decent man, colonel," he said. "Everybody knows that, and I've lived in this house long enough for you not to have to remind me of it."

When he stood up he didn't seem victorious. He only seemed satisfied at having been able to repay our attentions of eight years. I was the one who felt upset, the one at fault. That night, seeing the germs of death that were becoming progressively more visible in his hard yellow eyes, I understood that my attitude was selfish and that because of that one single stain on my conscience it would be quite right for me to suffer a tremendous expiation for the rest of my life. He, on the other hand, was at peace with himself. He said:

"As for Meme, have them rub her with alcohol. But they shouldn't give her any physics."

# X.

My grandfather's come back beside Mama. She's sitting down, completely lost in her thoughts. The dress and the hat are here, on the chair, but my mother's not in them anymore. My grandfather comes closer, sees that her mind's somewhere else, and he moves his cane in front of her eyes, saying: "Wake up, child." My mother blinks, shakes her head. "What were you thinking about?" my grandfather asks. And she, smiling with great effort: "I was thinking about the Pup."

My grandfather sits down beside her again, his chin resting on his cane. He says: "That's a coincidence. I was thinking about him too."

They understand their words. They talk without looking at each other, Mama leaning back in her chair and my grandfather sitting next to her, his chin still resting on his cane. But even like that they understand each other's words, the way Abraham and I can understand each other when we go to see Lucrecia.

I tell Abraham: "Now I'm tecky-tacking." Abraham always walks in front, about three steps ahead of me. Without turning around to look, he says: "Not yet, in a minute." And I say to him: "When I teck somebum hoblows up." Abraham doesn't turn his head but I can hear him laugh softly with a foolish and simple laugh that's like the thread of water that trembles down from the snout of an ox when he's finished drinking. He says: "It must be around five o'clock." He runs a little more and says: "If we go now somebum might hoblow." But I insist: "In any case, there's always tecky-tacking." And he turns to me and starts to run, saying: "All right, then, let's go."

In order to see Lucrecia you have to go through five yards full of trees and bushes. You have to go over the low wall that's green with lizards where the midget with a woman's voice used to sing. Abraham goes running along, shining like a sheet of metal in the strong light, his heels harried by the dog's barking. Then he stops. At that point we're by the window. We say: "Lucrecia," making our voices low as if Lucrecia was sleeping. But she's awake, sitting on the bed, her shoes off, wearing a loose nightgown, white and starched, that reaches down to her ankles.

When we speak, Lucrecia lifts her eyes and makes them turn around the room, fastening a round, large eye like that of a curlew on us. Then she laughs and begins to move toward the center of the room. Her mouth is open and she shows her small, broken teeth. She has a round head, with the hair cut like a man's. When she gets to the center of the room she stops laughing, squats down, and looks at the door until her hands reach her ankles, and she slowly begins to lift her gown, with a calculated slowness, cruel and challenging at the same time. Abraham and I are still looking in the window while Lucrecia lifts up her gown, her lips sticking out in a panting and anxious frown, her big curlew eyes staring and shining. Then we can see her white stomach, which turns deep blue farther down, when she covers her face with the nightgown and stays that way, stretched out in the center of the bedroom, her legs together and tight with a trembling force that comes up from her ankles. All of a sudden she quickly uncovers her face, points at us with her forefinger, and the shining eye pops out in the midst of terrible shrieks that echo all through the house. Then the door of the room opens and the woman comes in shouting: "Why don't you go screw the patience of your own mothers?"

We haven't been to see Lucrecia for days. Now we go to the river along the road to the plantations. If we get out of this early, Abraham will be waiting for me. But my grandfather doesn't move. He's sitting next to Mama with his chin on his cane. I keep watching him, watching his eyes behind his glasses, and he must feel that I'm looking at him, because all of a sudden he gives a deep sigh, shakes himself, and says to my mother in a low, sad voice: "The Pup would have made them come if he had to whip them."

Then he gets up from his chair and walks over to where the dead man is.

It's the second time that I've been in this room. The first time, ten years ago, things were just the same. It's as if they hadn't been touched since then or as if since that remote dawn when he came here to live with Meme he hadn't worried about his life anymore. The papers were in the same place. The table, the few cheap articles of clothing, everything was in the same place it's in today. As if it were yesterday when the Pup and I came to make peace between this man and the authorities.

By that time the banana company had stopped squeezing us and had left Macondo with the rubbish of the rubbish they'd brought us. And with them went the leaf storm, the last traces of what prosperous Macondo had been like in 1915. A ruined village was left here, with four poor, dark stores; occupied by unemployed and angry people who were tormented by a prosperous past and the bitterness of an overwhelming and static present. There was nothing in the future at that time except a gloomy and threatening election Sunday.

Six months before an anonymous note had been found nailed to the door of this house one morning. No one was interested in it and it stayed nailed here for a long time until the final drizzle washed away its dark letters and the paper disappeared, hauled off by the last winds of February. But toward the end of 1918, when the closeness of the elections made the government think about the necessity of keeping the tension of its voters awake and irritated, someone spoke to the new authorities concerning this solitary doctor, about whose existence there would have to be some valid evidence after such a long time. They had to be told that during the first years the Indian woman who lived with him ran a shop that shared in the same prosperity that favored even the most insignificant enterprises in Macondo during those times. One day (no one remembers the date, not even the year) the door of the shop didn't open. It was imagined that Meme and the doctor were still living here, shut up, living on the vegetables they grew themselves in the yard. But in the note that appeared on this corner it said that the physician had murdered his concubine and buried her in the garden, afraid that the town would use her to poison him. The inexplicable thing is that it was said during a time when no one could have had any reason to plot the doctor's death. I think that the authorities had forgotten about his existence until that year when the government reinforced the police and the reserves with men they could trust. Then they dug up the forgotten legend of the anonymous note and the authorities violated these doors, searched the house, dug up the yard, and probed in the privy trying to locate Meme's body. But they couldn't find a trace of her.

On that occasion they would have dragged the doctor out, beaten him, and he most surely would have been one more sacrifice on the public square in the name of official order. But the Pup stepped in; he came to my house and invited me to visit the doctor, certain that I'd be able to get a satisfactory explanation from him.

When we went in the back way we found the ruins of a man abandoned in the hammock. Nothing in this world can be more fearsome than the ruins of a man. And those of this citizen of nowhere who sat up in the hammock when he saw us come in were even worse, and he himself seemed to be covered by the coat of dust that covered everything in the room. His head was steely and his hard yellow eyes still had the powerful inner strength that I had seen in them in my house. I had the impression that if we'd scratched him with our nails his body would have fallen apart, turning into a pile of human sawdust. He'd cut his mustache but he hadn't shaved it off. He'd used shears on his beard so that his chin didn't seem to be sown with hard and vigorous sprouts but with soft, white fuzz. Seeing him in the hammock I thought: *He doesn't look like a man now. Now he looks like a corpse whose eyes still haven't died.*

When he spoke his voice was the same parsimonious ruminant voice that he'd brought to our house. He said that he had nothing to say. He said, as if he thought that we didn't know about it, that the police had violated his doors and had dug in his yard without his consent. But that wasn't a protest. It was only a complaining and melancholy confidence.

As for Meme, he gave us an explanation that might have seemed puerile, but which was said by him with the same accent with which he would have told the truth. He said that Meme had left, that was all. When she closed the shop she began to get restless in the house. She didn't speak to anyone, she had no communication at all with the outside world. He said that one day he saw her packing her bag and he didn't say anything to her. He said that he still didn't say anything when he saw her in her street clothes, high heels, with the suitcase in her hand, standing in the doorway but not speaking, only as if she were showing herself like that so that he would know that she was leaving. "Then," he said, "I got up and gave her the money that was left in the drawer."

I asked him: "How long ago was that, doctor?"

And he said: "You can judge by my hair. She was the one who cut it."

The Pup didn't say much on that visit. From the time he'd entered the room he seemed impressed by the sight of the only man he hadn't met after being in Macondo fifteen years. That time I noticed (and more than ever, maybe because the doctor had cut his mustache) the extraordinary resemblance between those two men. They weren't exact, but they looked like brothers. One was several years older, thinner and more emaciated. But there was the community of features between them that exists between two brothers, even if one looks like the father and the other like the mother. Then I recalled that last night on the veranda. I said:

"This is the Pup, doctor. You promised me you'd visit him once."

He smiled. He looked at the priest and said: "That's right, colonel. I don't know why I didn't." And he continued looking at him, examining him, until the Pup spoke.

"It's never too late for a good beginning," he said. "I'd like to be your friend."

At once I realized that facing the stranger, the Pup had lost his usual strength. He spoke timidly, without the inflexible assurance with which his voice thundered from the pulpit reading the atmospheric predictions of the Bristol Almanac in a transcendental and threatening tone.

That was the first time they'd seen each other. And it was also the last. Still, the doctor's life was prolonged until this morning because the Pup had intervened again in his favor on the night they begged him to take care of the wounded and he wouldn't even open the door, and they shouted that terrible sentence down on him, the fulfillment of which I've now undertaken to prevent.

We were getting ready to leave the house when I remembered something that I'd wanted to ask him for years. I told the Pup I was going to stay awhile with the doctor while he interceded with the authorities. When we were alone I asked him:

"Tell me something, doctor. What was the child?"

He didn't change his expression. "What child, colonel?" he asked. And I said: "Yours. Meme was pregnant when you left my house." And he, tranquil, imperturbable:

"You're right, colonel. I'd even forgotten about that."

My father was silent. Then he said: "The Pup would have made them come if he had to whip them." My father's eyes show a restrained nervousness. And while this waiting goes on, it's been a half hour already (because it must be around three o'clock), I'm worried about the child's perplexity, his absorbed expression, which doesn't seem to be asking anything, his abstract and cold indifference, which makes him just like his father. My son's going to dissolve in the boiling air of this Wednesday just as it happened to Martín nine years ago, when he waved from the train window and disappeared forever. All my sacrifices for this son will be in vain if he keeps on looking like his father. It won't be of any use for me to beg God to make him a man of flesh and blood, one who has volume, weight, and color like other men. Everything will be in vain as long as he has the seeds of his father in his blood.

Five years ago the child didn't have anything of Martín's. Now he's getting to have it all, ever since Genoveva García came back to Macondo with her six children, with two sets of twins among them. Genoveva was fat and old. Blue veins had come out around her eyes, giving a certain look of dirtiness to her face, which had been clean and firm before. She showed a noisy and disordered happiness in the midst of her flock of small white shoes and organdy frills. I knew that Genoveva had run away with the head of a company of puppeteers and I felt some kind of repugnance at seeing those children of hers, who seemed to have automatic movements, as if run by some single central mechanism; small and upsettingly alike, all six with identical shoes and identical frills on their clothing. Genoveva's disorganized happiness seemed painful and sad to me, as did her presence, loaded with urban accessories, in a ruined town that was annihilated by dust. There was something bitter, something inconsolably ridiculous, in her way of moving, of seeming fortunate and of feeling sorry for our way of life, which was so different, she said, from the one she had known in the company of the puppeteers.

Looking at her I remembered other times. I said to her: "You've gotten very fat." And then she became sad. She said: "It must be that memories make a person fat." And she stood there looking closely at the child. She said: "And what happened to the wizard with four buttons?" And I answered her right out, because I knew that she knew: "He went away." And Genoveva said: "And didn't he leave you anything but that?" And I told her no, he'd only left me the child. Genoveva laughed with a loose and vulgar laugh. "He must have been pretty sloppy to make only one child in five years," she said, and she went on, still moving about and cackling in the midst of her confused flock: "And I was mad about him. I swear I would have taken him away from you if it hadn't been that we'd met him at a child's wake. I was very superstitious in those days."

It was before she said good-bye that Genoveva stood looking at the child and said: "He's really just like him. All he needs is the four-button jacket." And from that moment on the child began to look just like his father to me, as if Genoveva had brought on the curse of his identity. On certain occasions I would catch him with his elbows on the table, his head leaning over his left shoulder, and his foggy look turned nowhere. He was just like Martín when he leaned against the carnation pots on the railing and said: "Even if it hadn't been for you, I'd like to spend the rest of my life in Macondo." Sometimes I get the impression that he's going to say it; how could he say it now that he's sitting next to me, silent, touching his nose that's stuffed up with the heat? "Does it hurt you?" I asked him. And he says no, that he was thinking that he couldn't keep glasses on. "You don't have to worry about that," I tell him, and I undo his tie. I say: "When we get home you can rest and have a bath." And then I look toward where my father has just said: "Cataure," calling the oldest of the Guajiros. He's a heavyset and short Indian, who was smoking on the bed, and when he hears his name he lifts his head and looks for my father's face with his small somber eyes. But when my father is about to speak again the steps of the mayor are heard in the back room as he staggers into the bedroom.

## XI.

This noon has been terrible for our house. Even though the news of his death was no surprise to me, because I was expecting it for a long time, I couldn't imagine that it would bring on such an upset in my house. Someone had to go to this burial with me and I thought that one would be my wife, especially since my illness three years ago and that afternoon when she found the cane with the silver handle and the wind-up dancer when she was looking through the drawers of my desk. I think that we'd forgotten about the toy by then. But that afternoon we made the mechanism work and the ballerina danced as on other occasions, animated by the music that had been festive before and which then, after the long silence in the drawer, sounded quiet and nostalgic. Adelaida watched it dance and remembered. Then she turned to me, her look moistened by simple sadness:

"Who does it remind you of?" she asked.

And I knew who Adelaida was thinking about, while the toy saddened the room with its worn-out little tune.

"I wonder what's become of him?" my wife asked, remembering, shaken perhaps by the breath of those days when he'd appeared at the door of the room at six in the afternoon and hung the lamp in the doorway.

"He's on the corner," I said. "One of these days he'll die and we'll have to bury him."

Adelaida remained silent, absorbed in the dance of the toy, and I felt infected by her nostalgia. I said to her: "I've always wanted to know who you thought he was the day he came. You set that table because he reminded you of someone."

And Adelaida said with a gray smile:

"You'd laugh at me if I told you who he reminded me of when he stood there in the corner with the ballerina in his hand." And she pointed to the empty space where she'd seen him twenty-two years before, with full boots and a costume that looked like a military uniform.

I thought on that afternoon they'd been reconciled in memory, so today I told my wife to get dressed in black to go with me. But the toy is back in the drawer. The music has lost its effect. Adelaida is wearing herself out now. She's sad, devastated, and she spends hours on end praying in her room. "Only you would have thought of a burial like that," she told me. "After all the misfortunes that befell us, all we needed was that cursed leap year. And then the deluge." I tried to persuade her that my word of honor was involved in this undertaking.

"We can't deny that I owe my life to him," I said.

And she said:

"He's the one who owes his to us. All he did when he saved your life was to repay a debt for eight years of bed, board, and clean clothes."

Then she brought a chair over to the railing. And she must be there still, her eyes foggy with grief and superstition. Her attitude seemed so decided that I tried to calm her down. "All right. In that case I'll go with Isabel," I said. And she didn't answer. She sat there, inviolable, until we got ready to leave and I told her, thinking to please her: "Until we get back, go to the altar and pray for us." Then she turned her head toward the door, saying: "I'm not even going to pray. My prayers will still be useless just as long as that woman comes every Tuesday to ask for a branch of lemon balm." And in her voice there was an obscure and over-turned rebellion:

"I'll stay collapsed here until Judgment Day. If the termites haven't eaten up the chair by then."

My father stops, his neck stretched out, listening to the familiar footsteps that are advancing through the back room. Then he forgets what he was going to tell Cataure and tries to turn around, leaning on his cane, but his useless leg fails him in the turn and he's about to fall down, as happened three years ago when he fell into the lemonade bowl, with the noise of the bowl as it rolled along the floor and the clogs and the rocker and the shout of the child, who was the only one who saw him fall.

He's limped ever since then, since then he's dragged the foot that hardened after that week of bitter suffering, from which we thought he'd never recover. Now, seeing him like that, getting his balance back with the help of the mayor, I think that that useless leg holds the secret of the compromise that he's going to fulfill against the will of the town.

Maybe his gratitude goes back to that time. From the time he fell on the veranda, saying that he felt as if he'd been pushed off a tower, and the last two doctors left in Macondo advised him to prepare for a good death. I remember him on the fifth day in bed, shrunken between the sheets; I remember his emaciated body, like the body of the Pup, who'd been carried to the cemetery the year before by all the inhabitants of Macondo in a compressed and moving procession of flowers. Inside the coffin his majesty had the same depth of irremediable and disconsolate abandonment that I saw in the face of my father during those days when the bedroom filled up with his voice and he spoke about that strange soldier who appeared one night in the camp of Colonel Aureliano Buendía during the war of '85, his hat and boots decorated with the skin, teeth, and claws of a tiger, and they asked him: "Who are you?" And the strange soldier didn't answer; and they asked him: "Where do you come from?" And he still didn't answer; and they asked him: "What side are you fighting on?" And they still didn't get any answer from the strange soldier, until an orderly picked up a torch and held it close to his face, examined it for an instant, and exclaimed, scandalized: "Jesus! It's the Duke of Marlborough!"

In the midst of that terrible hallucination, the doctors gave orders to bathe him. It was done. But on the next day you could only see a small change in his stomach. Then the doctors left the house and said that the only thing advisable was to prepare him for a good death.

The bedroom was sunken in a silent atmosphere in which you could hear only the slow and measured flapping of the wings of death, that mysterious flapping that has the smell of a man in the bedrooms of the dying. After Father Ángel administered the last rites, many hours passed before anyone moved, looking at the angular profile of the hopeless man. Then the clock struck and my stepmother got ready to give him his spoonful of medicine. That was when we heard the spaced and affirmative footsteps on the veranda. My stepmother held the spoon in the air, stopped murmuring her prayer, and turned to the door, paralyzed by a sudden blush. "I'd recognize those steps even in purgatory," she managed to say at the precise moment that we looked toward the door and saw the doctor. He was on the threshold, looking at us.

I say to my daughter: "The Pup would have made them come even if he had to whip them," and I go over to where the coffin is, thinking: *Since the time the doctor left our house I've been convinced that our acts were ordained by a higher will against which we couldn't have rebelled, even if we tried with all our strength, or even if we assumed the sterile attitude of Adelaida, who shut herself up to pray.*

And while I cover the distance that separates me from the coffin, looking at my men, impassive, sitting on the bed, I feel that I've breathed in the first breath of air that boils up over the dead man, all that bitter matter of fate that destroyed Macondo. I don't think the mayor will delay with the authorization for the burial. I know that outside, on the streets tormented by the heat, people are waiting. I know that there are women in the windows, anxious for a spectacle, and that they stay there, looking out, forgetting that the milk is boiling on the stove and that the rice is dry. But I think that even this last show of rebellion is beyond the possibilities of this crushed and flayed group of men. Their capacity for fight has been broken ever since that Sunday election day when they moved, drew up their plans, and were defeated, and afterward they still were convinced that they were the ones who determined their own acts. But all of that seemed to have been disposed, ordained, channeling the deeds that would lead us step by step to this fateful Wednesday.

Ten years ago, when ruin came down upon us, the collective strength of those who looked for recovery might have been enough for reconstruction. All that was needed was to go out into the fields laid waste by the banana company, clean out the weeds, and start again from scratch. But they'd trained the leaf storm to be impatient, not to believe in either past or future. They'd trained it to believe in the moment and to sate the voracity of its appetite in it. We only needed a short time to realize that the leaf storm had left and that without it reconstruction was impossible. The leaf storm had brought everything and it had taken everything away. After it all that was left was a Sunday in the rubble of a town and the ever-present electoral schemer on Macondo's last night, setting up four demijohns of liquor in the public square at the disposal of the police and the reserves.

If the Pup managed to hold them back that night in spite of the fact that their rebellion was still alive, today he would have been capable of going from house to house armed like a dogcatcher obliging them to bury this man. The Pup held them under an ironclad discipline. Even after the priest died four years ago— one year before my illness—that discipline could be seen in the impassioned way in which they all cut the flowers and shrubs in their gardens and took them to his grave in a final tribute to the Pup.

This man was the only one who didn't go to the burial. The only one, precisely, who owed his life to that unbreakable and contradictory subordination of the town to the priest. Because the night they set out the four demijohns of liquor on the square and Macondo became a town overrun by armed barbarians, a town in terror which buried its dead in a common grave, someone must have remembered that there was a doctor on this corner. That was when they laid the stretchers by the door and shouted to him (because he didn't open up, he spoke from inside); they shouted to him: "Doctor, take care of these wounded people because there aren't enough doctors to go around," and he replied: "Take them somewhere else, I don't know about any of that." And they said to him: "You're the only doctor left. You have to do a charitable act." And he answered (and still hadn't opened the door), imagined by the crowd to be in the middle of the room, the lamp held high, his hard yellow eyes lighted up: "I've forgotten everything I knew about all that. Take them somewhere else," and he stayed there (because the door was never opened) with the door closed, while men and women of Macondo were dying in front of it. The crowd was capable of anything that night. They were getting ready to set fire to the house and reduce its only occupant to ashes. But then the Pup appeared. They say that it was as if he'd been there invisible, standing guard to stop the destruction of the house and the man. "No one will touch this door," they say the Pup said. And they say that was all he said, his arms open as if on a cross, his inexpressive and cold cow-skull face illuminated by the glow of rural fury. And then the impulse was reined in, it changed direction, but it still had sufficient force for them to shout the sentence that would assure the coming of this Wednesday for all the ages.

Walking toward the bed to tell my men to open the door, I think: *He'll be coming any minute now*. And I think that if he doesn't get here in five minutes we'll take the coffin out without any authorization and put the dead man in the street so he'll have to bury him right in front of the house. "Cataure," I say, calling the oldest of my men, and he barely has time to lift his head when I hear the mayor's footsteps coming through the next room.

I know that he's coming straight toward me and I try to turn quickly on my heels, leaning on my cane, but my bad leg fails me and I go forward, sure that I'm going to fall and hit my face against the coffin, when I stumble across his arm and clutch it firmly, and I hear his voice of peaceful stupidity saying: "Don't worry, colonel, I can assure you that nothing will happen." And I think that's how it is, but I know he's saying it to give himself courage. "I don't think anything will happen," I tell him, thinking just the opposite, and he says something about the ceiba trees in the cemetery and hands me the authorization for the burial. Without reading it I fold it, put it in my vest pocket, and tell him: "In any case, whatever happens, it had to happen. It's as if it had been announced in the almanac."

The mayor goes over to the Indians. He tells them to nail up the coffin and open the door. And I see them moving about, looking for the hammer and nails which will remove the sight of that man forever, that unsheltered gentleman from nowhere whom I saw for the last time three years ago beside my convalescent's bed, his head and face cracked by premature decrepitude. He had just rescued me from death then. The same force that had brought him there, that had given him the news of my illness, seemed to be the one which held him up beside my bed saying:

"You just have to exercise that leg a little. You may have to use a cane from now on."

I would ask him two days later what I owed him and he would answer: "You don't owe me anything, colonel. But if you want to do me a favor, throw a little earth on me when morning finds me stiff. That's all I need for the buzzards not to eat me."

In the promise he made me give, in the way he proposed it, in the rhythm of his footsteps on the tile in the room, it was evident that this man had begun to die a long time back, even though three years would pass before that postponed and defective death would be completely realized. That day was today. And I even think that he probably didn't need the noose. A slight breeze would have been enough to extinguish the last glow of life that remained in his hard yellow eyes. I'd sensed all that ever since the night I spoke to him in his little room, before he came here to live with Meme. So when he made me promise what I'm about to do now, I didn't feel upset. I told him simply:

"It's an unnecessary request, doctor. You know me and you must know that I would have buried you over the heads of everybody even if I didn't owe my life to you."

And he, smiling, his hard yellow eyes peaceful for the first time:

"That's all very true, colonel. But don't forget that a dead man wouldn't have been able to bury me."

Now no one will be able to correct this shame. The mayor has handed my father the burial order and my father has said: "In any case, whatever happens, it had to happen. It's as if it had been announced in the almanac." And he said it with the same indolence with which he turned himself over to the fate of Macondo, faithful to the trunks where the clothing of all those who died before I was born is kept. Since then everything has gone downhill. Even my stepmother's energy, her ironclad and dominant character have been changed into bitter doubt. She seems more and more distant and silent, and her disillusionment is such that this afternoon she sat down beside the railing and said: "I'll stay collapsed here until Judgment Day."

My father hadn't ever imposed his will on anything again. Only today did he get up to fulfill that shameful promise. He's here, sure that everything will happen with no serious consequences, watching the Guajiros starting to move to open the door and nail up the coffin. I see them coming closer, I stand up, I take the child by the hand and pull the chair toward the window so as not to be seen by the town when they open the door.

The child is puzzled. When I get up he looks me in the face with an indescribable expression, a little upset. But now he's perplexed, beside me, watching the Indians, who are sweating because of the effort to open the bolts. And with a penetrating and sustained lament of rusty metal, the doors open wide. Then I see the street again, the glowing and burning white dust that covers the houses and has given the town the lamentable look of a run-down piece of furniture. It's as if God had declared Macondo unnecessary and had thrown it into the corner where towns that have stopped being of any service to creation are kept.

The child, who at the first moment must have been dazzled by the sudden light (his hand trembled in mine when the door was opened), raises his head suddenly, concentrated, intent, and he asks me: "Did you hear it?" Only then do I realize that in some neighboring courtyard a curlew is telling the time. "Yes," I say. "It must be three o'clock already," and almost at that precise moment the first hammer blow sounds on the nail.

Trying not to listen to the lacerating sound that makes my skin crawl, trying to prevent the child from noticing my confusion, I turn my face to the window and in the next block I see the melancholy and dusty almond trees with our house in the background. Shaken by the invisible breath of destruction, it too is on the eve of a silent and final collapse. All of Macondo has been like that ever since it was squeezed by the banana company. Ivy invades the houses, weeds grow in the alleys, walls crumble, and in the middle of the day a person finds a lizard in her room. Everything has seem destroyed since we stopped cultivating the rosemary and the nard; since the time an invisible hand cracked the Christmas dishes in the cupboard and put moths to fatten on the clothes that nobody wore anymore. When a door becomes loose there isn't a solicitous hand ready to repair it. My father doesn't have the energy to move the way he did before the collapse that left him limping forever. Señora Rebeca, behind her eternal fan, doesn't bother about anything that might repel the hunger of malevolence that's provoked in her by her sterile and tormented widowhood. Águeda is crippled, overwhelmed by a patient religious illness; and Father Ángel doesn't seem to have any other satisfaction except savoring the persevering indigestion of meatballs every day during his siesta. The only thing that seems unchanged is the song of the twins of Saint Jerome and that mysterious beggar woman who doesn't seem to grow old and who for twenty years has come to the house every Tuesday for a branch of lemon balm. Only the whistle of a yellow, dusty train that doesn't take anyone away breaks the silence four times a day. And at night the toom-toom of the electric plant that the banana company left behind when it left Macondo.

I can see the house through the window and I am aware that my stepmother is there, motionless in her chair, thinking perhaps that before we get back that final wind which will wipe out this town will have passed. Everyone will have gone then except us, because we're tied to this soil by a roomful of trunks where the household goods and clothing of grandparents, my grandparents, are kept, and the canopies that my parents' horses used when they came to Macondo, fleeing from the war. We've been sown into this soil by the memory of the remote dead whose bones can no longer be found twenty fathoms under the earth. The trunks have been in the room ever since the last days of the war; and they'll be there this afternoon when we come back from the burial, if that final wind hasn't passed, the one that will sweep away Macondo, its bedrooms full of lizards and its silent people devastated by memories.

Suddenly my grandfather gets up, leans on his cane, and stretches out his bird head where his glasses seem to be fastened on as if they were part of his face. I think it would be hard for me to wear glasses. With the smallest movement they'd slip off my ears. And thinking about that I tap my nose. Mama looks at me and asks: "Does it hurt you?" And I tell her no, that I was just thinking that I wouldn't be able to wear glasses. And she smiles, breathes deeply, and tells me: "You must be soaked." And she's right; my clothes are burning on my skin, the thick, green corduroy, fastened all the way up, is sticking to my body with sweat and gives me an itchy feeling. "Yes," I say. And my mother leans over me, loosens my tie and fans my collar, saying: "When we get home you can rest and have a bath." "Cataure," I hear.

At that point, through the rear door, the man with the revolver comes in again. When he gets in the doorway he takes off his hat and walks carefully, as if he was afraid of waking up the corpse. But he did it to surprise my grandfather, who falls forward, pushed by the man, staggers, and manages to grab the arm of the same man who'd tried to knock him down. The others have stopped smoking and are still sitting on the bed in a row like four crows on a sawhorse. When the man with the revolver comes in the crows lean over and talk secretly and one of them gets up, goes over to the table, and picks up the box of nails and the hammer.

My grandfather is talking to the man beside the coffin. The man says: "Don't worry, colonel. I can assure you that nothing will happen." And my grandfather says: "I don't think anything will happen." And the man says: "They can bury him on the outside, against the left wall of the cemetery where the ceiba trees are the tallest." Then he gives my grandfather a piece of paper, saying: "You'll see that everything will turn out fine." My grandfather leans on his cane with one hand, takes the paper with the other, and puts it into his vest pocket, where he keeps his small, square gold watch with a chain. Then he says: "In any case, whatever happens, it had to happen. It's as if it had been announced in the almanac."

The man says: "There are some people in the windows, but that's just curiosity. The women always look at anything." But I don't think my grandfather heard him, because he's looking through the window at the street. The man moves then, goes over to the bed, and, fanning himself with his hat, he tells the men: "You can nail it up now. In the meantime, open the door so we can get a breath of air."

The men start to move. One of them leans over the box with the hammer and nails and the others go to the door. My mother gets up. She's sweaty and pale. She pulls her chair, takes me by the hand, and tugs me aside so that the men can get by to open the door.

At first they try to turn the bolt, which seems to be soldered to the rusty catches, but they can't move it. It's as if someone were pushing with all his strength from the street side. But when one of the men leans against the door and pounds it, the room is filled with the noise of wood, rusty hinges, locks soldered by time, layer upon layer, and the door opens, enormous, as if a man could go through on another's shoulders; and there's a long creaking of wood and iron that's been awakened. And before we have time to find out what's happened, the light bursts into the room, backward, powerful and perfect, because they've taken away the support that held it for two hundred years with the strength of two hundred oxen, and it falls backward into the room, dragging in the shadow of things in its turbulent fall. The men become brutally visible, like a flash of lightning at noon, and they stumble, and it looks as if they had to hold themselves up so that the light wouldn't knock them down.

When the door opens a curlew begins to sing somewhere in town. Now I can see the street. I can see the bright and burning dust. I can see several men sitting on the opposite sidewalk, their arms folded, looking toward the room. I hear the curlew again and I say to Mama: "Did you hear it?" And she says yes, it must be three o'clock. But Ada told me that curlews sing when they get the smell of a dead man. I'm about to tell my mother just at the moment when I hear the sharp sound of the hammer on the head of the first nail. The hammer pounds, pounds, and fills everything up; it rests a second and pounds again, wounding the wood six times in a row, waking up the long, sad sound of the sleeping boards while my mother, her face turned the other way, looks through the window into the street.

When the hammering is over the song of several curlews can be heard. My grandfather signals his men. They lean over, tip the coffin, while the one who stayed in the corner with his hat says to my grandfather: "Don't worry, colonel." And then my grandfather turns toward the corner, agitated, his neck swollen and purple like that of a fighting cock. But he doesn't say anything. It's the man who speaks again from the corner. He says: "I don't even think there's anyone left in town who remembers this."

At that instant I really feel the quiver in my stomach. *Now I do feel like going out back*, I think; but I see that it's too late now. The men make a last effort; they straighten up, their heels dug into the floor, and the coffin is floating in the light as if they were carrying off a dead ship to be buried.

I think: *Now they'll get the smell. Now all the curlews will start to sing.*

(1955)

# The Handsomest Drowned
# Man in the World

## A TALE FOR CHILDREN ✳

The first children who saw the dark and slinky bulge approaching through the sea let themselves think it was an enemy ship. Then they saw it had no flags or masts and they thought it was a whale. But when it washed up on the beach, they removed the clumps of seaweed, the jellyfish tentacles, and the remains of fish and flotsam, and only then did they see that it was a drowned man.

They had been playing with him all afternoon, burying him in the sand and digging him up again, when someone chanced to see them and spread the alarm in the village. The men who carried him to the nearest house noticed that he weighed more than any dead man they had ever known, almost as much as a horse, and they said to each other that maybe he'd been floating too long and the water had got into his bones. When they laid him on the floor they said he'd been taller than all other men because there was barely enough room for him in the house, but they thought that maybe the ability to keep on growing after death was part of the nature of certain drowned men. He had the smell of the sea about him and only his shape gave one to suppose that it was the corpse of a human being, because the skin was covered with a crust of mud and scales.

They did not even have to clean off his face to know that the dead man was a stranger. The village was made up of only twenty-

*isolation*

98

*gloomy*

*pression*

odd wooden houses that had stone courtyards with no flowers and which were spread about on the end of a desertlike cape. There was so little land that mothers always went about with the fear that the wind would carry off their children and the few dead that the years had caused among them had to be thrown off the cliffs. But the sea was calm and bountiful and all the men fit into seven boats. So when they found the drowned man they simply had to look at one another to see that they were all there.

That night they did not go out to work at sea. While the men went to find out if anyone was missing in neighboring villages, the women stayed behind to care for the drowned man. They took the mud off with grass swabs, they removed the underwater stones entangled in his hair, and they scraped the crust off with tools used for scaling fish. As they were doing that they noticed that the vegetation on him came from faraway oceans and deep water and that his clothes were in tatters, as if he had sailed through labyrinths of coral. They noticed too that he bore his death with pride, for he did not have the lonely look of other drowned men who came out of the sea or that haggard, needy look of men who drowned in rivers. But only when they finished cleaning him off did they become aware of the kind of man he was and it left them breathless. Not only was he the tallest, strongest, most virile, and best built man they had ever seen, but even though they were looking at him there was no room for him in their imagination.

They could not find a bed in the village large enough to lay him on nor was there a table solid enough to use for his wake. The tallest men's holiday pants would not fit him, nor the fattest ones' Sunday shirts, nor the shoes of the one with the biggest feet. Fascinated by his huge size and his beauty, the women then decided to make him some pants from a large piece of sail and a shirt from some bridal brabant linen so that he could continue through his death with dignity. As they sewed, sitting in a circle and gazing at the corpse between stitches, it seemed to them that the wind had never been so steady nor the sea so restless as on *superstition*

that night and they supposed that the change had something to do with the dead man. They thought that if that magnificent man had lived in the village, his house would have had the widest doors, the highest ceiling, and the strongest floor, his bedstead would have been made from a midship frame held together by iron bolts, and his wife would have been the happiest woman. They thought that he would have had so much authority that he could have drawn fish out of the sea simply by calling their names and that he would have put so much work into his land that springs would have burst forth from among the rocks so that he would have been able to plant flowers on the cliffs. They secretly compared him to their own men, thinking that for all their lives theirs were incapable of doing what he could do in one night, and they ended up dismissing them deep in their hearts as the weakest, meanest, and most useless creatures on earth. They were wandering through that maze of fantasy when the oldest woman, who as the oldest had looked upon the drowned man with more compassion than passion, sighed:

"He has the face of someone called Esteban."

It was true. Most of them had only to take another look at him to see that he could not have any other name. The more stubborn among them, who were the youngest, still lived for a few hours with the illusion that when they put his clothes on and he lay among the flowers in patent leather shoes his name might be Lautaro. But it was a vain illusion. There had not been enough canvas, the poorly cut and worse sewn pants were too tight, and the hidden strength of his heart popped the buttons on his shirt. After midnight the whistling of the wind died down and the sea fell into its Wednesday drowsiness. The silence put an end to any last doubts: he was Esteban. The women who had dressed him, who had combed his hair, had cut his nails and shaved him were unable to hold back a shudder of pity when they had to resign themselves to his being dragged along the ground. It was then that they understood how unhappy he must have been with that huge body since it bothered him even after death. They could see him in life, condemned to going through doors sideways, cracking his head on crossbeams, remaining on his feet during visits, not knowing what to do with his soft, pink, sea lion hands while the lady of the house looked for her most resistant chair and begged him, frightened to death, sit here, Esteban, please, and he, leaning against the wall, smiling, don't bother, ma'am, I'm fine where I am, his heels raw and his back roasted from having done the same thing so many times whenever he paid a visit, don't bother, ma'am, I'm fine where I am, just to avoid the embarrassment of breaking up the chair, and never knowing perhaps that the ones who said don't go, Esteban, at least wait till the coffee's ready, were the ones who later on would whisper the big boob finally left, how nice, the handsome fool has gone. That was what the women were thinking beside the body a little before dawn. Later, when they covered his face with a handkerchief so that the light would not bother him, he looked so forever dead, so defenseless, so much like their men that the first furrows of tears opened in their hearts. It was one of the younger ones who began the weeping. The others, coming to, went from sighs to wails, and the more they sobbed the more they felt like weeping, because the drowned man was becoming all the more Esteban for them, and so they wept so much, for he was the most destitute, most peaceful, and most obliging man on earth, poor Esteban. So when the men returned with the news that the drowned man was not from the neighboring villages either, the women felt an opening of jubilation in the midst of their tears.

"Praise the Lord," they sighed, "he's ours!"

The men thought the fuss was only womanish frivolity. Fatigued because of the difficult nighttime inquiries, all they wanted was to get rid of the bother of the newcomer once and for all before the sun grew strong on that arid, windless day. They improvised a litter with the remains of foremasts and gaffs, tying it together with rigging so that it would bear the weight of the body until they reached the cliffs. They wanted to tie the anchor from a cargo ship to him so that he would sink easily into the deepest waves, where fish are blind and divers die of nostalgia, and bad currents would not bring him back to shore, as had happened with other bodies. But the more they hurried, the more the women thought of ways to waste time. They walked about like startled hens, pecking with the sea charms on their breasts, some interfering on one side to put a scapular of the good wind on the drowned man, some on the other side to put a wrist compass on him, and after a great deal of *get away from there, woman, stay out of the way, look, you almost made me fall on top of the dead man,* the men began to feel mistrust in their livers and started grumbling about why so many main-altar decorations for a stranger, because no matter how many nails and holy-water jars he had on him, the sharks would chew him all the same, but the women kept piling on their junk relics, running back and forth, stumbling, while they released in sighs what they did not in tears, so that the men finally exploded with *since when has there ever been such a fuss over a drifting corpse, a drowned nobody, a piece of cold Wednesday meat.* One of the women, mortified by so much lack of care, then removed the handkerchief from the dead man's face and the men were left breathless too.

He was Esteban. It was not necessary to repeat it for them to recognize him. If they had been told Sir Walter Raleigh, even they might have been impressed with his gringo accent, the macaw on his shoulder, his cannibal-killing blunderbuss, but there could be only one Esteban in the world and there he was, stretched out like a sperm whale, shoeless, wearing the pants of an undersized child, and with those stony nails that had to be cut with a knife. They only had to take the handkerchief off his face to see that he was ashamed, that it was not his fault that he was so big or so heavy or so handsome, and if he had known that this was going to happen, he would have looked for a more discreet place to drown in, seriously, I even would have tied the anchor off a galleon around my neck and staggered off a cliff like someone who doesn't like things in order not to be upsetting people now with this Wednesday dead body, as you people say, in order not to be bothering anyone with this filthy piece of cold meat that doesn't have anything to do with me. There was so much truth in his manner that even the most mistrustful men, the ones who felt the bitterness of endless nights at sea fearing that their women would tire of dreaming about them and begin to dream of drowned men, even they and others who were harder still shuddered in the marrow of their bones at Esteban's sincerity.

That was how they came to hold the most splendid funeral they could conceive of for an abandoned drowned man. Some women who had gone to get flowers in the neighboring villages returned with other women who could not believe what they had been told, and those women went back for more flowers when they saw the dead man, and they brought more and more until there were so many flowers and so many people that it was hard to walk about. At the final moment it pained them to return him to the waters as an orphan and they chose a father and mother from among the best people, and aunts and uncles and cousins, so that through him all the inhabitants of the village became kinsmen. Some sailors who heard the weeping from a distance went off course and people heard of one who had himself tied to the mainmast, remembering ancient fables about sirens. While they fought for the privilege of carrying him on their shoulders along the steep escarpment by the cliffs, men and women became aware for the first time of the desolation of their streets, the dryness of their courtyards, the narrowness of their dreams as they faced the splendor and beauty of their drowned man. They let him go without an anchor so that he could come back if he wished and whenever he wished, and they all held their breath for the fraction of centuries the body took to fall into the abyss. They did not need to look at one another to realize that they were no longer all present, that they would never be. But they also knew that everything would be different from then on, that their houses would have wider doors, higher ceilings, and stronger floors so that Esteban's memory could go everywhere without bumping into beams and so that no one in the future would dare whisper the big boob finally died, too bad, the handsome fool has finally died, because they were going to paint their house fronts gay colors to make Esteban's memory eternal and they were going to break their backs digging for springs among the stones and planting flowers on the cliffs so that in future years at dawn the passengers on great liners would awaken, suffocated by the smell of gardens on the high seas, and the captain would have to come down from the bridge in his dress uniform, with his astrolabe, his pole star, and his row of war medals and, pointing to the promontory of roses on the horizon, he would say in fourteen languages, look there, where the wind is so peaceful now that it's gone to sleep beneath the beds, over there, where the sun's so bright that the sunflowers don't know which way to turn, yes, over there, that's Esteban's village.

(1968)

# A Very Old Man
# with Enormous Wings

A TALE FOR CHILDREN

On the third day of rain they had killed so many crabs inside the
house that Pelayo had to cross his drenched courtyard and throw
them into the sea, because the newborn child had a temperature
all night and they thought it was due to the stench. The world
had been sad since Tuesday. Sea and sky were a single ash-gray
thing and the sands of the beach, which on March nights glim-
mered like powdered light, had become a stew of mud and rotten
shellfish. The light was so weak at noon that when Pelayo was
coming back to the house after throwing away the crabs, it was
hard for him to see what it was that was moving and groaning
in the rear of the courtyard. He had to go very close to see
that it was an old man, a very old man, lying face down in the
mud, who, in spite of his tremendous efforts, couldn't get up,
impeded by his enormous wings.

Frightened by that nightmare, Pelayo ran to get Elisenda, his
wife, who was putting compresses on the sick child, and he took
her to the rear of the courtyard. They both looked at the fallen
body with mute stupor. He was dressed like a ragpicker. There
were only a few faded hairs left on his bald skull and very few
teeth in his mouth, and his pitiful condition of a drenched great-
grandfather had taken away any sense of grandeur he might have
had. His huge buzzard wings, dirty and half-plucked, were forever

entangled in the mud. They looked at him so long and so closely that Pelayo and Elisenda very soon overcame their surprise and in the end found him familiar. Then they dared speak to him, and he answered in an incomprehensible dialect with a strong sailor's voice. That was how they skipped over the inconvenience of the wings and quite intelligently concluded that he was a lonely castaway from some foreign ship wrecked by the storm. And yet, they called in a neighbor woman who knew everything about life and death to see him, and all she needed was one look to show them their mistake.

"He's an angel," she told them. "He must have been coming for the child, but the poor fellow is so old that the rain knocked him down."

On the following day everyone knew that a flesh-and-blood angel was held captive in Pelayo's house. Against the judgment of the wise neighbor woman, for whom angels in those times were the fugitive survivors of a celestial conspiracy, they did not have the heart to club him to death. Pelayo watched over him all afternoon from the kitchen, armed with his bailiff's club, and before going to bed he dragged him out of the mud and locked him up with the hens in the wire chicken coop. In the middle of the night, when the rain stopped, Pelayo and Elisenda were still killing crabs. A short time afterward the child woke up without a fever and with a desire to eat. Then they felt magnanimous and decided to put the angel on a raft with fresh water and provisions for three days and leave him to his fate on the high seas. But when they went out into the courtyard with the first light of dawn, they found the whole neighborhood in front of the chicken coop having fun with the angel, without the slightest reverence, tossing him things to eat through the openings in the wire as if he weren't a supernatural creature but a circus animal.

Father Gonzaga arrived before seven o'clock, alarmed at the strange news. By that time onlookers less frivolous than those at dawn had already arrived and they were making all kinds of conjectures concerning the captive's future. The simplest among them thought that he should be named mayor of the world. Others of sterner mind felt that he should be promoted to the rank of five-star general in order to win all wars. Some visionaries hoped that he could be put to stud in order to implant on earth a race of winged wise men who could take charge of the universe. But Father Gonzaga, before becoming a priest, had been a robust woodcutter. Standing by the wire, he reviewed his catechism in an instant and asked them to open the door so that he could take a close look at that pitiful man who looked more like a huge decrepit hen among the fascinated chickens. He was lying in a corner drying his open wings in the sunlight among the fruit peels and breakfast leftovers that the early risers had thrown him. Alien to the impertinences of the world, he only lifted his antiquarian eyes and murmured something in his dialect when Father Gonzaga went into the chicken coop and said good morning to him in Latin. The parish priest had his first suspicion of an imposter when he saw that he did not understand the language of God or know how to greet His ministers. Then he noticed that seen close up he was much too human: he had an unbearable smell of the outdoors, the back side of his wings was strewn with parasites and his main feathers had been mistreated by terrestrial winds, and nothing about him measured up to the proud dignity of angels. Then he came out of the chicken coop and in a brief sermon warned the curious against the risks of being ingenuous. He reminded them that the devil had the bad habit of making use of carnival tricks in order to confuse the unwary. He argued that if wings were not the essential element in determining the difference between a hawk and an airplane, they were even less so in the recognition of angels. Nevertheless, he promised to write a letter to his bishop so that the latter would write to his primate so that the latter would write to the Supreme Pontiff in order to get the final verdict from the highest courts.

His prudence fell on sterile hearts. The news of the captive angel spread with such rapidity that after a few hours the courtyard had the bustle of a marketplace and they had to call in troops with fixed bayonets to disperse the mob that was about to knock the house down. Elisenda, her spine all twisted from sweeping up so much marketplace trash, then got the idea of fencing in the yard and charging five cents admission to see the angel.

The curious came from far away. A traveling carnival arrived with a flying acrobat who buzzed over the crowd several times, but no one paid any attention to him because his wings were not those of an angel but, rather, those of a sidereal bat. The most unfortunate invalids on earth came in search of health: a poor woman who since childhood had been counting her heartbeats and had run out of numbers; a Portuguese man who couldn't sleep because the noise of the stars disturbed him; a sleepwalker who got up at night to undo the things he had done while awake; and many others with less serious ailments. In the midst of that shipwreck disorder that made the earth tremble, Pelayo and Elisenda were happy with fatigue, for in less than a week they had crammed their rooms with money and the line of pilgrims waiting their turn to enter still reached beyond the horizon.

The angel was the only one who took no part in his own act. He spent his time trying to get comfortable in his borrowed nest, befuddled by the hellish heat of the oil lamps and sacramental candles that had been placed along the wire. At first they tried to make him eat some mothballs, which, according to the wisdom of the wise neighbor woman, were the food prescribed for angels. But he turned them down, just as he turned down the papal lunches that the penitents brought him, and they never found out whether it was because he was an angel or because he was an old man that in the end he ate nothing but eggplant mush. His only supernatural virtue seemed to be patience. Especially during the first days, when the hens pecked at him, searching for the stellar parasites that proliferated in his wings, and the cripples pulled out feathers to touch their defective parts with, and even the most merciful threw stones at him, trying to get him to rise so they could see him standing. The only time they succeeded in arousing him was when they burned his side with an iron for branding steers, for he had been motionless for so many hours that they thought he was dead. He awoke with a start, ranting in his hermetic language and with tears in his eyes, and he flapped his wings a couple of times, which brought on a whirlwind of chicken dung and lunar dust and a gale of panic that did not seem to be of this world. Although many thought that his reaction had been one not of rage but of pain, from then on they were careful not to annoy him, because the majority understood that his passivity was not that of a hero taking his ease but that of a cataclysm in repose.

Father Gonzaga held back the crowd's frivolity with formulas of maidservant inspiration while awaiting the arrival of a final judgment on the nature of the captive. But the mail from Rome showed no sense of urgency. They spent their time finding out if the prisoner had a navel, if his dialect had any connection with Aramaic, how many times he could fit on the head of a pin, or whether he wasn't just a Norwegian with wings. Those meager letters might have come and gone until the end of time if a providential event had not put an end to the priest's tribulations.

It so happened that during those days, among so many other carnival attractions, there arrived in town the traveling show of the woman who had been changed into a spider for having disobeyed her parents. The admission to see her was not only less than the admission to see the angel, but people were permitted to ask her all manner of questions about her absurd state and to examine her up and down so that no one would ever doubt the truth of her horror. She was a frightful tarantula the size of a ram and with the head of a sad maiden. What was most heartrending, however, was not her outlandish shape but the sincere affliction with which she recounted the details of her misfortune. While still practically a child she had sneaked out of her parents' house to go to a dance, and while she was coming back through the woods after having danced all night without permission, a fearful thunderclap rent the sky in two and through the crack came the lightning bolt of brimstone that changed her into a spider. Her only nourishment came from the meatballs that charitable souls chose to toss into her mouth. A spectacle like that, full of so much human truth and with such a fearful lesson, was bound to defeat without even trying that of a haughty angel who scarcely deigned to look at mortals. Besides, the few miracles attributed to the angel showed a certain mental disorder, like the blind man who didn't recover his sight but grew three new teeth, or the paralytic who didn't get to walk but almost won the lottery, and the leper whose sores sprouted sunflowers. Those consolation miracles, which were more like mocking fun, had already ruined the angel's reputation when the woman who had been changed into a spider finally crushed him completely. That was how Father Gonzaga was cured forever of his insomnia and Pelayo's courtyard went back to being as empty as during the time it had rained for three days and crabs walked through the bedrooms.

The owners of the house had no reason to lament. With the money they saved they built a two-story mansion with balconies and gardens and high netting so that crabs wouldn't get in during the winter, and with iron bars on the windows so that angels wouldn't get in. Pelayo also set up a rabbit warren close to town and gave up his job as bailiff for good, and Elisenda bought some satin pumps with high heels and many dresses of iridescent silk, the kind worn on Sunday by the most desirable women in those times. The chicken coop was the only thing that didn't receive any attention. If they washed it down with creolin and burned tears of myrrh inside it every so often, it was not in homage to the angel but to drive away the dungheap stench that still hung everywhere like a ghost and was turning the new house into an old one. At first, when the child learned to walk, they were careful that he not get too close to the chicken coop. But then they began to lose their fears and got used to the smell, and before the child got his second teeth he'd gone inside the chicken coop to play, where the wires were falling apart. The angel was no less standoffish with him than with other mortals, but he tolerated the most ingenious infamies with the patience of a dog who had no illusions. They both came down with chicken pox at the same time. The doctor who took care of the child couldn't resist the temptation to listen to the angel's heart, and he found so much whistling in the heart and so many sounds in his kidneys that it seemed impossible for him to be alive. What surprised him most, however, was the logic of his wings. They seemed so natural on that completely human organism that he couldn't understand why other men didn't have them too.

When the child began school it had been some time since the sun and rain had caused the collapse of the chicken coop. The angel went dragging himself about here and there like a stray dying man. They would drive him out of the bedroom with a broom and a moment later find him in the kitchen. He seemed to be in so many places at the same time that they grew to think that he'd been duplicated, that he was reproducing himself all through the house, and the exasperated and unhinged Elisenda shouted that it was awful living in that hell full of angels. He could scarcely eat and his antiquarian eyes had also become so foggy that he went about bumping into posts. All he had left were the bare cannulae of his last feathers. Pelayo threw a blanket over him and extended him the charity of letting him sleep in the shed, and only then did they notice that he had a temperature at night, and was delirious with the tongue twisters of an old Norwegian. That was one of the few times they became alarmed, for they thought he was going to die and not even the wise neighbor woman had been able to tell them what to do with dead angels.

And yet he not only survived his worst winter, but seemed improved with the first sunny days. He remained motionless for several days in the farthest corner of the courtyard, where no one would see him, and at the beginning of December some large, stiff feathers began to grow on his wings, the feathers of a scarecrow, which looked more like another misfortune of decrepitude. But he must have known the reason for those changes, for he was quite careful that no one should notice them, that no one should hear the sea chanteys that he sometimes sang under the stars. One morning Elisenda was cutting some bunches of onions for lunch when a wind that seemed to come from the high seas blew into the kitchen. Then she went to the window and caught the angel in his first attempts at flight. They were so clumsy that his fingernails opened a furrow in the vegetable patch and he was on the point of knocking the shed down with the ungainly flapping that slipped on the light and couldn't get a grip on the air. But he did manage to gain altitude. Elisenda let out a sigh of relief, for herself and for him, when she saw him pass over the last houses, holding himself up in some way with the risky flapping of a senile vulture. She kept watching him even when she was through cutting the onions and she kept on watching until it was no longer possible for her to see him, because then he was no longer an annoyance in her life but an imaginary dot on the horizon of the sea.

(1968)

# Blacamán the Good, Vendor of Miracles

From the first Sunday I saw him he reminded me of a bullring mule, with his white suspenders that were backstitched with gold thread, his rings with colored stones on every finger, and his braids of jingle bells, standing on a table by the docks of Santa María del Darién in the middle of the flasks of specifics and herbs of consolation that he prepared himself and hawked through the towns along the Caribbean with his wounded shout, except that at that time he wasn't trying to sell any of that Indian mess but was asking them to bring him a real snake so that he could demonstrate on his own flesh an antidote he had invented, the only infallible one, ladies and gentlemen, for the bites of serpents, tarantulas, and centipedes plus all manner of poisonous mammals. Someone who seemed quite impressed by his determination managed to get a bushmaster of the worst kind somewhere (the snake that kills by poisoning the respiration) and brought it to him in a bottle, and he uncorked it with such eagerness that we all thought he was going to eat it, but as soon as the creature felt itself free it jumped out of the bottle and struck him on the neck, leaving him right then and there without any wind for his oratory and with barely enough time to take the antidote, and the vest-pocket pharmacist tumbled down into the crowd and rolled about on the ground, his huge body wasted away as if he had nothing inside of it, but laughing all the while with all of his gold teeth. The hubbub was so great that a cruiser from the north that had been docked there for twenty years on a goodwill mission declared a quarantine so that the snake poison wouldn't get on board, and the people who were sanctifying Palm Sunday came out of church with their blessed palms, because no one wanted to miss the show of the poisoned man, who had already begun to puff up with the air of death and was twice as fat as he'd been before, giving off a froth of gall through his mouth and panting through his pores, but still laughing with so much life that the jingle bells tinkled all over his body. The swelling snapped the laces of his leggings and the seams of his clothes, his fingers grew purple from the pressure of the rings, he turned the color of venison in brine, and from his rear end came a hint of the last moments of death, so that everyone who had seen a person bitten by a snake knew that he was rotting away before dying and that he would be so crumpled up that they'd have to pick him up with a shovel to put him into a sack, but they also thought that even in his sawdust state he'd keep on laughing. It was so incredible that the marines came up on deck to take colored pictures of him with long-distance lenses, but the women who'd come out of church blocked their intentions by covering the dying man with a blanket and laying blessed palms on top of him, some because they didn't want the soldiers to profane the body with their Adventist instruments, others because they were afraid to continue looking at that idolater who was ready to die dying with laughter, and others because in that way perhaps his soul at least would not be poisoned. Everybody had given him up for dead when he pushed aside the palms with one arm, still half-dazed and not completely recovered from the bad moment he'd had, but he set the table up without anyone's help, climbed on it like a crab once more, and there he was again, shouting that his antidote was nothing but the hand of God in a bottle, as we had all seen with our own eyes, but it only cost two cuartillos because he hadn't invented it as an item for sale but for the good of all humanity, and as soon as he said that, ladies and gentlemen, I only ask you not to crowd around, there's enough for everybody.

They crowded around, of course, and they did well to do so, because in the end there wasn't enough for everybody. Even the admiral from the cruiser bought a bottle, convinced by him that it was also good for the poisoned bullets of anarchists, and the sailors weren't satisfied with just taking colored pictures of him up on the table, pictures they had been unable to take of him dead, but they had him signing autographs until his arm was twisted with cramps. It was getting to be night and only the most perplexed of us were left by the docks when with his eyes he searched for someone with the look of an idiot to help him put the bottles away, and naturally he spotted me. It was like the look of destiny, not just mine, but his too, for that was more than a century ago and we both remember it as if it had been last Sunday. What happened was that we were putting his circus drugstore into that trunk with purple straps that looked more like a scholar's casket, when he must have noticed some light inside of me that he hadn't seen in me before, because he asked me in a surly way who are you, and I answered that I was an orphan on both sides whose papa hadn't died, and he gave out with laughter that was louder than what he had given with the poison and then he asked me what do you do for a living, and I answered that I didn't do anything except stay alive, because nothing else was worth the trouble, and still weeping with laughter he asked me what science in the world do you most want to learn, and that was the only time I answered the truth without any fooling, I wanted to be a fortune-teller, and then he didn't laugh again but told me as if thinking out loud that I didn't need much for that because I already had the hardest thing to learn, which was my face of an idiot. That same night he spoke to my father and for one real and two cuartillos and a deck of cards that foretold adultery he bought me forevermore.

That was what Blacamán was like, Blacamán the Bad, because I'm Blacamán the Good. He was capable of convincing an astronomer that the month of February was nothing but a herd of invisible elephants, but when his good luck turned on him he became a heart-deep brute. In his days of glory he had been an embalmer of viceroys, and they say that he gave them faces with such authority that for many years they went on governing better than when they were alive, and that no one dared bury them until he gave them back their dead-man look, but his prestige was ruined by the invention of an endless chess game that drove a chaplain mad and brought on two illustrious suicides, and so he was on the decline, from an interpreter of dreams to a birthday hypnotist, from an extractor of molars by suggestion to a market-place healer; therefore, at the time we met, people were already looking at him askance, even the freebooters. We drifted along with our trick stand and life was an eternal uncertainty as we tried to sell escape suppositories that turned smugglers transparent, furtive drops that baptized wives threw into the soup to instill the fear of God in Dutch husbands, and anything you might want to buy of your own free will, ladies and gentlemen, because this isn't a command, it's advice, and, after all, happiness isn't an obligation either. Nevertheless, as much as we died with laughter at his witticisms, the truth is that it was quite hard for us to manage enough to eat, and his last hope was founded on my vocation as a fortune-teller. He shut me up in the sepulchral trunk disguised as a Japanese and bound with starboard chains so that I could attempt to foretell what I could while he disemboweled the grammar book looking for the best way to convince the world of my new science, and here, ladies and gentlemen, you have this child tormented by Ezequiel's glowworms, and those of you who've been standing there with faces of disbelief, let's see if you dare ask him when you're going to die, but I was never able even to guess what day it was at that time, so he gave up on me as a soothsayer because the drowsiness of digestion disturbs your prediction gland, and after whacking me over the head for good luck, he decided to take me to my father and get his money back. But at that time he happened to find a practical application for the electricity of suffering, and he set about building a sewing machine that ran connected by cupping glasses to the part of the body where there was a pain. Since I spent the night moaning over the whacks he'd given me to conjure away misfortune, he had to keep me on as the one who could test his invention, and so our return was delayed and he was getting back his good humor until the machine worked so well that it not only sewed better than a novice nun but also embroidered birds or astromelias according to the position and intensity of the pain. That was what we were up to, convinced of our triumph over bad luck, when the news reached us that in Philadelphia the commander of the cruiser had tried to repeat the experiment with the antidote and that he'd been changed into a glob of admiral jelly in front of his staff.

He didn't laugh again for a long time. We fled through Indian passes and the more lost we became, the clearer the news reached us that the marines had invaded the country under the pretext of exterminating yellow fever and were going about beheading every inveterate or eventual potter they found in their path, and not only the natives, out of precaution, but also the Chinese, for distraction, the Negroes, from habit, and the Hindus, because they were snake charmers, and then they wiped out the flora and fauna and all the mineral wealth they were able to because their specialists in our affairs had taught them that the people along the Caribbean had the ability to change their nature in order to confuse gringos. I couldn't understand where that fury came from or why we were so frightened until we found ourselves safe and sound in the eternal winds of La Guajira, and only then did he have the courage to confess to me that his antidote was nothing but rhubarb and turpentine and that he'd paid a drifter two cuartillos to bring him that bushmaster with all the poison gone. We stayed in the ruins of a colonial mission, deluded by the hope that some smugglers would pass, because they were men to be trusted and the only ones capable of venturing out under the mercurial sun of those salt flats. At first we ate smoked salamanders and flowers from the ruins and we still had enough spirit to laugh when we tried to eat his boiled leggings, but finally we even ate the water cobwebs from the cisterns and only then did we realize how much we missed the world. Since I didn't know of any recourse against death at that time, I simply lay down to wait for it where it would hurt me least, while he was delirious remembering a woman who was so tender that she could pass through walls just by sighing, but that contrived recollection was also a trick of his genius to fool death with lovesickness. Still, at the moment we should have died, he came to me more alive than ever and spent the whole night watching over my agony, thinking with such great strength that I still haven't been able to tell whether what was whistling through the ruins was the wind or his thoughts, and before dawn he told me with the same voice and the same determination of past times that now he knew the truth, that I was the one who had twisted up his luck again, so get your pants ready, because the same way as you twisted it up for me, you're going to straighten it out.

That was when I lost the little affection I had for him. He took off the last rags I had on, rolled me up in some barbed wire, rubbed rock salt on the sores, put me in brine from my own waters, and hung me by the ankles for the sun to flay me, and he kept on shouting that all that mortification wasn't enough to pacify his persecutors. Finally he threw me to rot in my own misery inside the penance dungeon where the colonial missionaries regenerated heretics, and with the perfidy of a ventriloquist, which he still had more than enough of, he began to imitate the voices of edible

animals, the noise of ripe beets, and the sound of fresh springs
so as to torture me with the illusion that I was dying of indigence
in the midst of paradise. When the smugglers finally supplied
him, he came down to the dungeon to give me something to eat
so that I wouldn't die, but then he made me pay for that charity
by pulling out my nails with pliers and filing my teeth down with
a grindstone, and my only consolation was the wish that life would
give me time and the good fortune to be quit of so much infamy
with even worse martyrdoms. I myself was surprised that I could
resist the plague of my own putrefaction and he kept throwing
the leftovers of his meals onto me and tossed pieces of rotten
lizards and hawks into the corners so that the air of the dungeon
would end up poisoning me. I don't know how much time had
passed when he brought me the carcass of a rabbit in order to
show me that he preferred throwing it away to rot rather than
giving it to me to eat, but my patience only went so far and all
I had left was rancor, so I grabbed the rabbit by the ears and
flung it against the wall with the illusion that it was he and not
the animal that was going to explode, and then it happened, as
if in a dream. The rabbit not only revived with a squeal of fright,
but came back to my hands, hopping through the air.

That was how my great life began. Since then I've gone through
the world drawing the fever out of malaria victims for two pesos,
visioning blind men for four-fifty, draining the water from dropsy
victims for eighteen, putting cripples back together for twenty
pesos if they were that way from birth, for twenty-two if they were
that way because of an accident or a brawl, for twenty-five if they
were that way because of wars, earthquakes, infantry landings, or
any other kind of public calamity, taking care of the common sick
at wholesale according to a special arrangement, madmen according to their theme, children at half price, and idiots out of gratitude, and who dares say that I'm not a philanthropist, ladies and
gentlemen, and now, yes, sir, commandant of the twentieth fleet,
order your boys to take down the barricades and let suffering

humanity pass, lepers to the left, epileptics to the right, cripples where they won't get in the way, and there in the back the least urgent cases, only please don't crowd in on me because then I won't be responsible if the sicknesses get all mixed up and people are cured of what they don't have, and keep the music playing until the brass boils, and the rockets firing until the angels burn, and the liquor flowing until ideas are killed, and bring on the wenches and the acrobats, the butchers and the photographers, and all at my expense, ladies and gentlemen, for here ends the evil fame of the Blacamáns and the universal tumult starts. That's how I go along putting them to sleep with the techniques of a congressman in case my judgment fails and some turn out worse than they were before on me. The only thing I don't do is revive the dead, because as soon as they open their eyes they're murderous with rage at the one who disturbed their state, and when it's all done, those who don't commit suicide die again of disillusionment. At first I was pursued by a group of wise men investigating the legality of my industry, and when they were convinced, they threatened me with the hell of Simon Magus and recommended a life of penitence so that I could get to be a saint, but I answered them, with no disrespect for their authority, that it was precisely along those lines that I had started. The truth is that I'd gain nothing by being a saint after being dead, an artist is what I am, and the only thing I want is to be alive so I can keep going along at donkey level in this six-cylinder touring car I bought from the marines' consul, with this Trinidadian chauffeur who was a baritone in the New Orleans pirates' opera, with my genuine silk shirts, my Oriental lotions, my topaz teeth, my flat straw hat, and my bicolored buttons, sleeping without an alarm clock, dancing with beauty queens, and leaving them hallucinated with my dictionary rhetoric, and with no flutter in my spleen if some Ash Wednesday my faculties wither away, because in order to go on with this life of a minister, all I need is my idiot face, and I have more than enough with the string of shops I own from here to beyond the sunset, where the same tourists who used to go around collecting from us through the admiral, now go stumbling after my autographed pictures, almanacs with my love poetry, medals with my profile, bits of my clothing, and all of that without the glorious plague of spending all day and all night sculpted in equestrian marble and shat on by swallows like the fathers of our country.

It's a pity that Blacamán the Bad can't repeat this story so that people will see that there's nothing invented in it. The last time anyone saw him in this world he'd lost even the studs of his former splendor, and his soul was a shambles and his bones in disorder from the rigors of the desert, but he still had enough jingle bells left to reappear that Sunday on the docks of Santa María del Darién with his eternal sepulchral trunk, except that this time he wasn't trying to sell any antidotes, but was asking in a voice cracking with emotion for the marines to shoot him in a public spectacle so that he could demonstrate on his own flesh the life-restoring properties of this supernatural creature, ladies and gentlemen, and even though you have more than enough right not to believe me after suffering so long from my evil tricks as a deceiver and falsifier, I swear on the bones of my mother that this proof today is nothing from the other world, merely the humble truth, and in case you have any doubts left, notice that I'm not laughing now the way I used to, but holding back a desire to cry. How convincing he must have been, unbuttoning his shirt, his eyes drowning with tears, and giving himself mule kicks on his heart to indicate the best place for death, and yet the marines didn't dare shoot, out of fear that the Sunday crowd would discover their loss of prestige. Someone who may not have forgotten the blacamanipulations of past times managed, no one knew how, to get and bring him in a can enough *barbasco* roots to bring to the surface all the corvinas in the Caribbean, and he opened it with great desire, as if he really was going to eat them, and, indeed, he did eat them, ladies and gentlemen, but please don't be moved or pray for the repose of my soul, because this death is nothing but a visit. That time he was so honest that he didn't break into operatic death rattles, but got off the table like a crab, looked on the ground for the most worthy place to lie down after some hesitation, and from there he looked at me as he would have at a mother and exhaled his last breath in his own arms, still holding back his manly tears all twisted up by the tetanus of eternity. That was the only time, of course, that my science failed me. I put him in that trunk of premonitory size where there was room for him laid out. I had a requiem mass sung for him which cost me fifty four-peso doubloons, because the officiant was dressed in gold and there were also three seated bishops. I had the mausoleum of an emperor built for him on a hill exposed to the best seaside weather, with a chapel just for him and an iron plaque on which there was written in Gothic capitals HERE LIES BLACAMÁN THE DEAD, BADLY CALLED THE BAD, DECEIVER OF MARINES AND VICTIM OF SCIENCE, and when those honors were sufficient for me to do justice to his virtues, I began to get my revenge for his infamy, and then I revived him inside the armored tomb and left him there rolling about in horror. That was long before the fire ants devoured Santa María del Darién, but the mausoleum is still intact on the hill in the shadow of the dragons that climb up to sleep in the Atlantic winds, and every time I pass through here I bring him an automobile load of roses and my heart pains with pity for his virtues, but then I put my ear to the plaque to hear him weeping in the ruins of the crumbling trunk, and if by chance he has died again, I bring him back to life once more, for the beauty of the punishment is that he will keep on living in his tomb as long as I'm alive, that is, forever.

(1968)

# The Last Voyage
# of the Ghost Ship

Now they're going to see who I am, he said to himself in his strong new man's voice, many years after he had first seen the huge ocean liner without lights and without any sound which passed by the village one night like a great uninhabited palace, longer than the whole village and much taller than the steeple of the church, and it sailed by in the darkness toward the colonial city on the other side of the bay that had been fortified against buccaneers, with its old slave port and the rotating light, whose gloomy beams transfigured the village into a lunar encampment of glowing houses and streets of volcanic deserts every fifteen seconds, and even though at that time he'd been a boy without a man's strong voice but with his mother's permission to stay very late on the beach to listen to the wind's night harps, he could still remember, as if still seeing it, how the liner would disappear when the light of the beacon struck its side and how it would reappear when the light had passed, so that it was an intermittent ship sailing along, appearing and disappearing, toward the mouth of the bay, groping its way like a sleepwalker for the buoys that marked the harbor channel until something must have gone wrong with the compass needle, because it headed toward the shoals, ran aground, broke up, and sank without a single sound, even though a collision against the reefs like that should have produced a crash of metal and the explosion of engines that would have frozen with fright the soundest-sleeping dragons in the prehistoric jungle that began with the last streets of the village and ended on the other side of the world, so that he himself thought it was a dream, especially the next day, when he saw the radiant fishbowl of the bay, the disorder of colors of the Negro shacks on the hills above the harbor, the schooners of the smugglers from the Guianas loading their cargoes of innocent parrots whose craws were full of diamonds, he thought, I fell asleep counting the stars and I dreamed about that huge ship, of course, he was so convinced that he didn't tell anyone nor did he remember the vision again until the same night on the following March when he was looking for the flash of dolphins in the sea and what he found was the illusory liner, gloomy, intermittent, with the same mistaken direction as the first time, except that then he was so sure he was awake that he ran to tell his mother and she spent three weeks moaning with disappointment, because your brain's rotting away from doing so many things backward, sleeping during the day and going out at night like a criminal, and since she had to go to the city around that time to get something comfortable where she could sit and think about her dead husband, because the rockers on her chair had worn out after eleven years of widowhood, she took advantage of the occasion and had the boatman go near the shoals so that her son could see what he really saw in the glass of the sea, the lovemaking of manta rays in a springtime of sponges, pink snappers and blue corvinas diving into the other wells of softer waters that were there among the waters, and even the wandering hairs of victims of drowning in some colonial shipwreck, no trace of sunken liners or anything like it, and yet he was so pigheaded that his mother promised to watch with him the next March, absolutely, not knowing that the only thing absolute in her future now was an easy chair from the days of Sir Francis Drake which she had bought at an auction in a Turk's store, in which she sat down to rest that same night, sighing, oh, my poor Olofernos, if you could only see how nice it is to think about you on this velvet lining and this brocade from the casket of a queen, but the more she brought back the memory of her dead husband, the more the blood in her heart bubbled up and turned to chocolate, as if instead of sitting down she were running, soaked from chills and fevers and her breathing full of earth, until he returned at dawn and found her dead in the easy chair, still warm, but half rotted away as after a snakebite, the same as happened afterward to four other women before the murderous chair was thrown into the sea, far away where it wouldn't bring evil to anyone, because it had been used so much over the centuries that its faculty for giving rest had been used up, and so he had to grow accustomed to his miserable routine of an orphan who was pointed out by everyone as the son of the widow who had brought the throne of misfortune into the village, living not so much from public charity as from the fish he stole out of boats, while his voice was becoming a roar, and not remembering his visions of past times anymore until another night in March when he chanced to look seaward and suddenly, good Lord, there it is, the huge asbestos whale, the behemoth beast, come see it, he shouted madly, come see it, raising such an uproar of dogs' barking and women's panic that even the oldest men remembered the frights of their great-grandfathers and crawled under their beds, thinking that William Dampier had come back, but those who ran into the street didn't make the effort to see the unlikely apparatus which at that instant was lost again in the east and raised up in its annual disaster, but they covered him with blows and left him so twisted that it was then he said to himself, drooling with rage, now they're going to see who I am, but he took care not to share his determination with anyone, but spent the whole year with the fixed idea, now they're going to see who I am, waiting for it to be the eve of the apparition once more in order to do what he did, which was steal a boat, cross the bay, and spend the evening waiting for his great moment in the inlets of the slave port, in the human brine of the Caribbean, but so absorbed in his adventure that he didn't stop as he always did in front of the Hindu shops to look at the ivory mandarins carved from the whole tusk of an elephant, nor did he make fun of the Dutch Negroes in their orthopedic velocipedes, nor was he frightened as at other times of the copper-skinned Malayans, who had gone around the world enthralled by the chimera of a secret tavern where they sold roast filets of Brazilian women, because he wasn't aware of anything until night came over him with all the weight of the stars and the jungle exhaled a sweet fragrance of gardenias and rotten salamanders, and there he was, rowing in the stolen boat toward the mouth of the bay, with the lantern out so as not to alert the customs police, idealized every fifteen seconds by the green wing flap of the beacon and turned human once more by the darkness, knowing that he was getting close to the buoys that marked the harbor channel, not only because its oppressive glow was getting more intense, but because the breathing of the water was becoming sad, and he rowed like that, so wrapped up in himself, that he didn't know where the fearful shark's breath that suddenly reached him came from or why the night became dense, as if the stars had suddenly died, and it was because the liner was there, with all of its inconceivable size, Lord, bigger than any other big thing in the world and darker than any other dark thing on land or sea, three hundred thousand tons of shark smell passing so close to the boat that he could see the seams of the steel precipice, without a single light in the infinite portholes, without a sigh from the engines, without a soul, and carrying its own circle of silence with it, its own dead air, its halted time, its errant sea in which a whole world of drowned animals floated, and suddenly it all disappeared with the flash of the beacon and for an instant it was the diaphanous Caribbean once more, the March night, the everyday air of the pelicans, so he stayed alone among the buoys, not knowing what to do, asking himself, startled, if perhaps he wasn't dreaming while he was awake, not just now but the other times too, but no sooner had he asked himself than a breath of mystery snuffed out the buoys, from the first to the last, so that when the light of the beacon passed by the liner appeared again and now its compasses were out of order, perhaps not even knowing what part of the ocean sea it was in, groping for the invisible channel but actually heading for the shoals, until he got the overwhelming revelation that that misfortune of the buoys was the last key to the enchantment and he lighted the lantern in the boat, a tiny red light that had no reason to alarm anyone in the watchtowers but which would be like a guiding sun for the pilot, because, thanks to it, the liner corrected its course and passed into the main gate of the channel in a maneuver of lucky resurrection, and then all the lights went on at the same time so that the boilers wheezed again, the stars were fixed in their places, and the animal corpses went to the bottom, and there was a clatter of plates and a fragrance of laurel sauce in the kitchens, and one could hear the pulsing of the orchestra on the moon decks and the throbbing of the arteries of high-sea lovers in the shadows of the staterooms, but he still carried so much leftover rage in him that he would not let himself be confused by emotion or be frightened by the miracle, but said to himself with more decision than ever, now they're going to see who I am, the cowards, now they're going to see, and instead of turning aside so that the colossal machine would not charge into him, he began to row in front of it, because now they really are going to see who I am, and he continued guiding the ship with the lantern until he was so sure of its obedience that he made it change course from the direction of the docks once more, took it out of the invisible channel, and led it by the halter as if it were a sea lamb toward the lights of the sleeping village, a living ship, invulnerable to the torches of the beacon, that no longer made it invisible but made it aluminum every fifteen seconds, and the crosses of the church, the misery of the houses, the illusion began to stand out, and still the ocean liner followed behind him, following his will inside of it, the captain asleep on his heart side, the fighting bulls in the snow of their pantries, the solitary patient in the infirmary, the orphan water of its cisterns, the unredeemed pilot who must have mistaken the cliffs for the docks, because at that instant the great roar of the whistle burst forth, once, and he was soaked with the downpour of steam that fell on him, again, and the boat belonging to someone else was on the point of capsizing, and again, but it was too late, because there were the shells of the shoreline, the stones of the streets, the doors of the disbelievers, the whole village illuminated by the lights of the fearsome liner itself, and he barely had time to get out of the way to make room for the cataclysm, shouting in the midst of the confusion, there it is, you cowards, a second before the huge steel cask shattered the ground and one could hear the neat destruction of ninety thousand five hundred champagne glasses breaking, one after the other, from stem to stern, and then the light came out and it was no longer a March dawn but the noon of a radiant Wednesday, and he was able to give himself the pleasure of watching the disbelievers as with open mouths they contemplated the largest ocean liner in this world and the other aground in front of the church, whiter than anything, twenty times taller than the steeple and some ninety-seven times longer than the village, with its name engraved in iron letters, *Halál-csillag,* and the ancient and languid waters of the seas of death dripping down its sides.

(1968)

# Monologue of Isabel Watching It Rain in Macondo

Winter fell one Sunday when people were coming out of church. Saturday night had been suffocating. But even on Sunday morning nobody thought it would rain. After mass, before we women had time to find the catches on our parasols, a thick, dark wind blew, which with one broad, round swirl swept away the dust and hard tinder of May. Someone next to me said: "It's a water wind." And I knew it even before then. From the moment we came out onto the church steps I felt shaken by a slimy feeling in my stomach. The men ran to the nearby houses with one hand on their hats and a handkerchief in the other, protecting themselves against the wind and the dust storm. Then it rained. And the sky was a gray, jellyish substance that flapped its wings a hand away from our heads.

During the rest of the morning my stepmother and I were sitting by the railing, happy that the rain would revive the thirsty rosemary and nard in the flowerpots after seven months of intense summer and scorching dust. At noon the reverberation of the earth stopped and a smell of turned earth, of awakened and renovated vegetation mingled with the cool and healthful odor of the rain in the rosemary. My father said at lunchtime: "When it rains in May, it's a sign that there'll be good tides." Smiling, crossed by the luminous thread of the new season, my stepmother told me: "That's what I heard in the sermon." And my father smiled. And he ate with a good appetite and even let his food digest leisurely beside the railing, silent, his eyes closed, but not sleeping, as if to think that he was dreaming while awake.

It rained all afternoon in a single tone. In the uniform and peaceful intensity you could hear the water fall, the way it is when you travel all afternoon on a train. But without our noticing it, the rain was penetrating too deeply into our senses. Early Monday morning, when we closed the door to avoid the cutting, icy draft that blew in from the courtyard, our senses had been filled with rain. And on Monday morning they had overflowed. My stepmother and I went back to look at the garden. The harsh gray earth of May had been changed overnight into a dark, sticky substance like cheap soap. A trickle of water began to run off the flowerpots. "I think they had more than enough water during the night," my stepmother said. And I noticed that she had stopped smiling and that her joy of the previous day had changed during the night into a lax and tedious seriousness. "I think you're right," I said. "It would be better to have the Indians put them on the veranda until it stops raining." And that was what they did, while the rain grew like an immense tree over the other trees. My father occupied the same spot where he had been on Sunday afternoon, but he didn't talk about the rain. He said: "I must have slept poorly last night because I woke up with a stiff back." And he stayed there, sitting by the railing with his feet on a chair and his head turned toward the empty garden. Only at dusk, after he had turned down lunch, did he say: "It looks as if it will never clear." And I remembered the months of heat. I remembered August, those long and awesome siestas in which we dropped down to die under the weight of the hour, our clothes sticking to our bodies, hearing outside the insistent and dull buzzing of the hour that never passed. I saw the washed-down walls, the joints of the beams all puffed up by the water. I saw the small garden, empty for the first time, and the jasmine bush against the wall, faithful to the memory of my mother. I saw my father sitting in a rocker, his painful vertebrae resting on a pillow and his sad eyes lost in the labyrinth of the rain. I remembered the August nights in whose wondrous silence nothing could be heard except the millenary sound that the earth makes as it spins on its rusty, unoiled axis. Suddenly I felt overcome by an overwhelming sadness.

It rained all Monday, just like Sunday. But now it seemed to be raining in another way, because something different and bitter was going on in my heart. At dusk a voice beside my chair said: "This rain is a bore." Without turning to look, I recognized Martín's voice. I knew that he was speaking in the next chair, with the same cold and awesome expression that hadn't varied, not even after that gloomy December dawn when he started being my husband. Five months had passed since then. Now I was going to have a child. And Martín was there beside me saying that the rain bored him. "Not a bore," I said. "It seems terribly sad to me, with the empty garden and those poor trees that can't come in from the courtyard." Then I turned to look at him and Martín was no longer there. It was only a voice that was saying to me: "It doesn't look as if it will ever clear," and when I looked toward the voice I found only the empty chair.

On Tuesday morning we found a cow in the garden. It looked like a clay promontory in its hard and rebellious immobility, its hooves sunken in the mud and its head bent over. During the morning the Indians tried to drive it away with sticks and stones. But the cow stayed there, imperturbable in the garden, hard, inviolable, its hooves still sunken in the mud and its huge head humiliated by the rain. The Indians harassed it until my father's patient tolerance came to its defense. "Leave her alone," he said. "She'll leave the way she came."

At sundown on Tuesday the water tightened and hurt, like a shroud over the heart. The coolness of the first morning began to change into a hot and sticky humidity. The temperature was neither cold nor hot; it was the temperature of a fever chill. Feet sweated inside shoes. It was hard to say what was more disagreeable, bare skin or the contact of clothing on skin. All activity had ceased in the house. We sat on the veranda but we no longer watched the rain as we did on the first day. We no longer felt it falling. We no longer saw anything except the outline of the trees in the mist, with a sad and desolate sunset which left on your lips the same taste with which you awaken after having dreamed about a stranger. I knew that it was Tuesday and I remembered the twins of Saint Jerome, the blind girls who came to the house every week to sing us simple songs, saddened by the bitter and unprotected prodigy of their voices. Above the rain I heard the blind twins' little song and I imagined them at home, huddling, waiting for the rain to stop so they could go out and sing. The twins of Saint Jerome wouldn't come that day, I thought, nor would the beggar woman be on the veranda after siesta, asking, as on every Tuesday, for the eternal branch of lemon balm.

That day we lost track of meals. At siesta time my stepmother served a plate of tasteless soup and a piece of stale bread. But actually we hadn't eaten since sunset on Monday and I think that from then on we stopped thinking. We were paralyzed, drugged by the rain, given over to the collapse of nature with a peaceful and resigned attitude. Only the cow was moving in the afternoon. Suddenly a deep noise shook her insides and her hooves sank into the mud with greater force. Then she stood motionless for half an hour, as if she were already dead but could not fall down because the habit of being alive prevented her, the habit of remaining in one position in the rain, until the habit grew weaker than her body. Then she doubled her front legs (her dark and shiny haunches still raised in a last agonized effort) and sank her drooling snout into the mud, finally surrendering to the weight of her own matter in a silent, gradual, and dignified ceremony of total downfall. "She got that far," someone said behind me. And

I turned to look and on the threshold I saw the Tuesday beggar woman who had come through the storm to ask for the branch of lemon balm.

Perhaps on Wednesday I might have grown accustomed to that overwhelming atmosphere if on going to the living room I hadn't found the table pushed against the wall, the furniture piled on top of it, and on the other side, on a parapet prepared during the night, trunks and boxes of household utensils. The spectacle produced a terrible feeling of emptiness in me. Something had happened during the night. The house was in disarray; the Guajiro Indians, shirtless and barefoot, with their pants rolled up to their knees, were carrying the furniture into the dining room. In the men's expression, in the very diligence with which they were working, one could see the cruelty of their frustrated rebellion, of their necessary and humiliating inferiority in the rain. I moved without direction, without will. I felt changed into a desolate meadow sown with algae and lichens, with soft, sticky toadstools, fertilized by the repugnant plants of dampness and shadows. I was in the living room contemplating the desert spectacle of the piled-up furniture when I heard my stepmother's voice warning me from her room that I might catch pneumonia. Only then did I realize that the water was up to my ankles, that the house was flooded, the floor covered by a thick surface of viscous, dead water.

On Wednesday noon it still hadn't finished dawning. And before three o'clock in the afternoon night had come on completely, ahead of time and sickly, with the same slow, monotonous, and pitiless rhythm of the rain in the courtyard. It was a premature dusk, soft and lugubrious, growing in the midst of the silence of the Guajiros, who were squatting on the chairs against the walls, defeated and impotent against the disturbance of nature. That was when news began to arrive from outside. No one brought it to the house. It simply arrived, precise, individualized, as if led by the liquid clay that ran through the streets and dragged household items along, things and more things, the leftovers of a remote catastrophe, rubbish and dead animals. Events that took place on Sunday, when the rain was still the announcement of a providential season, took two days to be known at our house. And on Wednesday the news arrived as if impelled by the very inner dynamism of the storm. It was learned then that the church was flooded and its collapse expected. Someone who had no reason to know said that night: "The train hasn't been able to cross the bridge since Monday. It seems that the river carried away the tracks." And it was learned that a sick woman had disappeared from her bed and had been found that afternoon floating in the courtyard.

Terrified, possessed by the fright and the deluge, I sat down in the rocker with my legs tucked up and my eyes fixed on the damp darkness full of hazy foreboding. My stepmother appeared in the doorway with the lamp held high and her head erect. She looked like a family ghost before whom I felt no fear whatever because I myself shared her supernatural condition. She came over to where I was. She still held her head high and the lamp in the air, and she splashed through the water on the veranda. "Now we have to pray," she said. And I noticed her dry and wrinkled face, as if she had just left her tomb or as if she had been made of some substance different from human matter. She was across from me with her rosary in her hand saying: "Now we have to pray. The water broke open the tombs and now the poor dead are floating in the cemetery."

I may have slept a little that night when I awoke with a start because of a sour and penetrating smell like that of decomposing bodies. I gave a strong shake to Martín, who was snoring beside me. "Don't you notice it?" I asked him. And he said: "What?" And I said: "The smell. It must be the dead people floating along the streets." I was terrified by that idea, but Martín turned to the wall and with a husky and sleepy voice said: "That's something you made up. Pregnant women are always imagining things."

At dawn on Thursday the smells stopped, the sense of distance was lost. The notion of time, upset since the day before, disappeared completely. Then there was no Thursday. What should have been Thursday was a physical, jellylike thing that could have been parted with the hands in order to look into Friday. There were no men or women there. My stepmother, my father, the Indians were adipose and improbable bodies that moved in the marsh of winter. My father said to me: "Don't move away from here until you're told what to do," and his voice was distant and indirect and didn't seem to be perceived by the ear but by touch, which was the only sense that remained active.

But my father didn't return: he got lost in the weather. So when night came I called my stepmother to tell her to accompany me to my bedroom. I had a peaceful and serene sleep, which lasted all through the night. On the following day the atmosphere was still the same, colorless, odorless, and without any temperature. As soon as I awoke I jumped into a chair and remained there without moving, because something told me that there was still a region of my consciousness that hadn't awakened completely. Then I heard the train whistle. The prolonged and sad whistle of the train fleeing the storm. *It must have cleared somewhere*, I thought, and a voice behind me seemed to answer my thought. "Where?" it said. "Who's there?" I asked looking. And I saw my stepmother with a long thin arm in the direction of the wall. "It's me," she said. And I asked her: "Can you hear it?" And she said yes, maybe it had cleared on the outskirts and they'd repaired the tracks. Then she gave me a tray with some steaming breakfast. It smelled of garlic sauce and boiled butter. It was a plate of soup. Disconcerted, I asked my stepmother what time it was. And she, calmly, with a voice that tasted of prostrated resignation, said: "It must be around two-thirty. The train isn't late after all this." I said: "Two-thirty! How could I have slept so long!" And she said: "You haven't slept very long. It can't be more than three o'clock." And I, trembling, feeling the plate slip through my fingers: "Two-thirty on Friday," I said. And she, monstrously tranquil: "Two-thirty on Thursday, child. *Still* two-thirty on Thursday."

I don't know how long I was sunken in that somnambulism where the senses lose their value. I only know that after many uncountable hours I heard a voice in the next room. A voice that said: "Now you can roll the bed to this side." It was a tired voice, but not the voice of a sick person, rather that of a convalescent. Then I heard the sound of the bricks in the water. I remained rigid before I realized that I was in a horizontal position. Then I felt the immense emptiness. I felt the wavering and violent silence of the house, the incredible immobility that affected everything. And suddenly I felt my heart turned into a frozen stone. *I'm dead*, I thought. *My God, I'm dead.* I gave a jump in the bed. I shouted: "Ada! Ada!" Martín's unpleasant voice answered me from the other side. "They can't hear you, they're already outside by now." Only then did I realize that it had cleared and that all around us a silence stretched out, a tranquillity, a mysterious and deep beatitude, a perfect state which must have been very much like death. Then footsteps could be heard on the veranda. A clear and completely living voice was heard. Then a cool breeze shook the panel of the door, made the doorknob squeak, and a solid and monumental body, like a ripe fruit, fell deeply into the cistern in the courtyard. Something in the air revealed the presence of an invisible person who was smiling in the darkness. *Good Lord*, I thought then, confused by the mixup in time. *It wouldn't surprise me now if they were coming to call me to go to last Sunday's Mass.*

(1955)

# Nabo

Nabo was lying face down in the hay. He felt the smell of a urinated stable rubbing on his body. On his brown and shiny skin he felt the warm embers of the last horses, but he couldn't feel the skin. Nabo couldn't feel anything. It was as if he'd gone to sleep with the last blow of the horseshoe on his forehead and now that was the only feeling he had. He opened his eyes. He closed them again and then was quiet, stretched out, stiff, as he had been all afternoon, feeling himself growing without time, until someone behind him said: "Come on, Nabo. You've slept enough already." He turned over and didn't see the horses; the door was closed. Nabo must have imagined that the animals were somewhere in the darkness in spite of the fact that he couldn't hear their impatient stamping. He imagined that the person speaking to him was doing it from outside the stable, because the door was closed from the inside and barred. Once more the voice behind him said: "That's right, Nabo, you've slept enough already. You've been asleep for almost three days." Only then did Nabo open his eyes completely and remember: "I'm here because a horse kicked me."

He didn't know what hour he was living. The days had been left behind. It was as if someone had passed a damp sponge over those remote Saturday nights when he used to go to the town square. He forgot about the white shirt. He forgot that he had a green hat made of green straw and dark pants. He forgot that he didn't have any shoes. Nabo would go to the square on Saturday nights and sit in a corner, silent, not to listen to the music but to watch the black man. Every Saturday he saw him. The Negro wore horn-rimmed glasses, tied to his ears, and he played the saxophone at one of the rear music stands. Nabo saw the black man but the black man didn't see Nabo. At least, if someone had known that Nabo went to the square on Saturday nights to see the Negro and had asked him (not now, because he couldn't remember) whether the black man had ever seen him, Nabo would have said no. It was the only thing he did after currying the horses: watch the black man.

One Saturday the Negro wasn't at his place in the band. Nabo probably thought at first that he wasn't going to play anymore in the public concerts in spite of the fact that the music stand was there. Although for that reason precisely, the fact that the music stand was there, he thought later that the Negro would be back the following Saturday. But on the following Saturday he wasn't back and the music stand wasn't in its place.

Nabo rolled onto one side and he saw the man talking to him. At first he didn't recognize him, blotted out by the darkness of the stable. The man was sitting on a jutting beam, talking and patting his knees. "A horse kicked me," Nabo said again, trying to recognize the man. "That's right," the man said. "The horses aren't here now and we're waiting for you in the choir." Nabo shook his head. He still hadn't begun to think, but now he thought he'd seen the man somewhere. Nabo didn't understand, but he didn't find it strange either that someone should say that to him, because every day while he curried the horses he invented songs to distract them. Then he would sing the same songs he sang to the horses in the living room to distract the mute girl. When he was singing if someone had told him that he was taking him to a choir, it wouldn't have surprised him. Now he was surprised even less because he didn't understand. He was fatigued, dulled, brutish. "I want to know where the horses are," he said. And the man said: "I already told you, the horses aren't here. All we're interested in is to get a voice like yours." And perhaps, face down in the hay, Nabo heard, but he couldn't distinguish the pain that the horseshoe had left on his forehead from his other disordered sensations. He turned his head on the hay and fell asleep.

Nabo still went to the square for two or three weeks in spite of the fact that the Negro was no longer in the band. Perhaps someone would have answered him if Nabo had asked what had happened to the black man. But he didn't ask and kept on going to the concerts until another man with another saxophone came to take the Negro's spot. Then Nabo was convinced that the Negro wouldn't be back and he decided not to return to the square. When he awoke he thought he had slept a very short time. The smell of damp hay still burned in his nose. The darkness was still there before his eyes, surrounding him. And the man was still in the corner. The obscure and peaceful voice of the man who patted his knees, saying: "We're waiting for you, Nabo. You've been asleep for almost two years and you refuse to get up." Then Nabo closed his eyes again. He opened them again, kept looking at the corner, and saw the man once more, disoriented, perplexed. Only then did he recognize him.

If the people in the house had known what Nabo was doing on the square on Saturday nights, they probably would have thought that when he stopped going he did so because now he had music at home. That was when we brought the gramophone to amuse the girl. Since it needed someone to wind it up all day, it seemed most natural that that person should be Nabo. He could do it when he didn't have to take care of the horses. The girl remained seated, listening to the records. Sometimes, when the music was playing, the girl would get out of her chair, still looking at the wall, drooling, and would drag herself to the veranda. Nabo would lift the needle and start to sing. In the beginning, when he first came to the house and we asked him what he could do, Nabo said that he could sing. But that didn't interest anyone. What we needed was a boy to curry the horses. Nabo stayed, but he kept on singing, as if we had hired him to sing and the business of currying the horses was only a distraction that made the work easier. That went on for more than a year, until those of us in the house grew used to the idea that the girl would never be able to walk, would never recognize anyone, would always be the little dead and lonely girl who listened to the gramophone looking coldly at the wall until we lifted her out of her chair and took her to her room. Then she ceased to pain us, but Nabo was still faithful, punctual, cranking the gramophone. That was during the time when Nabo was still going to the square on Saturday nights. One day, when the boy was in the stable, someone beside the gramophone said: "Nabo!" We were on the veranda, not concerned about something no one could have said. But when we heard it a second time: "Nabo!" we raised our heads and asked: "Who's with the girl?" And someone said: "I didn't see anyone come in." And another said: "I'm sure I heard a voice calling Nabo." But when we went to look all we found was the girl on the floor, leaning against the wall.

Nabo came back early and went to bed. It was the following Saturday that he didn't return to the square because the Negro had been replaced. And three weeks later, on a Monday, the gramophone began to play while Nabo was in the stable. No one worried at first. Only later, when we saw the black boy coming, singing and still dripping from the water of the horses, did we ask him: "How'd you get out?" He said: "Through the door. I've been in the stable since noon." "The gramophone's playing. Can't you hear it?" we asked him. And Nabo said he could. And we asked him: "Who wound it up?" And he, shrugging his shoulders: "The girl. She's been winding it for a long time now."

That was the way things were until the day we found him lying face down on the hay, locked in the stable and with the edge of the horseshoe encrusted on his forehead. When we picked him up by the shoulders, Nabo said: "I'm here because a horse kicked me." But no one was interested in what he might have said. We were interested in his cold, dead eyes and mouth full of green froth. He spent the whole night weeping, burning with fever, delirious, talking about the comb that he'd lost in the hay in the stable. That was the first day. On the following day, when he opened his eyes and said: "I'm thirsty," and we brought him water, he drank it all down in one swallow and twice asked for a little more. We asked him how he felt and he said: "I feel as if a horse had kicked me." And he kept on talking all day and all night. And finally he sat up in bed, pointed up with his fore-finger, and said that the galloping of the horses had kept him awake all night. But he'd had no fever since the night before. He was no longer delirious, but he kept on talking until they put a handkerchief in his mouth. Then Nabo began to sing behind the handkerchief, saying that next to his ear he could hear the breathing of the blind horses looking for water on top of the closed door. When we took out the handkerchief so that he could eat something, he turned toward the wall and we all thought that he'd fallen asleep and it was even possible that he had fallen asleep for a while. But when he awoke he was no longer on the bed. His feet were tied and his hands were tied to a brace beam in the room. Trussed up, Nabo began to sing.

When he recognized him, Nabo said to the man: "I've seen you before." And the man said: "Every Saturday you used to watch me in the square." And Nabo said: "That's right, but I thought I saw you and you didn't see me." And the man said: "I never saw you, but later on, when I stopped coming, I felt as if someone had stopped watching me on Saturdays." And Nabo said: "You never came back, but I kept on going for three or four weeks." And the man, still not moving, patting himself on the knees: "I couldn't go back to the square even though it was the only thing that was worth anything." Nabo tried to sit up, shook his head in the hay, and still he heard the cold, obstinate voice, until he no longer had time even to know that he was falling asleep again. Always, ever since the horse had kicked him, that happened. And he always heard the voice: "We're waiting for you, Nabo. There's no longer any way to measure the time you've been asleep."

Four weeks after the Negro had stopped coming to the band, Nabo was combing the tail of one of the horses. He'd never done that. He would just curry them and sing in the meantime. But on Wednesday he'd gone to the market and had seen a comb and had said to himself: "That comb is for combing the horses' tails." That was when the whole thing happened with the horse that gave him a kick and left him all mixed up for the rest of his life, ten or fifteen years before. Somebody in the house said: "It would have been better if he'd died that day and hadn't gone on like this, all through, talking nonsense for the rest of his life." But no one had seen him again ever since the day we locked him up. Only we knew that he was there, locked up in the room, and since then the girl hadn't moved the gramophone again. But in the house we had very little interest in knowing about it. We'd locked him up as if he were a horse, as if the kick had passed the sluggishness on to him and encrusted on his forehead was all the stupidity of horses: animalness. And we left him isolated within four walls as if we'd decided he should die of imprisonment because we weren't cold-blooded enough to kill him in any other way. Fourteen years passed like that until one of the children grew up and said he had the urge to see his face. And he opened the door.

Nabo saw the man again. "A horse kicked me," he said. And the man said: "You've been saying that for centuries and in the meantime we've been waiting for you in the choir." Nabo shook his head again, sank his wounded forehead into the hay once more, and thought he suddenly remembered how things had happened. "It was the first time I ever combed a horse's tail," he said. And the man said: "We wanted it that way so you would come and sing in the choir." And Nabo said: "I shouldn't have bought the comb." And the man said: "You would have come across it in any case. We'd decided that you'd find the comb and comb the horses' tails." And Nabo said: "I'd never stood behind them before." And the man, still tranquil, still not showing impatience: "But you did stand there and the horse kicked you. It was the only way for you to come to the choir." And the conversation, implacable, daily, went on until someone in the house said: "It must be fifteen years since anyone opened that door." The girl (she hadn't grown, she was over thirty and was beginning to get sad in her eyelids) was sitting looking at the wall when they opened the door. She turned her face in the other direction, sniffing. And when they closed the door, they said again: "Nabo's peaceful. There's nothing moving inside anymore. One of these days he'll die and we won't be able to tell except for the smell." And someone said: "We can tell by the food. He's never stopped eating. He's fine like that, locked up with no one to bother him. He gets good light from the rear side." And things stayed like that; except that the girl kept on looking toward the door, sniffing the warm fumes that filtered through the cracks. She stayed like that until early in the morning, when we heard a metallic sound in the living room and we remembered that it was the same sound that had been heard fifteen years before when Nabo was winding the gramophone. We got up, lighted the lamp, and heard the first measures of the forgotten song; the sad song that had been dead on the records for such a long time. The sound kept on, more and more strained, until a dry sound was heard at the instant we reached the living room, and we could still hear the record playing and saw the girl in the corner beside the gramophone, looking at the wall and holding up the crank. We didn't say anything, but went back to our rooms remembering that someone had told us sometime that the girl knew how to crank the gramophone. Thinking that, we stayed awake, listening to the worn little tune from the record that was still spinning on what was left of the broken spring.

The day before, when they opened the door, it smelled of biological waste, of a dead body. The one who had opened it shouted: "Nabo! Nabo!" But nobody answered from inside. Beside the opening was the empty plate. Three times a day the plate was put under the door and three times a day the plate came out again with no food on it. That was how we knew that Nabo was alive. But by no other means. There was no more moving inside, no more singing. And it must have been after they closed the door that Nabo said to the man: "I can't go to the choir." And the man asked why. And Nabo said: "Because I haven't got any shoes." And the man, raising his feet, said: "That doesn't matter. Nobody wear shoes here." And Nabo saw the hard, yellow soles of the bare feet the man was holding up. "I've been waiting for you here for an eternity," the man said. "The horse only kicked me a moment ago," Nabo said. "Now I'll throw a little water on my face and take them out for a walk." And the man said: "The horses don't need you anymore. There aren't any more horses. You're the one who should come with us." And Nabo said: "The horses should have been here." He got up a little, sank his hands into the hay while the man said: "They haven't had anyone to look after them for fifteen years." But Nabo was scratching the ground under the hay, saying: "The comb must still be here." And the man said: "They closed up the stable fifteen years ago. It's full of rubbish now." And Nabo said: "Rubbish doesn't collect in one afternoon. Until I find the comb I won't move out of here."

On the following day, after they'd fastened the door again, they heard the difficult movements inside once more. No one moved afterward. No one said anything again when the first creaks were heard and the door began to give way under unusual pressure. Inside something like the panting of a penned animal was

heard. Finally the groan of rusty hinges was heard as they broke
when Nabo shook his head again. "Until I find the comb, I won't
go to the choir," he said. "It must be around here somewhere."
And he dug in the hay, breaking it, scratching the ground, until
the man said: "All right Nabo. If the only thing you're waiting
for to come to the choir is to find the comb, go look for it." He
leaned forward, his face darkened by a patient haughtiness. He put
his hands against the barrier and said: "Go ahead, Nabo. I'll see
that nobody stops you."

And then the door gave way and the huge bestial Negro with
the harsh scar marked on his forehead (in spite of the fact that
fifteen years had passed) came out stumbling over the furniture,
his fists raised and menacing, still with the rope they had tied
him with fifteen years before (when he was a little black boy who
looked after the horses); and (before reaching the courtyard) he
passed by the girl, who remained seated, the crank of the gramophone still in her hand since the night before (when she saw
the unchained black force she remembered something that at one
time must have been a word) and he reached the courtyard (before finding the stable), after having knocked down the living-
room mirror with his shoulder, but without seeing the girl (neither
beside the gramophone nor in the mirror), and he stood with his
face to the sun, his eyes closed, blind (while inside the noise of
the broken mirror was still going on), and he ran aimlessly, like a
blindfolded horse instinctively looking for the stable door that
fifteen years of imprisonment had erased from his memory but
not from his instincts (since that remote day when he had combed
the horse's tail and was left befuddled for the rest of his life),
and leaving behind catastrophe, dissolution, and chaos like a blindfolded bull in a roomful of lamps, he reached the back yard
(still without finding the stable), and scratched on the ground
with the tempestuous fury with which he had knocked down the
mirror, thinking perhaps that by scratching on the ground he
could make the smell of mare's urine rise up again, until he finally

reached the stable doors and pushed them too soon, falling inside on his face, in his death agony perhaps, but still confused by that fierce animalness that a half-second before had prevented him from hearing the girl, who raised the crank when she heard him pass and remembered, drooling, but without moving from the chair, without moving her mouth but twirling the crank of the gramophone in the air, remembered the only word she had ever learned to say in her life, and she shouted it from the living room: "Nabo! Nabo!"

(*1951*)